The
Privateering Earl

HONI SOIT QVI MAL Y PENSE

COM̄ DE SKIPTON

N͞ISS͞ DN͞E

FORTIÆ BARO C͞L

GEORGIUS CLIFFORD CO

CUMBERLANDIÆ BARO C

The right Honorable GEORGE Earle of Cumber: land, Lo: Clifford of Skipton, Knight of the most noble Ordre of the Garter and one of her M͞tes most Honorable privy Counsell.

R·Vaus fe

The Privateering Earl

RICHARD T. SPENCE

ALAN SUTTON PUBLISHING LIMITED

First published in the United Kingdom in 1995
Alan Sutton Publishing Ltd · Phoenix Mill · Far Thrupp
Stroud · Gloucestershire

British Library Cataloguing in Publication Data

Spence, Richard T.
  Privateering Earl: George Clifford, 3rd
  Earl of Cumberland, 1558–1605
  I. Title
  942.055092

ISBN 0–7509–0892–0

Half-title illustration: The Earl's crest from Lady Anne's Book of Heraldry, *in the Hothfield MSS*
Frontispiece: Earl George, engraved by Robert Vaughan

Typeset in 11/12pt Erhardt.
Typesetting and origination by
Alan Sutton Publishing Limited.
Printed in Great Britain by
Hartnolls, Bodmin, Cornwall.

In memory of my parents

Contents

List of Illustrations

GENEALOGICAL TABLES

TABLES

MAPS

Acknowledgements

I am deeply grateful to the Duke of Devonshire and the Trustees of the Chatsworth Settlement for permission to examine and use for this biography the Bolton, Londesborough and Currey Papers at Chatsworth; the Duke of Northumberland for the Syon MSS at Alnwick; the Marquess of Salisbury for the Hatfield MSS; the Marquess of Tavistock and the Trustees of the Bedford Estates for the Woburn Abbey MSS; his Grace the Archbishop of Canterbury and the Trustees of Lambeth Palace for the Lambeth Palace archives, and Hugh T. Fattorini for the Skipton MSS deposited with the Yorkshire Archaeological Society. The United States Department of the Interior National Park Service kindly gave me access to the library and archives at Fort San Cristobal, Old San Juan, Puerto Rico.

Numerous archivists have aided me, with skill, understanding and courtesy. I am particularly indebted to the following: Peter Day, Keeper of Collections, and the Librarian and archivists Michael Pearman and Thomas Askey at Chatsworth; Peter Watkins and Hugh Steele-Smith at Bolton Abbey; Dr Colin Shrimpton at Alnwick Castle; Robin Harcourt-Williams at Hatfield House; Mrs Marie Draper at the Bedford Estate Office; Sheila MacPherson and Richard Hall at Kendal Record Office, and Mrs Sylvia Thomas, Mrs Maisie Morton and Dr William Connor of the West Yorkshire Archive Service. The Bibliography makes plain how many other archivists and librarians in the public as well as private service I have relied on in preparing this study.

The author and publishers gratefully acknowledge the grant towards the cost of publication from the Isobel Thornley Bequest of the University of London.

It gives me pleasure to acknowledge here the encouragement and help I have received from Professor Kenneth R. Andrews, Professor A. Hassell Smith, Dr J. Trevor Cliffe, W. Rhys Robinson, and Dick and the late Mary Clifford, founders of the Clifford Association. Many students of Tudor history besides myself will remember how greatly their researches were stimulated by Professors S.T. Bindoff, J.E. Neale and Joel Hurstfield in their seminars at the Institute of Historical Research, London University.

Abbreviations

Andrews	K.R. Andrews, *Elizabethan Privateering,* Cambridge, 1964.
APC	*Acts of the Privy Council of England*, ed. J.R. Dasent.
BL	British Library.
Bolton MSS	Chatsworth, Bolton MSS.
Clay	J.W. Clay, 'The Clifford Family', *Yorkshire Archaeological Journal*, xviii, 1905.
Clifford	Hugh Clifford, *The House of Clifford*, Chichester, 1987.
CPR	*Calendar of Patent Rolls.*
CRO	Cumbria County Record Office, Carlisle.
CSPD	*Calendar of State Papers, Domestic.*
CSP, Foreign	*Calendar of State Papers, Foreign.*
CSP, Scotland	*Calendar of State Papers, Scotland.*
CSP, Spanish	*Calendar of State Papers, Spanish.*
CSP, Venetian	*Calendar of State Papers, Venetian.*
Currey	Chatsworth, Currey Papers.
DNB	*Dictionary of National Biography.*
GEC	*The Complete Peerage*, ed. G.E. Cockayne, 1910–59.
HMC	*Historical Manuscripts Commission.*
KRO	Cumbria County Record Office, Kendal.
Lond.	Chatsworth, Londesborough Papers.
MSS	Manuscripts.
PCC	Prerogative Court of Canterbury.
PRO	Public Record Office.
PRO C54	Chancery, Close Rolls.
PRO C66	Chancery, Patent Rolls.
PRO LC4	Lord Chamberlain's Office, Recognizances.
PRO SP12	State Papers, Domestic, Elizabeth.
Spence 'Earls'	R.T. Spence, 'The Cliffords, Earls of Cumberland, 1579–1646: a study of their fortunes based on their household and estate accounts' (unpub. Ph.D. thesis, London University, 1959).
VCH	*Victoria County History.*
Whitaker	T.D. Whitaker, *The History and Antiquities of the Deanery of Craven in the County of York*, 3rd edn, ed. A.W. Morant, 1878.
Williamson	G.C. Williamson, *George, Third Earl of Cumberland (1558–1605) His Life and Voyages*, Cambridge, 1920.
YAS	Yorkshire Archaeological Society.
YAS, DD121	Skipton MSS.
Yorkshire Fines, Tudor	*Feet of Fines of the Tudor Period, 1486–1603*, ed. W. Brigg, 4 vols, YAS Record Series. II, V, VII, VIII, Worksop, 1887–90.

THE EARLS OF CUMBERLAND

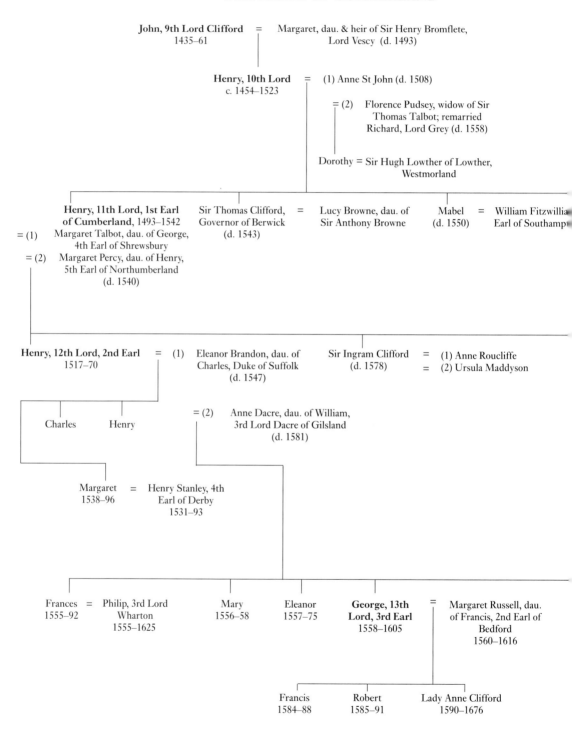

John, 9th Lord Clifford = Margaret, dau. & heir of Sir Henry Bromflete,
1435–61   Lord Vescy (d. 1493)

Henry, 10th Lord = (1) Anne St John (d. 1508)
c. 1454–1523

= (2)   Florence Pudsey, widow of Sir
Thomas Talbot; remarried
Richard, Lord Grey (d. 1558)

Dorothy = Sir Hugh Lowther of Lowther,
Westmorland

Henry, 11th Lord, 1st Earl   Sir Thomas Clifford, = Lucy Browne, dau. of   Mabel = William Fitzwillia
of Cumberland, 1493–1542   Governor of Berwick   Sir Anthony Browne   (d. 1550)   Earl of Southamp
= (1) Margaret Talbot, dau. of George,   (d. 1543)
4th Earl of Shrewsbury
= (2) Margaret Percy, dau. of Henry,
5th Earl of Northumberland
(d. 1540)

Henry, 12th Lord, 2nd Earl = (1) Eleanor Brandon, dau. of   Sir Ingram Clifford = (1) Anne Roucliffe
1517–70   Charles, Duke of Suffolk   (d. 1578) = (2) Ursula Maddyson
(d. 1547)

= (2)   Anne Dacre, dau. of William,
3rd Lord Dacre of Gilsland
(d. 1581)

Charles   Henry

Margaret = Henry Stanley, 4th
1538–96   Earl of Derby
1531–93

Frances = Philip, 3rd Lord   Mary   Eleanor   George, 13th = Margaret Russell, dau.
1555–92   Wharton   1556–58   1557–75   Lord, 3rd Earl   of Francis, 2nd Earl of
1555–1625   1558–1605   Bedford
1560–1616

Francis   Robert   Lady Anne Clifford
1584–88   1585–91   1590–1676

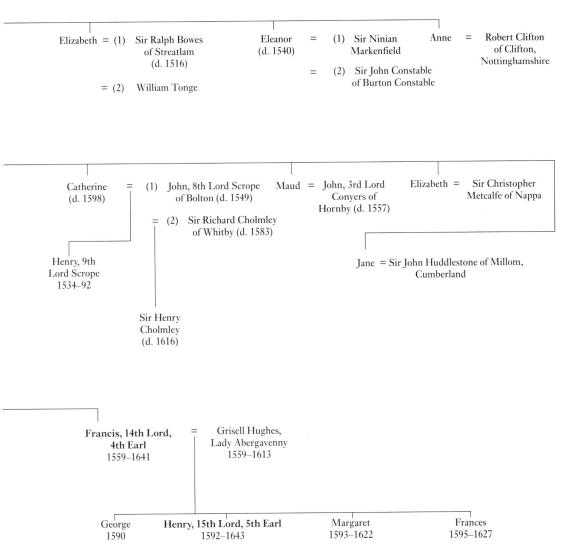

Elizabeth = (1) Sir Ralph Bowes
                 of Streatlam
                 (d. 1516)

        = (2)   William Tonge

Eleanor   = (1) Sir Ninian
(d. 1540)   Markenfield

          = (2) Sir John Constable
                  of Burton Constable

Anne = Robert Clifton
         of Clifton,
         Nottinghamshire

Catherine   =   (1) John, 8th Lord Scrope
(d. 1598)   of Bolton (d. 1549)

            =   (2) Sir Richard Cholmley
                     of Whitby (d. 1583)

Maud = John, 3rd Lord
         Conyers of
         Hornby (d. 1557)

Elizabeth = Sir Christopher
              Metcalfe of Nappa

Henry, 9th
Lord Scrope
1534–92

Jane = Sir John Huddlestone of Millom,
        Cumberland

Sir Henry
Cholmley
(d. 1616)

Francis, 14th Lord,   =   Grisell Hughes,
   4th Earl   Lady Abergavenny
   1559–1641   1559–1613

George   Henry, 15th Lord, 5th Earl   Margaret   Frances
1590   1592–1643   1593–1622   1595–1627

CHAPTER 1

George, Lord Clifford, and his Heritage: 1558–70

Rarely can a Clifford heir have been more welcome than George, the future 3rd Earl of Cumberland. His birth on 8 August 1558 at Brougham Castle in Westmorland eased the worst fears of his parents, Earl Henry and Countess Anne, about the survival of their noble line. A second son Francis, born on 30 October 1559 at Skipton Castle in the West Riding of Yorkshire, gave them the greater comfort of double assurance. They would still feel qualms about either or both boys escaping the perils of early childhood. The Earl's two sons by his first wife, Countess Eleanor, had died in infancy and only one daughter, Lady Margaret, survived. For ten years he had endured the real possibility that, should he himself die, the great Clifford inheritance in Yorkshire and Westmorland would be dismembered. His anxiety was not lessened after his second marriage in 1554 because Countess Anne gave birth to three daughters in as many years. George and Francis, therefore, brought a sense of relief about the succession and diverted attention away from the girls and the wealth they had stood to inherit.[1]

There would have been nothing remarkable about the collapse of a great noble house. The Tudor peerage were few in numbers, usually between fifty and sixty families, and ever-changing because their wastage rate was high. A quarter died out every twenty-five years from infant mortality, disease, death by accident or in battle and execution for treason.[2] Both Countess Eleanor's family, the Brandons, dukes of Suffolk, and Countess Anne's, the Dacres of Gilsland in Cumberland, came to an end for lack of a direct male heir and their estates fell into others' hands.[3] Even the possibility of failure brought its problems. A nobleman who only had daughters was vulnerable to predatory peers and needed nerve and acuity to fend them off. As will be seen, the difficulties Earl Henry faced were to make an impact on the course of George's life. A generation later, Earl George was himself afflicted by worries about who should succeed him because his sons died young and this left him with only one child, Lady Anne Clifford.

One of the themes of this study is the recurring concern of the Earls about the continuation of the male line and perpetuating the link between their inheritance and their earldom. The imperative which drove their determination over this was the long and honoured traditions and high prestige of their noble family. George's heritage comprised: high social status with ancient baronial titles adding lustre to the earl's coronet; martial ancestors in whose deeds he could take pride; a network of relatives among the peerage and knightly families; a royal connection and, upholding the whole edifice, extensive estates centred on Yorkshire and Westmorland. Nobility, his acclaimed ancestry and great landed wealth were George's birthright and set the framework for much of his outlook and actions throughout his adult life.

It is worth considering the chief elements of his enviable heritage. The Cliffords were a family of ancient noble lineage, lords by tenure on the Welsh Marches from the eleventh century, barons by writ of parliament from 1299 and earls by Henry VIII's creation in 1525. Their ancestry can be traced by tradition from the Viking Rollo, first duke of Normandy, and in certainty from the Norman Pons whose sons came over with the Conqueror. It was a third generation Pons, Walter (1127–87), who assumed the name Clifford from Clifford Castle in Herefordshire which he acquired by marriage. The pivotal career which elevated the Cliffords from Welsh marcher lords into northern barons was that of Robert, 1st Lord (1274–1314), who established his family first in Westmorland and then at Skipton-in-Craven. These estates were still the core of the inheritance to which George succeeded in 1579, maintained intact despite the vicissitudes and often brief lives of the later medieval barons. Lord Robert himself was killed in the English débâcle at Bannockburn in 1315. His successor, Roger, 2nd Lord, was executed for rebellion in 1322 and five of the next seven lords died in battle on the Continent or in the Wars of the Roses.

The family sank to its nadir with the death of the Lancastrian John, 9th Lord on the eve of the battle of Towton in 1461 and his posthumous attainder by Edward IV. His heir, Henry, 10th Lord, was denied his lands and titles for almost twenty-five years until, in 1485, after the Yorkist Richard III's defeat and death at the Battle of Bosworth Field, he was restored by the Tudor Henry VII. In 1487 he married the King's first cousin, Anne St John of Bletsoe, the first of the Cliffords' two royal marriages. From this time the Cliffords were Tudor men and this closeness brought the family to the peak of their royal favour under Henry VIII – the earldom for Henry, 11th Lord in 1525, the marriage of his heir to the King's niece, Lady Eleanor Brandon, in 1535 and the acquisition of big monastic and other estates by 1542.[4]

Great landed wealth and power were essential to command respect and sustain the peerage in their pre-eminence. The enormous expansion of the Clifford possessions between 1532 and 1542, mostly in Craven, raised their patrimony from a baronial estate into one worthy of their earldom and shifted its balance permanently away from Westmorland into Yorkshire. It probably reached its peak in value just before Earl Henry succeeded on 22 April 1542; not, however, its greatest extent – that was to come in James I's reign. Its three main locations were Westmorland, Craven, and Londesborough in the East Riding of Yorkshire.

With their barony of Westmorland and four castles the Cliffords had been the dominating landowners in that county since the early fourteenth century, succeeding the Lords Vipont whose inheritance fell to Lord Robert. Their properties were grouped round their castles along the line of the relatively low-lying Eden Valley from Brougham in the North to the river's source in the Forest of Mallerstang thirty miles to the South. Brougham Castle, a bulwark against Scottish invasion, was their favourite residence. Appleby's location made it the natural administrative centre for the whole estate. Pendragon was destroyed by the Scots in 1341 and Brough burnt down by fire after Christmas in 1521. In addition to the manorial courts and other rights within the jurisdiction of their barony, the Cliffords enjoyed the county-wide administrative authority and duties of their unique hereditary sheriffwick, which they exercised through a deputy. Appleby Castle housed the gaol and provided courtroom and lodgings for the judges of assize on their northern circuit. The parliamentary elections for the county were held there. Nearby in Cumberland, the Cliffords owned the manors of Skelton, Lamonby and Carleton with Penrith, all obtained by Lord Robert, which for convenience were also administered from Appleby.

Their second great original seigneury was the Clifford Fee in Craven, the Honour of Skipton granted by Edward II to Lord Robert in 1311 in exchange for estates in Monmouth. This property had comprised the castle and lordship of Skipton with its extensive demesnes, the manors of Stirton, Thorlby and Silsden and the large Forest of Barden. The manor of Marton had been added early in the fifteenth century. The big expansion in Craven came during Henry VIII's reign, first with the grant in 1512 of the manors of Carleton, Lothersdale, Bradley and Utley in the Aire Valley to the South of Skipton. Then, during the 1530s, Henry, 6th Earl of Northumberland, with the King's agreement, settled on them the Percy Fee in Craven, which lay contiguous to the Clifford Fee to its west and north. Besides its jurisdictions, the Cliffords obtained the manors of Settle,

Brougham Castle, Westmorland, from the north-west, from a drawing by Samuel and Nathaniel Buck, 1739

Giggleswick and Long Preston and the Forest of Langstrothdale. However, there were encumbrances. Northumberland reserved rents of £172 2s. 4d. per year. Because of the sixty years' leases he had made, the townships of Buckden and Starbotton in Langstrothdale did not come into the Cliffords' hands until much later in the century.

Important though the Percy Fee was, much the most valuable acquisition was the estates of the dissolved priories of Bolton and Marton, obtained through the agency of the Duke of Suffolk and with the purchase price reduced because of the King's goodwill. These monastic lands had been largely amortized by earlier lords of Skipton and so dovetailed into the Cliffords' existing properties. They enlarged and consolidated the Cliffords' possessions to the east of Skipton, a corollary to their westward and northern expansion with the Percy Fee. An incidental gain was the exclusion of rivals, their only competitors of standing being the Nortons of Rylstone. Their Craven estate now stretched in an almost continuous block from Storithes in the east to Giggleswick in the west, covering the Wharfe, Aire and Ribble valleys, and northwards to the watershed with Wensleydale. The heart of this great estate was the all-but-continuous demesnes and enclosed deer parks spreading from Barden and Bolton to the walls of Skipton Castle. Equally impressive were their all-embracing jurisdictions. With both the Clifford and Percy Fees in their hands the Earls were effectively lords of the whole of Craven.

This paramount position was reinforced by their authority, under the Crown, as bailiffs of Staincliffe wapentake which was virtually conterminous with Craven. The wapentake was a liberty from which the sheriff of Yorkshire was excluded. The Earls' steward of courts deputised for them in serving writs and other legal processes and presided over its courts. Furthermore, as stewards of the royal Forest of Knaresborough, the Earls had oversight of a huge area extending eastwards from the bounds of Bolton and Barden, their steward in practice doing the work for them. The courtroom survives intact amidst the ruins of Knaresborough Castle. The Earls now had four residences in Craven: the Castle, the smaller Barden Tower and the Biggin Lodge in Carleton Park much favoured by their ladies, and the gatehouse of Bolton Priory, the future Bolton Hall.

During Earl Henry's tenure the inheritance took its final shape, completing the shift to the North which had started as far back as the thirteenth century. He disposed of most of his separated properties, both the old Clifford holdings in the South and the scattered ex-monastic manors in Yorkshire. By 1570, Maltby in South Yorkshire, Hart in Durham with its strategic port of Hartlepool and Clifford's Inn in Fleet Street, used by lawyers, were the Cliffords' only outlying properties. Raising cash appears to have been the main reason for each of the Earl's sales, but his long-term objective was to consolidate the patrimony. Consequently, he systematically added to his Craven estates whenever he could. He bought the manors of Litton in Littondale in 1554, Gargrave in 1556 and Lady Drury's moiety of Grassington in 1559, his brother Sir Ingram already owning the other. He obtained more lands in Gargrave in 1556, Sutton and Glusburn in 1558, Arncliffe in Littondale in 1560 and Malham, Malham Moor and Scosthrop in 1561.[5]

Skipton Castle, Yorkshire, from the outer gatehouse, showing, left to right, the great drum towers (1195–1220) and the Long Gallery and Octagonal Tower erected in 1535 by the 1st Earl. The castle was slighted by the parliament of 1648–9 and later restored by Lady Anne Clifford

Potentially his most valuable acquisition was in 1553 when he paid £400 for Sir Thomas Chaloner's eighty years' lease of the tithes in Craven and the parish of Leeds granted only two years before by Christ Church, Oxford. From this time, the Christ Church tithes became virtually a perpetual tenancy for the Earls and their successors, the Earls of Burlington and the Dukes of Devonshire. What the lease gave them was the tithe crops, with the huge barns for storage, of the rectories formerly owned by Bolton Priory, that is Skipton, Broughton, Carleton, Preston-in-Craven (with the township of Long Preston) and Bolton itself. The rectorial tithes were the tenth part of the yearly corn and hay crops in the parish, the arable in Craven being mainly barley and oats with some wheat and rye. At Bolton the Earls also took the vicarial tithes of wool, lambs, eggs and hens. Every year they kept some of the nearby tithe crops for consumption in their household and stables at Skipton and Barden; the rest they leased for cash rents. Earl George was to consider them 'of so necessary use that they cannot convenyently be severed from the demeanes without apparent decay of howsekeeping or of the Earledome'.[6]

The third segment of the Cliffords' inheritance had come to them by the marriage of John, 9th Lord to Margaret Bromflete, daughter and sole heiress of Henry, Lord Vescy. The Vescy manors were spread over east Yorkshire, with the focus at Londesborough whose hall had formerly been the Vescy family's residence. Earl Henry extended them by purchasing from his daughter Lady Margaret, her husband Lord Strange and Frances, Duchess of Suffolk a twenty-one years' lease of two-thirds of the manor of Faxfleet on Humberside and Gayton Grange in Lincolnshire, which had descended to Margaret from the late Duke of Suffolk.[7] Faxfleet became an integral part of the Londesborough estate until well into the next century.

Though the Earl, on balance, bought fewer manors than he disposed of, his death interrupted his plans for making good the loss. He instructed his executors that, after paying his debts and legacies, they should use the other sums arising 'for purchasing of landes, in consideration of such lands I have sold.'[8] They were unable to do this, for reasons which will be explained in Chapter 3. Earl Henry had nevertheless taken the increase of the Craven and Londesborough properties one stage further and, by getting rid of the scattered manors, had made estate management throughout his possessions less costly and much more responsive to his own and his successor's direction.

The revenues Earl George stood to inherit on his father's death would rank him alongside or superior to most of his contemporaries among the nobility. They fell short of the incomes enjoyed by the handful of wealthiest families, including in the North the Talbots, earls of Shrewsbury, and the Percys, Earls of Northumberland. But he would be on a par with the Nevilles, Earls of Westmorland, and the Lancashire-based Stanleys, Earls of Derby, and easily surpassed his baronial relatives and neighbours, the Scropes of Bolton in the North Riding, the Dacres in Cumberland and the Whartons of Wharton Hall in Westmorland. Its great size and revenues apart, Earl George's landed heritage had two discernible influences on him. Firstly, sentiment towards the origins of the various parts of his estates determined to a large extent how he treated them, though value and legal title were bound up with that. Secondly, the policy of concentration on Craven ensured that, however short of cash he might be, George never missed a chance to purchase properties in Skipton town and adjacent manors. What otherwise befell the inheritance in his hands will loom large in considering his career and its consequences.

In the status-conscious Elizabethan Court, Earl George was never likely to be troubled by disparaging comments directed in resentment by some of the old-established peers towards newcomers, often royal servants or favourites raised to a barony or better. His earldom might be fairly recent, yet, with only one marquess, it ranked him ninth in order of precedence.[9] Moreover, his array of baronial titles was proof of antiquity and gave him added dignity and stature among his fellows. Displaying them revealed to the discerning eye his noble antecedents and kinship and also the origins of his family's landed wealth and the territorial power they had long enjoyed. The full emblazon bore eight quarterings, best interpreted as two quarterlies of four. The first was the Clifford coat, dating from the thirteenth century, which comprised the Clifford shield and its augmentation with the Vipont and Flint (from the Viponts) arms. The second quarterly was a late fifteenth-century addition, Lord Vescy's emblazon of Bromflete, Vescy, Atton and St John shields, the latter especially apposite for the Shepherd Lord after his marriage to Lady Anne and its hint of his royal connection. The supporters were dexter, a wyvern gules (Clifford), and sinister, a dog semée of roundlets (St John), though there were variations of the latter. The crest was a wyvern sejant within an earl's coronet, the motto Desormais, 'Henceforth'.[10]

Both the wyvern and the motto need further elucidation. Earl George, like his father and grandfather and their officers, termed the wyvern a red dragon. Until the end of the sixteenth century, no distinction was made between the two heraldic beasts and the Cliffords, with their post-conquest Welsh connections, may always have thought of their crest as a dragon. George's red dragon, as will be seen in chapters IV and V, was admissible as Arthurian symbolism, but, when it clashed with Queen Elizabeth's Tudor red dragon emblem, it was likely to cause her offence and sometimes did. When the Cliffords adopted their motto is uncertain. William Taylor, then the receiver-general in Craven, informed the antiquary Roger Dodsworth in 1620 that it signified the Cliffords' restoration following an attainder. If this tradition was based on fact, there are three possibilities, 1234, 1327 and 1485. The motto's first recorded use, by Henry, 10th Lord at the battle of Flodden in 1513, may give greater credence to his adopting it in 1485 but its medieval French suggests an earlier origin.[11] Earl George's usual choice of titles was calculated to carry the greatest weight among his associates and tenants on all his estates – Earl of Cumberland, Lord of the Honour of Skipton, Lord Clifford, Lord of Westmorland, Vipont and Vescy. As was the fashion, his signet ring was engraved with his crest.

In the young Lord George, an awareness of the high rank of his family and their renowned forebears would have been instilled by his courtesy title, the ceremonial of his father's noble establishment and the visual displays of the Clifford and Cumberland coats of arms in Skipton Castle and the other residences, all regularly visited on the household's peripatetic journeyings. Heraldry and portraiture gave moral instruction with a visual power not easy to appreciate today. The heraldry of the stained glass windows and stone plaques was a history lesson in George's older antecedents and also delineated the more recent family alliances with the St Johns and Percys. The furnishings listed in the 1572 Skipton inventory included richly ornate green, yellow and tawny hangings, testers and cushions, all decorated with the family's arms and crests. Three panes of cloth of gold and two of tawny velvet had a red dragon looking out of a white castle made of silver tessay, a depiction which will be recalled in chapter V. Tableware and many other household items would be stamped suitably with crest and coats. However, the emblems on furnishings, silverware, doors and perhaps other furniture which would make most impression on visitors and the young George and Francis would be the leopards and dragons, portcullises and roses of the Tudor kings. Two doors have survived in Skipton Castle with carvings of Henry VII's and Henry VIII's arms. Church monuments had the same educative effect. In Holy Trinity, Skipton the fine tomb to the 1st Earl with his coats of arms proclaimed his standing and marriage alliances and, most of all, the honour of Knight of the Garter bestowed on him by Henry VIII. John, 7th Lord's garter and coat were depicted in the brass of his tomb slab in Bolton Priory. The nave had been preserved as a chapel, serving the local community, its curate appointed and paid by the Earls. The priory was rich in heraldry, including that of English monarchs.[12]

George, indeed, was attuned from early childhood to take his rightful place among the Tudor nobility, a close-knit and distinctive group who enjoyed special privileges and a unique esteem and renown. In a society which was hierarchical in structure, in theory and also largely in practice, the peerage stood at the apex, under the Crown. Below them in descending order of rank came the knighthood and gentry, the yeomen in the countryside and merchants in the boroughs, down to the lower orders in the towns and rural areas. It was a deferential society in

The tomb of Henry Clifford, 1st Earl of Cumberland (1493–1542), with the brass of the 2nd Earl (1517–70), in Holy Trinity Church, Skipton

which men were expected to – and usually did – doff their caps to those of higher status, not just from custom but also because of ingrained attitudes of mind. Nevertheless, society from peers down to paupers was not, and could never have been, as rigid as contemporary theory laid down. The edges of the supposedly discrete ranks were blurred. There was much vertical mobility, while friendship, wealth and, conversely, poverty could make a mockery of birth and inherited status. Yet the nobility remained distinctive and their standing, upheld by demeanour, precedence and terms of address, amounted to a cleavage between them and all those of lower rank.[13] Episodes in Earl George's career amply illustrate the social relations of the Elizabethan peerage, the notions of rank, the gulf between them and the rest of society, and the circumstances, notably during the long years of the war against Spain, when the sharing of experiences and George's own bent of mind could temporarily bridge that gulf.

The peerage's natural affinity was with the monarch and when they had to defer to commoners it was usually to Privy Councillors or other office-holders who were acting with the authority of the Crown. For any nobleman, relations with his monarch were of paramount importance. Nearness in blood gave a special nexus, a source of strength at times, of danger at others, which often proved fateful under the Tudor rulers. Most noble families could point to some remote royal ancestry in their genealogy similar to George's via his great-grandmother, Lady Anne. Only the Earls of Hertford and Derby could claim as close a link with the Tudors as his, because his half-sister Lady Margaret was directly descended from Henry VII through his daughter Mary, widow of Louis XII of France and sister of Henry VIII. In view of the focus in this study on George's relationship with Queen Elizabeth I it is worth considering how Earl Henry and Lady Margaret fared in the years before her accession, which virtually coincided with George's birth. Princess Elizabeth was a sharply observant witness of their experiences which, while nerve-racking during Edward VI's reign, were comfortable under Mary I when Elizabeth herself, under restraint, could only look on the future with some foreboding. But there is a more compelling reason for looking at how Lady Margaret fared. Only a decade later George was to be as much a prisoner of political and religious developments as his sister had been, Earl Henry working hard on both occasions to safeguard his children's interests.

Earl Henry might have avoided his problems in the early 1550s when he was widowed and Lady Margaret was his only child and potentially a great heiress. He was still only in his early thirties and appreciated how imperative it was to find a second wife and beget a male heir. The stumbling block was the attitude of the chosen girl, the seventeen-year-old Anne, daughter of William, 3rd Lord Dacre. They discussed the proposed marriage during 1550 and Dacre got the support for the match of Lady Dacre's brother, Francis Talbot, 8th Earl of Shrewsbury, then Lord President of the Council in the North at York, and also of the royal Council in Westminster. However, young noble ladies had minds of their own and often got their way. For three and a half years Anne, in service in another household, would not agree, Dacre being convinced it was because of the 'evill Counsell' of some of her friends.[14]

For Earl Henry these waiting years were to prove almost fatal as he and Lady

THE TUDORS, BRANDONS AND CLIFFORDS

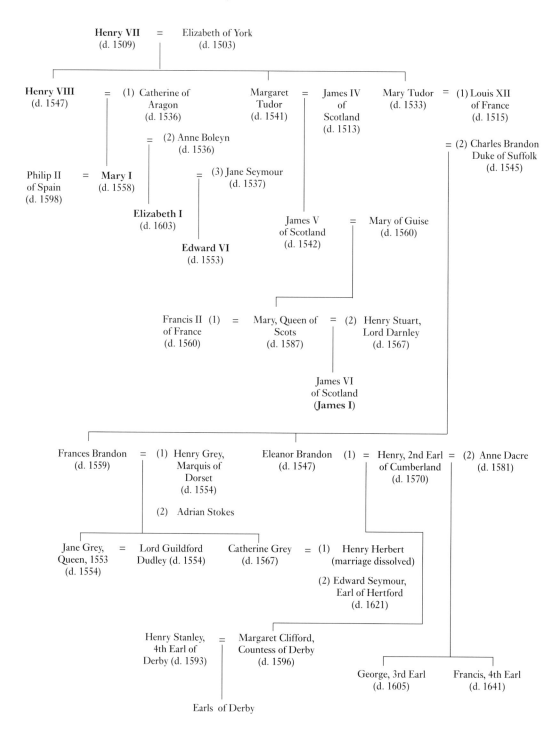

Margaret became ensnared in the religious, political and dynastic crises of Edward VI's reign and the ambitions of the Lord President, John Dudley, Duke of Northumberland, and his Protestant faction which dominated the young King's Council.[15] Under Northumberland, Earl Henry was to discover the drawbacks of a daughter who was both his heir and a blood-royal relation of successive Tudor monarchs. Furthermore, Lady Margaret was all the richer because of her share of her grandfather the Duke of Suffolk's wealth.[16] She was a catch indeed for any nobleman's son. Yet what gave her special appeal was her royal descent and her claim as eighth in line to the throne, recognised in Henry VIII's will. The story of how Northumberland tried to get control of the fourteen-year-old Margaret's inheritance and royal claim in his plot to exclude Queen Mary I from the throne and safeguard his Protestant regime has been well told by Mrs Stopes and summarised by Dr Williamson, so need not be repeated here. Earl Henry did his utmost with strength of mind and ingenuity to protect his daughter and the Clifford inheritance. Fortunately for him, Edward VI died on 6 July 1553, before the planned wedding of Northumberland's elder brother Sir Andrew Dudley with Lady Margaret could be held, indeed before Sir Andrew and his retinue could ride to Skipton Castle where the marriage was to take place. As soon as the news reached York of Queen Mary's accession, the Earl made his allegiance to the Tudors and the Queen's person explicit and for this overt display of loyalty, was well rewarded.[17]

During Mary's reign, Earl Henry's links with the Court through his daughter remained strong and his position safe. For her coronation Queen Mary issued 'to our Ryghte Dere and Entyerlye beloved Coosyn the Ladye Clyforde xv yardes of purple satten for oon ffrenche gowne'.[18] At Mary's marriage with King Philip in Winchester Cathedral in July 1554, Lady Margaret was her only female relative present and held her purse for Philip's gift of gold coins.[19] Princess Elizabeth was then a virtual prisoner and some commentators regarded Lady Margaret as having the better claim to the throne after Queen Mary.[20] When it came to Lady Margaret's own marriage, the Queen proved as sensitive as any Tudor to its dynastic and religious implications. If she did not actually dictate the choice of Henry, Lord Strange then she certainly gave her sanction. He was heir to Edward, 3rd Earl of Derby, a suitably Catholic nobleman with great estates centred on Lancashire. In 1554 it was quite foreseeable that the Derbys would eventually obtain the Cliffords' main Yorkshire and Westmorland properties and this would have held secure for the Catholic cause a huge region across the North of England; a Marian version of the Duke of Northumberland's scheme.

The wedding was one of the great Court events of 1555. The ceremony was performed on 12 February in the chapel of Whitehall Palace in the presence of Queen Mary and King Philip. The Queen presented the bride with a brooch of thirteen diamonds and all the apparel and household linen which Sir Andrew Dudley had purloined from Edward VI's wardrobe, so that Lady Margaret probably wore the robes of gold and silver tinsel which Dudley had chosen for her. After a great dinner, there were jousts and a tournay on horseback; after supper, the Spanish combat of 'jube the cane', a play with torch-lights, a masque and finally a banquet.[20] Following this sumptuous occasion, the Earl had more

Margaret Clifford, Countess of Derby   *Queen Mary I, 1554, by Hans Eworth*
(1540–1596), artist unknown

reason than most peers to hang in his chamber at Skipton Castle the portraits of King Philip and the Emperor Charles V. This would be a matter of paternal pride in his daughter's connection with the greatest of the European rulers rather than endorsement of Queen Mary's marriage because there are grounds for thinking he was not happy with a foreigner as consort.[22]

Lady Margaret's marriage was to bring Earl George close relatives in the Stanley family and responsibilities towards them when they in turn struggled with inheritance difficulties during the 1590s. He would become aware of Lady Margaret's spendthrift nature and marital problems which led to the break-up of her marriage in 1567 but it was her later extravagances and Queen Elizabeth's treatment of her which impinged on him far more. Elizabeth and the Privy Council had to step in to curb her improvidence. Lady Margaret never escaped the bonds set by her blood-royal link. Portraits of her show that she was uncomfortably close in looks and physique to Mary Tudor, a constant reminder to Elizabeth of her sister's reign and her years of custody and danger. Elizabeth tended to be harsh and unforgiving with her Brandon cousins who had both a claim to her throne, which could become a focus of opposition, and also crossed her by rash actions. Lady Margaret was to outlive them all and continue to offend Elizabeth by her uncontrolled spending and behaviour up to her death in 1596. Unhappy in her marriage and closely supervised at Court by the Queen, Lady Margaret was frequently without joy or comfort.[23] It is Elizabeth's memories of events before her accession and her feelings towards Lady Margaret and the whole Clifford family, in so far as they may be surmised, which have to be borne in mind when the fluctuating nuances of her ties with Earl George are pondered.

Earl Henry's own second marriage was solemnised soon after his daughter's. Anne Dacre made up her mind in August 1554 and at last agreed. Details were settled in February 1555. Because Dacre could not afford more, the Earl was content to take only £1,000 as Anne's 'portion', that is the substantial sum in cash which fathers provided for their daughters on marriage. In return for this, the groom's father (or he himself) guaranteed her an annual allowance and an income, that is a jointure, if she were widowed. Earl Henry provided Anne with a jointure estate of all the Westmorland castles and properties apart from the sheriffwick, with Brougham Castle as her chief dower house, a generous endowment and suitably close to her Dacre homeland but a sign of the downgrading of that estate now compared to Craven. The wedding took place at Kirkoswald, Cumberland. The first child of this union, Frances, was born at Skipton in 1555 and two more daughters followed in 1556 and 1557.[24]

Faced after Frances's birth with an even remoter prospect of the male line being continued, Earl Henry executed a special deed either in 1555 or 1556 to ensure that a large part of the Clifford patrimony would not fall, via his daughters, into the hands of the Derbys or any other family. It reveals the Earl's strong sense of family history and obligation to his brother and the male line. Now, unless a son inherited, the Cliffords' original Westmorland and Skipton properties would go to Lady Margaret and Lord Strange. The rest of his possessions, that is all the additions since 1311 including the Vescy, Percy and monastic lands and the tithes lease, would be inherited by Sir Ingram who, as heir male, would succeed to the earldom. Sir Ingram had big properties of his own in Yorkshire, Derbyshire and Nottinghamshire. Combined with the lands he would receive by the deed, they would amply sustain the earldom. Even more interesting is the Earl's recognition of the claims of his natural brother Thomas Clifford of Bolton, because, should Sir Ingram die without male heir, he would inherit in his place. The Earl looked to more distant branches of his family for the other possible inheritors. Next in line came Thomas Clifford of the Aspenden, Hertfordshire branch, his brother George, then William of London, all descended from Thomas, 8th Lord (1414–55), and finally the Cliffords of Borscomb in Wiltshire. So concerned did Earl Henry remain about the male succession that, even a decade after George and Francis were born, he incorporated the dispositions of this entail in his will, drawn up on 8 May 1569. It was fortunate for the earldom that George and Francis did survive. Both Sir Ingram, despite two marriages, and Thomas of Bolton died without direct heirs. The earldom would have counted for far less in the hands of the Aspenden or other minor gentry branches of the family.[25]

Earl George's heritage, with all its advantages and concomitant responsibilities, was one of the two dominating influences upon his development from boyhood to manhood and his eventual succession to the patrimony. The second, equally inescapable, was the political and religious circumstances of the late 1560s during which he grew up. These were to shape the course of his life to a greater degree than even his sister's had been by those of the early 1550s. This was no fault of Earl Henry's, although after his marriage he rarely visited London or the Court and instead devoted himself to provincial and private affairs, spending his time on

Robert Dudley, Earl of Leicester (1533–88),
by Steven van der Meulen, c. 1565

estate matters and his scholarly pursuits of alchemy and astrology.[26] Just as he had for Countess Margaret, he calculatedly chose the best options for George as he and Lady Anne interpreted them, warding off as far as they could the damaging intrigues of Court politics. Elizabeth I's Court in the 1560s was rent with personal rivalries and factions, the older nobility resenting the parvenues, northerners the southerners, Catholics the Protestants. Deep issues roused passions and animosity, especially the questions of her marriage and the succession to the throne, religion, foreign relations, and the treatment of Mary, Queen of Scots after she fled to England in May 1568. All aspects of courtier in-fighting were eventually to impinge on Earl Henry – the personal, political and religious – and in the end he was compelled to play his part in their violent denoument, the 1569 Rebellion.

First to affect Lord George's future was another Dudley intrusion into Earl Henry's affairs, this time not necessarily unwelcome. Those members of Northumberland's family who had been spared execution and later released by Queen Mary had been restored by Elizabeth. It was the Duke's youngest son Robert, Earl of Leicester, by then Elizabeth's favourite, who sponsored George's marriage; not, however, for altruistic motives. When George reached an age for formal marriage agreements, Leicester seized the chance to draw Earl Henry and his heir closer to him and his Protestant friends at Court and in particular to Francis Russell, 2nd Earl of Bedford. In 1565 Leicester engineered the marriage of his twice-widowed elder brother Ambrose Dudley, Earl of Warwick, to Bedford's eldest daughter Anne. Then Leicester 'motioned' the matching of

George with Bedford's youngest daughter Margaret, the children being seven and five years old respectively. Leicester was picking up the threads of his father's policy towards the Cliffords, drawing into his fold their northern wealth and connections. He may also have been trying to neutralise Earl Henry's possible adhesion to Lord Dacre and the Earls of Northumberland and Westmorland, all four northern noblemen being Catholics and so considered by Mary, Queen of Scots and her advisers to support her succession to the English throne. Perhaps, too, Leicester had in mind countering the close marriage links which his rival Thomas Howard, 4th Duke of Norfolk already enjoyed with the Earls of Westmorland and Derby and Lord Scrope.

Bedford was one of the new nobility, his title an Henrician creation, a loyal subject to Queen Elizabeth, in religion a Puritan, the 'hotter' sort of Protestant as a contemporary called them, who based their faith on the Scriptures.[27] He had fled abroad during Queen Mary's reign to escape her persecution and became imbued with the extreme reformist notions of John Calvin in Geneva. For his daughter to marry an earl's heir from an ancient noble family was the kind of match he would most aspire to. He obviously discounted the potential religious harm to Margaret from her future Catholic relatives; in fact, Leicester's circle may have regarded her as a means to spread Protestantism into the North. Earl Henry appointed his brothers-in-law Anthony Browne, Viscount Montagu, and Leonard Dacre (both Catholics) to settle preliminary marriage articles. He sent his cousin Sir Gervase Clifton of Clifton, Nottinghamshire, to view the girl. The report was satisfactory and, in January 1566, the Earl, following protocol, wrote from Appleby Castle to Leicester to 'open the matter to the Quenes Majeste for her hignes assent'. It was now tacitly assumed that at the appropriate age Lord George and Lady Margaret would be married.

There may have been more to Leicester's sponsorship of the match than his own or his supporters' political and religious ambitions. It had too much in common with royal policy towards the North to discount collusion with the Queen herself. The power of the traditional great office-holders there, Northumberland, Westmorland, Dacre and the Cliffords themselves, had been whittled away by Henry VIII. Elizabeth went a step further, replacing them by noblemen of more certain allegiance, Lord Scrope in the West March and southerners elsewhere, including Thomas Radcliffe, 3rd Earl of Sussex, as the Lord President at York and Bedford, who, in 1564, was appointed warden of the East Marches and governor of Berwick. Of all the northerners, the Cliffords had proved themselves the most loyal to the Tudor Crown. In the 1536 Pilgrimage of Grace, Earl Henry had helped rally Carlisle to resist, his father had defied the rebels from Skipton Castle, and Sir Ingram had held Berwick-on-Tweed. The marriage alliance would signal the Earl's leaning towards Leicester's circle at Court and be interpreted as affirming his fidelity to Queen Elizabeth.

Earl Henry and Countess Anne must have been content with the prospect of George being linked with the Puritan Russells and their own overt political connections now with Leicester's Protestant faction. But the Earl did not compromise his family's Catholic stance. During this first decade of Elizabeth's reign conservative religious beliefs and practices were still deeply entrenched in the North and royal policy was inclined to accommodate them. The men the Earl chose as members of Parliament for Appleby and Westmorland, such as his servants Christopher Monckton, John Eltoftes and Gerard Lowther, were Catholics. According to Bishop Best of Carlisle in 1564, he used his influence as sheriff to impede the implementation of the Protestant Elizabethan Church Settlement in the north-west with his Dacre relatives as his natural henchmen. He and Countess Anne were probably planning for George a future as a Catholic in conviction combined with unswerving loyalty to the Queen, like themselves and Viscount Montagu, who was a Privy Councillor highly esteemed by Elizabeth. This would have been at that time an entirely feasible and legitimate prospect. Granted that role, for George to have a father-in-law such as Bedford and friends within Leicester's circle would be all to his advantage.

A second development had disturbing implications immediately for Earl Henry and in the long run for his heir. The political equilibrium in the north-west was upset by the Duke of Norfolk. Successive dukes had always supported the Dacres and, in January 1567, the twice-widowed Duke seized the opportunity to marry as his third wife Lady Elizabeth, the widow of Thomas, 4th Lord Dacre. This gave him the guardianship of her five-year-old son, George, 5th Lord, and her four daughters. Politically, it enabled Norfolk to extend his power into the North and build up his own clientele among the gentry, especially in Cumberland, Westmorland and on the Borders. After Lady Elizabeth's death in childbed in September, the Duke exploited his control over his step-daughters (as guardians were wont to do), consolidating his family's position by matching his sons with the Dacre girls. How Earl Henry and Countess Anne reacted to the Duke as their brother-in-law, in charge of their nephew and nieces, is not known. Most likely they would have been unhappy at the establishment of so powerful a courtier in the north-west. A great peer like Norfolk would overshadow all.[28]

In the meantime, George, Lord Clifford was made aware of the duties which fell on boys of noble standing at an early age. On 6 August 1567, still only eight years old, he entered into his first legal transaction in fulfilment of an agreement made between his father and John Lambert Esq. of Calton in Craven. This was the settlement by Lambert of a jointure estate, comprising Airton Hall and its lands, on his son and heir Benjamin and his wife Elizabeth Clifford, the Earl's natural daughter. It was commonsense to pass to George the responsibility for his half-sister's future welfare and he was given the support of seven of the Earl's senior officers, Thomas of Aspenden, Matthew Redman Esq. of Flasby, William Lister Esq. of Midhope, William Arthington gent. of Arthington, George Clapham gent. of Beamsley, Laurence Preston and Christopher Carr. The Earl's other natural daughter, Joan, had married in 1563 Edward Birkbeck Esq. of Hornby who for many years was to be a diligent officer of the Earls in Westmorland.[29]

The Bedford marriage agreement and Norfolk's northern intrigues would have been pondered by the Earl and Countess before they decided in 1569 where and under whose guidance Lord George should now be brought up. He had probably been tutored in the household by the schoolmaster William Hartley and his father's officers Henry Denton and Lancelot Marton who taught his sister

Eleanor, his elder by only a year. Now eleven years old, it was time for him to leave home. His placing was for the Earl and Countess Anne a matter for careful judgement. Both the Earl and his father had been educated at Court, but George was too young for that and, in any case, opportunities for boys to serve the monarch's person were restricted with a queen on the throne. The best his parents could do was place him with his relatives in the South where he could become familiar with another noble house and royal occasions. Their solution was ideal in its religious, social and political aspects. He was sent to live with his aunt Magdalen Dacre and her husband Viscount Montagu whose residence was Battle Abbey, near the Sussex coast. As Lady Anne Clifford related, Lord George was 'bred up there for a while so that he might see the renowned Queen Elizabeth and her court and the City of London and the Southern parts of England.' At Battle, the young lord would be subjected to a strict Catholic regime of divine prayers, festivals, fasts and diet and the company of so many visiting Catholics that Lady Magdalen's household was called Little Rome.[30]

This move was timely. Earl Henry's health deteriorated during 1569 and in May he made his will. In this he looked to protect his widow and four under-age children. He chose his executors wisely. Viscount Montagu and Sir Edward Saunders, chief baron of the Exchequer, could keep an eye on their affairs at Westminster. Sir William Ingleby of Ripley Castle and the lawyer William Tankard of Boroughbridge, his steward of the Courts at Knaresborough, had influence in the Council at York. His two most trusted household officers, his groom of the chamber William Ferrand and auditor Laurence Preston, would support Countess Anne in dealing with estate and financial business. He

Battle Abbey, Sussex

appointed his Dacre and Montagu brothers-in-law as assignees of the lands to pay his debts and legacies, and Leonard Dacre with Ferrand and Preston as the custodians of the three keys of the 'treasure house' in Skipton Castle, where the irreplaceble estate records were stored. Lord George was to inherit the main Clifford properties; Francis enjoy a life interest in the east Yorkshire manors; Lady Frances got a suitable cash sum as her portion, depending on the rank of the man she married, and Lady Eleanor 800 marks as her portion. The Earl made the usual charitable bequests and preferment by lease, legacies or annuities to 115 estate and household servants, including twelve keepers, an indication of the size of his establishment and patronage.[31]

All his careful planning and his aspirations for George's future were shattered by the Great Northern Rebellion in November 1569. The Earls of Westmorland and Northumberland and their Catholic followers rose in support of the Duke of Norfolk with the intention of overthrowing Queen Elizabeth and establishing Mary, Queen of Scots on the throne. Earl Henry, then residing at Brougham Castle, remained completely loyal to Queen Elizabeth. He had a spy in the rebels' camp distinguished, as Northumberland was to recall, by his fine white gelding, though his name was not known. The Earl, with Leonard Dacre and Thomas, 2nd Lord Wharton, assisted his nephew Henry, Lord Scrope, the West March warden, to raise forces against the rebels. Brougham and Carlisle Castles were the centres of their operations. It was to the Earl and safety at Brougham that Sir George Bowes's horsemen rode, early in December, after escaping through the rebel lines besieging Barnard Castle. By the time the insurgents retreated towards Scotland, Scrope and Earl Henry had about 1,000 men ready to attack them. Their actions were commended to the Queen and Council: 'my Lord of Comberland, & my Lord Scrope, and Leonard Dacre have shewed them selfs honorable and diligent in ther service at the rebels entring into the West Marches, and upon the scaling of the rebels: there be great nombers of them taken in the West Marches'; in fact, 300 or more.[32]

Less than two weeks later, on 8 January 1570, the Earl died at Brougham, aged fifty-two. He had been 'not helthefull in bodie' when he made his will in May. Queen Elizabeth was aware of his infirmity when she wrote to him on 7 December urging him to raise men against the rebels and doubted that he would be able to take any 'vehement travaile abroad.' Indeed, it may have been these exertions in winter which led to a rapid deterioration in his condition. The Earl of Bedford had heard by 3 January that he was in some danger and petitioned the Queen to have the wardship of Lord George because, he explained, it was well known that 'ther hath bene communication betwene my lord of Cumbrelande and me for the marryinge of his son to one of my daughters.' The Queen granted him the wardship at once. Within a week of his father's decease, Earl George was removed from Montagu's at Battle and placed in Bedford's charge.[33]

His uncle Leonard Dacre straightaway paid his respects to Bedford. He wrote on 19 January to convey 'the verie good hope that I conceyve of your honorable care over the younge Erle, to his owne advancement and his frends Comforth'. Then he added, in phrases of hard realism:

Francis Russell, 2nd Earl of Bedford
(1527–85), English School

as nature fastynethe me to the roote of that young ymppe: So I shall accounte my selfe bownde to all those which further his welthe and honor. And as his whole estate in tyme to come, now restithe moche in your Lord: so I ame nowe humbly to crave of your honor, to accompte me, as one which will depende of hym, and of those which do for hym, and that to the uttermoste of my power.[34]

Dacre in one respect did his duty by George. Before he himself rebelled less than a month later, he assigned to Countess Anne his share of the responsibility for overseeing some of the Craven estates, so they would escape any possible royal retribution. His revolt was caused by despair. The accidental death of the young George, Lord Dacre in the previous June had delivered into the hands of Norfolk and his sons the rich Dacre inheritance. Leonard's right title to the barony had been denied him by a commission set up by Norfolk as Earl Marshal. Angered, he defied the Council with the forces he had raised against the northern earls in a vain attempt to regain his family's estates. The defeat of Dacre's borderers by Lord Hunsdon's royal army ended the old order in the North. The traditional great nobility of Nevilles, Percys and Dacres and many of their gentry followers were now dead, exiled or in custody and their estates confiscated. Among them were the Nortons of Rylstone, the Cliffords' awkward neighbours in Craven.

Only three of the northern nobility fully survived the debacle of 1569, Earl George, who was under age and a royal ward in the South, his relatives the loyal

Scropes of Bolton, and Lord Wharton. When the latter died in 1572 the wardship of his heir Philip, 3rd Lord was granted by the Queen to the Earl of Sussex. The execution of the Duke of Norfolk in 1572 effectively neutralised the Howard influence in the north-west until the end of the century because, for the sake of tranquillity, the Queen excluded his sons from their Dacre properties and confined them to the South. By the time Earl George, his brother Francis and the young Lord Wharton entered into their estates, the North was politically a calmer and safer region, but one from which many of its traditional features had been erased. The changes were, indeed, to be so profound that it was almost a new environment for Earl George and Francis and their generation of northern gentry, except that they were themselves to contribute to the metamorphosis which had occurred by the start of the Jacobean era.

Much depended for the Clifford family's future on how Earl George fared under the surveillance of the Earl of Bedford: this is considered in the following chapter. His mother managed as best she could in looking after her other children and the Clifford estates, aided only by her senior officers. She was diminished and exposed by the death or exile of so many of her once-powerful relatives and friends and governmental suspicion of many of those who survived. Leonard died in extreme poverty in Brussels in 1573 and her younger brothers were only minor gentry. Montagu, her highest placed relative, served her well if intermittently because he lived so far away. He, Earl George and Francis were to take over the obligations to tend for the next generation of disinherited and impoverished Dacres.[35]

The Cliffords were denied their due reward for holding firm for the Crown in 1569. Earl Henry's death early in 1570 and George's minority – the family's first for over a century – precluded them from sharing by purchase, lease, or offices in the Queen's redistribution of the lands forfeited by the rebels, even greater in some areas of the North than those of the dissolved religious houses. For Earl Henry to have obtained some of the Nevilles's and Nortons's manors would have been an appropriate epilogue to a career praiseworthy for its devotion to his family and inheritance and for maintaining the Cliffords' unswerving fidelity to successive Tudor monarchs. He had consolidated the patrimony and preserved it intact. If he had needed some luck to weather the mid-century political crises, he showed judgement as well as resilience.

His later career as an undemonstrative, provincial nobleman was a legitimate and understandable alternative to his frenetic younger days spent in Henry VIII's service. He could not escape courtier machinations, as has been seen, yet he surmounted the ensuing dangers. Earl George was to take the contrary course, abandoning the North for the hurly-burly of life at Court. By opting for a role centre stage he was to dissipate the landed wealth so painstakingly built up by generations of his forebears and bequeath to his successors, his brother Earl Francis and nephew Earl Henry, greater financial burdens and discord than the family had ever experienced before. He would have done well to reflect on how tenaciously his father had laboured to keep the great Clifford inheritance secure for him.

CHAPTER 2

Guardianship and Tutelage: 1570–9

Only one year separated Earl George from his brother Francis and they remained to the end close in spirit if not in temperament. Much hinged on their relationship and there is justification for regarding George's tenure of the earldom as a partnership with Francis in managing the Clifford estates and then, increasingly, the fortunes of the family. Their upbringing was not comparable; George's followed the usual noble habit of lavishing the best on the heir: in his case reasons of state reinforced that practice. During his most formative years, from eleven until twenty-one, the influences on him were almost entirely southern, at first by his parents' wish through the Montagues, as has been seen, and then by royal design. From January 1570 for at least seven years George was a member of the Earl of Bedford's family rather than his own, brought up in some isolation from his mother, brother and sisters and their northern relatives, friends and officers. Interwoven with the Bedford influences were those of Trinity College, Cambridge, Christ Church, Oxford and then, increasingly, Elizabeth I's Court. Only once before his marriage, for six weeks in June and July 1576, is he known to have stayed with his mother, at Barden Tower for a family celebration, her fortieth birthday perhaps.

By contrast, Francis, a second son not expected to inherit the earldom (though he in fact did), was reared in his mother's household until 1576 when he lived for a time in London, most likely rooming in Clifford's Inn, although he too journeyed north for the family get-together that summer.[1] He did not attend university, nor undertake legal instruction at the Inn. Yet, however different the social, religious and political atmosphere of Countess Anne's home compared with Bedford's, it is hard to distinguish any traits in outlook or behaviour separating the brothers other than George's naturally greater energies and intellectual gifts and his more exuberant lifestyle and activities. In his younger days Francis regularly accompanied George and, even after his own marriage in 1589 when he settled down at Londesborough, he gave at least as much attention to his brother's affairs in Craven and the capital as to his own.

With the Bedfords Earl George was brought up at Chenies in Hertfordshire, although he also stayed at Russell House on the Strand and Tavistock in Devon.

At Chenies he had his own chamber in the now demolished wing of the manor house. It had not changed when the inventory was taken on 20 September 1585. It was adequately furnished for a young nobleman although inferior in decor to the room he would have used in Skipton Castle. It was wainscoted under the window, had a fireplace with an endiron and fireshovel. The turned wainscot bedstead had a tester and head with a valance of yellow satin of bridges [Bruges] wrought with black velvet. The three old curtains were of black and yellow sarsenet. The other contents comprised an old livery wainscot cupboard and a walnut chair. The furniture was not of much value but the three pieces of hangings of imagery, one of them bordered with bells, fifty-four ells in length (sixty-seven and a half yards) which would cover the walls, were priced at £3 12s. Next to the main chamber was a closet containing a table with a folding trestle and another table with a pair of trestles, perhaps used as a study and for private tutoring by Bedford's resident schoolmaster who would guide his studies for fifteen months until he went to Cambridge.[2]

Bedford's was an almost ideal household for completing Earl George's education in aristocratic duties, demeanour and the social graces. The Russells were a large family, with four sons and three daughters by Bedford's first wife, the younger children being of an age with George. With the eldest daughter Anne, Countess of Warwick, George was to develop a particularly close affinity, a bond of disposition not merely of kinship or because of Anne's exploitable intimacy with Queen Elizabeth. Bedford's second wife, Countess Bridget, daughter of

The now ruined nursery at Chenies manor house, Buckinghamshire, where Earl George's chamber was located

Lord Hussey, was herself twice widowed, most recently relict of Henry Manners, 2nd Earl of Rutland. Bedford's other ward, John Chudleigh of Devon, may also have stayed at Chenies. Besides enjoying the society of the large, highly educated and cultured Russell family and their many relations, Earl George grew up within the orbit of one of the great officers of state, a privy councillor at the heart of royal government and highly regarded by the Queen. He would meet and perhaps sit at the table with distinguished guests, absorbing awareness of current national and overseas issues and in turn becoming familiar to the visitors and treated as his future station in life befitted.[3] Most of all, he would have met the Queen, not on her visit to Chenies in 1570, but while attending Bedford at Court. In the order of procession to parliament at Westminster on Thursday 8 May 1572 George walked beside the young Edward Manners, 3rd Earl of Rutland, nine years older and just senior to him in precedence, who was to be a close friend over the next fifteen years.[4]

An understanding of the mainsprings of Tudor power, the Court, Council and parliament, was essential for Earl George's political education and cementing his allegiance to the Tudor throne. A prime expectation was his religious conformity. In this the Russell family had for the Queen, Burghley and the Council the special requirement of being firmly Protestant in their beliefs. Bedford was one of the influential group of councillors and courtiers, including the Earls of Huntingdon, Leicester and Warwick and Secretary Walsingham, who both protected and sponsored Puritan preachers and their publications. He gave the lead in this in Devon and other south-western counties where his standing has been termed 'all but viceregal.' His son, Lord John, a career diplomatist, had married Elizabeth, daughter of Anthony Cooke and widow of Sir Thomas Hoby, a woman renowned for her linguistic abilities and Calvinistic piety. Both his younger daughters, Elizabeth and Margaret, were to be noted for their Puritan persuasion.[5]

George was, therefore, brought up from 1570 in another very strict household in the religious sense, yet one far removed from the Catholic environment of his Montagu, Dacre and Clifford relatives. An instance of the efforts to insulate the Earl from the doctrines whose treasonable temptations had infused the recent Northern Rebellion is shown in the letter Bedford wrote to Burghley from Coventry on 23 July 1570. He reported that he had sent George away to Oxford for a while 'and, according to your advice, have given as great charge as I can [to those who had care of him], to avoid from him such popish wasps and bees as will be buzzing in his ears, to confirm in him a deafness to true religion' – irony in that phrase – 'whereof I hope there will be great care had.'[6]

However, it was less the precise Calvinist convictions of the Russells and the preachers they patronized which brought about George's conversion than the more restrained Puritanism of his tutors at Cambridge: John Whitgift, master of Trinity College, and William Whitaker. Whitgift was a firm believer in the Calvinist notions of predestination and the salvation of God's elect but, like Elizabeth herself, was more forgiving of those with Catholic inclinations. It was the Queen's personal decision that George should be a pupil of Whitgift, who was then also dean of Lincoln and prebendary of Ely and a decade later became her most trusted Archbishop of Canterbury. Whitgift it was, George later affirmed,

Archbishop John Whitgift (?1530–1604), artist unkown

who 'wanne [him] from Poperie' and so confirmed that personal reformation which was a principal cause of retaining him in the South.[7] In protestation and seemingly in belief, too, Earl George for the rest of his life adhered closely to Whitgift's own religious outlook.

Whitgift's regime in college was strict both in the moral sense and in religious observance, for noblemen as for all his pupils. Sir George Paul wrote that he held his titled scholars and the rest 'to their publique disputations, and exercises, and prayers which he never missed, chiefly for devotion, and withall to observe others absence, alwaies severely punishing such omissions and negligences.' The Master dined and supped in the common Hall so as to keep a watchful eye over them, control their manners and by his example 'teach them to be contented with a scholler-like Colledge diet'. Earl George, Edward Somerset, 4th Earl of Worcester, and Edward, 11th Lord Zouche together affirmed 'that everye nighte they Came to his Chamber, & reade a chapter, & hearde prayers; & he laboured more to instructe them in true groundes of religion' than any other person since.

Whitgift's accounts for his private pupils have survived, including Earl George's. He matriculated in May 1571 and went into residence on 9 May, a carrier bringing his stuff from Chenies to the college. His study at Trinity was barer than his chamber at Chenies. Besides his bed, he had a desk with pen and inkhorn, a cupboard, hourglass and a gittern lute bought for him by Whitgift. The room had glass windows, painted cloths on the walls, a grate to burn wood and coal which were supplied to him along with candles and a key to the privy door. He had one manservant, Tom. Whitgift bought such clothes as George needed, his rather plain attire of jerkin, doublet and hose, linen stockings, 'pomps and pantocles', shoes and boots, a velvet girdle, a Sclavonian cloak and gloves. When George was sick, in July 1572 and again in July 1573, Whitgift met the bills of the doctors and apothecaries who treated him. A man was paid to teach him to dance in November 1573. His recreations included archery with a bow, arrows and archery gloves the Master obtained for him, hawking (the hawk a gift) and riding. But there was also travel in Whitgift's company, both ecclesiastical and social in flavour, on his official visits to Ely, Lincoln and to the courtier Roger, 2nd Lord North at Kirtling, Cambridgeshire.

Earl George came from a studious home, his father having an excellent collection of books, and his private tutoring would have continued at Bedford's. At Trinity he may not have strictly followed the normal four-year course for a bachelor's degree, rather a course devised for him by Whitgift, but the main elements were there. The first year of the degree was a study of mathematics, that is cosmography, arithmetic, geometry and astronomy, including Ptolemy and Euclid. The second year covered dialectic and rhetoric, the final two years philosophy. All students had to be competent enough in Latin at the outset to study the texts. Lady Anne Clifford commented that her father 'never attained to any great perfection in the Latin tongue, yet he had a general knowledge and insight into all the arts specially the Mathematicks wherein he took great delight.' What books Bedford provided for him are not known, but in June 1571 Whitgift bought for him the *Dialogues of Sebastian Castalio* (or Castellion) and the *Colloquies of Erasmus* and in November 1573 Cicero's *Orationes Philippicae* and Giustiniani's *Epistolae*. Erasmus had popularised Latin texts which were in 'free, conversational style, pleasant, easy and of terse discourse.' Castalio's dialogues required scriptural knowledge and sound Latinity. Cicero's orations were essential because they embodied 'grace, insight and all the qualities of good style'. George had the command of language to express himself incisively in speech and correspondence: this would have owed something to his Trinity education. A number of his fellow students became much more fluent in contemporary and classical Latin and also Greek. George's relative and, it would appear, deliberately chosen companion, Richard Musgrave of the Edenhall, Cumberland family (a ward of Thomas, 2nd Lord Wharton) studied the New Testament in Greek. The intellectual fare Whitgift provided for Francis and Anthony Bacon included Plato, Aristotle, Xenophon and Sallust. Earl George ought also to have studied Greek before taking his MA on 15 November 1576 but neither Lady Anne nor any other source mentions that he had even a smattering of the language.[8]

One of the benefits of a university education for the nobility was the chance to mix with other men. Trinity was a college whose endowments favoured scholars from Westmorland and Yorkshire.[9] Earl George was to keep in touch with some of these northern contemporaries throughout his life. First and foremost, Richard Musgrave, who was to remain his friend, officer and, for a time, creditor. At the Earl's instance, he became master of the royal ordnance in the North and was knighted by James I in 1603. The Earl may have sponsored Christopher Shute MA, an ecclesiastical writer with Puritan leanings who, in 1577, republished *Testimony of a True Faith* and dedicated it to him. Shute had become vicar of

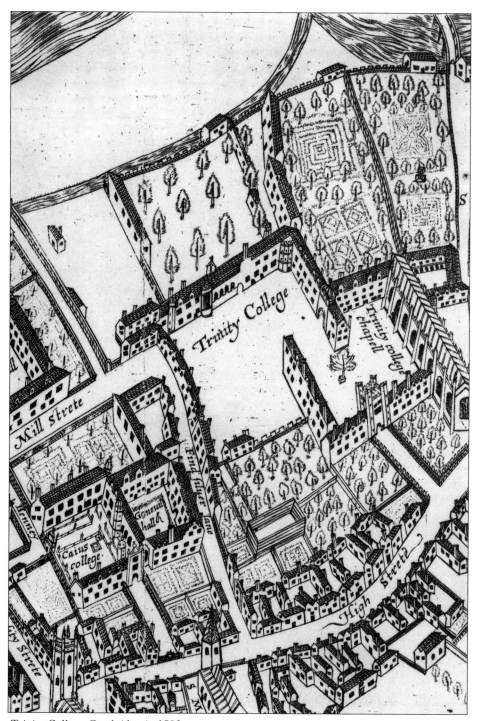

Trinity College, Cambridge, in 1592

Giggleswick in 1576 on the Queen's presentation, master of Giggleswick School and one of the Earl's wealthier tenants in the lordship. William Brogden, who matriculated sizar in 1573 but did not graduate, was curate at Bolton by 1575 under the Earl's patronage, though unlicensed, and became rector of Burnsall in Craven in 1579, where he remained until his death in 1618. Other sons of northern gentry with whom George and his brother were connected were Thomas Brogden, Robert Hutton, nephew of the Archbishop of York, Edmund Ferrand and William Mallory of Studley.[10] Of Whitgift's other private pupils, the Earl of Worcester and Francis Bacon were to be life-long friends.

Earl George's scholarly bent was not to philosophy or classics. It was mathematics and geography which aroused his curiosity and excitement and these remained his passion throughout his life. In his daughter's words, he devoted his attention so earnestly to mathematics 'as to abstract it wholly from all other studies'. His studies at Trinity furthered his mathematical and geographical interests but the initial stimulus to the latter almost certainly came from Bedford and his circle of courtiers dedicated to overseas expansion. They patronized the small group of propagandist writers advocating English exploration and colonisation and invested in the voyages; a corollary of their Puritan and anti-Spanish stances. Bedford was godfather to Francis Drake and it was Warwick who introduced the Yorkshire mariner Martin Frobisher to Court.[11]

Bedford's maritime involvement was displayed at Chenies. In one of his chambers was a parchment map of a fort in the West Indies. Another chamber was called 'The Scollope shell chamber' (possibly a precursor of the Jacobean grotto at Woburn) which also contained two pieces of imagery of men of war. Bedford's own withdrawing chamber had two pieces of hangings depicting a shipwreck.[12] Oceanic exploration and trading and the imperial threat of Spain and Portugal – a common theme of anxiety to the Puritan privy councillors – had, from the 1560s, become the new frontier of English horizons, catching the imagination of the younger generation; it would have been a constant topic of conversation and analysis among Bedford's ministerial and religious intimates.

The 1570s were a stirring time for a young nobleman to come to maturity because of the heightened involvement of the English in oceanic trade and exploration and the clash with Spanish naval power engendered by the voyages of Hawkins and Drake. Oxford University had become the centre for the study of cartography, geography and navigation. The Earl was already connected with and, no doubt welcome at, Christ Church because of his lease of their Craven and Leeds tithes, but it was the presence there of Richard Hakluyt the Younger which was the great appeal. His lectures were arousing excitement at the outset of his unique career as the great publicist and recorder of English maritime enterprise. The Hakluyts, Richard and his brother Thomas, were the actual and also symbolic link with the Earl's extended education at the universities. Both had been at Cambridge and Thomas left Trinity with the Earl to take up residence at Christ Church.

Hakluyt explained in dedicating his *Principall Voyages* in 1589 to Sir Francis Walsingham that his 'publike lectures was the first, that produced and shewed both the olde imperfectly composed, and the new lately reformed Mappes,

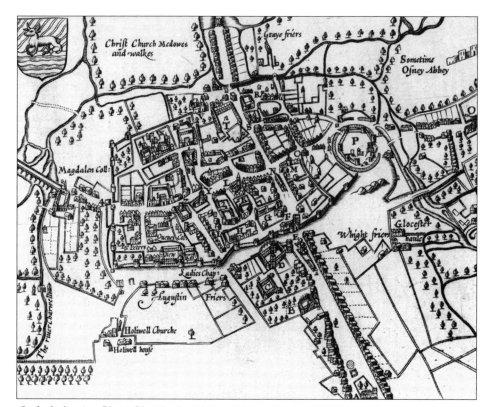

Oxford, showing Christ Church, the college, and Queen's College: a detail from John Speed's map of Oxfordshire, 1610

Globes, Spheares, and other instruments of this Art for demonstration in the common schooles, to the singular pleasure, and generall contentment of my auditory'. Among the avid listeners was Earl George. From the lectures the Earl developed a great theoretical understanding of geography and navigation which he, more than any other nobleman and more than most mariners, was to translate into practical realities by the discipline and rigours of oceanic privateering.

Inspired first by Bedford and then the Hakluyts, Earl George became one of that particular group of university-educated men who contributed enormously to both English overseas expansion and the defeat of Spain during the last two decades of Elizabeth I's reign. Besides the Hakluyts, those at Oxford comprised the future Lord Chief Justice Sir John Popham who was a prime mover in North American colonisation; Sir Edwin Sandys of Virginia fame; the courtier and investor in exploration, Edward Dyer; Sir Philip Sidney, Walsingham's son-in-law; Sir Julius Caesar and his brother Thomas, stepsons of the adventurer Michael Lok; and the explorer Thomas Cavendish.[13]

Earl George's own considerable impact on maritime affairs is looked at in subsequent chapters. His first imaginative contribution came in 1577, when he was nineteen. Bedford, Warwick and Edward Dyer were among the courtiers who invested in Martin Frobisher's second voyage which set off on 26 May that year, gripped by the prospect of gold from the rocks he had brought back from North America on his previous year's sailing in search of the north-west passage to Asia. Earl George, Lord Wharton and Thomas Caesar invested £25 apiece. All were to lose their money, the supposed ore proving worthless. The Earl sensibly followed Bedford's lead in not risking his cash in Frobisher's third voyage, unlike the Earl and Countess of Warwick.[14] The rocks survive, in a large wall built round Elizabeth I's Dartford Manor in Kent, a testimony to misdirected, toiling yet pioneering endeavour.

The most immediate and fruitful outcome of the Frobisher voyages is attributable to Earl George's scholarly interests, worthy of Hakluyt himself. He was the patron of Dionyse Settle who sailed on the 1577 voyage and wrote the first English eye-witness account of America. Settle's *A true reporte of the late voyage into the west and northwest regions* is a description unusual in its objectivity when most publications were unashamedly promotional in purpose. He ascribes the objectives of the voyage to the search for gold first, then for the north-west passage, and he also argues with conventional enthusiasm for religious dissemination and the conversion of the natives. Settle's first-hand account was precisely what the English reading public needed if they were to appreciate fully what the Atlantic and American worlds held in store for them.

In dedicating his book to the Earl, Settle wrote 'I am not oblivious, neither careless, when, and how, your Honour (above my noble expectation) nobly satisfied the request of me your humble servant.' Nothing is known about Settle apart from the book, although his is not an unusual name in Craven and a Robert Settle Esq. acted for Bedford in 1585. He only became the Earl's 'servant' with the sponsorship and he was clearly pleasantly surprised at the Earl's favourable response. But the Earl knew Lok and Frobisher and was probably also instrumental in getting him a place on the voyage. Settle called Frobisher 'your Honours worthie Countrieman'; this was not strictly correct, the Earl being a son of Westmorland not Yorkshire. Through the dedication and the quickly produced foreign editions of the work – French in 1578, Latin and German in Nuremburg in 1580, Italian in Naples in 1582 – Earl George became widely known abroad as well as at home as a nobleman with a special concern for overseas expansion. A decade elapsed, however, before other writers on English voyages obtained his patronage and by then he had begun his own maritime adventures.[15]

During his years of tutelage Earl George was sustained financially in theory by grants from the Court of Wards, in practice mainly from Bedford's pocket. For fiscal reasons the Tudors had revived the feudal rights of monarchs over the lands and disposal in marriage of any tenants-in-chief who inherited, like George, as a minor. The Court had been set up to exploit the income the Crown could get by selling both wardships and the rights over marriage, for which there was often great competition from would-be purchasers. George's wardship cost Bedford dearly, as he would have anticipated. His initial outlay was heavy enough. Bureaucratic expenses to do with obtaining the wardship came to £250, a sum which possibly conceals a gift to Burghley as Master of the Court of Wards.

Sir Martin Frobisher (c. 1537–94), by Cornelius Ketel, 1577

Queen Elizabeth is rarely mentioned when rewards and the incipient corruption of the wardship system are discussed, her personal gifts being mostly undocumented. When the bill was signed for the wardship, Bedford gave her a present of a cup of lapis lazuli, garnished with gold and the garnishing set with diamonds and rubies, worth £140.[16]

The Crown claimed a third of the yearly rental of a ward's estates, just over £600 in George's case, and from this paid exhibitions for his maintenance. Bedford received £200 a year for George's exhibition, a total from 1 January 1570 to 29 June 1579 of £1,644 19s. 0¼d. But against this he had to pay the Crown £1,600 for the purchase of the wardship, likewise in annual instalments. As often happened, Bedford fell behind in his payments, still owed £200 at his death in

1585 and this debt was not cleared for a further four years. Earl Henry had requested the Queen and the Master of the Wards to allow his son £40 a year over the third of his revenues due to the Court, but they seem to have ignored the plea.[17] Bedford could well afford the little extra.

The initial investment was just the start of the financial commitments Bedford undertook when he purchased Earl George's wardship. Indeed, in contrast to Whitgift's austere regime, Bedford indulged his ward grossly, almost certainly more than his parents or the Montagues would have done. Besides the £200 a year exhibition which supported George's education at Trinity and Christ Church (the source of Whitgift's funds), Bedford allowed him £300 annually for his own expenses which over the seven and a half years amounted to £2,250.[18] Much of this would have been spent out of term. Political and religious objectives apart, Bedford could only have justified such an investment in his ward if, as was his right, he married him to one of his daughters, always a noble guardian's aspiration. This did happen but only after tribulation for Earl George and worry for his guardian.

Bedford's investment in his ward might, indeed, have been in vain. Though Earl George was at first attracted to Lady Margaret Russell, which Bedford disliked because he wished him to marry her elder sister Elizabeth, he later fell 'exceedingly in love' with Sir William Holles's daughter Gertrude, by repute a very handsome lady. The Earl's and Holles's friends, in the accustomed fashion, asked Sir William to consent to her marriage but he would not agree to it, claiming that he did not want a son-in-law before whom he would have to stand cap in hand. He would, he declared, see her married to an honest gentleman with whom he could have friendship and conversation. No argument by the advocates could shift Sir William. He was as good as his word. Gertrude was married to Walter Stanley Esq. of West Bromwich on 20 January 1578.[19] Thus the Clifford titles which would have honoured the Holles family fell to the daughter of a house more noble if not more proud.

It may be that the Earl's verses which Anthony Holborne set to a lute accompaniment express his anguish at losing Gertrude Holles. When the words were penned is uncertain yet no other known liaison would have occasioned such depth of feeling. Robert Dowland published Holborne's setting in *A Musicall Banquet* in 1610, well after the lutenist's death in 1602 and the Earl's in 1605. The authors of the three other poems Dowland gives as Sir Philip Sidney, Robert Devereux, 2nd Earl of Essex, and Sir Henry Lee, all among the closest of George's later associates:

> My heavy sprite, opprest with sorrow's might,
> Of wearied limbs, the burthen sore sustains,
> With silent groans and heart's tears still complains,
> Yet I breathe still and live in life's despight.
>
> Have I lost thee? all fortune I accurse
> Bids thee farewell, with thee all joys farewell;
> And for thy sake this world becomes my hell.[20]

Gertrude was, indeed, lost to him. Dr Williamson hints at one of George's later affairs with a Stanley but he may have confused his dates. In the event it was Lady Margaret whom Earl George agreed to marry, not Bedford's preferred choice Lady Elizabeth. She had to wait until 7 August 1582 for her marriage to the widowed William Bourchier, 3rd Earl of Bath, who was but one year older than Earl George. All three of Bedford's daughters were therefore matched into the high Elizabethan noble families. Lady Margaret was two years younger than George. Her mother had died when she was young and she had been brought up until the age of eight by her mother's sister Mrs Alice Elmers. Then she was returned to Bedford's family where her step-mother took charge of her at about the time Earl George became Bedford's ward. Like all the Russell children, she was intelligent and well-educated. Though she never learnt a foreign language, she read widely in translation throughout her life. Her daughter described her as 'truly religious, devout and conscientious, even from her very childhood, and did spend much time in reading the Scriptures and other good books, and in heavenly meditations, and in prayers, fastings and deeds of Charity.' She was, continued Lady Anne, naturally high-spirited, but tempered this by civil and courteous behaviour, instilled in her no doubt by her genteel as well as precise upbringing. Portraits of her, made in later life and poor in quality, display some primness and sadness but otherwise accord with Lady Anne's recollection of her mother as having 'a very well favoured face with sweete and quick gray eyes and a comely personage.'[21]

The wedding ceremony at St Mary Overy, Southwark, on 24 June 1577 was a dual one because George's elder sister Lady Frances was married at the same time to his close friend and frequent companion Philip, 3rd Lord Wharton.[22] Queen Elizabeth, whose attendance made it a royal occasion, would have had quiet satisfaction at the symbolic ending of the old Clifford-Wharton hostility, the conversion of both her wards to the established church and their allegiance to herself and the Tudor throne, a patent success for her political manipulation of these young northern lords and the dedication of Burghley, Bedford, Sussex and Whitgift. She and her advisers had shrewdly been making the most of the chances to remould northern politics after 1569, but with caution and patience. In the new order which was emerging, Cliffords and Whartons were to be instrumental over the next thirty years in bringing calm and order to the North and the Scottish Border region.[23]

Bedford was lavish in his gifts to the young Earl and Countess of Cumberland, besides meeting the big expense of the wedding celebrations. He spent over 1,000 marks on Countess Margaret's apparel and, in addition, bought jewelry for her worth £300. He gave them his mansion house at Chiswick as their London home, later valued at £400. On 6 July he also granted them for life all the swans and cygnets on the River Thames and wood growing on two acres of woodland below his manor of Acton to burn in the mansion. Furthermore, he provided, at a cost of £267 10s. 8d., the gilt and silver plate for their tables and their journeys so that they would continue to have their meals at home and in transit in the splendour they were used to and also be able to entertain in appropriate style. This tableware comprised in gilt plate a pair of fair livery pots weighing 200 oz.; a large pair of flagons 200 oz.; a large basin and ewer of chase work 250 oz.; a large nest of bread bowls 200 oz.; two saltcellers 80 oz.; a fair standing cup and ewer 80 oz.; a deep bowl and ewer 60 oz.; twelve large spoons 24 oz.; three lesser bowls 60 oz., and a casting bottle of 12 oz. For these, Bedford paid, at 7s. 6d. an ounce overall, £169 10s. In silverware they had a deep basin weighing 60 oz.; a nest of bowls 60 oz.; a jug 30 oz., and a poringer and spoon 16 oz.. For their travelling Bedford provided a carrying case of bowls, dishes, plates, basin, spoons and other pieces, all silver and weighing 190 oz. The silverware cost him £98 0s. 8d. All would be engraved with the Clifford and Bedford crests.

Earl George had wedding expenses of his own. For these, he borrowed £120 on 11 June from the London jeweller John Mabbe junior, his friend Sampson Ingleby of Ripley standing surety with him for repayment. Yet this bond and the Earl's other debts to mercers and tailors, totalling £460, were also met by Bedford. An account of Bedford's whole expenditure on the wardship and marriage, correct in the details which can be checked, gave the huge sum of £6,267 10s. 8d. over and above the moneys he received from the Court of Wards. And yet this figure did not include much of the incidental outlay for Earl George as a member of Bedford's family, treated like one of his sons, such as law charges, the gifts of horses, geldings, hawks and similar presents, the payments on journeys for George and his attendants and, not least, 'his sportes, which were verie chargeable.'[24]

Nor were the gifts to cease when Earl George came of age, although now Bedford could in turn enjoy his son-in-law's hospitality. Bedford's bequests in his will dated 7 April 1584 included 100 marks to Earl George in plate or money and to Countess Margaret his 'best bedd of clothe of golde and silver in the lower chamber at Cheynies withe King Henry the eightes armes in yt'. This was an appropriate remembrance for both families whose service to the awesome monarch had been rewarded with such great munificence. But it had far greater significance. Beds and bedchambers were highly charged with emotions and symbolism and the state beds of nobility held a special status. This might even have been where George and Margaret were first bedded, with all the ceremony and boisterous celebrations that newlyweds then had to endure. By 1585, when Margaret inherited the great bed, her memories would have been bitter-sweet; she and her husband already drifting apart.[25]

An arranged marriage assured Countess Margaret of the high status to which she was accustomed yet neither her father's oversight nor his generosity could guarantee contentment. Except for one brief period the marriage was not a mutually happy one, although there were longer spells of friendly relationship before an eventual abrasive separation. They had married for their common good rather than liking for one another. As the Countess confided to Dr Layfield, though God 'matched us in lawful manner in one, our minds met not, but in contrarys and thought of discontentment.' For Earl George, Gertrude Holles would not be forgotten.

Shortly after the wedding, the Earl and his seventeen-year-old Countess travelled north to take up residence with his mother in Skipton Castle. If the Earl was now, in early manhood, reunited with his kindred and welcomed in those regions his family had long dominated, his young wife had for the first time left the lusher southern counties which had always been her home. It was not merely in the strange surroundings, bleak moorlands and harsher climate that she found little to comfort her. She was separated from all she had hitherto known,

> one servant rather for trust, than wit, about me, only acquainted with mee, in a country contrary to my religion, his mother and friends all separate in that opinion, himself not settled but carried away, with young mens opinions.

But she was not completely isolated, at least in her beliefs. On 24 November Christopher Shute preached a 'verie Godlie and necessary Sermon' before her, which he subsequently published. And she was back in London for a while with the Earl that Christmas and exchanged New Year's gifts with the Queen, receiving a cup of silver and gilt with a cover, Brandon, 20½ oz. weight.[26]

It was not just loneliness but indifference and neglect Countess Margaret suffered in her early marriage. The Earl was often in the South attending Bedford and the Court. Either from natural causes or from her situation his Countess was recurrently in poor health during 1578. It was his sister, Lady Derby, who intervened on her behalf. She wrote to George from Isleworth on 27 September – and at greater length to his mother – pleading with him to bring his wife nearer London where medical help was at hand. She pointed out that he need not escort her with a full train because the journey was for sickness not for show, seven or eight persons and enough furniture would do. Then he should seek the opinions of the most learned physicians. Bedford and his daughter had offered to bear the expenses but, Lady Derby urged, it would be better for the Earl to do that even though he had not yet assumed his inheritance. By doing so he would publicly display his affection for his wife, whom she was certain he loved and would care for as any man may, and would be 'honorably esteemed of the worlde' and all the more favoured, if that were possible, by the Countess's friends.[27]

Lady Derby was, of course, expressing not just her own worries but the Bedfords and was less concerned with the Earl's inner feelings than his outward behaviour and the Clifford family's credit. Whether he and his mother were persuaded is not certain. That autumn he accompanied the Bedfords and Lords Wharton and Norris to Plymouth, probably to see Drake fitting out his ships which left on 15 November on what became his great circumnavigation voyage.[28] In any case, Countess Margaret's sickness and discontent continued for several years. She visited Buxton for treatment. Although she gradually grew accustomed to the unfamiliar and the forbidding stronghold which was her home, it was not until 1583 that her plight improved. She then observed with delight how her husband's attitude to her 'turned from a strange manner and carriage to much and very much love and kindness known to all and most comfortable found to mee.' Her health improved and she experienced the joy of motherhood.[29]

Moreover, she was no longer isolated in her religion. The Earl of Huntingdon, Lord President of the Council in the North from 1572, was a Puritan who used his position to extend godly beliefs in the North. In one instance at least Earl George and Countess Margaret aided and abetted him. Robert Moore had left

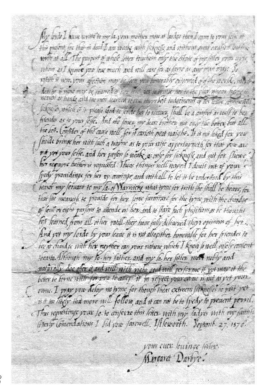

The Countess of Derby's letter to Earl
George from Isleworth, 27 September 1578

Cambridge at the age of twenty-three and at the request of the Earl and his wife had gone to Skipton Castle and remained there for a year and a half, preaching in Craven. When the rector of Guiseley resigned, Huntingdon requested the Earl and Countess to make this opportunity for a living for Moore known to the Earl of Bedford. They did so, and Bedford, Warwick, Oxford, Lord Willoughby and Sir Francis Walsingham, who were then all at Court, jointly bought the advowson of Guiseley in 1581 and presented Moore to it. For sixty years, until his death in 1640, Moore preached the Puritan gospel and did much to make the southern part of Craven a Protestant area. Granted that Leicester's circle had viewed Countess Margaret as an instrument for the spread of Puritanism in the North, this was a fulfilment of their ambitions.[30]

If Earl George's personality and attitudes were shaped in any way by his long years of tutelage and his marriage, then it was by contradiction and extremes – his family's Catholicism and the Montagues' devotions against the Puritan piety of the Bedfords and their circle; the strictness of Whitgift's regime at Trinity contrasting with the indulgence of his guardian; the passion for Gertrude Holles dashed by her father's rebuff and the arranged marriage which satisfied Bedford and the Queen but neither George nor Margaret. In adult life the Earl exhibited the religious persuasions of Whitgift and the careless courtier extravagance cultivated at Chenies and Russell House. In a marriage which was often strained

Henry Hastings, 3rd Earl of Huntingdon (1536–95), artist unkown

and eventually broke down, Countess Margaret sought solace in her devotions, the comfort of her sisters and their families and her beloved and dutiful daughter Lady Anne.

The intellectual ferment implanted in the Earl by Hakluyt and the new horizons of oceanic geography and expansion was dormant for several years as his private concerns took precedence. Then the outbreak of the sea war with Spain in 1585 aroused his maritime enthusiasms and enabled him to indulge them to the full in the legitimate guise of royal service in defence of the realm. This was to accord with his guiding apothegm, classical and traditional in inspiration, from Homer's *Iliad*, Book VI, in Cowper's translation,

> That I should outstrip always, all mankind
> In worth and valour, nor the house disgrace
> Of my forefathers, heroes without peer.[31]

For Francis Clifford, the future 4th Earl, there was neither the lavish attention nor scholarly education Earl George experienced. By their father's death he was to miss some of the grander features of high noble life, the large and peripatetic household and prolonged visits to relatives and friends which were an education in themselves. He tended to be reared on his own, alongside the younger of his two sisters, Lady Eleanor, because George was in the South and Lady Frances absent in service elsewhere. But he was well cared for by his mother, financially supported by the 100 marks a year his father had bequeathed him, and as much thought was given to his upbringing as an earl's second son could expect, privileged indeed beyond most of his fellows. The earliest mention of him is as a twelve-year-old borrowing £250 on 7 November 1571 from one of his family's servants, Robert Aske Esq. of Aughton, with another, Robert Oglethorpe gent. of Rawden, standing surety with him, the purpose unstated.[32] What he wore as a youth is hinted at in his dun hat and cloak of tawny chequered velvet decorated with two globes or balls of gold lace and squirrel fur which were in the wardrobe at Skipton Castle when the inventory was taken in 1572.

Francis would be privately tutored, first by William Hartley the schoolmaster and probably also by Henry Denton and Lancelot Marton.[33] In 1576 at the age of seventeen he was sent to London to complete his informal education in the capital, as mentioned above. He was admitted to Gray's Inn in 1583–4, though he may have regarded it only as a convenient place to room in the city near to his brother because, by his own confession, he was 'unlearned in the Lawes of this Realme' and could not 'reade or understand any lattyn conveyance'.[34] Less able than George and lacking his intellectual bent, he was nevertheless a literate man with cultural interests. He enjoyed mainly music and drama, nourished in Countess Anne's household, because Barden Tower was on the itineraries of players who sought patronage and lodging in noble houses which she readily and frequently gave. Moreover, the provincial and more parochial nature of Francis's youth fitted him better than George for sympathetic management of the Clifford properties and dealings with their tenants. Family conversation, his gentry tutors and local journeyings in Craven gave him a knowledge of and feeling for the patrimonial estates and their people. From the 1580s, first as steward of Craven and later as earl, his understanding and sensitivity and his very familiarity with the local inhabitants distinguished his whole approach from that of his elder brother.

Francis was necessarily reared in an atmosphere of religious conservatism. As Countess Margaret discovered, the Clifford household in Yorkshire still clung to its older doctrinal allegiances. The most frequent visitors, Countess Anne's relatives and officers, were almost all Catholic in sympathy – her younger brother Francis Dacre Esq. of Croglin, Cumberland and his wife, her sister-in-law Lady Katherine Scrope, Sir Ingram and Dame Ursula, Christopher Monckton Esq., who was tenant of Londesborough Hall, Sir William Ingleby and Thomas Clifford of Aspenden.[35] They could, however, no longer worship with the same assurance and security as before the Rebellion. That crisis and the bull *Regnans in Excelsis*, issued in 1570, which proclaimed Elizabeth's excommunication and deposition, threw English Catholics' allegiance into doubt and compelled counter-measures from the government. Countess Anne, old Lady Wharton, Lady Anne Ingleby and Monckton were all named by Archbishop Sandys of York in October 1577 as 'disobedient' in religion, that is Catholic recusants. Monckton was to be imprisoned for his recusancy. Countess Anne eventually bowed to ecclesiastical pressure. She promised the Archbishop in August 1580 'that hir whole family shalbe dutifull' in matters of religion, hardly necessary for Earl George and his wife. Not so old Lady Wharton and Lady Scrope. They continued in their 'stowte obstinacie', giving an 'evil example' complained the authorities, Lady Scrope maintaining a recusant household at Whitby with her second husband, Sir Richard Cholmley, until her death in 1598.[36]

Nevertheless, Francis did not follow his relatives down that path, his loyalty to the established church being unquestioned. Rather it gave him an appreciation of the breadth of contemporary religious experience which made him comfortable with gentry of all shades of belief. This tolerance was a characteristic of all the last three Clifford earls, friendship with families long related or linked with theirs counting for more than sectarian fervour and its unhappy social divisiveness. In the North, where older and newer religious attitudes existed side by side up to the Civil War, this was a commonsense and practical outlook. Amicable relations with the network of gentry and other estate officers were of mutual advantage and with the now sparse northern nobility and higher clergy one of the pillars of their social relationships.

By 1578, on the eve of his majority, Earl George had completed his formal education, married and was in regular attendance at Court. He had joined the exclusive ranks of the Elizabethan peerage and found his natural niche in the company of Bedford, Warwick, Rutland and other fellow-noblemen and their attendants. His upbringing had fitted him for any role he might, as a nobleman, wish or be allowed to play. Its precise nature, however, was still within his choice. He was already familiar with his place in the order of precedence alongside Rutland, another earldom created in 1525. Once he came of age, he would enjoy, among the privileges of his exalted rank, a seat in the House of Lords with its say on legislation, separate taxation, the right to trial by his peers, the right to bear weapons and arm his servants, and the superior placing anywhere and at any time over men of lesser rank.[37]

Guiseley Rectory, a crucked building stone-clad in 1601 by Robert Moore

Moreover, as head of the House of Clifford, Earl George was himself at the apex of a particular social pyramid of men – and women – who looked to him and depended on him in varying respects. Much the closest to him was his own small group of relatives and friends, his brother Francis, brother-in-law Lord Wharton, William and Sampson Ingleby, and Richard Musgrave. For a time the Earl was in touch with his uncle Francis Dacre. Henry Cholmley, Lady Katherine's son, was drawn to him and also Robert Bowes gent. of Streatlam, Durham, an older family link there. These were precious few in numbers, explicable because George had been absent from his estates for so long and the leading northern families where he might have naturally found associates had collapsed because of their part in the Northern Rebellion. As his career developed, many more from outside his immediate family were drawn within his aegis. In contemporary social philosophy, women were subordinate to men, dependent on them legally and financially. This was also true of Countess Margaret. She in turn had her own little clutch of attendants responsible to her. Her noble rank and descent gave her the edge, in theory, over her husband's senior gentry officers. In practice, her relations with them would depend, as for all noblewomen, on her personality, her perception of her role and, most of all, her husband's attitude towards her and her place in his activities.

At a lower level in terms of intimacy with the Earl were gentry who stood out from the many who acted as Clifford estate and household officers. Earl George inherited from his parents their senior officers, such as the Listers, Eltoftes, Prestons, Ferrands, Martons and Tempests in Craven; in Westmorland, the Birkbecks of Hornby and Blenkinsops of Helbeck Hall; in Cumberland, the Salkelds of Little Salkeld, and at Londesborough the Leemings of Weighton. At a lower rank were dozens of men and women in the Earl's regular employ. Noble houses were great enterprises, with multifarious concerns and responsibilites. Upkeep of the residences, management of the household, purchases and sales of goods, farming, leasing, collection of rents, holding manorial courts, supervision of mining, and many other activities called for staff who would dedicate themselves to a nobleman's service. Without them, great houses could not have functioned, let alone survived. Successive generations of officers and other servants found employment under the Clifford lords and earls, parallel dynasties almost but with a constant influx of new men. Theirs was an organic relationship, mutually interdependent. Other gentry might be drafted in, as the Russells and Manners were for a particular purpose at the outset and then the close of Earl George's career. But it was the loyalty, hard and willing work, even financial aid when called for, of George's regular officers and servants which sustained the House of Clifford for him.[38] Any study of his career encompasses theirs, more fleetingly perhaps but with equivalent merit. In the end they were deservedly among the gainers as he frittered away the great landed assets which fell to his charge in 1579 when he attained his majority.

CHAPTER 3

Landowner and Courtier: 1579–86

Earl George, wrote Charles Chester somewhat sourly in 1593, was 'the rudest Earle by reason of his northerly bringen up & great societe'.[1] Rude in the sense of blunt he most likely was, a trait often associated with northerners which Bedford's household and Whitgift's regime appear not to have softened. Prejudice and perhaps envy explain the rest of Chester's comment. Backbiting was the lot of those high in social rank and office and Earl George was to endure his share. Similarly disparaging is Dr Whitaker's oft-quoted judgement that George was a great but unamiable man.[2] At first sight there may be some substance to this view. Contemporary writers and eulogists are eloquent about Earl George's 'honour', more reticent about pleasing traits in his personality. Yet the Earl inspired affection as well as respect and loyalty both during his lifetime and in recollection. The most unexpectedly emotional was Robert Cecil, 1st Earl of Salisbury's confession to James I, 'I loved him living and now admire him dying' he wrote, when the Earl was on his deathbed in the autumn of 1605.[3]

Portraits, not all idealised, show him to have been a tallish, slim, dark-haired man, with a rather severe countenance. As James Lea commented, 'His looks were stern, his looks do fear afford.'[4] His build, in which he resembled his father,[5] is confirmed by his jousting armour and by Whitaker, who examined his body in the Skipton vault. His appearance was impressive in an age when dignity in stature was enhanced by the fastidious elegance of manly habit. His daughter wrote that he 'was endued with many perfections of Nature befitting so noble a personage as an excellent quicknesse of wit and apprehension, an active and strong body and an affable disposition and behaviour.'[6] Only the last adjective might be questioned and, even then, the Earl's letters and other sources suggest that 'affability' could well have been his demeanour in private and among family and friends as distinct from when exercising authority. Much will be revealed about his personality and outlook as his activities and attitudes are described in this study.

Earl George was, indubitably, a man of intelligence and accomplishment with much of the ideal courtier's breadth of scholarly and cultural attainments and, equally, disposition to action. His letters are vivid and pithy in the high Renaissance style, a joy to read. His career was to give him opportunities to display his administrative and martial skills no wit inferior to those of his greatest forbears. Yet if his strengths brought him renown it was the flaws in his personality which came to dominate, with ultimately regrettable consequences for his family and the Clifford inheritance. It is easy to predict in retrospect, even during his years in Bedford's care, some of the weaknesses in his character and the fateful lure of the Court which were eventually to bring about his financial downfall. But it was the precise circumstances of Elizabeth I's reign in the 1580s which largely account for the direction Earl George's career took and these were not foreseeable except in the most general sense and in the worst fears of the Protestant, anti-Spanish group of her councillors. Moreover, he was perpetually at the mercy of the Queen's policies and her manipulation of her servants whose destinies were in her grasp no whit less than their predecessors' under previous Tudor monarchs. She must bear some part of the blame for the downward spiral in his fortunes in the 1590s.

Natural attributes, social status and education apart, Earl George could hardly have been better placed to make an impact on national affairs in the last decades of the Tudor era. He entered one of the great noble patrimonies in the kingdom. The net rental of his father's estates at his death had been estimated for wardship purposes at £1,821 8s. 3d. This total comprised £1,092 17s. for the Yorkshire properties; £580 5s. 6d. for Westmorland; £24 5s. 9½d. for Cumberland; £120 for the manor of Hart, and £4 for the rent of Clifford's Inn. There is independent evidence for the accuracy of these figures.[7] What they ignore are the casualties such as entry fines, wardships, leases, timber and mineral resources and farming which added appreciably to the annual revenues of any great landowner. Much will be said subsequently about the Earl's finances, yet, because very few of his accounts survive, his expenditure and income are largely a matter of impression and guesswork although there is much detail which is soundly-based.

How a family's estates were tended during a minority could make or mar the inheritance because they were easily exploited by the unscrupulous. On balance, Earl George's Craven lands were well-managed by his mother and her officers for nine years whereas the Westmorland and Londesborough properties suffered to some extent from lack of firm control. Besides the third of the rents due to the Court of Wards and the Westmorland revenues reserved for the Countess's jointure income, there were other heavy calls on the estate. Earl Henry's executors, in accordance with his will, raised moneys to pay both his debts and the 2,000 marks he bequeathed to Lady Frances if, as happened, she married a baron. He had provided separately for Lady Eleanor, depositing 800 marks for her child's or marriage portion with Simon Musgrave in Westmorland for safe keeping, protected by a £2,000 recognizance from Musgrave. When Eleanor died at Appleby aged eighteen in the summer of 1575 she left that money to Countess Anne and, in a touching manner, jewels to her brothers and sister and various other relatives and presents to her gentlewomen and schoolmasters.[8]

The Countess generously waived the larger income of a widow's third she could have demanded from her late husband's properties, taking only the Westmorland jointure revenues to support her and her household. Her biggest capital outlays were in 1571 re-building the toll-booth in Skipton and the lodge in

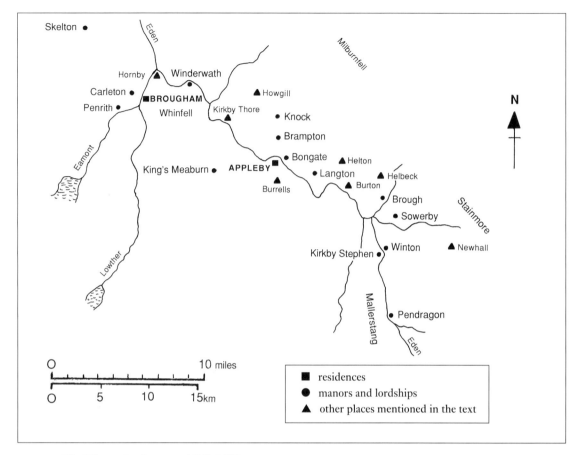

The Westmorland estates, 1570–1605

Carleton Park, henceforward called the Newbiggin. She lived well, though within her means, her household of forty-three servants alternating between Barden Tower and the Newbiggin.[9] She either could not, or could not afford to, obtain manors to replace those her husband had sold, but she did purchase leases. In her most important land transaction, she took advantage of Thomas Proctor's move to Warsill near Ripon, buying from Proctor and Charles Holte their remaining interest in the forty-one years' lease of Friarhead in the manor of Winterburn granted by Edward VI. Proctor demised Warsill Grange to her as security to keep the bargain. On 31 January 1575 she leased Friarhead to Christopher Marton Esq. for twenty-one years but, with an eye on the Cliffords' long term interests, required him to enter into £1,000 bond not to seek a new lease of the property. In return, Marton assigned to her the lease of Birks and Firth in Langstrothdale, which still had twenty-one years to run, and agreed to pay her £233 6s. 8d. in cash over a period of five years. At last these two large Percy Fee holdings were in Clifford hands, though reserved rents of £15 6s. 4d. were due from them to the Earl of Northumberland.[10] She purchased successive leases of Silsden tithe corn

The Craven estates, 1570–1602

from the lessee of Kildwick parsonage, which Christ Church, Oxford, had granted out in 1559, and sub-let it for £40 a year.[11]

Countess Anne was assiduous in taking whatever legal action was needed to protect her sons' inheritance and her own jointure estate. For instance, she initiated a suit in the Court of Wards against Richard Sandford Esq. of Howgill Castle, Westmorland who, espying an opportunity during George's minority, challenged the Cliffords' traditional rights on Milburn Fell. This dispute was eventually settled by arbitration in 1580 to the Cliffords' satisfaction.[12] The one obvious failure of Countess Anne and her advisers was in not appointing a new steward at Londesborough after the death of William Babthorpe. This may well have been due rather to the laxity of the Court of Wards. The consequence was a lack of direction over that estate which later contributed to Francis Clifford's problems of dealing with the neighbouring landowner Marmaduke Threlkeld and his tenants and led to recurrent litigation with him.[13]

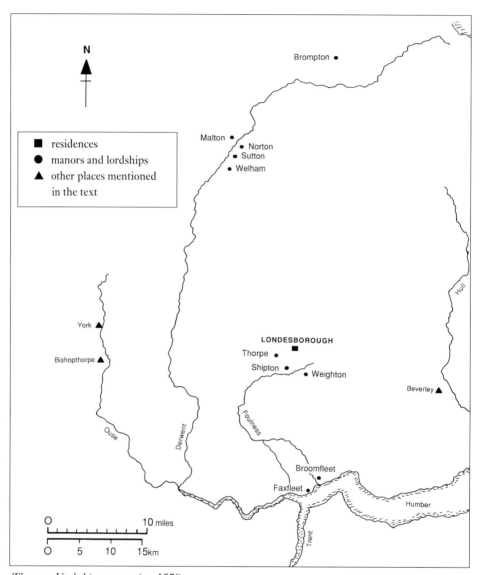

The east Yorkshire properties, 1570

Even as a minor Earl George could be called on to take severe steps to protect his interests, with his guardian's formidable support. One case was his imprisonment in Skipton Castle in May 1576 of Thomas Frankland gent., the latter agreeing to it as the alternative to prosecution in the Court of Wards for hunting and killing the Earl's wild deer in Craven. The indenture between them was witnessed by Bedford, Sir Edward Russell and Edmund Eltoftes. The Countess and her officers were conscious of the rights of the young Earl as incoming lord. They postponed the major and some of the minor decisions as he approached manhood. In practice, George began to take over the reins of management in the summer of 1578, well over a year before his wardship formally ended. Unusually, he had the advantage of entering a patrimony largely clear of encumbrances other than legacies and annuities and his mother's Westmorland jointure. This freedom to act and the death of his uncle Sir Ingram early in 1578 enabled him to anticipate some of the revenues which would legally become his in August 1579. This made him independent of Bedford and accustomed his future estate officers and tenants to his style of lordship. But the stated purposes, 'ffor the dischardge of suche debtes as I nowe owe as also for the mentenance of my estate and Chardges during my mynoritie', were to become ominously familiar to his officers in subsequent years.

On 31 May he appointed George Salkeld Esq. of Rosgill, John Brisco Esq. of Crofton, Reynold Hartley of Appleby and William Ferrand to raise money from the tenants of his Cumberland manors. In return, he promised to repay the borrowed sums by reducing the tenants' gressums, that is entry fines, for the new leases he would grant when he took over the estates. On 1 June he authorised his senior officers Sir William Ingleby, Edmund Eltoftes, Christopher Monckton, Leonard Preston and Ferrand to do the same for Hart and Hartlepool, which Sir Ingram had previously occupied. He gave similar instructions on 6 June for Maltby and its woods and for Leeds tithes, with the added inducement in the latter of preferment for new leases for those tenants who agreed to lend him cash.[14]

These formal processes marked the beginning of the natural co-operation between the young Earl and his father's trusted officers who eased George into his inheritance. Already by 1578 petitions from tenants, which Countess Anne had hitherto dealt with, were being deferred so that George could make the decisions, a long delay for the supplicants and an accumulation of matters requiring his attention in the autumn of 1579. Some agreements were reached *pro tem*. For instance, on 8 April permission was granted for an enclosure of arable in Gargrave but an obligation was required from the tenant with a penalty clause of £40 to prevent any change without the Earl's licence. Many called for tricky ethical consideration, the blind scholar down from university with a dubious claim on a farmstead, the woman with elderly and infirm parents formerly removed from their farmstead, suspicions of partiality and venality by manorial officers, all best left to the Earl and his advisers to determine.[15]

The most vexed and protracted issue for George and Francis was asserting their claims to their uncle's estate. Sir Ingram had vested the reversion of his lands in Earl Henry who in turn had devised them to his sons. After the Earl's death, Sir Ingram had assured his possessions to them 'for the good Love and zeale' that he always had for the noble house from which he was descended, wishing its better continuance and better maintenance. His estates, said to be of the clear yearly value of £1,000 or more, were to bring Earl George and his brother a big accession of landed wealth but only after fighting off legal challenges to their right title which started before either came of age, indeed before their uncle's death. Prospective changes of ownership or when an occupant was already under pressure from rivals were the best, often the only, chances of pressing claims with any hope of success, as George and Francis now learnt and themselves later applied.

Sir Ingram's large properties had come to him through his first wife, Anne Roucliffe, an astute marriage engineered for him by his father the 1st Earl. Anne was a joint heiress of the great Plumpton estate whose division in the later fifteenth century had caused recurrent litigation. The contestants against George and Francis were Margaret Yaxley, widow, and Marmaduke Constable Esq. of Wassand, Yorkshire (then a minor), who counter-claimed all Sir Ingram's properties by virtue of similar descent to Anne's in what was virtually the last phase of the century-old squabble over the Plumpton inheritance. Seizing on the rare opportunity, they initiated a suit against Sir Ingram and his beneficiaries, George and Francis, and pursued this after the former's decease. Eventually the dispute went to arbitration and at the highest level. Lord Chancellor Bromley, Viscount Montagu, the Earl of Rutland and John Popham, by then the Queen's Solicitor General, were all friends, even relatives of the Cliffords though not necessarily partial to their cause. Their award on 28 June 1580 in favour of Earl George and his brother was almost certainly legally sound. Margaret Yaxley covenanted to allow them quiet possession. Constable likewise abandoned his claim on payment of the £50 the arbitrators settled on him. Another rival claimant, Thomas Hawley, agreed on 11 December 1581 to allow Francis quiet possession of Sir Ingram's Derbyshire and Nottinghamshire lands under the award, on payment of £100. The legal costs over the three years must have been heavy and were met in part, possibly entirely, after Sir Ingram's death by Countess Anne.[16]

Earl George received all his uncle's Yorkshire lands, four manors and the moieties of five others, that is the Craven manors of Nesfield and Westhall and the moieties of Steeton and Grassington (the two halves of Grassington now being united) and other West Riding lands, the manors of Cowthorpe and Bickerton and the moieties of Idle, near Bradford, Clotheram and Studley Roger near Ripon and Snaith near Selby. The Earl did not immediately take possession of all these. Sir Ingram had asked him to make provision for his second wife and widow, Dame Ursula, and this George did by making over to her Nesfield, Westhall and Cowthorpe for life. There were minor incumbrances on two of Sir Ingram's properties. He had let Clotheram and Studley Roger to Thomas Clifford of Bolton who had sub-let them to Christopher Marlow and Christopher Malham for a rent of 40 marks per annum. Earl George and Francis bought out the lessees' interest for £40 on 10 December 1580.[17] The Grassington moiety, likewise, had been sub-let.

When Earl George came of age in August 1579 he entered into an enviably huge patrimony. He took possession in Yorkshire of thirty-four manors and the moieties of four, with other holdings, and also Hart, his Cumberland lands, and Clifford's Inn. He held the reversions of his mother's and Dame Ursula's jointure estates and of the east Yorkshire properties, where his brother had only a life interest. Indeed, until Francis attained his majority on 30 October 1580 they jointly administered them. George had to wait less than two years to take over the Westmorland lordships on his mother's death at Skipton on 3 July 1581 (he and Countess Margaret being with her at the time) and little longer for Dame

TABLE 1 *The inheritance of Earl George and Francis Clifford, 1579–80*

EARL GEORGE

Yorkshire

CRAVEN
Castle and manor of Skipton
Manors of :

Gargrave	West Hall	Coat
Silsden with Holden	Steeton (moiety)	East Marton
Barden Forest	Bolton	West Marton
Stirton & Thorlby	Halton	Settle
Elso & Crookrise	Storithes & Hazlewood	Giggleswick
Embsay	Woodhouse cum	Long Preston
Eastby	Appletreewick	Gisburn
Cononley	Cracoe & Threapland	Langstrothdale
Carleton	Grassington	Buckden
Lothersdale	Scosthrop	Starbotton
Bradley Over and Nether	Litton	
Nesfield & Langbar	Littondale with Arncliffe	

Lands in: Skibeden, Malham, Newhall, Cowling, Eastburn, Glusburn, Utley, Herton and Draughton.

WEST RIDING
Manors of:
Cowthorpe
Maltby
Idle (moiety)
Studley Parva

Lands in: Bickerton, Hensall, Snaith, Thorpe, Wrays and Rotherham.

EAST RIDING
Manors of:

Londesborough	Welham (moiety)
(Market) Weighton	Sutton (moiety)
Shipton & Thorpe	Broomfleet (part)

NORTH RIDING
Castle and manor of Malton (third part)
£84 reserved rent from Brompton cum membris

Net rental of the Yorkshire lands   £1,157   11s.   4d.

TABLE 1 continued

Westmorland

	Rents		
	£	s.	d.
Mallerstang	41	12	11½
Kirkby Stephen	27	9	0½
Winton	32	13	7½
Sowerby	23	19	3¼
Brough Over and Nether	35	15	10½
Stainmore East, with corn mill and Newhall	121	9	10
Stainmore South, with £5 8s. profits of one coal mine	37	4	1½
Appleby, with Scattergate and Burrells	21	3	3
Bongate, with Southfield	41	4	6
Kings Meaburn	28	5	11
Brampton	5	0	0¾
Knock, with £5 rent of Fenfield	24	7	8
Moorehouse with Hornby and Woodfield	17	4	6
Burton and Helton (one tenement)	0	7	4
Langton lands and tenements	12	19	6
Brougham demesnes, coney warren (£28 9s.) and corn mill (£11 16s. 8d.)	40	5	4
Whinfell Forest	37	0	0
The free rents of Westmorland called cornage and serjeant food, with the office of sheriff of the county	52	5	7
Milburnfell and Sandfordwood	2	18	2
Net rental of Westmorland	£580	5	6

Cumberland

Manors of:			
Skelton	14	3	6
Lamonby	7	12	2
Carleton with Penrith	2	9	11½

Durham

Hart and Hartlepool	120	0	0

London

Clifford's Inn	4	0	0
Total net rental	£1,886	2	7½

TABLE 1 continued

FRANCIS CLIFFORD ESQ.

Yorkshire

A life interest only with reversion to Earl George and his heirs of Londesborough, Weighton, Shipton and Thorpe, Welham, Sutton, Malton, Broomfleet and £84 rent from Brompton, listed above.

Derbyshire

The moieties of the manors of:

Wormhill	Pilsley
Wheston alias Iveston	Edensor
Tideswell	Darley
Flagg	Calton cum Lees
Martinside	Bakewell
Combs	Stanton
Betfield	Chaddesden
Hardlow	Herbenger Meadow
Chelmorton	Spondon
Wardlow	Broughton
Castleton	Duffield
Haslop alias Hassop	Woodhouse

Nottinghamshire

Kinoulton (moiety)

(*Sources*: PRO, Wards 9/140, fols 291–94; Alnwick MSS, X, II, 3/7/h/1; Clay, pp. 380, 385–6)

Ursula's manors. By the age of twenty-five, he had full control of all the Clifford patrimony except for the east Yorkshire manors and had not yet assigned any to Countess Margaret as her jointure estate, nor was he to do so until 1591. Few nobleman, and none of his forbears since John, 9th Lord, enjoyed such untramelled command of their inheritance at so young an age as Earl George.

When Francis Clifford attained his majority in 1580, he was hardly less well placed. He had the biggest landed endowment of any Clifford second son since the Conquest, which had accrued from his father's provision, his uncle's bequests and his mother's generosity. He had received in April 1577, when he was seventeen, the goods and chattels of his half-uncle Thomas of Bolton, who had made him his sole executor, though not his lease of Clotherham and Studley. By then, Francis had begun to farm on his own account in Craven. On 20 September

1581 Dame Ursula released Sir Ingram's former lands due to him, the moieties of twenty-four manors in Derbyshire and one in Nottinghamshire.[18] With these properties, Francis became a considerable landowner in his own right. But his income was more than doubled by the revenues from his life interest and leasehold tenancies, which lifted him into the ranks of the wealthier northern gentry. In October he took over the east Yorkshire lands with Londesborough Hall. From his mother he received several valuable sources of income. Kirkbythure tithes in Westmorland, worth £84 a year, were Francis's due when he came of age. The others had been purchased by his mother. The lease of Birks and Middlesmoor in Langstrothdale brought him £50 in annual income. His mother's interest in Silsden tithes and, after Christopher Marton's tenure elapsed, in Friarhead passed to him. In his early years of manhood Francis described himself as of Grassington, not Londesborough. This was because Countess Anne also left to him the twenty-one years' lease Sir Ingram had made to her in August 1561 of his moiety of Grassington, its manor house and demesnes, for £26 11s. 8d. rent per annum. Its term was almost complete but Earl George was happy to allow him continued occupancy so that he remained the single biggest tenant in the manor until 1604 and, moreover, rent-free.[19] In return, as has been seen, George took over Francis's interest (through Thomas Clifford) in Clotheram and Studley Roger.

This exchange was part of an amicable settlement within the family of matters relating to Francis's upbringing in his mother's care. After Thomas Clifford's death, Countess Anne had used the Clotheram rents and also the profits of the Kirkbythure tithes to meet the costs of Francis's education and his lawsuits during his minority, which as his guardian she could justify. Two days before she died, Francis made an indenture of release to her, her executors and assigns of any demands for the moneys from these sources she had spent on him.[20] This formal document is no reflection on his character, rather the usual Elizabethan prudence in matters of law and finance and perhaps as much a protection for him as for her executors because, as has been seen, Earl George had the reversionary interest in Clotheram and Studley. The sequence of ownership and sub-tenancies from Sir Ingram through Thomas and Francis Clifford, Marton and Marlow to Earl George was complicated enough without the Countess's executors being involved. Fortunately, George and his brother were on the best of terms and sorted out their rights and finances as they thought fit.

For the first four years after reaching full manhood, Earl George gave every indication of settling down in his northern inheritance. There was a great deal for an incoming lord to do. In 1579 almost all the tenancies fell in. He and his council of senior estate officers were busy negotiating new agreements to hold for the life of the tenant or himself, or in the case of demesnes and tithes, annually or for twenty-one years. The many delayed petitions from men and women with aspirations or grievances were dealt with. Francis, whom he made steward of Craven, and his friends John Manners Esq. and Sir Francis Russell were among the commissioners he appointed to survey his lands. Household and estate officers and humbler folk looked to him for renewal of their positions or preferment. Brian Garnett, for instance, failed in his petition to become the Earl's auditor but Francis took him into his service instead.

A great deal of patronage was dispensed and friendships gratified, obligations being repaid or created. Richard Musgrave was one of the Earl's officers awarded profitable leases which supplemented their fees and expenses, grants which brought goodwill and gave recompense for devotion to his service. The Earl demised to him for twenty-one years at a yearly rent of £20 the Hawhouse, one of the biggest holdings in the Bolton demesnes, with a covenant to supply an 'hable and sufficient horsse and Competant furnyture' for the musters. Men of standing interceded with the commissioners to obtain what otherwise might be denied. Sir Gervase Clifton, for instance, petitioned them on behalf of one Needham, a servant of his brother-in-law, who already held Clifton's moiety of a farm in Steeton and wanted the Earl's moiety also. In return, in the usual fashion, Clifton promised to favour them or any of their friends in any way, as they should command him.[21] Care, thought and equity were called for in making almost every lease. With the Westmorland estates falling to him in 1581, this time-consuming and absorbing activity of appointing officers, holding courts, examining juries of survey and deciding new tenancies held the young Earl's attention until well into 1582.[22] There would have been ample opportunities for him to show whatever toughness, generosity or compassion he deemed fitting and for his commissioners, gentry and other tenants to assess his style of landlordship.

The new leases realised large amounts of cash over a three-year period. Earl George sensibly used some of the money to add to his properties. In 1580 he bought two messuages in Old Coney Street, York, as town houses, thus qualifying as a burgage holder. Only four days after his mother's death, he purchased for £1,600 (to be paid over two years) the lordship of Winderwath with 350 acres of land, which adjoined his Brougham Castle estate. The vendor was Thomas Knyvet Esq., gentleman of the privy chamber to Queen Elizabeth, who was to achieve fame as the officer who arrested Guy Fawkes in 1605 and become Lord Knyvet of Escrick, Yorkshire. A proviso in the agreement was that his mother, Dame Anne, whose property this was, should enjoy a life occupancy. Earl George also reached agreement in 1581 with William Nesfield gent. to buy the manor of Flasby in Craven for £1,000, likewise allowing Nesfield a life tenancy. The next year a mutually satisfactory exchange brought him the large manor of Eshton, which adjoined Flasby, and gave Christopher Marton Esq. the manors of East and West Marton and £500 in cash to make up the difference in value.[23] Francis used Eshton Hall for a time as a residence on his estate work in Craven.

What is discernible in these transactions is a desire to consolidate the Clifford estates, just as Earl Henry had done, with good properties which also had halls of quality and appeal to potential tenants. A similar intention is evident in the disposal of some of the inconvenient outlying parts in 1582 and 1583. The Rotherham holding brought in £80. George's solicitor, Anthony Wright, bought the capital messuage of Studley, also for £80. The Earl disposed of most of his Cumberland properties. Robert Southaik Esq. of Skelton and the Harrisons of Penrith bought messuages in Skelton, Lamonby and Unthank. Sir Thomas Carleton took Carleton Hall, though the Earl retained the mill probably because it served Brougham Castle. The only apparent aberration from this centralising policy was the Earl's purchase of the 300-acre Lingfield in Haughton Fields in County Durham in 1584. This was, in fact, a transaction on behalf of the Pudsey family, to whom he was related, and he re-sold the field to William Pudsey of Bolton-by-Bowland two years later.[24]

During his minority his father's offices had been exercised by Crown nominees, but rank and wealth carried obligations, foremost being regular employment as one of the Crown's cadre of unpaid, executive officers in the provinces. Gradually Earl George assumed the role expected of him in northern affairs. In 1579, because of Hart, he was involved with Lords Lumley and Wharton and local inhabitants in negotiations with the Bishop of Durham over the repair of the Tyne Bridge.[25] In Westmorland he formally took over the shrievalty from the Crown appointee, Sir Simon Musgrave, who continued to exercise the office as his deputy. He was appointed steward and constable of Knaresborough for life in 1580, but had to wait until 10 May 1586 for a separate twenty-one years' lease of Staincliffe wapentake. He was appointed to the commissions of the peace for the northern counties and, in 1581, was nominated as one of the royal commissioners to survey the forts and castles of the West Marches.[26]

A more prestigious position was his membership, from 1582, of the Council in the North at York. This was proof indeed that he was considered politically trustworthy by the Queen and her advisers. That year, on 23 November, he was included, with the Lord President, the Earl of Huntingdon, and other dignitaries, on the commission of enquiry into congregations and conventicles, an aspect of the Queen and Council's effort to enforce conformity in religion. Privately, Earl George disliked Huntingdon holding the greatest position in the North, more because he was an outsider than for his personality or Puritan persuasion. Earl George, although linked with the Bedford, Leicester and Huntingdon group through his marriage, displayed at this time no allegiance to any particular Court faction, his interests being social rather than political. However, his political patronage was less casual than has been thought. In the election of members for the House of Commons, he always reserved the premier place in Westmorland for his relatives – his brother in 1584 and 1586, Francis Dacre in 1588, Sir William Bowes in 1593, Henry Cholmley in 1597 and his nephew George Wharton in 1601. He clearly sponsored Robert Constable for Appleby in 1586, Laurence Lister in 1588 and Robert Bowes in 1589. The other places he was happy to let the Bedfords and their friends take, Countess Margaret having some say in the choice. He also evinced concern with northern affairs and a practical involvement to which he was to return after the southern distractions of his privateering career. In the north-west there was a distinct Clifford gentry following, but issues there remained low key until near the end of the century when they looked to him for leadership over Border problems.[27]

Military preparedness was a matter for serious concern. There were worries on two fronts for Elizabeth I and her Council: in Scotland where control of the young King James VI and his kingdom oscillated between the French-supported Catholic party and their Protestant opponents, and in the Low Countries where the nearness and weight of Philip II's armies fighting the Dutch rebels caused increasing alarm. In the musters ordered in May 1584, the Earl was required to levy 300 men out of the West and North Ridings nearest to Skipton Castle. In November 1585 he was called on to play an active part with troops near the Borders, ready to support the Scottish Protestants after they had destroyed the French party. Both crises passed without offering him the chance to fight. Moreover, with the wardenships filled and the government's cautious policy towards Scotland and the Marches, there was no obvious role for energetic young men like the Earl or Lord Wharton on the northern frontier. The West March was in the experienced hands of George's cousin Henry, Lord Scrope. Nor is it conceivable that he would have readily taken to the restraints the Council set on wardens' actions in maintaining law and order and good relations with Scottish border officials.[28]

By 1583 Earl George was beginning to chafe at the lack of colour and excitement in his life. He was frustrated by the lack of suitable employment in northern administration for a man of his vitality, most of his offices being honorary or temporary and always subject to Huntingdon's oversight. He indulged the usual noble relaxations of hunting, hawking and visiting relatives, especially Wharton Hall, but they were not enough. After the initial demanding work on his estates, there was little challenge and much routine administration in managing them which was best left to his officers. In later years, he was to reveal, if humorously,[29] the low view nobility had of mere rustics, whom Shakespeare wickedly parodied in *A Midsummer Night's Dream*.

It is no surprise, then, that during 1583 he forsook his country pursuits, Skipton and Brougham and the environment of his estates, for the bustling atmosphere of Elizabeth I's Court. His brother, Lord Wharton and the Earl of Rutland were of similar mind and his regular companions, all young men alike, staying at Wharton's house in Cannon Row or the one he rented in Westminster. For George, this was a return to the life he had relished in his youth, mingling with men of his own rank and the great officers of state, no longer remote from the frenetic issues and buzz of news and gossip as he had been at Skipton. As a courtier, he had the advantage of the Queen's long-standing goodwill, the proximity of his mentors Burghley and Bedford, and the renewed closeness to his sister, the Countess of Derby, and his sisters-in-law the Countesses of Warwick and Bath, all three royal ladies-in-waiting and more influential than is often thought. Except for a few months in 1585, the Earl sojourned at Court on his own. Countess Margaret was pregnant in the summer of 1583 with their first child Francis, named after his brother, who was born at Skipton Castle on 10 April 1584.[30]

Capital and Court together had a unique attraction in early modern England and there was a continuous influx from the provinces of people of all social ranks, accomplishments and qualities, some permanent, much temporary and for a purpose, either trade or litigation or curiosity or ambition. Whether at the royal palaces of Richmond, Greenwich and Westminster or on progress, Elizabeth I's Court was the cultural concourse of the realm, displaying the best and latest in fashions and in musical entertainment and pageantry. Here congregated the great in the land, competing for power and favour, innumerable suitors jostling for gifts, grants, lands, offices and preferment of all kinds and seeking the redress of grievances. Here were played out personal rivalries and religious and political factional struggles reaching down from the high officers of state and privy councillors deep into the provinces and shires. Suitors of all kinds thronged to Chancery, Common Pleas, the Exchequer and other lawcourts in Westminster Hall, mingling with a mass of lawyers. The great city and port of London, now approaching 300,000 in population, offered the best and most varied goods and exotic imports which appealed to the wealthiest in the land on a scale which dwarfed York, Hull, Bristol, Newcastle and Norwich. Very few of the titled and wealthy could escape the pull of the metropolis at some time in their lives and for young noblemen the opportunities of advancement through royal favour in the 1580s were unsurpassed.

This decade was to be the climacteric of Elizabeth I's reign. The older generation of courtiers and officers who had made her secure on the throne passed away – Leicester, Bedford, Walsingham and Hatton among them. Only Burghley was to survive to the later 1590s. The younger men who established themselves at Court stood to take their places, Earl George among them. He did not neglect political affairs and attendance at parliament; he could hardly have avoided awareness of current issues in the milieu in which he now circulated. Yet

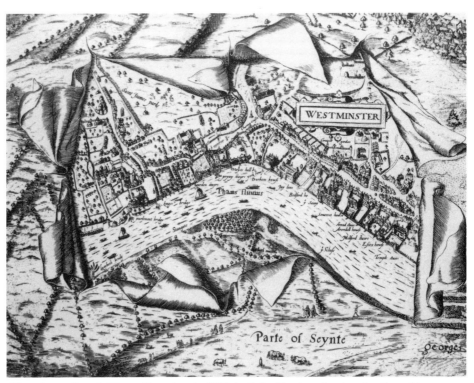

Westminster, from A View of London in 1600 *by John Norden, showing the tiltyard in Whitehall, and Durham, Bedford and Essex Houses*

in the early years it was indulgence in pastimes and pleasures which dominated. Honour and pride as well as winnings were at stake in every activity, whether horse-racing, bowls, archery, board-games or jousting, all keenly competitive.

Rutland aroused some jealousy in the Earl of Warwick and Sir Philip Sidney by lending George a fine horse in February 1584, which Warwick claimed was worth £1,000 in times of need. It would be with this priceless steed that George won a golden bell worth £50 given by the mayor and city of Salisbury at a race at the Furseys, near Harnham Hall in Hampshire, attended by many eminent courtiers including Warwick and Pembroke, the young Robert Devereux, Earl of Essex, the Howards and Lord Chandos. George promised on his honour to return with the cup for the same race the following year, but it was his conceit over his success which still rankled with Charles Chester and others of Essex's supporters ten years later.[31]

Earl George had another triumph over Essex, his life-long friend and sporting rival, at the great archery contest they put on in York that same year. Crowds of spectators, among them three Russian ambassadors, gathered in the fields of York to watch knights, esquires, gentlemen and others take part in a series of ten archery matches which lasted a full week. Earl George's Cumberland archers – Walmsley, Bolton and Ratcliffe – won this famous competition against the men entered by Essex and the York merchant Christopher Maltby. William Elderton effusively saluted the Earl in *A New Yorkshire Song Intituled Yorke, Yorke for my monie*:

> God save the good earle of Cumberlande
> His praise in golden lines shall stande,
> That maintains archerie through the land,
> As well as they do at London.
> Whose noble minde so courteously
> Acquaintes himself with the communaltie,
> To the glory of his nobilitie,
> I will carie the praise to London.

Elderton bravely championed York in his verses yet he underlines the rareness of the occasion and the chasm between London and the northern capital in staging such events, not least the regret that the Queen never travelled north to see the city for 'the comfort great of that countree'.[32]

With £20 a bow winnings and side-bets wagered, Earl George would have won handsomely at York as at the Furseys. Yet Walmsley, the supreme archer, did not get his due reward. He came to Londesborough on 18 March 1622 claiming the debt still owed him and was paid to his satisfaction by Earl Francis.[33] Gambling was endemic among the courtiers. One of the fashionable dares for young gallants was to undertake the dangerous journey to Constantinople and back, no doubt on the big Levanters which often had to fight their way through the Mediterranean against the Barbary pirates, the route having just been re-opened to English merchantmen. In May 1583 and again in March the next year, the Earl entered into two wagers, one with William Hodges Esq. of Weston Underhedge,

Gloucestershire, the other – in which Francis also was bound – with Nicholas Mosley, citizen and clothworker of London, who was to be Lord Mayor in 1599 and build Hough End Hall near Manchester. In these, the Earl pledged to pay 200 marks to Hodges, £300 to Mosley within three months of notice being given at Lord Wharton's house that George Gifford Esq. of London had travelled to Constantinople and brought back a certificate or testimony as proof. Henry Cavendish Esq. of Chatsworth made a similar wager with Gifford. How serious the bets were is proved by the fact that they were formally recorded in the Close Rolls of Chancery. Both would be lost, like the Earl's with Henry Astell who successfully completed the return journey in May 1586 and then rode to Masham in the North Riding to claim his £20 winnings from Sir Thomas Danby who held George's Portuguese gold coin as pledge.[34]

Earl George made his mark quickly in the great show-piece events of the Court, the royal tournaments, the most magnificent public spectacles of the reign. He was to become pre-eminent in the jousting which was the heart of the display of prowess and flamboyance held under the discerning eyes of the Queen and distinguished visitors. As his daughter declared, 'in the exercises of Tilting, Turning, and course of the ffield' he excelled all the nobility of his time and matched Sir Henry Lee whom he replaced as Queen's Champion in 1590. The Earl made his first appearance at the Accession Day tilts on 17 November 1583. His early success and popular esteem were other causes of envy among his fellows at Court.[35]

Participating in these lavish jousting festivals was an expensive pastime, requiring armour and arms of quality, fine horses and their trappings, and rewards to the heralds who stage-managed the whole proceedings. The superbly damascened armour, decorated with gold stars and shown in portraits of the Earl, was his first, and obviously costly, jousting and field armour dating from these early years at Court. This was the armour he was to wear throughout his career, at first in jousts and then in all the military actions in which he was engaged. The decoration was deeply symbolic. There was visual power, it was held, in women's eyes and especially the Queen's. The stars were her eyes, through which shone the strength of the sun's golden rays. On 17 November 1583, he gave the officers of arms £6 because he 'had not his Coullers to give', that is his heraldic scarves or plumes. His renown in tournaments was thus achieved at a price, but one all leading courtiers were willing and committed to paying. Where he had honed his skill in arms is not recorded, though by tradition there was a jousting field in Skipton Castle's grounds.[36]

His brother was constantly at hand for the Earl to turn to when his own purse was empty. Among the debts which accumulated between 1583 and 1587 were sums Francis had loaned him for card-playing, for horse-racing at Newmarket and for bowls at Archbishop Hutton's palace at Bishopthorpe, near York.[37] Not even an earl could sustain extravagant living for long without running into debt. Noblemen's wealth was tied up in capital and not easily converted into cash. Perennial charges such as reserved rents, fees and annuities to servants, legacies, upkeep of castles, food and drink and furnishings for a large household all greatly diminished an apparently huge estate income. Earl George's disposable cash,

Tilting at the barriers, Whitehall

swollen artificially by entry fines and some minor sales, had sufficed to maintain him and his Countess in the North between 1579 and 1583 and even to buy new properties, as has been noted. Thereafter, his cash resources proved insufficient to maintain him and his entourage at Court and in London, where lodgings, food, fuel and finery, not to mention rewards and gambling losses, made the cost of living inordinately high, and in addition support Countess Margaret's necessary household in Craven.

From the first, George and Francis had to subsidise their living expenses by borrowing and by selling land. Obtaining credit was no problem for anyone with landed wealth. There were five standard ways of acknowledging debts. Bills, written in English on paper, were usually given short-term for small debts, as to tradesmen. The snag for the latter was that they could easily be lost, denied or ignored and interest was often not demanded. Bonds, written obligations in Latin, were securer for the creditor because both the original debt and the accumulated legal ten per cent interest could be more easily recovered by litigation. Recognizances entered in the Close Rolls in Chancery were preferable, if the incidental costs were acceptable, since they were enforceable by that court, which could levy the debt from the debtor's properties. Statutes, likewise, were recorded and subject to tougher enforcement. The statutes merchant and staple were mostly used by the mercantile community; statutes of a similar type recorded in the Lord Chamberlain's office were more favoured by landowners. Finally, lending against property, with land mortgaged for security, allowed the creditors to take possession on default to recover the debt and interest. The debtor had to be careful because mortgaged land was not often valued to its full amount and he stood to lose far more than the loan if he had to sacrifice the land. Easy though obtaining credit was, cumulative borrowing would eventually compel the disposal of property to stave off litigation for debt and foreclosure on mortgaged lands, as was to happen to Earl George.[38]

Initially he turned for loans mainly to men with northern connections. He and Lord Wharton had done so in 1580 when they paid for their living expenses in London with £250 lent by Cuthbert Buckle, vintner and later Lord Mayor, whose family were Clifford tenants in Westmorland and whom the Earl rightly regarded as 'a countryman of mine'. In 1583 the Earl and his brother-in-law entered into a recognizance for £1,600 for repayment of £800 they jointly borrowed from Marmaduke Wyvill Esq. of Constable Burton in the North Riding, with Wharton also taking a separate £200 loan. All the money was repaid as Wyvill requested at his mansion on 11 November. From 1584, however, the Earl sought loans from a much broader range of lenders, London merchants, officials and gentry who had plenty of cash to put out at interest, and his repayments became tardier. In February, he borrowed £400 from Richard Tailford, citizen and upholsterer of London, with Francis, Anthony Wright and William Ferrand acting as joint sureties with him. This loan was periodically extended and not re-paid for three years, with the interest which had been allowed to accumulate.[39]

Complementary to the borrowing was selling land, but the first choice is surprising. The Earl and his Countess sold their wedding gift of the Chiswick mansion house for £340 on 15 August 1583 to her brother Sir William Russell. It stayed in the family, so no doubt Bedford gave his approval.[40] The Earl and Francis negotiated minor sales in Derbyshire in 1583 and then in June 1584 authorised their commissioners to sell all the Derbyshire properties. Immediate sales of the greater part of the manors raised almost £3,000 between 1584 and 1586. These were Francis's manors, held in his own right, yet the initiative came from George and he benefited from the cash raised as much as his brother. Here is an instance of the dominance over Francis which lasted throughout his life.

There was, it is true, a case for getting rid of these wide-spread moieties of manors but only if Clifford were adequately recompensed. In time this did happen, George satisfying his brother in 1587 for at least £1,169 owed on these sales and in a way which was to Francis's advantage. Afterwards, there was no point in Francis retaining the rest of the Derbyshire and Nottinghamshire lands and he sold them in later years for his own purposes and benefit and not the Earl's. With such widespread sales litigation could have been predicted. An unhappy legacy was a protracted dispute over Edensor with the Countess of Shrewsbury, Bess of Hardwick, a Star Chamber suit ended by an award in her favour in 1605.[41] There was one minor sale in Craven about December 1584. William Nesfield purchased six messuages for £200 in Arncliffe Coat and Hawkswick.[42]

The strain of living above his means became all the greater for Earl George during the summer of 1585. Countess Margaret began to suffer from the many small debts he was incurring. 'My dear Lord', she wrote, 'I receive on every side your cost for this time and I fear much you measure not my bills by your powers which I desire may ever govern'.[43] Besides these, the Earl was raising large sums with increased signs of urgency, by mortgages and sales now as well as loans. In May he borrowed £500 for a year on a bond from Jonas Feld. His sureties were Francis, Anthony Wright, Thomas Markham Esq. of Kirby Bellars, Leicestershire, and Henry Constable Esq. of Burton Constable in the East Riding. George gave Constable a bond for 2,000 marks to indemnify him against Markham's bond. His first mortgage was of the manor of Cowthorpe which had reverted to him on Dame Ursula's death. He had bought back minor portions alienated at some earlier date and the whole of the manor was now in his hands. In June 1585 he raised £1,500 from Thomas Walmesley of Clayton-le-dale, Lancashire, then a sergeant-at-law and his legal adviser, with Cowthorpe as security for the loan.

In July, the Earl empowered his commissioners to sell his manors of Hart and Maltby and his lands at Welham, Sutton, Broomfleet, Stainton, Hutton and Idle. The two manors had been in the family's hands since the time of Robert, 1st Lord Clifford. Welham, Sutton and Broomfleet were former Vescy properties, held by Francis on his life tenancy. As one of the commissioners, he must have been willing to sell them, though Welham and Sutton were not disposed of at this stage and the Earl later satisfied him for the £200 Broomfleet brought. The rest were Sir Ingram's former properties owned by the Earl himself. Within two years the main holdings had been sold.

The first step, in August 1585, was the Earl's mortgage of Maltby for £1,000 to Humphrey Weld (or Wylde), grocer of London. In November, he sold messuages in the manor of Idle for at least £400, but this sum did not satisfy his need then for ready money. On 27 November he borrowed another £400 for a year from Richard Tailford and on 7 December £900 for eight months from Ralph Radcliffe, mercer. On the last day of the year Peter Van Lore, jeweller, acted as intermediary or broker to enable the Earl to borrow £700 from two foreign merchants, Martyn Vande Sande and Wolfart van Byler. Bound with the Earl and Francis in an obligation for repayment was Francis Morley, a London goldsmith, who was now acting as one of his financial aids.[44]

By the late autumn of 1585 Countess Margaret had in effect left her husband to pursue his pleasures at Court on his own, spending most of her time in Yorkshire interspersed with visits to Chenies and the Warwick's house North Hall at Northaw in Hertfordshire, a curious reversal of her attitude only eight years earlier. Her emotions were in conflict in these months: joy at the birth of her second son, Robert, at Northaw on 21 September and the better health of her first, sickly child, tempered with sorrow at her father's death on 28 July and, even worse, her favourite brother Lord Francis's murder by Scots on the Borders the

Anne Russell, Countess of Warwick (1548–1604), by the Master of the Countess of Warwick, c. 1565

day before. Earl George had been appointed by Bedford a trustee in his settlement of his properties on 20 July during his last illness. The Earl was one of the chief mourners at the funeral at Chenies on 14 September and joined those who vowed revenge for Francis Russell's death. The Countess and her sisters had been in mourning when her son Robert was born, but it is clear that it was her husband's profligacy which was casting the biggest shadow over her life in the closing months of the year.[45]

The spring of 1586 was to be the first critical period in Earl George's finances. These now got increasingly convoluted as he tried to stave off the threatened loss of his mortgaged lordships and at the same time turn his mind to a spectacular means of restoring his fortunes, that is by privateering. Countess Margaret later lamented to Dr Layfield that her husband had

> lost with many goings back and forwards and turnings many for the worse, but few for the better, till we had wasted our land and substance, which in hope of better fortune of the sea, than we had of the land, he ventur'd many thousands, which we saw come empty home.[46]

There can be no doubt, therefore, that the attraction of plunder to clear his debts and bring greater riches was a compelling motive in the Earl's decision to invest in a privateering expedition in the spring of 1586. His financial juggling had this objective in mind. In February he managed to postpone until 20 April the redemption of Cowthorpe. Maltby he had to sacrifice but it was worth much more than its mortage price. Humfrey Weld reconveyed it to him and then he

Francis, Lord Clifford (1584–9), artist unknown

Robert, Lord Clifford (1585–91), artist unkown

sold its manor house to his solicitor, Anthony Wright, for £320 and the manor itself for £1,480 to Edward Stanhope Esq. of Gray's Inn, a member of a prominent Yorkshire family and a friend of the Cliffords. From the proceeds, the Earl satisfied Weld for the £1,000 loan and £50 for six months interest and received almost £750 in cash.

To redeem Cowthorpe he took another drastic step, selling the manor of Hart on 19 April for £3,000 to two officials of the Court of Exchequer, Robert Petre Esq., a teller, and John Morley Esq. This enabled him to repay the £1,600 due to Walmesley. The day after he pledged Cowthorpe again for a bigger, more realistic sum, £2,500, to Petre and Morley for six months. There was an odd proviso in the pledge that the Earl would be able to choose on 29 September whether to redeem Cowthorpe or Hart; odd, because Petre and Morley took the precaution of binding him in a recognizance with a penalty of £6,000 to keep to his agreement over Hart. They had good reason for doing so. They sold the manor for £5,350, a huge profit, on 16 May 1587 to John, Lord Lumley, proof of careless under-valuation by George and his advisers, in effect a double loss by him.[47] Altogether, these transactions provided him with £4,650 in cash. Some of this would be for current living expenses. Most, however, was for the purchase of two merchant ships, refurbishing them and equipping them with the extra and heavier cannon and munitions which privateers carried.

It is worth assessing the consequences after less than three years of the Earl's abandoning his rural existence for what Countess Margaret called the 'pleasant delights of court'. Funding their lavish life-style had already made serious inroads into the Clifford brothers' inheritance. They had sold Hart, Maltby, Broomfleet and much of the Derbyshire and Nottinghamshire property. Cowthorpe was at risk. The Earl owed £3,900 on the other, recorded loans and there would have been many smaller but cumulatively worrying debts to tradesmen, craftsmen, servants and friends both in London and Yorkshire which would be hard to meet. Nobility with ready money were also among his creditors. For instance, the Earl and Countess of Shrewsbury lent him two separate sums of £500 in late 1585 or early 1586 on a mortgage of part of Francis's Derbyshire property and George was also paying interest on £20 borrowed from Henry, 9th Earl of Northumberland.[48] These debts are known because the bonds have survived in the respective family archives, not in those of the Cliffords. What else Earl George owed at that time, and who his creditors were, may never be fully revealed.

Considering his estate income, it is fair to say that by 1586 the Earl could have barely covered the £600 a year interest owed on the known debts, let alone make provision for his current living costs, had he not constantly deferred satisfying his creditors. That is a generous view, as there are other signs both of indebtedness and avoidance of payment. He had fallen behind on the annual instalments due to the Court of Wards for his livery – the fine of half their annual rental required from wards when they entered their estates. He did not manage to pay the sum due for 1581 until 1586. He also began to default in 1584 on the reserved rents due to the Earl of Northumberland on his Percy Fee lordships. By 1594, after frequent non-payment, he owed Northumberland over £824.[49]

If anything, Francis Clifford had come off relatively worse than his brother by consorting with far richer men than himself. His only major capital assets, the Derbyshire and Nottinghamshire lands, which were essential if he were to marry and endow a wife, had rapidly shrunk. What was left, his life-interest estates, would not appeal to a prospective father-in-law and trustees. In that respect, Francis's personal fortunes were bound up with his brother's and he was at the mercy of whatever direction they would take. In an elliptical and unforeseeable way, Francis was eventually to benefit from his brother's profligacy and re-establish himself as a substantial gentleman, with his seat at Londesborough. If he had qualms about throwing away his inherited landed estate in a spendthrift life-style, he left no record of his feelings. Moreover, because he constantly acted as George's surety, there was a legal risk to his own possessions from his brother's indebtedness which endured well beyond his abandonment of a courtier life in 1589.

Had Earl George wished, he could have sought a less drastic remedy to his financial dilemmas, as his father had done, by withdrawing from Court to tend his estates and coping as best he could. But the outbreak of the war with Spain late in 1585 focused and fused the strands in his enthusiasms: the excitement aroused by Hakluyt in the oceanic world, mathematics, cartography and navigation; the renowned feats and rich takings of Sir Francis Drake; the lust for honour and service to the Queen and the element of personal risk, the gambling, which epitomised his temperament and characterized men of his rank in the Elizabethan age. The maritime war was to be the outlet for the pent-up energies he had wasted hitherto in courtier frivolities. At twenty-seven, he was at the peak of his physical and mental powers. He had ambitions to go to sea himself, but could not do so for two more years. In 1586 his motive was primarily mercenery – to fill his coffers and restore his landed estate. But, compared with his great properties in Craven and Westmorland, what he had sold and mortgaged was peripheral and recoverable by retrenchment. The course he adopted not only resulted in the loss of the manors he hoped to save but ultimately compelled him to surrender a far great portion of the Clifford patrimony than was at stake in 1586.

CHAPTER 4

Promoter and Commander: 1586–8

The long, dangerous and exhausting war with Spain was to endure throughout almost all of the last twenty years of Earl George's life and provide a continual challenge to his honour, energies and resources. Yet, unlike nobility such as the Howards, Leicester and Essex, his fame was not to be attained on official or semi-official expeditions on land or sea. Royal command eluded him, except briefly against the Spanish Armada. His distinctive contribution to the defeat of Spain was his own privately-financed ventures, that is privateering.

It must be stressed that Earl George was neither pirate, arch-pirate nor buccaneer, though he is often deemed such. Privateering was 'private anti-Spanish enterprise at sea', legally authorised or permitted by Elizabeth I's government. In essence, it was commerce-raiding against Spain and her allies and anyone trading with them and extended into attacks against Spanish and Portuguese settlements overseas. This sea-warfare enabled many of Elizabeth I's subjects to fulfil their traditional obligations of worsting their sovereign's enemies, and profitably. Sir Francis Drake had shown how much damage could be done to, and plunder wrested from, Spain's overseas possessions and rich trade from the Indies and the Americas. Earl George was to be at the forefront of those who tried to emulate him.

The term 'privateer' can denote ships, promoters or commanders at sea and here is used in all three senses. Privateering was formalised by the grant of letters of reprisal or licences by the Lord Admiral, or by letters of marque from friendly foreign rulers. The Queen profited directly by collecting customs on the prize-goods and the Lord Admiral took a tenth share of the remaining value in goods which he then sold, sometimes to the owners and victuallers of the privateers concerned. Ports like Southampton took their own toll of the goods. This system, like much of Tudor administration, was open to abuse and corruption, local officials colluding with owners and victuallers at the expense of the Queen and the Lord Admiral, though it is easy to exaggerate the extent.

The government were at pains to minimise annoyance to countries not directly involved in the sea war. Consequently, the legal structure within which privateers operated accommodated friendly or neutral traders aggrieved at losing goods and vessels. Such traders could seek redress against the offending privateers by appealing to the Privy Council and courts with final litigation in the Admiralty Court. However, getting privateers to pay recompense when judgements went against them was more difficult, as Dutch and French merchants who suffered at Earl George's hands were to discover.[1]

The Earl's prominence was in some respects a disadvantage, making him far less likely to escape customs, tenths or lawsuits than many lesser operators. Furthermore, he was constricted in his activities to a far greater degree than most privateers. Usually for his projected voyages he had to obtain a royal commission or letters patent from the Queen herself. In practice this meant she could prompt, co-operate with or prohibit them. The Earl was regularly subjected to royal direction and was not a free agent, rather an instrument of whatever offensive or defensive action Elizabeth and her Council favoured at any particular moment. The extent of the Queen's influence on the Earl may only be guessed because much passed in private conversation between them. However, there are clear illustrations of her interference and of Council direction and, sometimes, their open disapproval and criticism of his actions. On the other hand, the Queen had obligations to those who served her, especially financial and moral support when justified, and this the Earl was not slow to exploit. In the early years too, besides lending him royal warships, she sometimes invested with him, giving a kind of official status to his private actions. But he never enjoyed the royal backing such as Drake had, clandestinely, on his circumnavigation in 1577–80 and openly for his subsequent voyages.

For his initial venture as promoter, Earl George decided against hiring vessels and, like Sir Walter Raleigh, obtained ships of his own. With the cash raised in April 1586 he purchased two merchantmen and prepared them, spurred by news of Drake's exploits in the West Indies. The 300-ton *Assurance* he re-named the *Red Dragon* – Clifford and Arthurian, or perhaps Tudor, sentiment here – and made her admiral with a crew of 230 commanded by Captain Robert Widdrington. She was a powerful ship, equipped as a privateer with the ship-destroying demi-cannons, culverins and demi-culverins, besides the smaller minions, sakers and falcons. The 130-ton *Bark Clifford*, armed with minions and falcons, was vice-admiral, with a crew of 70 under Captain Christopher Lister, son of William of Midhope in Craven, one of the Clifford's gentry tenants.[2]

What victuals were supplied to the ships is not recorded. Indeed, the only surviving list for any of the Earl's enterprises is one he drew up for a projected voyage of 1600 which did not take place. Each man's allowance then was to be a pound of bread and a gallon of beer per day; a pound of beef per day on four days in the week; on the other three days two messes of fish daily, every mess to be one third part ling, and on each fish day four men were to share half a pound of butter at dinner and a pound of cheese at supper. In addition, there were to be other foods such as pease, oatmeal for sick men, mustard seed and large stores of water in casks.[3] One problem in victualling privateers was the extra provisioning they needed compared with merchantmen because they were much more heavily manned, with gunners and, in particular, soldiers. The latter were essential for musket-fire as the ships closed on their enemy and then in the hand-to-hand

TABLE 2 *Elizabethan naval guns*

Type	Calibre (in)	Weight (lb)	Shot (lb)	Point blank range (paces)	'Random' range (paces)
Demi-cannon	6¼	4,500	32	340	1,700
Culverin	5¼	4,000	17	400	2,500
Demi-culverin	4¼	2,850	9	400	2,500
Saker	3½	1,800	5	340	1,700
Minion	3¼	1,200	4	320	1,600
Falcon	2¾	900	2¾	260	1,200
Falconet	2¼	400	1¼	220	1,000
Robinet	1½	300	1	150	700

fighting after boarding which was often the only way larger vessels could be forced to yield.

The Earl obtained authorisation for this first voyage of plunder not from the Lord Admiral but the exiled King of Portugal, who supplied letters of marque.[4] Since Spain had taken over Portugal and its wealthy trade and overseas possessions in 1583, the King and his supporters had been Elizabeth's allies. The Earl's ruse helped hoodwink Spanish spies who continually, though often inaccurately, passed onto Madrid whatever they could glean of English enterprises. Bernado de Mendoza, the Spanish ambassador, was himself deceived. He informed Philip II that the Earl's ships were bound for Portuguese lands, Brazil and then the Moluccas – the Spice Islands in the East Indies. In fact, the Earl had instructed Widdrington to repeat Drake's great and profitable voyage of 1577 to the South Seas, stop at Bahia in Brazil only to re-victual and, he stressed in their last conference, return with £6,000 worth of plunder. The Earl had appointed as pilot for the Straits of Magellan a professional mariner, Thomas Hood, who knew the route from sailing with Drake. The merchant John Saracold, member of the Drapers' Company who kept a journal of the voyage, was eager to reach the Pacific after sailing on Drake's *Elizabeth* in 1577. She had rounded Cape Horn but then put back, returning to England via the River Plate estuary. A Spanish informer, writing on 24 June, warned that the Earl's ships were in excellent order and well-provided with men and necessary stores for the voyage.[5]

On the eve of departure, the Earl was elated by the news of Drake's capture of 'one of the chiefest towns in all the Indies called Santo Domingo' with 300,000 ducats (at least £100,000) and 'infinite other wealth.' He wrote to Countess Margaret that his ships were on the point of going 'lucklier now to speed well than ever'. They set sail from Gravesend on 26 June, calling at Dartmouth and Plymouth, where they were joined by two of Raleigh's ships, the *Roe* as rear-admiral under Captain Hawes and his fine pinnace, the *Dorothy*, this being the first of a number of projects in which the Earl and Sir Walter collaborated. Contrary winds prevented their small fleet from leaving Plymouth until 17 August.[6]

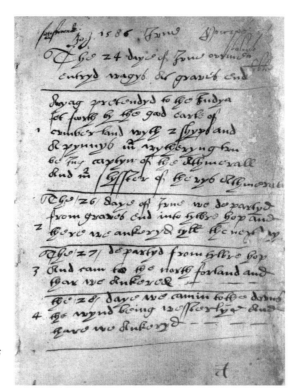

Thomas Hood's log of Cumberland's
fleet setting out from Gravesend,
26 June 1586

The cost of preparing his ships greatly added to the Earl's financial commitments during June. He borrowed £500 on the 8th for four months from Sergeant Walmesley, £1,000 on the 17th from the London mercers Thomas Cordell and Bartholomew Barnes, both of whom were notable privateering promoters, and, on the 20th, £1,000 from the lawyer Arden Waferer and £1,000 more on a mortgage of the manor of Gargrave to Richard Tailford. He used £900 of this cash to repay Radcliffe for the loan taken up in December.[7] The remaining £2,600 represents a part of his investment in the voyage. The size of the total cost is hard to estimate. Between April and June he had raised £7,250, most of which would have been spent on purchasing, equipping and victualling the ships: on Kenneth Andrews' estimates for only a six months' voyage the *Dragon* would have cost about £3,000 and the *Clifford* £1,000.[8] In addition, with the delay in sailing from Plymouth, victuals would have been consumed and have to be replaced. The Earl would have given bills and bonds to chandlers and other suppliers in Gravesend, Dartmouth and Plymouth. Even if Widdrington did return with £6,000 worth of plunder, the Earl might do no more than break even on his venture.

The Earl was fully aware that, whatever its success, his first enterprise would give no relief from his current indebtedness. He anticipated a long voyage by making the term of the loans from Cordell and Barnes a year and that from

Tailford eighteen months. Yet, if he were to redeem Cowthorpe on 29 September and repay the loans falling due to Walmesley and Van Lore, he would need a great deal of cash from some source which avoided adding to his already stretched credit in London. Consequently, he turned to the Queen for help. She generously responded with a gift of property in the North, possibly the lordship of Brancepeth and manor of Whitworth in Durham (formerly the Earl of Westmorland's lands, forfeited after the 1569 Rebellion), though the grant for that is dated April 1587. But, whatever it was, the Earl discovered on a visit that he could not convert it quickly into ready money. He probably again sought Elizabeth's aid in person, only to be rebuffed. His only hope now was for the Lord Treasurer to intercede with her on his behalf.

Writing from Court on 27 September, he appealed to Burghley, requesting that the Queen lend him £10,000 at £1,000 a year interest. For security, he promised either to pawn as much land as Burghley required or put as many gentlemen in bond as he thought sufficient, or resign up to the Queen her recent gift to him. From the latter, he rather brashly asserted, she would get more benefit than she would lose by lending him money. He stressed the urgency, 'my dayes of payement beinge soe neare, and the forfetures greate, which I shall faule into' if he were not relieved, through Burghley's support, by the grant of 'this, as I thyncke, my resonable sute'.[9]

The Earl's plea was unrealistic, even naive, considering the state of the royal Exchequer. Whether or not Burghley approached the Queen over the matter, which might not have been in George's best interests, nothing came of his supplication. Its failure marked the end of the early period of his courtier

Sir William Cecil, 1st Lord Burghley (1520–98), artist unkown

extravagance. He was unable to redeem Cowthorpe and it passed out of his possession. Petre and Morley found an immediately buyer in Sergeant Walmesley who, as usual, was well placed to make a bid. The Earl did manage at the end of 1586 to repay the money due to Van Lore and the £1,000 debt to the Earl and Countess of Shrewsbury, but only by a new mortgage. John Morley lent him £1,000 for six months on 6 December with the manors of Nesfield, Westhall and Langbar as security.[10] Despite the Earl's loss of Hart, Maltby and Cowthorpe, his recorded debts were as high as a year earlier, at £5,969.

From autumn 1586 to spring 1587 Earl George was continually at Court or employed, like so many peers and ministers, in the arraignment and then execution of Mary, Queen of Scots. He was a commissioner at her trial at Westminster and Fotheringhay Castle in Northamptonshire during October and carried news of the proceedings to Elizabeth. If he was specially chosen as courier, it would be because of his sister's cousinage with both Queens. He attended parliament in November when Mary's indictment was approved. He was one of the earls to whom the warrant for her execution was addressed and was present at Fotheringhay in February 1587 when she was beheaded. At the subsequent Star Chamber trial of the second secretary, William Davison, Elizabeth's scapegoat for her cousin's execution, the Earl again acted as a commissioner.[11] In April he was jousting at Court, running the course of the field with Sir Henry Lee and Sir Thomas Gage.

That summer, with the intensification of the war with Spain, Earl George came much nearer to achieving his ambition of active service. He was named in June as general of a fleet which the Queen intended should relieve Drake in his great attack on Cadiz, but in the event, frustratingly, it did not sail.[12] Before then, near the end of July, his eagerness for battle had got the better of him, but only after he had been required to put his finances in order to the satisfaction of his creditors and, most of all, the Queen. During the first half of the year, the Earl had increased his indebtedness largely to meet his living costs at Court. He borrowed £1,200 in March from his friend and servant William Ingleby on a two-years' mortgage of the manor of Eshton, the long term another indication of his growing insolvency. In June, he was unable to redeem the Nesfield manors from John Morley, who agreed to defer payment, with interest. The one loan the Earl did repay was the first £500 due to Cordell and Barnes.[13]

Countess Margaret was later to describe her anxiety over the risks her husband took with his life in 1587 and even more during the Armada battle the following year. If he had died then, his estates would have been exposed to litigation by his creditors, a worry for his Countess which was to increase over the coming years. Yet his brother, friends and servants bound with him as sureties were equally vulnerable. Most of all, the Queen was an interested party both for what he owed the Court of Wards and other, large, unspecified sums. The Earl had not used the lordship of Brancepeth and manor of Whitworth, granted in April, to repay his debts as she had intended. Her hand can now be perceived behind Burghley's action in forcing the Earl to make a formal arrangement to clear his debts.

In this, Earl George assigned to Burghley and Francis Clifford, to hold for ever, his Craven properties of Grassington, Steeton, Carleton, Cononley, Lothersdale,

The execution of Mary, Queen of Scots, at Fotheringay Castle, 8 February 1587. The Queen is shown, left, entering and, centre, being disrobed

Bradley, Utley, Settle, Giggleswick, Long Preston, Threapland and Cracoe, Woodhouse and Appletreewick, Litton and Littondale, and also Idle: in other words most of his Craven lands not already mortgaged or part of the 1311 Skipton Castle estate or of the Bolton Abbey demesnes. All had been accretions to the inheritance during the sixteenth century. The purpose was twofold. Burghley and Clifford were to sell the properties to pay his debts while his sureties – Francis himself, Anthony Wright, William Ferrand and the goldsmith Francis Morley – were safeguarded from his creditors. Sensibly, Ferrand's own leasehold tenancy of the manor house, demesnes and park of Carleton was excluded from this and subsequent assignments. At the end of two years, Francis was to be seized of whatever manors and lands had not been sold, to the use of the Earl and his heirs.[14]

Because the Queen had priority, Burghley procured on 1 August a royal protection for Francis, Wright, Ferrand and Morley from legal proceedings by the Earl's creditors to allow them to satisfy the Crown for 'certain great sums to be paid at a future date'. What these were is not specified, probably his debts to the Court of Wards and the £100 14s. 3½d. reserved rents on Brancepeth and Whitworth. Nevertheless, despite all the claims on the Earl's strained cash resources, Francis was able to avoid the major sales envisaged in the grant. The only land disposed of was the Earl's small property at Bickerton, which Sergeant

Walmesley bought for about £150.[14] Most of the creditors were happy to extend the loans as long as interest was paid or added to the principal. Indeed, the effect of the grant, far from restricting the Earl's commitments, was to strengthen his credit because the Craven properties had been assigned as security and, it would be common knowledge, with royal approval.

These financial arrangements put a rather different slant on Robert Carey's terse and stirring recollection of how he and Earl George stole away from Court near the end of July and crossed the Channel in a bark obtained by George with the intention of helping defend Sluys against the Duke of Parma's Spanish army, as did several other courtiers excited by the warfare just across the Channel. On reaching Ostend, they learnt Sluys had fallen. Carey stayed on in the port, where his brother was living, while the Earl left in his bark for Flushing and then Bergen-op-Zoom to visit the Earl of Leicester, commander of the English army supporting the Dutch rebel states. He got no chance to bloody his sword and achieved little by this quest for combat apart from setting foot on shipboard for the first time and witnessing in person the poor state of the English forces. Yet, in view of his own later attitudes and actions as a commander, this may have been a valuable insight into how not to conduct a campaign overseas.[16]

While the Earl's thoughts were on battle, his enthusiasm for exploration was being given a permanent and, appropriately, cartographic memorial by the famous navigator John Davis on his third and final attempt to reach Asia via the north-west passage. On 23 July, Davis recorded,

> having sayled 60 leagues Northwest into the streights, at two a clocke after noone, we ankered among many Isles in the bottome of the gulfe, naming the same the erle of Cumberlands Isles . . .

This is now called Cumberland Gulf in the Davis Strait. The place names in that region of Canada read like a roll-call of Elizabethan worthies who either supported or invested in Davis's voyages of exploration. Earl George was one of them and, conceivably, regarded as a sponsor in the wider sense as the foremost noble and courtier member of Hakluyt's circle of expansionists. He was the recipient of another maritime dedication in 1587, Thomas Greepe's description in verse of the exploits of Sir Francis Drake. Greepe commended Cumberland's fame and love 'of all vertuous attempts' and wished him long life and increase of honour 'with happy and eternall felicitie'. His choice of the Earl was apposite, though not his timing for the Earl's own first 'vertuous attempt' sadly did not match his exemplar's.[17]

His optimism that oceanic privateering would rescue him from his creditors was dashed when the ships arrived back on 29 September 1587. The delayed start, constant need to search for water and victuals off Sierra Leone and Brazil and Widdrington's lack of resolution meant they made no attempt to round the Straits and, instead, looked for plunder off the Brazilian coast and the Azores. They were skilfully resisted in Brazil and captured only a few hulks of little value. Captain Lister had urged the Admiral to let him have Thomas Hood and he would go to the South Seas alone in the *Bark Clifford*. Widdrington refused. It was with grief, wrote John Saracold, that they saw 'my lords hope thus deceived, and his great expenses and costs cast away.'[18] Earl George had undertaken the enterprise in circumstances of risk which resembled a reckless gamble. Not for the last time in his career, it was a gamble which failed. The plunder his ships gained did little to recoup his investment, let alone restore his fortunes, which plunged him even deeper into debt.

As usual, the Earl performed in the November celebrations at Court. On Coronation Day, he and Essex made challenge that on 26 February next, 1588, they would run against all-comers to maintain that the Queen was 'most worthiest and most fairest Amadis de Gaule', the legendary hero of the French chivalric romance published in 1540 and as popular in England as across the Channel. Again, on 24 November, he and Essex were 'the chiefe that ranne' at the tilt. Early next month he had better hopes of military action. He was made marshal of the field in the force gathered on the northern frontier with Huntingdon in command, Sir Henry Lee general of the horse and Sir Robert Constable general of foot, to guard against the Scottish troubles spilling over: the crisis soon passed. This was to be the pattern of the Earl's career. Although considered for and occasionally appointed to command by the Queen, he was fated never to see active service except on his own initiative. However, his obvious martial instincts and intentions attracted authors seeking patronage. It was this, as well as the approbation his rank would give, which led Edward Aggas to dedicate to him late in 1587 his translation *The Politicke and Militarie Discourses of the Lorde De La Noue*. Its timely publication would make the Earl's interests known to a wide readership in the way that Settle's work had done a decade earlier.[19]

At the very end of the year Earl George had to deal with another financial quandary. John Morley, on his deathbed in November, assigned the mortgage of the Nesfield manors to two more officials, Robert Freke Esq., a teller in the Exchequer, and Thomas Crompton, head of the fine office, and their associates, William Spencer Esq. and Edward Downing Esq. The Earl stood to lose the manors because his new creditors wanted the principal and interest repaid, not Yorkshire property which would be an encumbrance to them, and he was in no position to satisfy them. His most important and supportive noble creditor, the Earl of Shrewsbury, came to his rescue, taking over the mortgage in January 1588 and giving him a five-year period of grace before requiring repayment in 1593.

Shrewsbury, a great landowner, had a different attitude to real estate from that of most of Earl George's London creditors, as is shown by the negotiations between his officer, Leonard Bamforth, and the Earl and his legal adviser, Sergeant Walmesley, over details in the mortage agreement. These illustrate both the hidden dangers of a landowner securing loans on property and general awareness of the risks lenders took in providing the Earl with cash on credit. Earl George, sensibly, wanted to protect his manors by covenants restraining Shrewsbury from behaving as landlord by felling woods, making waste and ploughing the ground, which Bamforth claimed, dubiously, were always permitted in mortgages. Some mortgages did, indeed, allow occupation and exploitation of the assets but only in lieu of interest, not in addition. Bamforth was acting as a shrewd servant should, maximising opportunities for his master's good.

Bamforth was on firmer ground in his concern that Shrewsbury stood to lose all his money should Earl George die, because the Nesfield manors could be sold to discharge the statutes acknowledged by the Earl which took precedence over other forms of debt. Technically he was correct and with all Earl George's lands entailed to his elder son, so Bamforth thought, he was right to point this out. How the difficulties were resolved is not documented. What is most revealing is that Bamforth knew of statutes entered into by the Earl. These would be statutes merchant or staple which the trading community normally demanded as security. Since the only reference to one concerning the Earl is in Tailford's loan, other creditors besides him must have taken out collateral security with statutes, a common sense procedure when dealing with big debtors, but which, like so many bills and bonds, would be unknown but for incidental mention of this kind.[20]

The spring and early summer of the fateful year of 1588 were dominated for Earl George by financial affairs. It was a matter of honour, as well as a practical necessity now, that he settle his debts to his brother. Francis was his chief surety and, as steward of Craven, his senior officer in the Council which managed his estates. Between 1583 and September 1587 the Earl had accumulated debts to him totalling £1,669 4s. 10d., comprising moneys he had lost gambling, rents which Francis should have had, the interest on the borrowings from the Earl and Countess of Shrewsbury and £940 for the sales in Derbyshire and Nottinghamshire. All these had left Francis without an heritable estate and out of pocket too. It was impossible for George to make a cash settlement of this debt. Instead, in July 1588 he granted Francis the reversion of the Londesborough and other east Yorkshire properties; in effect, a sale.[21]

This was a drastic solution for George and his sons since these former Vescy lands would now pass from the main inheritance. Countess Margaret also was adversely affected; the third of her husband's estates to which she would be entitled at common law as a widow would be diminished. For Francis, on the other hand, it was ideal. He now had a Yorkshire seat and estate which would attract a wife of gentry status. Within two years, in July 1589, he married the widow Grissell Hughes, Lady Abergavenny, and built for her a fine mansion at Londesborough.[22] His lifestyle altered to that of a country gentleman residing in the East Riding but with responsibiities and also property of his own in Craven. He remained George's principal financial associate, often visiting London on his business, without ever, it seems, risking his own cash on his brother's privateering enterprises.

In April the Earl resorted for the first time to raising money by what later became one of his favourite methods, effectively selling individual messuages to the sitting tenants. A legal loophole in the assignments of the manors may have made this an attractive alternative to outright sales; certainly it was in the immediate sense far more productive. Following agreements made in April, twenty-seven tenants of Carleton and Lothersdale paid a total of £1,500 during May for grants of their tenements 'for ever' at the existing rents. Effectively these were sales which made them independent farmers, though they covenanted to attend the manorial court, have their corn ground at the manorial mill and do no harm to the Earl's deer and other game. The cost to the Earl and his successors

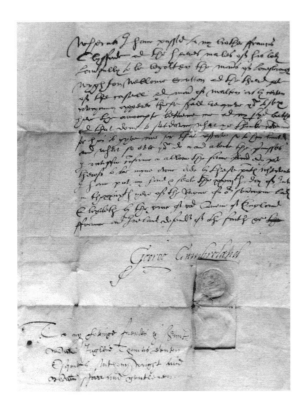

Earl George's instructions to his officers after passing his Londesborough estates to his brother Francis, 23 July 1587

was the loss of any future income from entry fines and of the option to increase revenues by switching from ancient to economic rents, though that was not estate practice at this time. The initiative for the grants probably came from Francis and the other estate commissioners, but the Earl would approve.[23]

Even with this money, he lacked the means to redeem Gargrave from Richard Tailford. To do this, he mortaged on 21 June the former royal lordship of Brancepeth and manor of Whitworth in Durham for £2,000 for six months to the officials Petre, Freke and Crompton. After re-paying the £1,000 principal and £200 accumulated interest owed on Gargrave, the Earl had £800 in ready money to meet his living expenses at Court.[24] His finances were stable for the moment, though at the expense of a personal estate shrunk to its medieval core of Westmorland and the Honour of Skipton, plus the contiguous and valuable Bolton Abbey demesnes. Most of the other manors in Craven were variously in the hands of Burghley and Clifford, Ingleby and Shrewsbury and might yet be lost if the downward spiral in his finances could not be arrested. Now that the outlying properties had gone, the Tudor acquisitions were the next most vulnerable of his family's possessions, already close to being sacrificed to his creditors. He had, moreover, begun to make inroads into the value of the manors by selling messuages, an erosion which in the short term had advantages over his usual practice of outright sales. However, such matters must have appeared trifling to him when set against the looming national crisis of an imminent Spanish seaborne invasion and the call to arms for the whole nation in defence of the Queen's realm.

The great Armada campaign was to give the Earl the long-awaited opportunity to thrust himself into the limelight, take part in naval action and command a royal warship, indeed a squadron. His was to be a noteworthy and varied contribution to both the English triumph and the celebrations which followed, together lasting almost the entire second half of 1588. Yet without his driving eagerness to take part, he would have been little more than a bystander in the land forces gathered at Tilbury to repel the invaders. On 22 July, as the Armada approached the Cornish coast, he was named to serve with other noblemen under the Lord General, the Earl of Leicester. Unable to bring down his own tenants – the militia of the five northern counties being ordered to stand guard there – he, like many courtiers, collected his own band of horsemen whom he lodged and maintained at his own expense near London, ready to join the royal army. He and Essex, general of the horse, entertained the mustered troops by running courses of the field, other jousters joining in their display.[25]

Nevertheless he still itched to take part in the expected great sea encounter. Countess Margaret successfully lobbied the Queen, through Secretary Walsingham, to allow him to join Lord Admiral Howard's fleet. She urged him to prepare to go quickly because if he tarried Elizabeth might change her mind. In the meantime, the Council was scouring the southern ports for ships which could immediately be got ready to strengthen Howard's fleet or act as supply vessels. They wrote on Wednesday 24 July to the Earl of Sussex, who was at Portsmouth in charge of supply, about Earl George's two ships and informed the Queen about them. She, however, was loth to use them without the Earl's prior assent.

The news had just reached the Court at Richmond Palace that the Armada had been sighted. On hearing this the Earl and Robert Carey took post horse for Portsmouth, calling at Richmond on their way, where the Council told him they wanted to employ his ships. He explained that, in his opinion, they were not fit for service, but he ordered his servant to see that the powder, munitions and shot in them were delivered to Sussex. When he and Carey arrived at Portsmouth later that day, he probably sought out Sussex from courtesy and to discuss how the *Red Dragon* and *Bark Clifford* and their stores could be most effectively used.

At the port the Earl and Carey found a frigate which took them to sea, searching in vain for the rival fleets off the Isle of Wight until nightfall. They blundered into the Spanish formation early next morning, realised their error, tacked about and lighted on the English fleet not far behind. They boarded Howard's flagship the *Ark Royal* but, finding it crowded and short of cabins, took boat to another royal warship, the 448-ton, 37-gun *Elizabeth Bonaventure* with a crew of 250 captained by George Raymond, an experienced seaman who had sailed on Drake's 1587 Cadiz expedition. They stayed in the *Bonaventure* and, Carey recalled, were very welcome and made much of.

This reception eased the somewhat anomalous working relationship and duality of command between the professional mariner and the high-ranking courtier. Raymond acted as the sole captain, in receipt of royal wages, the 'captain's diet'. The Earl, an unpaid volunteer, was held to be commander and the Lord Admiral brought him into his Council of War. It may be that this was a political move by Howard to give him weight against Drake and the other sea-dogs. But Howard was accountable to the Queen and Council for his actions and George's closeness to her was to prove useful. The Earl flew 'a bluddey flagge' as his colours on the *Bonaventure* (his red dragon crest not permissible), along with the two flags of St George, a silk ensign and two streamers which the ship sported throughout the conflict, the ensign afterwards bestowed on Raymond as his memento of the action.[26]

The weather was so calm on their first day with the fleet, Thursday 25 July, that in Carey's remembrance, nothing was attempted on either side. Indeed there was no set battle, rather skirmishes in which the *Bonaventure* may not have been involved. Both Howard and Hawkins, in the centre of the fleet, used their long boats to tow their ships to attack isolated Spanish vessels and, as the wind freshened, Frobisher's squadron on the left went into action against the Spanish flagship, the *San Martin*, but it was rescued by others. Drake thrust at the Armada's right flank to edge the Spaniards towards the Owers bank but Medina Sidonia realised the danger and the tactic failed.

During the next two days both fleets held their formation and course without a shot being fired, until Medina Sidonia anchored off Calais on Saturday evening. The English followed suit and were re-inforced by Lord Henry Seymour's squadron. There they remained until, in the darkness at about two o'clock on the morning of Monday 29 July, the spectacular attack of the fireships forced the Armada hastily to abandon their moorings to escape the burning hulks. The stalemate was broken at last, the Armada was scattered and the stage set for the decisive Battle of Gravelines.

With the Spaniards in disorder, Carey writes, 'we made ready to follow them, where began a cruel fight, and we had such advantage both of wind and tide, as we had a glorious day of them; continuing fight from four o'clock in the morning, till almost five or six at night'. After fleeing the fireships, the Armada recovered remarkably into a half-moon. Sir William Winter in the *Vanguard* charged at the starboard wing, firing at point-blank range six-score paces away, the *Rainbow* under Lord Seymour and the *Bonaventure* following suit. They set on and surrounded a great Spanish galleon, 'yet she saved herself valiantly.' All day the assault continued and only ceased when the English ships had spent their ammunition, the Spanish galleons being battered and their casualties grievous.

A change in wind to south-south-west on the Tuesday saved the Armada from the complete disaster of being wrecked on the Flemish sandbanks. They regrouped and sailed north, with the English following at a distance. They were off Flamborough Head on Wednesday 31 July. That night, according to Carey, the English resolved on a new fight as a farewell to Medina Sidonia's fleet. Only then was it realised how little ammunition any of the English ships had. By two o'clock on the morning of Thursday 1 August, a flag of council hung out of the vice-admiral's ship, Drake's *Revenge*, for a conference about what could be done. Earl George was one of the six commanders, along with Drake, Hawkins, Frobisher, Thomas Fenner and Edmund, Lord Sheffield, who signed with Lord Admiral

The battle off Gravelines, 29 July 1588, from the (lost) House of Lords Armada Tapestries engraved by John Pine, 1739. In the depictions of the commanders, Earl George is third from the right at the top

Howard the bold declaration of their determination to pursue the Spanish fleet until it had cleared the English coast and reached the Firth of Forth and then turn back 'to revictuall oure ships (which stand in extreme scarsitie) and also to guard and defend oure owne coaste at home'. If victuals and ammunition were supplied, they would pursue the Spaniards to the furthest, as far as the Armada dare go. In the event, they kept them in sight until 'a mighty storm', in Carey's words, drove the Spaniards away north and the English, having endured the gale at anchor, set sail southwards towards the Downs.[27]

Six days later, Earl George set foot on land again. The Lord Admiral had despatched him on Wednesday 7 August, when the English fleet was ten leagues east of Harwich, with letters for the Queen, Burghley and Walsingham. The Earl and Carey took a pinnace to Harwich and then post horse to Tilbury, arriving at midday on Thursday 8th while the Queen was at dinner with Leicester in his tent following her famous review of the forces mustered there. The Earl brought the first news the Court had heard of the Armada since its northward progress began and also the unwelcome, but as it transpired incorrect, reports that the Duke of Parma was about to cross the Channel with the army of Flanders. He also informed Burghley that the fifteen victuallers sent by Sussex from Portsmouth to supply the fleet had reached Harwich. The Queen knighted the Earl for his part in the battle and, by tradition, it was here that he picked up the glove she dropped which he henceforth wore in his hat. Robert Carey missed his reward, falling ill with fever which prevented his journeying to Scotland as the Queen's ambassador.[28]

Resolution of the Council of War, 1 August 1588, to pursue the Spanish Armada until they had cleared the English coast, then return to revictual and resume guard

Earl George quickly returned to the *Elizabeth Bonaventure*. He had joined it as a novice, been brought into the Council of War, fought in the thick of battle at Gravelines, and now had his first taste of independent command. The Lord Admiral divided his squadron into three groups as the fleet remained on guard in the Downs during August in case the wind changed and the Armada returned or, indeed, Parma tried to force a crossing. Howard had ten ships in his group, Sir Richard Grenville six in his and Earl George six with two pinnaces of watch. Like the rest of the fleet, his group was a mixture of royal and private vessels. He commanded in the *Bonaventure* and had under him another royal warship, the *Swiftsure* 232 tons, two Levanters – the *Merchant Royal* 400 tons and *Edward Bonaventure* 300 tons – the *Prudence* 120 tons and the *Sampson* 300 tons.[29] This last was his own *Red Dragon*, renamed by Sussex (perhaps with his approval while at Portsmouth) most likely because of sensitivity about a private ship in the Queen's service and under the royal flag bearing a name with such obvious Tudor connotations. From then on the ship was usually known as the *Sampson*, an inspired choice mindful of the destructive strength of the Biblical hero, but sometimes by its original name, the *Assurance*.

The *Sampson* was much the largest of the twenty-three voluntary ships brought into the royal navy after the Armada appeared. Her captain was Mr John Wingfield, master gunner William Maddock, boatswain Morris Jones, and she had a complement of 108 men, necessarily smaller than normal for a ship of her burden. The Earl's opinion of her fitness for service after her long voyage and then ten months laid up was justified, but Sussex acted with commendable speed and efficiency to get her ready once he was assured she was available. Starting on Thursday 25 June, the day after he received the Privy Council request, he prepared the *Sampson* and a Rotterdam flyboat of 40 tons to join Howard's fleet in only five days and, in addition, four small vessels to carry munitions and the other victuallers.

On that first day, eight demi-culverin crossbar shot were delivered to the *Red Dragon*, as she was still called, and 247 crossbars, round and chain shot for her sakers, minions and falcons. Later, 50 rounds each were taken aboard for her demi-cannon, culverins and demi-culverins; 218 more crossbar and chain shot for the sakers and minions; and eighteen barrels and 110 demi-barrels of gunpowder, some from the shire's provision and the Tower of London. From the *Dragon*'s store, held securely ashore, came six more demi-barrels of gunpowder a hundred-weight apiece, three humber barrels and various handweapons. Her sails and the topsails of the *Bark Clifford* were delivered from the store. Sails and other equipment were brought from the *Prudence* which was stripped to supply the *Dragon* and the flyboat. The *Bark Clifford*'s two cast iron minions, two bonnets and possibly two falcons were transferred to the flyboat.

At the same time, on Sussex orders, the *Dragon* was victualled with beef, fish, beer, wine, biscuit and bread bought from local tradesmen. Essential repairs were done. Her cooking hearth had to be rebuilt with 400 bricks, the back of the ship with 1500 planks, the tops fitted with trussing hoops and the main tops with fittings. Other necessary equipment included three lanterns, ropes, padlocks, candlesticks, a great copper kettle, a great bowl, frying pan and many small items such as royal paper, glue and bowstrings. The total cost of preparing the *Dragon*, besides her own equipment and store, came to £106 17s. 6d. All the entries were checked and approved by Sussex himself and the Crown met the whole expense along with the outlay for keeping her at sea for a whole month.[30] The Queen, as is seen, found a means of compensating the Earl for volunteering his ships and their stores.

The *Sampson* entered royal service as one of the 197 ships officially held to constitute the naval force against the Armada. Only eighteen were of greater burden, hence the Council's concern to make her available, and, as a privateer, she was heavily armed. She had no part in the fighting because she did not sail until the day after the Battle of Gravelines. She joined Howard's squadron in better shape than most of the ships which had taken shot and musket-fire in the battles and then were severely buffeted by the North Sea gales, and certainly she was better provisioned. Hence, the *Sampson* was one of the last privately-owned vessels to be discharged from royal service. There is no comment about whether her crew suffered from the pestilence which spread rapidly through Howard's squadron during August and, with its high mortality, made them a 'pitiful sight' to behold. Most likely they did. Sadly, the mariners' death-rate was far greater than it need have been because of a typical Tudor bureaucratic impasse; the Council was unable to discharge the crews without first paying them yet unable to pay them from lack of cash.[31]

Earl George's brave showing against the Armada ushered in a period of nearly four years when he most enjoyed royal favour. He was called back to Court from his squadron to play a leading part in the celebrations of the victory. On 26 August, at the last of the great reviews of royal forces in Whitehall organized by Essex, a joust was held in the fields. Essex and the Earl ran two tilts with the Queen watching from an open window. A Spanish informer present wrote that the spectators were highly pleased with the contest, because they were two of the best horsemen in the country. Other gentlemen joined in, but always Essex ran against the Earl. After they finished with the lances, they drew their swords, ignoring the Queen's sign to desist, and when they set to she shut the window in dismay at the danger courted by these pugnacious young noblemen.[32]

Effusive literary plaudits on the victory invariably include Earl George in the pantheon of heroes. James Aske, in his *Elizabetha Triumphans*, wrote of his part at Gravelines and after:

> And Comberland, a Wondrous forward Earle,
> But new imbarkt, attayning to this flight
> Did shewe himselfe, and shewing made them feele
> His power, not felt before of Spanyards.[33]

James Lea, in *An Answer to the Untruthes, Published and Printed in Spaine*, drawing inspiration from Greek mythology which all his readers would understand, compared the Earl to Alcides, that is Hercules:

> Next him the matchlesse Clifford shakes his sword,
> (Like to Alcides, faire Alcmenas sonne)
> His lookes are sterne, his lookes do feare affoord,
> Within his breast doth manly courage woone,
> Upon his crest the dragon list to frowne,
> Empaled and compast with a golden crowne.[34]

Cumberland's looks apart, what catches the eye in Lea's verse is mention of his crest, still regarded as a dragon and not yet a wyvern. The Earl featured in various depictions of the Armada's defeat, such as Robert Adam's charts which Augustine Ryther engraved and the Lord Admiral had woven into tapestries, later to be hung in the House of Lords and lost in the great 1834 fire. In Charles II's reign, the Earl was to figure on one of a set of Armada playing cards, the five of clubs. He was shown with the Earls of Oxford and Northumberland and other nobility and gentry going to visit the English Fleet; historically inaccurate, but a welcome recollection of the part they played in the overthrow of King Philip's grand design.

In the euphoria mingled with relief at fending off invasion, Earl George quickly turned his high standing with the Queen to his advantage. Although there was no concerted effort to complete the ruin of the Armada such as Horatio Palavicino proposed with the Earl as general and Frobisher his lieutenant, Elizabeth in effect joined him in a private operation against the Spaniards. His commission, granted on 4 October, stated his voyage was for both the service of the realm and, significantly, the recovery of his former losses. She lent him two of

1

2

3

*Three miniatures of George Clifford, 3rd Earl
of Cumberland, by Nicholas Hilliard.
Clockwise from top left: in 1589, 1591 and
1597 respectively.*

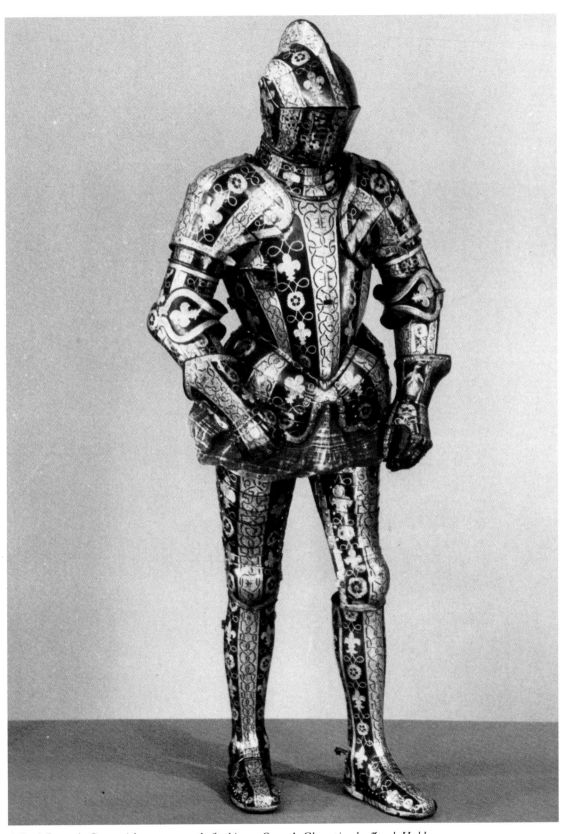

4 *Earl George's Greenwich armour, made for him as Queen's Champion by Jacob Halder*

*Armada playing-cards, c. 1676–1700. The V of Clubs shows the Earls of Oxford,
Northumberland and Cumberland visiting the English fleet*

the warships which had fought against the Armada, the 600-ton, 38-gun *Golden
Lion* which, with a crew of 200, cost £500 a month at sea, and the 120-ton *Scout*
which had a crew of over 60 and was armed with 20 light guns, sakers and smaller
armaments. These he manned with volunteers and equipped 'at his own Charge
and adventure'.[35] He did not need to use the *Sampson*, just de-commissioned, or
the *Clifford*, which was in no condition to go to sea.

Before he sailed, once more risking his life, Earl George entered into new
formal arrangements for the payment of his debts and the protection of his
brother and senior officers. In an indenture tripartite on 1 October 1588, he again
authorised Francis, Wright and Ferrand to sell the Craven manors assigned in
July 1587, adding to them Gisburn and Langstrothdale so that the grant now
included most of the Percy Fee lordships. With the royal protection expired,
Francis needed a new safeguard for his own inheritance. This was all the more
necessary because the Earl had increased his borrowing from Shrewsbury by a
further £1,000 and the latter held a bond for £2,000 for the repayment in which
Francis and William Ingleby stood bound with the Earl. They had no counter-
bond to protect their own lands should Shrewsbury (or his heirs and executors
if he died) demand repayment. Consequently, the Earl assigned to them, on

2 October, part of his valuable lease of the Craven and Leeds tithes held from Christ Church, Oxford, covenanting to pay the rents to the Dean and Chapter out of his own pocket. The remainder of the lease, Skipton, Long Preston and other township tithes and the income from them, he demised on 7 October to his relatives Henry Grey, 6th Earl of Kent (a Brandon and also Shrewsbury connection) and Lord Wharton to use to maintain his 'howse' and pay his debts.[36]

On this second privateering venture the Earl sailed and commanded in person. Spanish informants reported to Philip II that he intended robbery in the West Indies and the South Seas. However, the Queen would never have allowed such a voyage with her warships. His much more modest object was to intercept Channel shipping carrying contraband to Spain. He had an early success. About 20 October the *Lion* captured after a 'stout fight' a Dunkirker, the *Hare*, en route to Spain with merchandise. This he sent to Plymouth in Captain Lister's charge. Its cargo paid for the continuing costs of the venture. He received intelligence of four other Dunkirkers carrying ordnance and rich cargoes to Spain. Before he could locate them, a storm of such intensity blew up that even at anchor in Freshwater Bay he could only save the *Lion* by casting the main mast. After the return to Portsmouth, John Thomas, clerk of the prick and check, reported to Lord Admiral Howard on 15 November that the ship's main mast, yard, topmast and yard and topsail had all been lost. He asked whether replacement was at the Queen's charge or the Earl's.[37] Almost certainly the Queen stood the cost, another kindness to him in her benign post-Armada mood but one which she could hardly have avoided in view of her free use of his ships in the greatest crisis of her reign.

While at Plymouth the Earl and Robert Carey went in search of one of the big Armada hulks which had been beaten into harbour at Hope, twenty-three miles away. There proved to be no duke or treasure aboard, as had been rumoured, but their action, he informed Secretary Walsingham, had stopped the local people from plundering her. He was directly employed by the Council during November to search for Spanish goods which, it was thought, had been brought into the country in foreign ships. He sent down 'certaine dyscreete and trustie' servants to seek out such ships. On 22 November the Council requested Admiralty officers and local officials to assist the Earl's men in their work. His prominance had now brought him popularity and a ballad published on 14 November, *A Dytty of thexploit of Therle of Cumberland on the Sea in October 1588. and of thouerthrowe of 1600 Spaniardes in Irland*, exploited the two latest maritime events at a time when the English were still at the summit of their self-congratulation.[38]

Armada year, which had brought Earl George the excitement and strain of battle, command at sea and renown, ended as it had begun, with more financial pressure, this time resulting from his losses on his second privateering venture in October. Either for personal reasons or perception of George's difficulties, the Earl of Shrewsbury reached a new agreement with him and Francis on 30 November by which he could request repayment of the £1,000 loan on the Nesfield mortgage two years earlier than previously arranged, in 1591 instead of 1593. More immediately, the Earl was unable to repay the £2,000 with £100 interest due to Petre, Freke and Crompton on 23 December on the Brancepeth mortgage. They now foreclosed, paying him a further £500 for outright ownership as by the mortage agreement.[39] The surrender of Brancepeth and Whitworth was the price Earl George paid for the failure of his second enterprise. His known debts had risen to £6,800 and the catalogue of his lost properties was mounting. Without a change in his privateering fortunes much else was endangered, a sobering thought for him as he contemplated the disastrous course so far of his maritime adventuring which he had self-assuredly anticipated would restore his landed wealth.

CHAPTER 5

Privateer and Queen's Champion: 1589–91

The Earl was in the North in the early weeks of 1589 and, with his usual large following, graced the city of York with a visit in February, where the corporation presented him with their speciality, mayne bread, a gallon of hippocras – wine flavoured with spices – and a gallon of muscadel. He returned the compliment with gifts of venison to the Lord Mayor and aldermen. His mind must already have been on another enterprise. The prospects for successful privateering by the English were now far more propitious than previously. The shattering of the Armada had left Spain's trade routes denuded of their protective galleons. Privateers and investors were eager to exploit this temporary weakness. The Earl was determined to share in the onslaught, the imperative to obtain riches now greater than ever. As Countess Margaret recalled, his 'mind not altered with cross fortunes wrought still for means to go' and with a strength of purpose which overcame her opposition.[1] A Hilliard miniature of 1589 shows the Earl at his happiest and most relaxed. He is depicted wearing either an otherwise unknown suit of armour or, more likely, a composite of his starred and fleur-de-lis suits, suggesting the latter had already been designed in anticipation of his creation as Queen's Champion.

His third enterprise was one of several fleets sent out in 1589, straining Spanish defences all the more and inflicting damage on habitations and shipping. The Earl's fleet was given precedence over the others in one respect. The English counter-attack, the great Portugal expedition under Sir John Norris and Sir Francis Drake, occupied the early summer months, though it proved to be an expensive strategic failure. The Earl's fleet was the only other one allowed to pass south of France until Drake returned, though many other privateers were already at sea.[2] Its destination was the Azores, formerly Portuguese islands which had been conquered by Spain in 1583 after the mainland had been subjugated. Its objective was the interception of the rich Spanish and Portuguese fleets, or *flotas*, which passed through the islands in the summer on their way back to Iberia. Every year five or more huge Portuguese carracks set off from Lisbon with cargoes of European goods to sell in the East Indies on their three-year round voyage. For their return, they were laden with spices and pearls and oriental luxury goods. Two Spanish *flotas* left Seville annually, one in the spring bound for Mexico, the other for Panama, with goods to supply their American colonies, and returned the following year with American produce and, especially, silver and gold bullion. Many other vessels of varying sizes plied their settlements in the West Indies and on the American mainland. The carracks and the Spanish plate fleets linked up at Havana to cross the Atlantic in convoy and put into one of the fortified harbours in the Azores for repairs, revictualling and safe escort by the galleons (absent in 1589) to Iberia. Atlantic storms often scattered the *flotas*, making them all the more vulnerable to attack. The Azores were the trysting ground for the prowling English privateers for whom the capture of just one of these great vessels was the summit of their ambition.

Earl George's 1589 voyage is of unusual interest for several reasons.[3] It was a joint venture with the Queen who invested by lending her warship the *Victory*, 565 tons, a sign of her confidence in him and the reason for the exception. The *Victory*, one of the four oldest royal navy ships which in 1591 were described as its 'cheifest strength', was captained by Christopher Lister who had proved his worth on the 1586–87 and 1588 voyages. The Earl supplied the equipment, ammunition, other supplies and victuals for the *Victory* and its three supporting ships, his newly purchased *Meg* and *Margaret*, both of 60 tons, under Captains William Monson and Edward Careless, and a carvel of 40 tons, perhaps captured on the last voyage, under Captain Pigeon. He assembled a force of about 400 gentlemen, soldiers and sailors to man the ships. Victualling was under way at

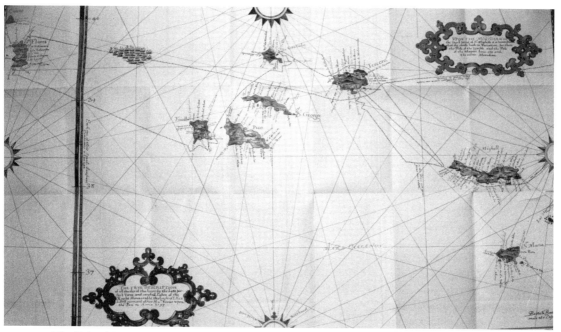

The 'Islands' (the Azores) in 1597. West to east: Corvo, Flores, Fayal, Pico, St George, Graciosa, Terceira, St Michael and St Mary

Southampton as early as 25 March. The Earl's total investment can hardly have been less than £2,000, taken up probably entirely on bills and bonds. The Queen's participation put a greater onus of reponsibility on him, not just for the financial success of the voyage but also the safety of the *Victory*. To enlarge the scope for plunder, he obtained letters of marque from the French Protestant leader Henry of Navarre (from August King Henry IV of France), whom Elizabeth was supporting militarily against his French and Spanish enemies. French ships from St Malo and other ports in league with Spain would be legitimate prizes for Cumberland's privateers.

For John Richards, a Hull sailor aged forty and one of the *Victory*'s crewmen, the hazard of impressment brought him before the Admiralty Court. Early in April he was walking in Tower Street towards London when he was accosted by a pressman who asked him in which ship he was serving. Richards answered none and continued on his way. The fellow pursued him and told him if he wasn't already pressed he would press him to serve in the Queen's ship the *Antelope*. He wouldn't believe Richard's claim that he was already pressed to serve in Cumberland's *Victory*, forced 12d. into his hand and when Richards threw it down swore he would drag him before a constable and he would serve the Queen or be killed. As they argued, the pressman struck Richards with the flat of his sword in its scabbard, cut the seaman's hand as he tried to protect his head and in doing so broke his own sword. Richard Sharp, a wax chandler, hearing the fight intervened with his shop staff. With both threatening to kill each other, Sharp told the pressman he had no commission to kill Richards and this led to a general argument about whether swords could be used when pressing, all the issues ultimately being judged by the Court.

This, of all Cumberland's enterprises, epitomised the confluence of his scholarly, practical and financial concerns. Aware from personal experience of the deficiencies of Tudor navigational methods, he persuaded the mathematician Edward Wright to obtain leave of absence from Gonville and Caius College, Cambridge and sail with him in the *Victory*. At his call now was the academic precision of an excellent scholar. It was the understanding Wright gained of charts and instruments on this voyage which, combined with his theoretical knowledge, enabled him to make two of the great practical advances of the era, his improvement on Mercator's projection and his perfection of the spherical navigation charts of the cosmographer Alomo de Santa Cruz. As Sir Geoffrey Callender has commented, all 'so-called Mercator's charts today are drawn on the projection of Edward Wright, to whom the world owes a profound and unacknowledged debt.' Wright, in dedicating his *Certain Errors in Navigation* to the Earl in 1599, paid tribute to him for diverting him from his theoretical speculation in the university to the 'practicall demonstration of the use thereof in Navigation by experience at sea' and for providing his maintenance during the voyage.[4]

The enterprise is unusual, too, in that three eye-witness accounts were written and subsequently published. Wright appended his own detailed narrative to his work on navigation. Captain (later Sir) William Monson, the vice-admiral, left manuscript descriptions of this and several of the Earl's later voyages which were published in 1902. Of even greater interest, the great Dutch chronicler Jan Huyghen van Linschoten was a passenger in one of the East Indiamen, the *Santa Cruz*, bound for Lisbon. His *Discourse*, based on what he saw and also learnt at Angra in Terceira, complements the English views with details of which they were unaware and a Spanish and Azorean perspective of the actions of the Earl's fleet. He also produced a careful plan of the town, haven and defences of Angra which gives visual confirmation of Wright's description of it as viewed from the *Victory*.

Earl George set sail from Plymouth on 18 June 1589. Three days out he lawfully captured three French leaguer ships as prizes. Part of their Newfoundland fish cargoes he added to his ships' store, the rest he sent to England in two of the vessels. He met several of the English fleet returning from the Portugal expedition and provided them with much-needed victuals. Cruising off the coast of Spain he intercepted a north-bound convoy of eleven Baltic merchantmen, taking from them only contraband pepper and cinnamon from Lisbon worth £450. Crossing to the Azores, on 1 August he reached St Michael, the largest and one of the easternmost islands. At the haven at Ponta Delgada he left alone a London ship, the *Falcon*, under a Scottish pilot, but at night his boats stole three small Spanish vessels freighted with oil and wine from Seville, the castle's gunners only able to fire randomly and harmlessly in the dark. However, he had the misfortune, though he was only to learn it later, of being misled by a captured letter into believing that the carracks had departed from Terceira eight days previously. Because of this, he sailed past the haven at Angra, where they still lay, en route to the most westerly island, Flores, the first landfall available for eastbound shipping from the Americas. Linschoten tells of the fear they had at Angra because they knew of the Earl's presence in the islands and, even more, as they watched his fleet sail by. Quickly the carracks were re-laden and, re-inforced by 400 Spanish soldiers, they hastened towards Lisbon, just escaping again because they dropped anchor in the harbour one day before Drake passed Cascais with his large fleet.

At Flores the Earl peacefully traded some of his captured oil, wine and sugar for water and fresh victuals. There was little, in any case, to plunder, the only town of size, Santa Cruz, having been destroyed by privateers two years before. But he now learnt (again mistakenly) that the carracks were still at Terceira, so he took his fleet eastwards again. Reaching first the haven of Horta in Fayal, his boats braved fire from its fort to draw away a 250 ton ship laden with sugar, ginger and hides from St Juan de Puerto Rico and five other small ships. The four best of these he sent to England as prizes. While off Fayal his fleet was strengthened when ships owned by Raleigh and John Davis joined him. They sailed in consort for Terceira which they sighted on 31 August. There – by happy chance – he rescued eight Englishmen who had just escaped from custody in a small boat, and they informed him, correctly, that the carracks had sailed for Lisbon. Without hope of them now, the Earl set out on 31 August to try to take Horta by surprise. With contrary winds and then calm it took ten days to return to Fayal, by which time the islanders were aware of his presence.

The fort of Santa Cruz at Horta had been constructed in 1567 by the military engineer Gaspar Ferraz as a defence against Moorish pirates. It was (and still is) low-built of stone – Wright called it a platform – but well equipped with fifty-eight iron cannon, twenty-three of which were mounted on carriages and placed on a wooden platform behind barricadoes facing the sea. Until recently it had been manned by Spanish troops but the townsmen, over-burdened with taxes to meet the cost, had persuaded Madrid to let them garrison the fort themselves. The Earl sent Captain Lister to negotiate with them, offering them peaceful occupation of town and fort without plunder or, alternatively, face an assault with all that would follow. Some of the leading townsmen were favourable, wanting above all to escape looting, but the garrison proclaimed their allegiance to King Philip and prepared to fight, an instance of the divided allegiances of the islanders which made the privateers' dealings with them unpredictable.

Consequently, Cumberland landed his soldiers a mile and a half north of Horta and led the attack down the beach and through the town while the *Victory* and its consorts bombarded the fort. The garrison fired their cannon at both the land-force and the fleet but then fled, like groups of horsemen who also resisted, when the Earl's troops closed in. His soldiers scaled the walls of the fort and raised the red cross of St George over it. He took its cannon as prizes and then knocked down its walls. He set guard on the churches, which turned to his advantage later because the 2,000 ducats [£600–£1,000] he raised from the governor in ransom was mostly in church plate. He gave orders that the houses should not be spoiled but, unguarded, they were ransacked by the soldiers and mariners, who helped themselves to chairs, coverlets, hangings and apparel, all the precious goods having been taken by the inhabitants as they dispersed into the countryside. Cumberland entertained four of the leading townsmen on the *Victory*. These may have been the men who, as Linschoten describes, were later arrested and punished by the Spanish authorities for failing to resist the Englishmen, the disunity among the defenders being held to blame for Horta's capture. Re-victualled and with more prizes, but still without sufficient water, the Earl weighed anchor on Tuesday 16 September.

Four days later, Linschoten relates, six of the West Indian *flota* arrived at Horta, temporarily put ashore four million ducats of gold and silver and then, having speedily got their ships ready again, sailed with their rich cargoes less than two days before the Earl's fleet again came to the haven. As Linschoten concluded, it appeared that God would not let the English have the treasure because once seen it would have been theirs. With a gold ducat worth about 9s. and a silver over 3s., this was a fortune missed. The Earl continued to ply the islands, looking for prizes, food and water. He was resisted at first at Graciosa before negotiating purchases of beasts, hens and other victuals, and repulsed at St Marie and St George with casualties, he himself being wounded at the first according to Linschoten. A St Malo ship, the *Flowerdeluce*, laden with Newfoundland fish, putting into Graciosa for repairs with its main mast overboard, was taken and sent to England with a prize crew.

Then on Thursday 9 October, off Terceira, he spied fifteen of the West Indian *flota* taking refuge in the haven at Angra. When the strong winds abated, he took his fleet closer with the intention of entering the haven in boats to drag out some

Angra Haven, Terceira, guarded to the west by Mount Brasil Castle and to the east by San Sebastian Fort. From Linschoten's 1593 map

of the big ships. This proved too dangerous because the haven was protected at its westerly end by the castle on Mount Brasil with its twenty-five pieces of ordnance and at the other the fort with about fourteen great brass pieces. The fleet hovered within sight of Angra for five more days, then seeing the West Indiamen had furled their sails and let down their masts rightly concluded they would not leave. So, the Earl continued his search for water and stray merchantmen at St Marie, where they took another prize, and then at St George, before setting sail for the coast of Spain on 31 October in the hope of obtaining water and more prizes there. In this he was successful. He captured a Brazil ship of 110 tons laden with sugar and brazilwood and then tackled a much larger Brazilman of 3–400 tons. A tough encounter followed in which the Earl was wounded in the side, head and legs and Captain Lister shot in the shoulder. But it had a rich cargo of hides, cochineal, sugar, china dishes and some plate and silver estimated as worth £100,000. The Earl sent it to England with Lister in charge of the prize crew.

Praise of Earl George's third enterprise has been muted because his fleet failed in its main objective of capturing a great prize. Although he scoured the islands throughout August, September and October, the carracks and the West Indian plate fleet eluded him. Michael Oppenheim, following Monson, concludes that the Earl's fleet did not maintain its right station on the *flota* track west of Terceira which allowed them to slip through and take refuge at Angra. His inability to maintain a constant vigil has been attributed to inexperience, poor navigation, Lister's ill-judgement and bad provisioning, with the need constantly to search for fresh water and food. There is some substance to this, yet what is not fully appreciated are the difficulties which Wright explains with scholarly attention to detail: the poor intelligence of the *flotas'* whereabouts; contrary winds and rough weather; the opposition of the inhabitants wherever food and water were sought; and a surprising shortgage of water in islands where rainfall is frequent. At Angra, the defences were far too strong for his force to tackle head on. Privateers, over-manned by normal standards, quickly consumed whatever water, wine and victuals their holds could store. Linschoten, more fatalistic after experiencing on the *Santa Cruz* the unpredictability of oceanic voyaging, restricted his comments to what he termed the Earl's 'hard fortune'. Timing was all-important. Drake, like Cumberland, missed the carracks whereas all but two of the West Indiamen which escaped the Earl at Angra fell victim to other English privateers off the coast of Spain.

As the fleet approached the Channel, the *Victory*'s crew were looking forward to watching the Queen's Day tilting and anticipating Christmas at home when gale-force easterly winds drove them west of Ireland. From then on they were in 'great extremitie' from dire shortage of water, and because of that, could not eat their victuals; the Earl shared their suffering. After making landfall on the northern Irish coast, they sailed down the Irish Sea, reaching Falmouth on 30 December where the Earl learnt of a great misfortune. The rich Brazilman had gone down on the rocks at Hell Cliff in Mount's Bay, Cornwall, in the great storm which had scattered his ships, when almost within sight of shore. Captain Lister and all but six of the prize crew had drowned. However, some of its goods were saved onshore by Sir Francis Godolphin and other gentlemen in the county. The news from his Countess also brought him grief. His elder son and heir, Lord Francis, had died on 8 December in Skipton Castle and been buried in Holy Trinity parish church. The sadness of this loss was lightened somewhat when the Countess gave birth on 30 January 1590 to a daughter, Lady Anne, who had been conceived on 1 May 1589 at Channel Row in Westminster just before her father left to board the *Victory* for the Azores.[5]

Estimates of the value of the prize goods taken on this voyage include £4,500 to £8,000 in spices and £9,000 in sugar, with the carvels, fish, cannon and plate not listed. The Earl wrote to his Countess on 5 January 1590 from Warwick House in London that he did not yet know the nature of the goods he had brought back 'but I look they should discharge all my debts, though I desire not to have it thought so'. His caution was sensible and not just because of the Queen's and his creditors' interest in the financial outcome. The fiscal and legal restraints on adventurers who operated in the public gaze whittled down their often apparently rich hauls. At sea, the crews had rights of pillage and on this voyage, despite the Earl's orders, the soldiers and mariners did loot at Horta and would freely pocket belongings from the captured crews.

Once in port, the residue of the prize goods, after deduction of the Queen's and Lord Admiral's dues and tolls, was normally divided into three parts. One part went to the crews because they sailed for a share of the booty in lieu of wages. The investors took the remaining two-thirds, which in this case meant agreed portions going to Raleigh and Davis as well as the Earl, and possibly the Queen herself for the *Victory*. Henry IV, also, may have been entitled to some reward from the French ships captured by the terms of his letters of marque. Dealing with such matters was time-consuming and often tiresome. Captain Lister and other seamen who lost their lives had to be allotted their share which their relatives received after probate. Godolphin and the other gentlemen needed commending, perhaps rewarding, for their action to protect the Earl's goods from the Brazilman.[6]

Seeing to the crews' claims delayed the Earl's journey to Skipton in January. 'I have so many men lying upon my charge', he told his wife, 'that I can no wise stir till these be despatched.'[7] Sales of the captured goods in the south coast ports to raise the cash for this could be slow, especially where a sudden glut lowered prices. Stephen Taylor (about whom much more will be heard) had rented extensive storage in Southampton in anticipation of captured merchandise and prizes would be unladen also in Portsmouth, Plymouth and Falmouth. The Earl's choice of Southampton as his chief base had a purpose. His admittance as a burgess in June meant he could trade there toll-free.[8] The one certain market was for cannon, though export permits were obligatory. The Earl obtained a warrant from the Queen to transport to Holland and Zealand the 100 tons of iron ordnance he had taken, which the Dutch rebels would now turn on King Philip's forces in the Low Countries. The men who actually shipped the cannon had to enter into a £1,000 bond to the Crown not to send them anywhere else.[9]

Even after all possible had been raised from the plunder, there was for Earl George a long-term doubt about how much he would retain as assured profit. Accusations and litigation against his fleets dogged his career and he was to encounter the first both during and following his 1589 enterprise. While he was in the Azores, various Dutch merchants complained about the *Golden Lion* taking their merchandise and wine from the *Jonas* of Purmerend and the *Hare* of Middleburg the previous year. Commissioners in September referred their claims against the Earl, his receiver Francis Morley and Captain Raymond to the Privy Council. In this case, the complaints were upheld and the Earl had to recompense the Dutch – a belated addition to his losses on the 1588 voyage. The Earl was an obvious target for Lubeck, Hamburg, Dutch and French merchants who suffered from English privateers because he was so well known. Regularly, claims were made against him and his captains which proved groundless, but far too many succeeded for his reputation or his financial good.[10]

Indeed, by a calculated afterthought in altered political circumstances and after the privateering war had effectively ended, French claims were made against the Earl's actions in 1589. Josselyne and Julyan Crosnere of St Malo commenced suit against him on 21 October 1601 for their ship the *Flowerdeluce* of 130 tons burden, which the *Victory* had taken. Julyan claimed he had laden 300,000 fish in Newfoundland for Josselyne to sell in Spain and purchase with the proceeds oil and cochineal for shipment to St Malo. When captured by the Earl, they said, the vessel was valued at £2,680 and the fish £3,420. Thomas Crompton, counsel for the Earl, had no difficulty proving that in 1589 St Malo was in revolt against Henry IV and, if not in league with Spain at that time, certainly was afterwards and the Crosneres' foodstuffs contravened the English government's ban.

The dispute well illustrates the murky features of such litigation which the Court constantly had to clarify. Had the Frenchmen won, the wrangle over values and compensation would have been intense. Crompton's argument for the Earl that the *Flowerdeluce* had spent her main mast, was leaking and her fish were in poor condition, is supported in part by Wright's account of its capture. However, the marked discrepancy between the Frenchmen's claims about the value of the fish and the petty customer's entries in Southampton is less easy to judge.[11] Falsifying was commonplace in the legal and administrative practices of the Elizabethan privateering era, a contributory factor to the ethical climate in which the Earl and his servants operated and to which they contributed. Granted the Earl's status as a burgess who could cast his vote for the town's mayor and member of parliament, the customer would more happily err in his favour than foreigners'. Yet in this instance, both the customer and the Crosneres may have been correct if, as seems likely, Cumberland's ships and then the prize crew helped themselves to the *Flowerdeluce*'s store of fish.

When all had been settled, Earl George could be well-satisfied with his third voyage. Despite its lost opportunities, Cheyney concluded, this 'must be considered one of the most successful, as it was one of the most representative of the voyages of attack upon the commerce and outlying possessions of Spain.'[12] His fourteen prizes and other booty realised for him a profit double that of the cost of equipping his ships. It did not, as he had hoped, repay all his accumulated debts. Yet it enabled him to buy back Brancepeth and Whitworth on 16 February 1590 from Petre, Freke and Crompton, paying them the principal and interest accumulating since June 1588, in all about £3,000.[13] This recovery is interesting not just as indicative of the success of the enterprise – and what else he might have repaid in bills and bonds may only be guessed – but as the first of only two occasions when his privateering profits diminished the total of his recorded debts. They now fell to just below £3,000, as near as he ever came to achieving the original financial objectives of his maritime adventures.

It was only when the Earl was in the depths of his financial misfortunes in November 1600 that he bethought himself to try to recover the goods which had been looted from the wrecked Brazilman. Thomas Penrose of Manacon in Cornwall, a gentleman of high standing whose family claimed rights on the shore in Mount's Bay, had kept others away, asserting he was rescuing the goods for the Earl while he was in fact 'busily and craftily' purloining them for himself. What he had saved from the wreck was said to be valued at £2,000. The miscellaneous items included an anchor worth £15, an iron gun of 13 cwt £7, two calivers £1, an arquebus of crock 12s., a piece of iron from the rudder 10s., a piece of camlet 50s., and a hundred Indian hides £50. But he had also managed to take off the wreck three bags of cochineal weighing 500 lbs each with a sale price of 20s. a pound, a scarf with pearls in it which were worth £200 and – what would most hurt the Earl in retrospect – 10,000 Spanish reals, then rated 2s. apiece in sterling. Penrose had kept the coins under lock and key in his study. Cumberland's lawyers claimed restitution but there was little to hope for at so late a date. The surprise is that he had taken no action in 1589 when eye-witnesses would have been easy to interrogate and other gentry like

Godolphin were at hand to testify. Instead, the act of providence which robbed the Earl filled Penrose's coffers with gold.[14]

One or two instances are mentioned later of the merchants and mariners who suffered personal and financial ruin because of aiding the Earl on his privateering voyages. For William Scot, merchant of Kirkcaldy in Scotland, the Earl's Azorean venture was his sudden downfall. Scot had traded contentedly in the Azores in partnership with several London merchants for four or five years. In July 1589 he was at Angra in St Michael with his ship the *Christopher* (Wright named it the *Falcon*), laden with wine and salt, when the Earl arrived and captured the Portuguese barks. Scot had fired his cannon briefly to deceive the garrison and then came aboard the *Victory* to offer his services to the Earl, provisioning the fleet with wine and fresh water. When the Portuguese governor heard of this, he clapped Scot in prison. His ship's master and crew sailed the *Christopher* back to London where his merchant colleagues arrested it, thinking Scot would not escape. But, after two and a half years, he got free and returned to England only to have the merchants refuse to hand over his ship claiming (possibly speciously) that he owed them money. King James VI interceded with Burghley on his behalf on 30 January 1593 to help him recover the vessel.[15]

Earl George was in London in the spring of 1590 when preparations were going ahead for the official expedition under Hawkins and Frobisher to put into effect the former's plan, which the Queen had been persuaded was feasible, of stationing a fleet in the Azores to cut off the flow of treasure which funded Spain's great military and maritime strength and war effort on the mainland of Europe. The Earl wrote to Countess Margaret on 1 April that, despite great competition for the vice-admiral's position, Lord Admiral Howard had stood by him and kept him in it. The Queen, he said, had welcomed him most kindly and, having much to discuss with him, had requested him to come to her again. But, he added, her 'minions me choose and bound.'[16]

Once again, however, the Earl was passed over for royal command. Instead, he resumed his own private operations, small scale this year because Hawkins's presence in the Azores restricted opportunities. He sent out two ships, the *Robert* of London captained by Nicholas Downton and the *Delight* of Southampton under Thomas Covert. Privateering separately, they took good prizes, the *Robert*'s laden with sugar, ginger and hides worth £2,580. One report described how a flyboat sent out by the Earl seized a Breton vessel in the Narrow Seas, then fought a Flushing man-of-war which tried to rescue it and later struck a Rotterdam man-of-war underwater and forced it to save itself in Calais. Fighting spirit as much as gunpower often gave English privateers the edge in such sallies against the enemy. This one was lauded in a popular publication on 5 August, *A ballad made vppon the late fighte at the Sea betwene 2 ships of Dunkerke, and a small ship of 80 Tunne apperteyninge to the Erle of Cumberland, the 26 of July 1590.*[17]

The Earl adventured £15 in Sir William Sanderson's *Moonlight* 80 tons which, in consort with four ships under John Watts in a West Indian and Virginian voyage, took prizes of hides, wood, sugar and spices valued at £6,800. The return for the Earl would have been £13; of little import because he never actually paid over his investment to Sanderson.[18] On balance, the Earl probably made a useful profit this year. There was no perceptible change in his financial position for better or worse, so that his living expenses at Court, particularly heavy during November, were probably sustained by his receipts from his privateering.

It was in November that Earl George achieved his greatest distinction as a courtier, the supreme honour of his appointment as Queen's Champion in succession to Sir Henry Lee who, now aged forty-seven, was feeling the physical demands of jousting beyond his strength. The ceremonial handing over was in the elaborate Accession Day Pageant in the tiltyard in Whitehall Palace. Lee and the successor he had chosen presented themselves to the Queen at the foot of the stairs under the gallery window, with music playing. The royal guests there included the French ambassador, Viscount Turenne, many ladies and the leading nobility.

A pavilion had been made of white taffeta (a royal colour) with a crowned pillar at the door of a temple constructed like the sacred Temple of the Vestal Virgins where presents were laid for the Queen, handed to her later by three Virgins. Latin verses were extolled. In the procession, Earl George appeared attired in white as the Knight of Pendragon Castle, riding upon his pageant car representing the castle and attended by actors or servants as the magician Merlin and possibly Uther Pendragon, the legendary father of King Arthur. The historical and literary allusions in the presentation to Tudor Arthurianism, to Geoffrey of Monmouth's *Historia Regum Britanniae* and Edmund Spenser's recently published *The Faerie Queene* are too many to re-iterate here, but that the Earl was deeply conscious of the links through his own antecedents and his family's dragon crest is a *sine qua non* of this recurrent theme in his pageantry. The Skipton Castle furnishings are vividly brought to mind.

His speech, delivered by Merlin, for all its light-toned Arthurian allusions and patriotic sentiments, was markedly personal and political, a resumé of his services against the Queen's enemy – his red dragon fighting against the black eagle of Spain – his losses from privateering and, pointedly, the lack of royal recognition of his sacrifices. 'Oftentimes', he declared,

> with great courage, but with noe lookd for successe, hath this Draggon pulled some feathers, but not seized on ye Bodie of this displayed Eagle, wherewith being discontented, but not dismayed, he began to mistrust old sawes, as idle tales, and on ye Seas his crosses have bin many; so on ye Land his love hath bin thwarted; in somuch that his affections were grown as desperate as his fortunes, receiving neither for his Loyalty, regard, nor for his labours profett.

In verse of similar allusory vein he prophesied the Queen's ultimate success, the thought of which pulled up his heart, and implored that with her eyes, 'his two Starres', she would vouchsafe him 'a gracious aspect'. His speech ended on a lighter note with the idea, dismissed as quickly as it came, of inviting her to the real Pendragon Castle, a ruin, and a vow that 'his devotion shalbe equall to his desires, his desires with his Loyalty, and all infinite.'

Laying bare his innermost feelings on so festive and public an occasion is a reminder of the constant open as well as covert pressure on Elizabeth I from her ministers and courtiers for favours and recognition of their services. As Champion, Earl George was to use pageants to proclaim his unwavering loyalty for all to hear but also, unashamedly, his financial plight and its causes. It says much for his close bond with the Queen that in his early years as Champion he could take liberties in his speech to which she did not take offence. In fact, he overpleaded his cause this time. Elizabeth had been generous with her land-grants and the loan of her warships. It has been suggested that the Queen also paid for the magnificent Greenwich armour elaborately incised with Tudor roses, fleurs-de-lis, strapwork, love-knots and Es, all symbolic references to her, the masterpiece of Jacob Halder, which the Earl subsequently wore as Champion (see colour plate). But he may have had the cash in 1590 to commission it himself as well as pay his share of the costs of the pageant.

In the tilting, the Earl, Essex and Lord Burgh challenged all comers, six courses apiece. Lee ran against the Earl and, as Richard Brakinbury reported to Lord Talbot, it was all honourably performed. George Peele, in his *Polyhymnia*, describes the Earl's appearance:

> Worthy Cumberland
> Thrice noble Earl accoutred as became
> So great a warrior and so good a knight
> Encountered first, y-clad in coat of steel
> And plumes and pendants all as white as swan
> And spear in rest right ready to perform
> What 'longed unto the honour of the place.

Afterwards, they approached the Queen together, Lee offered his armour to the Queen at the foot of the pillar, besought her to accept the Earl as her new Champion, armed the Earl, perhaps with his own armour, and set him upon his own horse. Earl George was now installed as Champion, which he was to remain until Elizabeth I's death in March 1603.[19]

To commemorate his elevation, the Earl commissioned a full-length miniature from Nicholas Hilliard in which he poses in his starred armour holding his lance, as if barring the way. The Queen's bejewelled glove is sewn onto his hat and his gauntlet is thrown down in challenge for her defence. On the tree of chivalry nearby hangs his pasteboard *impresa* shield adorned with sun and moon and the words '*Hasta quan[do]*', its meaning interpreted as that he would wield the lance (hast) as Champion until the sun, moon and earth went into eclipse. The linings of his surcoat and hat are patterned with symbols associated with Elizabeth, armillary spheres and branches of olive and caducei representing the globe, peace and ancient heralds' wands. In the background a panorama across the River Thames from the South bank towards Westminster and Whitehall shows Westminster Hall and Abbey, the Tower of London and Baynard's Castle.

Either then or soon after, Hilliard also painted an oval, shoulder-length miniature of Earl George bare-headed and wearing his new Greenwich armour with a blue favour tied to his right arm – blue being another of the Queen's colours. The portrait proclaims his achievements in his other role, that of privateer, a scourge of the Spanish enemy. The emblem of the thunderbolt amidst the stormy sky matches the motto *Fulmen aquasque fero* – 'I bear lightning and water'. The symbolism of the decoration of the Greenwich armour is the link between his dual roles as Queen's Champion on land and defender against Philip II at sea. In both Hilliard portraits he is shown at the peak of his powers and success. Yet there is in the oval portrait a sense of uncertainty and frankness much closer to the reality of his situation, Hilliard getting the essence of the sitter, the special power he claimed for his limning. George's high nobility was beginning to ring hollow with his persisting financial troubles. The Earl of Essex, royal favourite and brazenly self-glorying, was to upstage him by lavish spending on tournaments and pageants. Essex has been deemed Sir Henry Lee's authentic successor, yet Earl George was to prove not just the titular, but also the wiser and safer choice.[20]

In his speech the Earl had made explicit to the Queen his intention of continuing privateering. Early in December, he and Raleigh were considering a joint attack on the carracks over-wintering in the West Indies, but it did not materialise, possibly because of plans for another royal enterprise. There was much pressure on the Earl to be content with the honour he had already won by his maritime exploits. It was in vain. As his daughter explained, although the miseries and misadventures of his last voyage were enough to have deterred him, his desire for profit and honour was such that even the entreaties of many of his friends could not dissuade him from attempting yet another voyage in person. He was, in the gambling sense, on a winning streak and Spain was still vulnerable at sea, though much less so than during 1589 and 1590 because of her rapid building of galleons to replace those lost in the Armada.

In 1591 the Earl was planning his fourth voyage. His intention was to put to sea before Lord Thomas Howard left with the royal fleet in April to await the carracks in the Azores. The Queen agreed to lend him one of her warships as his flagship, the first choice being his Armada command the *Elizabeth Bonaventure*. Instead, the bigger, 600-ton, 38-gun *Garland* requiring a crew of 300 was made available. Its service began on 1 April at a monthly charge of £420, not including the wastage of cordage, canvas, sea-store, shot, powder and other provisions which were supplied at a cost to the navy of £259 from the arsenal in the Tower of London. In addition, the Earl equipped his own ships the *Sampson* 300 tons, captained by John Morton, the *Allagarta* 80 tons (a French vessel he had captured in 1589) under Captain Baylie, and his 12-ton pinnace the *Discovery* commanded by Nicholas Lynche.[21] The total monthly charge may have exceeded £900. His initial outlay was met by borrowing £2,500 on 27 February, with Clifford, Wright and Ferrand as sureties, from the Yorkshire gentleman Henry Lindley, son of Lawrence of Leathley near Otley. The Earl of Essex was the connection here, Lindley being his receiver in Yorkshire and financial adviser.[22]

The Earl's decision to court danger by commanding his fleet called for a series of new legal and financial dispositions in the interests of his family and associates which were quickly drawn up from the end of February. Besides his heir, Lord Robert, he had now to make provision for his daughter, Lady Anne, and the other daughter expected – though how is not revealed – when Countess Margaret,

*Sir Walter Raleigh (1554–1618), attributed
to monogrammist 'H', 1588*

again pregnant, eventually gave birth. In the first new conveyance, drawn up on
28 February, the day following the loan from Lindley, the Earl renewed his 1589
indenture, adding to Grassington and the numerous other Craven manors which
his brother, Wright and Ferrand already occupied, the two valuable capital
messuages or granges of Holme and Elso in Skipton demesnes, to be held for
twenty-one years in reversion after the existing leases. This, his first use of the
lands of the Honour of Skipton, was extended by the second and much more
important transaction completed three days later.

In this, the Earl and Countess Margaret entered into an indenture tripartite
with two groups of his officers; the first comprising Richard Musgrave, Robert
Oglethorpe, Laurence Lister and George Clapham Esq. of Beamsley; the second
his brother, John Taylor, Wright, Ferrand and James Ryther Esq. of Harewood
Castle. The Earl conveyed to them for thirty years Skipton Castle with its huge
demesnes, including Holme and Elso, and his two other Craven houses, Barden
Tower and the Newbiggin. The assignees were to use the profits from these
properties to repay his two major debts when they fell due; the £2,614 5s. 2d.
owed to Lindley and, by 1593, the principal and accumulated interest, totalling
£4,000, on the Nesfield mortgage to the executors of the Earl of Shrewsbury, who
had recently died. Furthermore, should the Earl lose his life, they were to support
Lady Anne with 100 marks a year for her education until she reached the age of
seventeen or married and, likewise, the expected second daughter.[23] One effect of
the increasing funnelling of the estate resources as by this indenture into servicing
the Earl's debts, his privateering expenses and his peripatetic household was the
neglect of his northern residences, which were to need heavy renovation after his
death.

Both conveyances had implications for Countess Margaret's prospects as a widow, especially as she was unable to deflect her husband from his dangerous maritime adventures. A large part of the hitherto sacrosanct 1311 Skipton estate, the core of the Clifford inheritance, had now been assigned. Her common law entitlement of a widow's third certainly would not now sustain her in the style either her father or she would have anticipated in 1577. It is a reflection on Earl George that over thirteen years elapsed before he endowed her with a jointure. Partly this was the result of his wardship and their under-age marriage, but equally perhaps his desire for freedom to manipulate his landed resources as he chose. There is no evidence of overt pressure on George early in 1591 to give the Countess the protection of a jointure, as there was a year later, but it must for long have been an issue within his family and close advisers which did not make for easy relations between him and his wife.

In fact he did take the preliminary step towards a jointure on 6 March with an indenture tripartite between himself and Countess Margaret of the one part, his servants Francis Morley and John Taylor of the second, and the lawyers John Piggott Esq. and Richard Hutton Esq. of the third. This stated that the Earl 'by her Majesties appointment and for her service' was determined to make a voyage upon the seas. To provide a jointure for his lady and for the education and preferment of his children, he covenanted that he and the Countess would, before Christmas 1591, convey all his Yorkshire and Westmorland estates by fine to Morley and Taylor with recovery from them to the use of the Earl and Countess during their lives and remainder to Lord Robert and his heirs; in default to the Earl's heirs male; then to the use of Francis Clifford and his heirs male; with remainder to the Earl's right heirs, that is his daughters.

The first proclamation for the fine was entered in the Common Pleas in June and completed in April 1592, by which time the Earl's circumstances were vastly changed, as will be seen. Apart from the fact that almost all Earl George's remaining estates had now been conveyed, what stands out in the indenture is the emphasis on the male inheritance because, after Lord Robert or any other of the Earl's sons, it was Francis Clifford and his sons who were given precedence over Lady Anne and the expected other daughter. The assumption was that Earl George had an absolute estate which he could dispose of as he wished, a notion inherited from his father's will which his lawyers Piggott and Hutton accepted unquestioningly. This was the Cliffords' first employment of the young Richard Hutton, who was to become their chief legal adviser and a distinguished judge in the Common Pleas under the Stuarts. Obviously the junior man, it was nevertheless an inauspicious beginning, because from the unverified certainty about George's title to the estates sprang the errors which brought about the great inheritance dispute under Earl Francis.[24]

On 22 March it was reported that Cumberland's ships were still detained for lack of money, because 'a great part of the preparation is at his own Charges.' He resolved this the next day by re-mortgaging Brancepeth and Whitworth, this time for £3,000 to James Gardiner Esq., Bartholomew Young gent., both resident in the Middle Temple, and Edmund Standen, one of the clerks of the Petty Bag in the Court of Chancery. On this occasion, the property was to remain continuously in mortgage for over six years. The Earl was admitted a burgess of Portsmouth at an assembly in the Guildhall on 3 May. Permission to sail came later that month; Burghley's memorial dated the 17th included the comment to 'instruct the Earl of Cumberland to employ himself against the Spaniards'. It is not clear whether the Earl heard before he set out or while at sea the sorrowful news of the death of his heir Lord Robert on 24 May, the burial being in the Bedford mausoleum at Chenies.[25] Francis Clifford was now his designated heir.

When the Earl weighed anchor his fleet was his largest and most powerful so far and he was joined by three ships owned by London merchants – John Bird and John Newton's *Golden Noble* 160 tons and *Moonshine* 50 tons, and the *Golden Dragon* 150 tons. He may have acted in consort with Lord Thomas Howard, his own strong force harrying shipping off the Spanish coast while Howard with the main fleet awaited the *flotas* in the Azores. The Earl was successful at first. The *Black Bull*, a great ship of Lubeck carrying masts, and three other well-laden hulks, Hamburg ships, were attacked, overcome and sent home under the escort of Captain Norton and the *Sampson*. He was confident that, if well-handled, they would make him 'a favour for the charge of the voyage.' He took the precaution of writing on 13 July to Julius Caesar, Master of Requests and judge of the Admiralty Court, whose brother Thomas he put in charge of the first hulk (both men old college friends), to use his influence to ward off any legal challenges to his right to the prizes and their cargoes. Two other ships laden with sugar were taken but both were subsequently lost while the cargo of a third, a wine ship, was divided among the privateers. Several Dutch ships carrying spices for the Portuguese were captured. William Monson was put in charge of them and they were sent to England with the *Golden Noble* guarding them.

This voyage, which had begun so propitiously, ended less happily. The *Golden Noble* failed in its duties, unable to prevent six Spanish galleons recapturing the Dutch vessels and with them the unfortunate Monson. The *Garland* was damaged in a storm and became separated from the *Golden Dragon*. It was on its first long expedition and proved 'a slugge of sail'. Thus the Earl, says Purchas, being much weakened, was forced 'without better proffitt or success' to return to England. Before he did so, he learnt that a great Spanish fleet under Admiral Bazan had set sail from Ferrol. He ordered the *Moonshine* under the capable Captain Middleton to shadow them until it was certain Bazan was destined for the Azores and then race ahead to warn Howard of the enemy's approach. Because of this timely action, all but one of Howard's royal navy ships moored at Flores managed to escape, including the *Revenge* in Sir Richard Grenville's epic last fight. With Bazan at sea, there was worry in England for the safety of the Earl and other privateers but he reached England without further trouble in September.[26]

This fourth voyage, though undertaken against the advice of his friends, delayed at its inception by the costs of victualling and dogged by misfortune, was not the complete failure some writers have considered it to have been. The cargoes of the Hamburg ships – copper, lead, corn, ash, deal boards, pipe staves and other war materiel – were declared contraband and they were acknowledged lawful prizes. A Brazilman carrying sugar was also landed. Nevertheless, the Earl was unlikely to have covered costs, let alone made a profit, because the proceeds would have been shared with the owners of the consort ships. Who paid for the victualling and wages of the Queen's ship, as of those sent out under Howard, was long unresolved. The Earl did not repay any of the £5,500 he had borrowed to equip his fleet, so 1591 saw a more than two-fold increase in his recorded debts to £9,500. In the short term, too, he lacked cash. He had to travel to Skipton and wait for Robert Leigh to bring the Michaelmas rents from Westmorland so that he could pay off 'the poor men which wrought in the *Garland* and other places'.[27] Yet the sale of the contraband goods may have produced enough ready money, or at least credit, towards the end of the year for him to victual and prepare his 1592 enterprise.

The Earl's depredations in the summer of 1591 brought strong diplomatic complaints as well as the usual legal challenge over his prizes. From Holland he was accused of taking all the goods of value from the Dutch ships, such as pepper, spices, rings, pearls and silver, of personally torturing the shipmasters to sign that their cargoes belonged to the enemy and, more credibly, seizing one vessel (throwing its cargo of salt overboard) to carry home the prize goods he had taken. He was, by allusion, called a pirate and a thief. Danish claims included one from Albert Albertson, consul of Copenhagen, who had goods worth 2,500 thalers (a silver coin, perhaps worth 3s.) despatched to him by his factor in Flushing seized by the Earl. There was both anger in Lubeck over the capture of the *Black Bull* and relief from merchants who had not sent out their ships along with her. The cause of the *Black Bull* was not heard in the Court of Arches under Sir Julius Caesar until February 1592.[28]

It would, therefore, be doubly gratifying for Earl George to receive confirmation, while still at sea in September, of the Queen's continuing high regard for him. In an intimate, even teasing letter to him, a 'Person of Rogish Condition' whom she was wont to chasten rather than commend, she expressed her great desire to hear of his well-doing and wished him good and perfect health, good success and a safe return. Yet she cautioned him not to let her partiality towards him reach the ears of the Earl of Essex lest he grow bold thereafter in favouring his supporters, real rogues 'whom we wold not have him suffer to pass uncorrected for divers their Misdemeanours.' The Queen took delight in giving nicknames and hereafter the Earl was known as her 'roge'.

Kindly thoughts and seductive words were the least she owed him for spending his fortune in her service, and news of how he had saved Howard's fleet may not then have reached Court. But the letter is proof she had taken to heart the sentiments of Merlin's speech at the great ceremony in the previous November. Even so, Tudor goodwill was fickle and, if Queen Elizabeth was not as unpredictable and malevolent in her moods as her dread father, events could quickly sour her relations with the leading courtiers and were to do so for Earl George within a year. The causes and the consequences of that and the implications of his heir's death were to dominate his affairs during 1592 and well beyond. In the November pageants he again appeared as the Knight of Pendragon and made public vows to return. What speeches and themes and special pleading diverted the Queen this time are not know, no details having survived of that year's Accession Day celebrations.[29]

CHAPTER 6

The Elusion of Riches: the Capture of the *Madre de Dios*, 1592

If any one year was the climacteric of Earl George's career, then it was 1592. Both his private and public actions and events beyond his control gave a severe wrench to his privateering fortunes, his relations with Queen Elizabeth, and the future course of his family and patrimonial affairs. It was to be the most fateful year, in terms of missed opportunities, in his entire life, though how that happened is explicable in terms of the pressures on him as a leading courtier. He was absorbed during the early months of 1592 in two interlinked matters: amending the jointure provisions for Countess Margaret and preparing another fleet. New dispositions had to be made because of the death of Lord Robert and he would wish now to free his Yorkshire properties fully for use as collateral. Consequently, on 28 February he revoked the existing deed and then assured to Countess Margaret the Westmorland castles and lordships as her jointure estate, the same officers and lawyers acting for them as in 1591.[1]

However, there was now insistent pressure for Countess Margaret to be given greater security for her jointure than a fine and recovery. According to Lady Anne Clifford, her mother's friends, appreciating that her two sons were both dead, her husband destroying his estate and Francis likely to succeed him in the earldom, thought it better for her to have a proper jointure rather than the uncertainty of her thirds. Lady Anne is correct about the reasons, awry about the issue which, in early 1592, was to persuade the Earl to provide his Countess with the ultimate safeguard for her jointure, an act of parliament. Their arguments prevailed. On the same day as the Earl signed the new deed, he petitioned the Queen for the enactment of a jointure, its terms as stated in the deed, so as to avoid 'all doubtes and ambiguytes and questions that maie here affter arise', and she concurred.[2]

An immediate consequence was the return of warmth in the Countess's relations with her husband. As he remarked 'I well perceive by thy kind lines our once most happy love will again be recovered, which only in this life above all I desire.'[3] In the longer term, after the private bill had been approved by Lords and Commons and given royal assent the following year, the Westmorland estates, alone of the Clifford inheritance, were fully protected from the Earl's creditors and, even more important, his own later depredations. When, on his death in 1605, the Countess entered them, they had been virtually untouched since he took them over in 1581.

The enterprise Earl George planned in 1592 was the most ambitious since 1586 and he intended to take command himself. His objective was to sail to the West Indies, most likely in collaboration with Sir Walter Raleigh's powerful force of fourteen ships to which the Queen and London merchant privateers contributed. They probably had a joint design on Havana, where the Spanish plate ships put in for shelter before they ran the gauntlet of the eastward crossing of the Atlantic. Letters patent were granted on 21 February empowering the Earl 'to annoy the King of Spain and his subjects and to burn kill and slay as just and needful cause shall require.' He decided this time against borrowing royal warships because he had been hampered in their use by the Queen's prohibition against laying them alongside to board, which imperilled their safety. Instead, he hired the *Tiger* 600 tons from St Malo at a cost of £300 a month, a rather quixotic choice because he had constantly preyed on merchantmen from the port. He equipped this large vessel and his own *Sampson* and *Discovery*. His co-investors, John Bird and John Newton, as in 1591 provided the *Golden Noble* and the *Moonshine*, and the fifth ship was the *Sunshine* 50 tons.

The Earl left Weymouth with this fleet in March and put into Plymouth harbour. He had sent ahead from Weymouth a scouting party consisting of the *Moonshine* under Captain John Middleton and the *Sunshine* captained by Robert Frost. The latter foundered on leaving harbour but off the coast of Spain the *Moonshine* captured a Spanish vessel of 30 tons which Frost took over. Together they crossed the Atlantic, reaching Trinidad in June. More will be said of their exploits later. The Earl's plan to follow with his main force was frustrated by continuous bad weather and contrary winds which prevented his ships from leaving Plymouth. He was stuck there when the saddest moment of the year happened, the death of his sister Lady Frances at Wharton Hall on 16 April, and he was unable to attend her funeral in Kirkby Stephen. After three months of inactivity, which meant he had missed the carracks leaving Lisbon for the East Indies and was too late to cross the Atlantic, he lost hope of commanding in person and gave instructions to Captain Norton to make for the Azores as soon as conditions became favourable. Five Portuguese carracks were expected to return from the West Indies that summer and Norton's task was to waylay them. Raleigh's fleet likewise was held up, so that when it set sail he too was forced to alter its strategic objectives.[4]

Quitting his fleet was a decision Earl George was long to rue. Yet he could not justify dallying with them as they languished at anchor, neglecting attendance at Court, especially as, at the Queen's instigation, he was twice honoured that summer when he was at the peak of royal favour. He had the unusual distinction of being named by the Queen Knight of the Garter on St George's Day while absent at Plymouth, his creation and installation being on 25 June. He was the third and last of his family to be awarded the garter. George was in the Queen's splendid retinue on her six-day visit to Oxford in late September. His election as honorary MA by Oxford University on 27 September could hardly have been more apposite, his studies at Christ Church being at the heart of his oceanic interests. As it happened, his ships had been instrumental in the capture of a great carrack, the *Madre de Dios*, only a few weeks earlier, so that both Queen and Earl would have had cause to commend the academic inspiration for his maritime endeavours.[5]

The Earl was also the recipient of a literary eulogy, worthy of comment here because of its sentiments and the light it incidentally throws on shipboard life on his fleets. His education at Cambridge under Archbishop Whitgift was recalled in glowing terms by Simon Haward, one of his chaplains on the previous voyage, who dedicated jointly to them his religious and patriotic verses in Latin, *The Solace for the Souldier and Saylour*. Haward wrote that 'certaine godly and valiant Capitaines and Shipmasters' with whom he had sailed the Spanish seas under the Earl had sought his aid 'that they might with better confidence call upon God'. This service he had done in both public sermons and private conference, a testimony to the attention to religious observance customary on the Earl's ships. Haward's discourse praised the valiant attempts of the noblemen and gentlemen of England 'which incurre so many daungers on the sea to cut off or abridge the proud and haughtie Power of Spayne.' The Earl might have recalled Haward's concluding apostrophe to him with a sardonic smile in the years to come:

Earl George's garter plate, St George's Chapel, Windsor Castle

> Therefore under favourable auspices continue to prosper,
> O noble hero. Prosper, unconquered Earl! with favourable
> breezes prosper . . . [6]

On Saturday 6 May, Francis Seall writes, the Earl's fleet managed at the third attempt to leave Plymouth harbour.[7] Its seven ships now comprised the *Tiger* as admiral under Norton, the *Sampson* vice-admiral captained by Abraham Cocke, the *Golden Noble* rear-admiral under George Cave, the *Discovery* and three new additions – the *Phoenix* 70 tons of Dartmouth, a bark of Barnstaple, and the *Grace of Dover* 50 tons which had to stay behind but re-joined later at Terceira. Their total tonnage was reckoned at 1,235 and they had a complement of nearly 500 'brave captains, gentlemen, soldiers and mariners'. Norton reached Finisterre and, according to one account, engaged two Spanish galleons, but could not hold them. In the action the *Golden Noble* was badly shot about, but recovered, captured a 900 ton argosy bound for Lisbon with a cargo of wine and rice and returned to port with its big prize.

Raleigh had also weighed anchor on 6 May, though he was compelled to quit his command and return to Court on the Queen's orders brought in the Lord Admiral's pinnace by Sir Martin Frobisher. He split his fleet, giving Frobisher in the *Garland* charge of the larger force to cruise off Cape St Vincent awaiting the carracks there while Sir John Burroughs in the *Roebuck* 300 tons led the warship *Foresight* 230 tons under Captain Crosse and a 60-ton bark of Bristol under Captain Hopkins to the Azores with the same purpose. Frobisher captured and sent home a Biscayan, the *Santa Clara*, of 600 tons off the Spanish coast, her cargo worth £6–7,000. From a flyboat near Lisbon, Burroughs learnt that King Philip, aware of Raleigh's intended thrust at the West Indies, had ordered Admiral Bazan with a big armada to escort the carracks from the Azores. Indeed, Bazan was already at sea, all but trapped Burroughs's ships and then, having assessed their size, made the mistake of concluding that the carracks could easily deal with them. This decision, as fateful for him as Cumberland's earlier, left the carracks unprotected at a time when, unbeknown to him, Norton as well as Burroughs was converging on them. He was to be dismissed for failing in his duties.

Passing St Michael, Burroughs took a number of carvels – small, square-rigged merchantmen mostly of 50–60 tons – without getting any intelligence about the carracks. He arrived at Flores on Thursday 21 June, negotiated the purchase of water and victuals at Santa Cruz and waited for Crosse and Hopkins to catch up. From the islanders he learnt that no West Indiamen were expected but that one carrack had already sailed past three days earlier on its way to Lisbon and the other four were following behind. Flores was to be their only port of call and they were to be met there by a Spanish fleet to escort them to Lisbon; Bazan's, which did not come. That same day, near Flores, the *Sampson* espied a vessel which Norton learnt from the islanders was the carrack the *Santa Cruz*. He gave chase and was joined by Burroughs's fleet. After a great storm scattered them, the carrack's crew beached the great vessel to avoid capture, unloaded most of its cargo and then set fire to it, taking up defensive positions in trenches to protect the precious goods. The English captains agreed to send their boats ashore fully manned to get the carrack's goods, which the islanders were carrying to safety. A hard march over craggy terrain brought them to the place. Carpets, quilts, raw silk, taffetas and calicoes were the chief commodities which Burroughs took into custody for the Queen and the other adventurers of his fleet. Much pillage was got by men who dived into the sea to recover jettisoned goods.

This success was happy enough but a richer prize, the 1,600 ton *Madre de Dios*, one of the greatest of the carracks, was known to be in the vicinity. Burroughs, Norton and the other commanders met in council on Flores, devised a plan to capture the carrack and agreed a consortship for the proper division of the spoils. The two barks had now departed (perhaps with the plunder from the *Santa Cruz*) but three other ships besides the *Grace of Dover* now increased the combined force to ten in number, Sir John Hawkins's *Dainty* 200 tons under Thomas Thompson, the *Golden Dragon* 150 tons captained by Christopher Newport, and the *Prudence* 70 tons under Hugh Merrick, both the latter newly arrived from the West Indies. They cast their net wide on 3 August at about four o'clock in the morning, spreading out some fifteen leagues west of Flores, a league and a half apart from north to south. The *Dainty*, being windmost, was the first to catch sight of the *Madre de Dios*, closed on her and opened the attack at about eleven in the morning, the *Golden Dragon* at two o'clock and the *Roebuck* at four o'clock, following up with their great ordnance and musket fire.

The *Dainty*, according to Thompson, boarded the carrack three times before it was knocked out of the fray when its main mast was hit and it had to stand off. With the *Madre de Dios* 'disdainfully' maintaining its steady course, its high decks, masts and rigging towering above the English ships and fending them off with its 32 cannon, Burroughs and Crosse agreed, at about eight o'clock in the evening, that if they were to capture the carrack they would have to close on her. First, the *Roebuck* lay aboard the carrack's windward side, then Crosse brought up the *Foresight* and in the confusion of the battle laid alongside the *Roebuck* instead of the carrack. The *Roebuck*, buffetted between them and holed under water by a cannon perrier, managed to disentangle itself but was now, like the *Dainty*, effectively out of the action. To prevent the carrack escaping, Crosse was now forced to take the additional risk with a royal ship of laying the *Foresight* directly aboard the carrack's bowsprit and lashing her fast, his soldiers leaping to attack the Portuguese on deck and rigging in dangerous and bloody hand-to-hand fighting.

Last to reach the battle were Earl George's two large ships and their weight and numbers made the capture secure. The *Sampson* discharged four or five of its cannon and a volley of small shot at the carrack and then laid alongside its starboard quarter, by the *Foresight*'s stern. Her men eagerly joined in the already fierce struggle with the carrack's defenders. Finally, from the larboard three companies of the *Tiger*'s soldiers, in Francis Seall's words, 'with a great noise and shout (of at the least nine score men), who crying "God and Saint George for England, a Cumberland, a Cumberland," advanced themselves on her shrouds and nettings, fighting pellmell with sword and pike'. The Portuguese, hemmed in from all quarters, suffering heavy casualties and frightenedly crying 'A quo deabala est a Cumberland', yielded between one and two o'clock in the morning. The carnage among the carrack's crew had been such that 'no man could almost steppe but upon a dead carkase or a bloody floore but specially about the helme where very many of them fell suddenly from stirring to dying.' Burroughs sent his own surgeons to give aid to the stricken Portuguese.

In the elation of victory and survival after the brutal conflict, the English soldiers and mariners surged into a scramble for spoils from the fabulous wealth of the *Madre de Dios*'s cargo and the private belongings of the Portuguese passengers and crew. All joined in. Officers and mariners alike rifled pearls, diamonds, rubies and sapphires in bags, chains and encrusted settings of gold and silver and any other precious goods they could lay their hands on and fled to shore in whatever ship they could. Captain Crosse got away with £10,000 worth in the *Foresight*. Sir John Burroughs, coming aboard the day after, claimed the carrack and its contents in the Queen's name though the Earl's men at first challenged his right. Burroughs and his few officers had acted too slowly to prevent the worst pilfering. They managed to retrieve a pitifully small amount of the jewels from some of the sailors they caught, but were not above helping themselves also. It was the *Tiger* and *Sampson* which escorted the *Madre de Dios* with its prize crew to Dartmouth, where they arrived on 7 September. In common parlance, it was the Earl who was held to have taken the carrack and his men were said to have had 'the cheefest pillage'.[8]

News of the great capture was swiftly brought to port by the fast-sailing *Discovery* which stole away from the fleet, to Burrough's chagrin. Word spread rapidly so that when the other ships reached the South coast harbours the mariners, all too eager to rid themselves of their booty, were met onshore by local and London jewellers and traders who bought for ridiculously cheap prices many of the precious stones and other pickings. Behind them came Sir Robert Cecil and other royal officials, spurred on by the Queen's anger at the plundering of the carrack. Among the numerous mariners they and the customs officers held and interrogated was Alunso Gomes, a Portuguese employed by Earl George possibly as a pilot in one of his ships. He confessed to Cecil and Sir Francis Drake that he had taken 320 sparks of diamonds, a collar of threefold roll of pearl with six tags of crystal garnished with gold, a small string of pemell with a pelican of gold, a small round pearl garnished with gold, also two chains of fold pearl with buttons of gold and and two small jewels hanging on the ends thereof. He had three silver hafts for knives and a silver fork and, with Antonio Martyne, had made £42 10s. by selling calico and other pillage in Plymouth. He deposed that the master of the *Sampson* had 150 diamonds, the master's mate, one Sousa, a packet of diamonds as big as his fist, and Corporal Edward Tonks of the *Tiger* a packet of rubies. Yet most of the carrack's precious contents disappeared without trace, dispersed through England and the Continent, many of the best pieces fetching good prices from English, French and Dutch dealers in London.

The size of the *Madre de Dios* caused amazement. Robert Adam, who surveyed it, measured its length from beakhead to stern at 165 ft and its widest breadth (at the second close deck) at 46 ft 10 in. The keel was 100 ft, the main mast 121 ft and its greatest circumference 10 ft 7 in, the main yard 106 ft. It had seven storeys (against the four of English galleons); a main orlop, three close decks, a spar deck of two floors, and a forecastle. Even more remarkable was its cargo which for the first time displayed for the English made them wonder at and envy the multifarious produce of the Indies and the wealth brought yearly and in abundance to the Iberian powers. The spices were pepper, cloves, maces, nutmegs, cinnamon and green ginger; drugs such as benjamin, frankincense and camphor; the cloths silks, sleeve silks, damasks, taffetas, sarsenets, counterfeit cloth of gold, and seven types of calico. There were manufactures – canopies, coarse diaper-towels, quilts and carpets. The many other wares included elephants' teeth, porcelain vessels, coconuts, hides, ebony wood and bedsteads. With the jewels purloined, it was this bulky cargo which was left, most of all pepper, which Thomas Middleton, treasurer of the commission appointed to handle the carrack and its goods, estimated as worth £150,000. Merchants purchased carpets and other moveables at Dartmouth and Plymouth. The *Sampson* was one of the ten ships hired to transport the 7,101 quintals [cwts] of pepper in 3,652 bags to London for appraisal at Leaden Hall and eventual disposal. The Earl would get some income from the freighting paid at 20s. per ton.

Earl George's absence while his fleet fought for this, the greatest prize of the whole privateering war, was to prove doubly unfortunate. By the terms of his patent, he alone was entitled to a share of the prizes taken and only so if he commanded in person. He had made no provision in the commission for Captain Norton or any other substitute. If he had commanded, if his strict but just control, incisive action and, most of all, his high standing had prevented the mariners to some degree from relieving the *Madre de Dios* of its precious contents and reducing its original value of £500,000 by over two-thirds, then his would have been a staggering reward. Instead, with no paramount claim at all to what remained, he had to compete for a share and most of all against the Queen. The bickering and legal contention were not to his liking. 'Long before this', he told Countess Margaret on 15 September, he would have written to her,

> if I had not been so troubled with this exceedingly great business, as twenty times I have wished the ship had never been taken, the spoil in her hath been unreasonable, yet there is so much left as I have will make me a free man.

But he could not stand aside and expect satisfaction when constant soliciting of his claims alone would give him a just return for his endeavours. Not only him. The men who served in his ships, who went for shares not wages, 'were wonderfully discontented fearing that the Earl losing all, they should have nothing.'[9] They, after all, had hazarded their lives in the dangerous mêlée aboard the carrack and had taken it forcibly 'with the dint of sword and push of pike'. Twenty-two of them riposted at accusations of their looting by formally complaining on 29 September of the pillage liberally taken by Sir John Burroughs and his officers and men.[10] The Earl's concern was praised by Francis Seall who wished every man 'would be as ready to reward the painful soldier and seafaring man as that noble Earl of Cumberland.'[11] His persistence warranted a rebuke

from Burghley, to which the Earl replied tersely, truthfully and without hyperbole
on 12 December,

> My Lord, I protest, my heart is free from the poison of ambitious humours,
> only the desire to relieve my friends and servants in danger of bonds for me, my
> credit from dying and my house from falling, kept but in the estate it was left
> me which God knows in this time will hardly maintain an Earl and for more (if
> God send it) I will ever be ready to spend it and my life (in any cause you shall
> wish or give allowance to) for the gain of Her Majesty and my country.[12]

Neither the Queen nor Burghley was eager to relinquish such a windfall as the
carrack's £141,000 actual value provided. She wanted all, though by the careful
reckoning of tonnage of the ships and investments by the privateers she was
entitled at most to £20,000, compared with Earl George's £66,000, the remainder
due to Raleigh, his co-investors the London merchants, and Hawkins for their
proportions. By the established rules of consortship, Earl George could have
expected even more than that, half the value. The contention between the Earl
and the Queen was seen as his claim by common law against hers by the royal
prerogative. Sir John Fortescue, Chancellor of the Exchequer, remonstrated with
her that if the Earl and the other adventurers were not 'princely considered of'
they would never be induced to further enterprises. It was this argument which
eventually prevailed on the Queen. She kept £80,000 for her treasury and
grudgingly gave up the remainder. This was divided into six equal parts, three
assigned to Earl George so that he received £36,000, two to Raleigh, £24,000, and
the other to the London merchants, £12,000.[13]

Nevertheless, what the Earl received was by the Queen's bounty, not his by
right. Her attitude had been that his ships did no more than was the duty of any
of her subjects, for which they were to be recompensed at her pleasure. Moreover,
the size of the sum granted is misleading. Included in it was the pillage known to
have been taken by his mariners, which he had to recover by litigation. He
certainly pursued one of the main culprits, Abraham Cocke, captain of the
Sampson. Cocke had a long record of maritime service, most recently with several
of the Earl's fleets following his capture, rather than rescue, from a Portuguese
vessel off Brazil by Captain Widdrington on the 1586–87 voyage.

The Earl had hired his services in 1592 for £100, paying him £30 cash in hand
while John Bird had given him a bond for the other £70, which sheds some light
on the methods of financing his fleet. After the carrack's capture, Cocke had
purloined 'many' of its goods, quit the *Sampson* and fled to the *Golden Dragon*,
which was partly owned by his father-in-law, William Bygate, where he stayed for
two months. Alunso Gomes, as mentioned above, asserted that Cocke had taken
150 diamonds. Another deponent, John Hampton, chief pilot of Raleigh's fleet
who had been wounded in the fighting, revealed more of Cocke's role in the
action. He described how the captain had bravely led the *Sampson*'s men onto the
carrack and, when the Portuguese surrendered, entered the pilot's cabin, rifled it
and also part of the pilot's chest. Sir John Hawkins had searched Cocke's house
but found nothing there. The Earl and his fellow plaintiff, John Bird, initiated

A detail from the portrait of Queen Elizabeth I, celebrating the defeat of the Armada (shown in the insets), by or after George Gower, c. 1588

proceedings in Chancery against both Cocke and Bygate and their bill was proved on 25 January 1593. Cocke was obliged not only to return the stolen goods but the £30 fee on the grounds of dereliction of duty in that he had failed to perform the service he had been hired to do.[14]

Although, because of the examinations and meticulous inquisitiveness of the royal officials into all aspects of the *Madre de Dios* affair, more is known about Earl George's 1592 fleet than any apart from his great Puerto Rican expedition, much remains unanswered. His costs, receipts and profits are still imponderable. The total investment by him and his partners in the ships which fought the carrack was estimated at £19,000. In Kenneth Andrews's opinion, such huge costs in relation to the tonnage are proof that the Earl, like so many of his kind, was 'ruthlessly cheated' by the provisioners.[15] Yet it is not clear whether this figure was based on the accounts of the fleet's nominated treasurer whose records, like all the Earl's, have not survived.

There is the question, too, of the changing composition of his fleet and the added claims of the merchants and other promoters of his consort vessels, which were subsumed in his claim. Moreover, the Earl and his servants were now much cannier in all aspects of privateering; inflation of figures, especially in the torridly competitive lobbying for shares of the £141,000 at the Queen's disposal, cannot be ruled out. One of the chief reservations about accepting so large an apparent outlay by the Earl and his fellow investors is that he did not in 1592 enter into any recorded loans. All his investment must have been raised on bills, bonds and conceivably statutes staple and merchant, no mention of which survives in his family papers.

What profit Earl George actually made from the capture of the *Madre de Dios* is impossible to say. On paper, he and his partners should have shared £17,000. The lawsuit against Cocke indicates the slowness of the process of recovering the value of the plundered goods. Nor is it clear how much they were required or failed to recover. There was a long delay before the Earl and Raleigh received the portions of the carrack's goods due to them. These were held back on 20 February 1593 on the Queen's instructions because they were thought to be overweight and the surplus could be used to compensate other investors.[16] When the Earl was able to sell his share of the goods and for what price – the glut in the market having forced down the value of pepper and other spices – is not known. The only verified fact is that he was able for the second and last time in his privateering career to lessen his recorded debts. These fell by £4,000 when he redeemed the Nesfield manors from Shrewsbury's successors, Edward Talbot and his wife Jane, in April 1593. Moreover, he had money to spare and curiously, since his own debts were still heavy enough, turned creditor, lending his friend the Earl of Essex £1,207 without demanding interest.[17]

For one of the young mariners who fought and survived the bloody encounters the return home was far from welcoming. Michael Mansell was an apprentice to Edmund Stephens, a waterman of the parish of All Hallows, Barking. He had been ordered by Stephens to go to sea in a merchantman. Instead, he had skipped away to sail 'with the Lord of Cumberland, and being come home he refused to serve and to give his pay to his sayd mistress.' On 28 January 1593 Mansell and a surety were bound over in the sum of £20 at Middlesex Sessions for his appearance at the next sessions to answer the Stephens's complaint of breaking his apprenticeship terms.[18] Mansell would not have been alone; the thrills of battle and pearls and ducats in his pouch would have unsettled many a young man tied to the humdrum coasting trade.

No episode in the life and death struggle of Elizabethan England against Imperial Spain, perhaps no event in the whole of the Queen's reign, so transparently reveals her people and the Tudor system at their best and worst as does the capture of the *Madre de Dios*. The fight for the great carrack and its aftermath brought out qualities of high courage, daring and self-sacrifice; conversely, greed, deceit and self-interest. The death, maiming, fear and pain were mollified to a degree by compassion and care for the defeated and for those in suffering. Human virtues and failings aplenty, with the Queen herself in one of her harsher moods interpreting the better good of her nation as lying in replenishing the treasury's coffers rather than her adventurous subjects' pockets. Fortescue's was the balanced, pragmatic view, but if the Queen acquiesced she did not concede the principle. Her government's yearly income was only £250,000.

The long-term impact of the capture of the *Madre de Dios* and its influence on England's own future quest for eastern trade was emphasised by Richard Hakluyt. 'I cannot but enter into the consideration and acknowledgement of Gods great favor towards our nation', he wrote, ' who by putting this purchase into our hands hath manifestly discovered those secret trades and Indian riches, which hitherto lay strangely hidden, and cunningly concealed from us'. Before, only a few Englishmen had glimpsed and even then imperfectly what was now plain for all to see. Hakluyt advocated the English opening up lawful traffic to obtain those East Indian treasures for themselves; not, however, just for material gain but 'to better our meanes to advance true religion and his holy service.'[19] First, however, the sea-war had to run its course. Then, when the East India Company was founded in 1600 to wrest a part of that trade in Oriental wealth for the English, Earl George was to be closely involved.

From the summer of 1592 there had been the familiar crop of complaints about the Earl's ships pillaging friendly or neutral merchantmen and restitution against him was pursued as usual through the Privy Council and the courts. Noel de Caron, the United Provinces' agent in England sought cash recompense on 14 August for £1,200 worth of goods taken the previous year by two ships of Lord Thomas Howard and the Earl from the *Hawk* of Amsterdam. Howard had dealt honourably with the deprived merchants. The Earl's comments were not yet known. He was still to answer for £400 taken by Captain Batten from an Amsterdam ship sailing from Barbary. The story of how this and other cases were dealt with is a salutary one for assessing both the attitudes and behaviour engendered by the privateering war and the impotence of royal officers to enforce decisions. The Privy Council and commissioners had debated the matter for three months before the Councillors ordered the ship's release. But the commissioners were resisted and the ship and its goods forcibly carried away so that the merchants had no choice but to seek compensation.

The Doge of Venice wrote in person to the Queen on 23 September requesting payment to his subjects of the value of the galleon *Tizzone*, which one of the Earl's warships had taken off Cascais on their way to the Azores. Its wine cargo had been transferred to the Earl's fleet and the galleon unfortunately wrecked while being brought to England by a prize crew. Caron's next list of complaints, on 4 February 1593, included the filching of nine tapestry hangings from a ship of Holland by one of the Earl's vessels on the 1592 voyage. On being landed, they were seized for the Queen by an informer, Michael Clattin, but the Earl's men took them away, again obstructing royal administration, albeit one of its most unpopular facets.[20]

Earl George would have taken particular pleasure in 1592 in Thomas Hood's dedication of his revised edition, with corrections, of the Gravesend gunner William Bourne's *A Regiment for the Sea . . .*, a practical guide to all aspects of marine affairs. Hood was a mathematician and contemporary of the Earl at Trinity College where he was now a Fellow. He had devoted himself to charts and instrument making and teaching the art of navigation. His dedication is revealing. What inspired his choice was the inclination of the Earl's mind to studies of that kind and to marine causes in general; 'the honorable favour', including the employment Hood had always found at his hands; and most interestingly, his first reason, 'the generall consent of many, who wish you well & iudge you a fitte patrone for suche a worke'. Whatever his origins, Cumberland was no landlubber. He earned respect and goodwill the hard way, with professional competence and by sharing with his mariners the adversities as well as the elations of shipboard life. He also shared, when need be, the hard physical work, such as hauling at the helm. That year Hood dedicated his *The Marriners guide* on the use of the sea-card, a form of chart, to Sir John Burroughs.[21]

What, meanwhile, of the *Moonshine* and its equally tiny consort? While the great drama of the *Madre de Dios* was being played out, Earl George's two scouts were in a world apart. They had crossed the Atlantic and reached Trinidad in June, being numbered among the twenty or so English privateers infesting the Spanish Caribbean during the early summer. Middleton and Frost attacked a Spanish frigate near Cartagena and, though beaten off, forced it aground. A fleet of four vessels sent out by Lord Thomas Howard under Benjamin Wood joined them on 22 June and together they looted the frigate. The next day, Frost's ship foundered and he was captured with thirteen of his men when they landed to survey the frigate with the idea of taking it over. Middleton in the *Moonshine* parted company with Wood and continued on his own course. He reached the South coast of Haiti in late June, captured a carvel off Santo Domingo and sent it home. He returned to the Spanish Main in August. He was still in the West Indies on 18 December 1592 and probably over-wintered there to conclude an intrepid and, tonnage for tonnage, highly successful privateering voyage. [22]

5 *Earl George as Queen's Champion, by Nicholas Hilliard, c. 1590*

6 *Margaret Russell, Countess of Cumberland, Constant in the Midst of Inconstancey', by Laurence Hilliard,* c. *1603–5*

CHAPTER 7

The Undaunted Earl: 1593–94

The destruction of two great carracks in 1592 and the anguish that caused to King Philip made no impression on the military priorities of the Queen and Privy Council. The land war against Spain on French soil took precedence and was to continue for two more years, even after Henry IV converted to Roman Catholicism to gain his kingdom in July 1593. It was a costly campaign and absorbed resources which might otherwise have gone into building up England's naval power.[1] Councillors would not have failed to grasp that the capture of the *Madre de Dios* had proved that a variant of Hawkins's strategy of 1590 could work, even if by default. Frobisher's fleet had distracted Bazan sufficiently to give Burroughs and Norton a free hand. What had altered perspectives and perhaps worried Bazan was the fire-power and aggressive spirit of the *Revenge* which the previous year had fought fifteen of his ships, sank four and caused him to lose two senior commanders and hundreds of men. However, that ratio of success, as Raleigh explained in his description of the fight, the royal navy could not sustain if England's defences were to remain secure. Granted the primacy of the land-war, the way forward was not a cohesive strategy combining royal and private finances and ships, but reliance as before on Cumberland, Raleigh and other privateers challenging the enemy at sea. Earl George did not need subtle persuasion from the Queen, Burghley and the Lord Admiral to spur him on, but there were to be ample occasions of it in the coming years.

The Earl spent the early months of 1593 at Court resolving the unfinished matters concerning the last voyage and sitting on two commissions by royal appointment. In one, he was involved with other noblemen dealing with the affairs of William Vaux, 3rd Lord Vaux of Harrowden, a Roman Catholic fined for recusancy who had spent the bulk of his fortune on his religious cause. In the other, of wide social import, he was joined with Howard, Drake, Raleigh and other commanders to enquire into the dire condition of the many poor soldiers and seamen crippled in the wars, the inevitable and sad outcome of the conflict with Spain. Their recommendations were embodied in statutes which placed the onus of supporting the maimed soldiers and mariners on the shires, cities and boroughs, the commissioners of the peace and city fathers being empowered to levy a special rate for that purpose.[2]

The companion issue of what to do with discharged healthy but footloose men was beyond the compass and competance of early modern and, indeed, much later governments. Francis Seall's complaint in 1592 was to echo down the ages; 'martial men are not accounted of in England longer than present occasion serves to employ them, and for that time (neither) but even scarcely recompensed.' But fear of maiming or of discharge into begging did not put off many a young man lured to the sea from the inland shires as well as the maritime. One of those eager to serve under Earl George in 1593 was a Nottinghamshire lad called Sydnam. His mother Margaret wrote from Worksop on 10 February asking the Earl of Shrewsbury's furtherance to enable him to go on Cumberland's forthcoming voyage, news of which must by then have become widely known.[3]

Heartened by his fleet's resounding success against the carracks, the Earl was preparing this, his sixth expedition in late spring. Captain Crosse's gamble with the *Foresight* had paid off, so he reverted to hiring two of the Queen's warships, the *Golden Lion* and the *Elizabeth Bonaventure*, both of 561 tons and costing £379 a month at sea. The rest of the fleet comprised two ships he probably purchased from the proceeds of the carracks – the *Anthony* 250 tons, captain James Langton, and the *Pilgrim* 100 tons, captain Francis Slingsby of Scriven in Yorkshire – the *Bark Chaldon* and his pinnace the *Discovery*. For the victualling, he borrowed another £1,000 on 15 May from Henry Lindley and £200 for a year from John Lacye, citizen and clothworker. The terms for the warships' hiring sought to avoid a repetition of the legal wrangling of 1592. The special commission granted on 28 May reserved to the Queen her due out of any prizes taken according to the tonnage of her ships and to the Lord Admiral his tenths. The rest of the profit was to be distributed between the Earl and his co-investors. As was normal with borrowing royal vessels, the Earl did not need to meet the costs of hiring until the voyage was completed, a short-term financial advantage which on this occasion was to rebound against him. The commission spelt out the powers normally accorded the Earl, like other commanders, to maintain discipline shipboard by inflicting on any offenders 'suche Punyshment, either by losse of Lymme or member, or by Death according to Martiall Lawe, or otherwise' as he deemed fitting.[4]

Earl George took command himself of this small but well-gunned force. He sailed about 23 June with the aim of repeating the 1592 voyage by intercepting the Spanish treasure ships in the Azores. The start was propitious. He captured two rich Leaguer ships from St Malo, one of which was added to the fleet, the other prize being sent home. He fought twelve hulks and made them give up large quantities of contraband goods, powder and ammunition. En route to the Azores, the Earl went in pursuit of a convoy of Spanish and Portuguese vessels, but on sight of them discovered they were too strong to attack.

Then, approaching Flores, the cruise was suddenly cut short. The Earl was taken ill and his recovery despaired of until Captain Monson, at great risk, secured a cow from the island of Corvo to supply him with milk; an act which probably saved his life. 'Valuing the earl's safety above all the profits of the voyage', the ships hastened home. Even with this mishap, the enterprise was one of the more profitable the Earl undertook because a Spanish sugar ship was also taken in August on the return journey. Since the business in the Azores had ended prematurely, the Earl could employ his own ships elsewhere. He despatched the *Anthony*, *Pilgrim*, *Discovery*, and the *Hope Bonadventure*, captain Thomas Smith, which he may have hired, to the West Indies.[5] Their voyage was to last until May 1594, so their activities and the financial implications are more properly described later in this chapter.

The Earl recovered to play his customary role at the Accession Day celebrations held that year at Windsor Castle, though he referred to the illness in his speech to the Queen. The Earl repeated the conceit of the last celebration two years before, arriving in the guise of the Knight of Pendragon Castle to find that by a miracle the old castle itself, founded in Westmorland and once removed to Westminster, had now been 'strangely erected' in Windsor – that is, his 1590 pageant car refurbished for this performance. The eloquent phrases, declaimed for him by a squire, did not mask the sober thought of the speech's content which was to re-iterate his vows of loyalty made at his first appearance as Queen's Champion, explain the presence with him of seamen and draw attention again publicly to his unhappy financial situation and dependence on the Queen's generosity. His position at Court was now more vulnerable than in 1590. Pique and envy among rival courtiers towards him had grown with his renown as Champion, his capture of the great carrack and the almost private division of its spoils between the Queen, Raleigh and himself. He had been in open conflict with the Queen over that and she was not immune to innuendo against him. He reminded her and all within earshot that his enterprises in the past two years had been dangerous and his actions honourable. 'Lett not Jelousie suspect', he warned, 'what Loyalltie and Love have undertaken.'

In his long absence from home and hard adventure, he continued, he had conversed for the most part with seamen and mariners, 'a kinde of people by nature painefull, by practise couragious, Loving to their Captaine, mindefull of their Countrie, and profitable to the Comon Wealth, yet earnest expectors of reward'. His own mariners had clamoured to accompany him at this celebration and he had condescended provided that only a few, the multitude being too many for the occasion, should attend him on behalf of the rest. Such a spontaneous urge by his crews to share the stage with him before the Queen and honoured guests, as in the companionly bonds of shipboard existence, would be sourly dismissed by some watchers. Witness Essex's supporter, Charles Chester, who spied an ulterior motive in Earl George's courting popularity with mariners to get 'thear good wills, as he thincketh to make him admirall on[e] day which may be never.' For her part, the Queen, with an avowed concern for all her subjects of whatever station in life, may have found the seamen's presence more gratifying.

The burden of the closing part of the Earl's speech was that only the Queen's grace would 'presage of his better fortune which cannot be amended without a mirracle'. This he phrased first with characteristic Arthurian imagery but in uncouth verse, for which he apologised,

>   When Windesore and Pendragon Castle doe Kiss
>   The Loyon shall bring the Red Dragon to Bliss.

In his concluding prophesy, lauding the Queen in conventional manner, the allusions pointed also to the setting of his pageant car and his mariners,

>   When duety shall move very castles of stone. . .
>   And when the Red Dragon led shipmen on dry land
>   Then blest be the Earth for a maide in an Iland.[6]

Earl George had reason for despondency at the close of 1593 and belief that only a 'mirracle' would restore his fortunes, a confession so self-evident now that it fails to astonish. Since the Armada, all but his 1591 enterprise had more than covered costs, yet only in 1589 and 1592 had he managed to reduce his known debts and even then temporarily. He had increased them in 1593, despite a successful voyage, so that they now stood at £8,320. True, he had built up some assets over the years in his substantial private fleet, but the liabilities had correspondingly grown and continued to do so almost inexorably over the next few months.

The coming year, 1594, was also marked by a downturn in his career. His position at Court had already been undermined by intrigues against him, mainly a result of what was perceived as favoured treatment over the *Madre de Dios*'s spoil. In part for the same reason, the Earl's stock with Elizabeth had fallen from the high point of the 'roge' letter of September 1591. Yet what cost him her favour even more, in a decade of unremitting and draining royal expenditure on the Spanish war, was his reluctance or inability to pay his debts to the Crown following Elizabeth's act of generosity over the carrack. Most recent was the £1,620 he owed for hiring the *Lion* and *Bonaventure* in the previous summer, a debt which neither he nor his successor ever paid, and, on top of that, the profit she should have received from that voyage by the terms of the commission. One long-standing Crown debt which touched his honour and his friends' attitude was his livery fine, now fallen so far in arrears that the Court of Wards (was this a warning shot by Burghley?) levied £58 owed on an obligation of 2 February 1583 from the lands of his surety, Lord Wharton.[7]

There were also his private debts to his friends and relatives. By Michaelmas 1594 he owed £824 to the Earl of Northumberland for arrears of the Percy Fee rents in Craven. He had borrowed £400 from his sister-in-law Lady Warwick which he was slow to refund. She wanted it paid by warrant out of the Westmorland revenues but, he explained, he had appointed those to redeem a mortgage in June; the latter an obligation unknown except for that comment. In promising on 17 February that he would pay her, he ascribed his financial difficulties to 'the long burden of making an offensive war'. This letter also makes plain that his Countess was again dissatisfied at his treatment of her. He had been almost continuously absent from the North and there was a perennial shortage of cash for her necessary housekeeping in Craven.[8]

One reason for Earl George's financial quandary now was that his room for manoeuvre was much more constricted. The Westmorland estate was beyond his reach except for rents and entry fines and the separate lordship of Winderwath. Brancepeth and Whitworth were mortaged. His Craven estates were his only major capital assets and most of those, with the lease of tithes, were already assigned to pay existing debts and interest charges. His chance to withdraw from Court and emulate his father had long passed. The Queen's attitude towards him over the carrack and his Crown debts extinguished any hopes he might have had of exploiting her munificence by seeking lucrative offices like Essex, Raleigh and other courtiers. As Champion he was wedded to Court and committed to costly annual outlays on tilt-days. He might lament his succession of ill-fortune, yet he was impelled to continue on the same hazardous courses of privateering and have faith that one year his luck would dramatically change for the better as it so nearly had done in 1592.

It was probably because of this lack of financial scope for action that a noticeable change occurred in Earl George's privateering associations which was to become more pronounced as the years passed. Hitherto, he had borrowed from a wide range of creditors, relatives, friends, gentlemen, lawyers, officials, London tradesmen and merchants, at first those with northern connections and latterly men predominantly London based. In addition, there were the many suppliers of naval stores in Gravesend and the southern ports. Outstanding among his creditors by 1594 were several big London merchants, especially the Levant and Barbary traders like the mercers Cordell and Barnes, the clothier John Bird and John Newton, who in addition had been co-investors on his enterprises, hired their ships to him and helped provision his fleets. Such merchant privateers, whose activities Kenneth Andrews has delineated, were ideally placed to take advantage of the multifarious aspects of the sea war against Spain. They owned powerful, well-armed ships, were used to co-operating in both trading and privateering, were adept at provisioning and at marketing captured merchandise and had a fast-developing role as financiers. They were promoters on a grand scale both of plunder at sea and English mercantile expansion in Europe, the Mediterranean and, later, on the long trans-oceanic routes to India and the Moluccas.[9]

The combination of all these activities on an extensive scale is uniquely observable from 1594 in the final years of Earl George's privateering career. His greater reliance on them probably dates from the previous year and the disposal of his share of the carrack's cargo for which he would have to call on their good offices. There is one caveat in considering the merchant privateers' nexus with the Earl. Although they increasingly helped fund his enterprises, with his Craven estates as collateral, he was in these last years to cast his net even wider for credit and draw on sources which he could hardly have contemplated when he first embarked on his quest for rich booty in the wake of Sir Francis Drake.

As was now customary, Earl George set forth another privateering fleet, his eighth, on 6 April 1594. Its fighting strength was three 300-ton ships, his own *Sampson*, captain Nicholas Downton, and two merchantmen, the *Royal Exchange* owned by the merchant privateers Thomas Cordell, William Holliday and William Garraway, which was the admiral with George Cave in command, and the *Mayflower* of Limehouse, captain William Anthony. Two small vessels, a carvel and a pinnace, the *Violet*, made up the fleet. The destination was the island of Terceira in the Azores, there to prey on the richly-laden Portuguese and Spanish shipping. For his share of the victualling, the Earl first borrowed £1,000 in March from the beerbrewer John Bird of Southwark for one year and, on 14 May, a further £1,000 for six months from Cordell, John Bird the clothier and their associate Thomas Paradine, haberdasher. The latter sum had been raised by them on 20 April, probably on the Earl's behalf, from William Offley, merchant tailor, and Peter Trieoner; an instance of the deep and intricate arrangements to make credit available in the city of London which was a feature of its rapid development in the war years of Elizabeth's reign. The Earl did repay one small debt in June, the £200 borrowed in 1593 from John Lacye.[10]

The return of the *Pilgrim* and its four consorts in the middle of May at Portsmouth after their long voyage and over-wintering in the West Indies should have been an occasion for pride and acclamation. Theirs was one of the most successful privateering cruises completed during the Elizabethan war and for Earl George his most profitable apart from the capture of the carrack. At Margarita island their plunder included £2,000 worth of pearls and they received 2,000 ducats worth of ransom more. At Santo Domingo they captured a frigate and added it to the fleet. From there they sailed to Jamaica, where they captured two barks, and then to Cuba. The *Pilgrim* then left for England with some of the captures.

The *Anthony, Hope Bonadventure*, and the frigate *Discovery* sailed to Central America. In the harbour of Puerto de Caballos in the Gulf of Honduras the *Anthony* gave what Kenneth Andrews describes as 'one of the best demonstrations of the persuasive powers of a privateer's broadside'. After a night of bombardment, the Earl's ships captured a fleet of seven Spanish vessels. They equipped themselves with the superior brass (that is, bronze) ordnance from their captures, brought home the largest, a 250 ton vessel, and disabled the rest. The Earl's fleet caused such consternation that a squadron was sent from Spain to pursue them. It reached the West Indies just as the *Pilgrim* and its fellows with their captures sailed into Plymouth amidst great rejoicing. Their haul of prizes was worth £10,350, besides the superior brass cannon with which they were now armed.

The Earl's delight at the haul was quickly turned to discontent by an incident of the kind that came to dominate his later years. The Queen took this occasion to demonstrate her displeasure at his failure to pay his debts to the Crown by ordering that his prizes should be searched and their value certified. He protested to the Lord Admiral and Sir Robert Cecil on 26 May that he had been singled out undeservedly for these 'unusual courses' and that many far richer prizes had not been searched. He told them that in time the Queen would blame those who advised her and continued:

Those who adventure with me I know by proof do trust me, your lordship for your tenths I doubt not will, and if Her Majesty do not for so little a part as her custom, I have lived to an unhappy hour and hazarded my estate and life very vainly.

The Lord Admiral had told him that this was done for his good. The Earl forbore to answer except to the Queen 'to whom when I have uttered what I am bound in duty, I will wish myself with Him that only knows what will be the end of these courses.' After the valuation at Portsmouth, which seems no different from the care usually taken, the tenths were paid to the Lord Admiral except for his share of the pearls which the Earl delivered to him in person, the details of these and the wide range of commodities captured shown in Table 3.[11]

In little over two months the Earl's mood of disgruntlement turned to one of dismay. The profit his seventh fleet had brought was wiped out by the losses on his eighth and the manner of its failure would give him just cause for depression and the feeling that fate was against him. Of all his enterprises, this came nearest to accomplishing the feat that tantalised a generation of Elizabethan seamen. The *Sampson* and its consorts set sail on 6 April from Plymouth for Terceira in the Azores. The carvel and pinnace with 50 musketeers were sent to search the shipping route round St Michael and the small Isle of Franca. Then, fanning out west of Fayal, the big ships sighted on Wednesday 12 June the richest of all the East Indian carracks, the 2,000 ton *Cinco Chagas*, the 'Five Wounds', in full sail eastward of them and gave pursuit. The *Mayflower* was first to close on her, four days later in the afternoon of Sunday 16 June, and battered her with great and small shot so that she lost her main top sail which forced her to steer broadside. The *Sampson* joined in about ten o'clock that night and they continued to bombard her.

When the *Royal Exchange* reached them at one o'clock, the commanders agreed that at dawn all three ships would lay aboard the carrack and this they managed with heavy fighting, now badly missing the absent 50 musketeers. Both attackers and defenders resorted to 'fier works', the *Mayflower* firing the carrack's stern, the *Sampson* her forecastle, while their own fore and top sails were set on fire and the *Royal Exchange*'s crew were busied quenching flames on her decks. With her sails burning, the *Mayflower* had to cut herself adrift and then help pull off the *Sampson* which was in similar plight and had become entangled with the carrack's masts. The fire had got such a hold on the carrack that its company besought their Captain General, a Spaniard, Don Francisco de Melo, to yield, but he refused to give in.

The *Cinco Chagas* was now ablaze and quickly sank, drowning 'manie hundreds of the passengers soldiers and saylers even then also verie manie of their bravest Spanish gallants men and weomen goodlie personages gorgeiously apparrelled yea and decked with rich chaynes of gold, Jewelles perles and pretious stones of great price'. Stripping themselves of their riches, they jumped into the sea naked in vain hope of saving themselves. Their struggles and drowning were a pitiful and lamentable sight for the Englishmen, a harsh reality of the sea-war against Philip II. The English ships' boats managed to save only two of the carrack's chief men, Captains Nuno Velio Perira and Bras Corea, who had swum for their lives. They were brought back to England and resided with the Earl and his family at his London home, the Charterhouse, for nine months until they were ransomed.

The privateers regarded themselves as fortunate that their own losses had been no heavier than twenty soldiers and seamen killed, who were all buried at sea.

TABLE 3 *Prizes brought into Portsmouth by the Earl of Cumberland's ships, May–June 1594*

MAY

By the *Hope Bonaventure* of that port, Thomas Smith captain, Richard Brown master.

1. Two Brazil prizes, which had in them:
    465 chests of white Brazil sugar
    25 chests of Muscanadoes [muscavado]
    16 chests of pannealoes [panele, brown unpurified sugar]
    10 tons, 19 cwt of brazil wood

    Tenths   46½ chests of white sugar, 2½ of Muscandoes, 1½ of pannelus, valued at £7 10s. per chest, and 21 kintalls [cwt], 3 qrs, 6 lbs of brazil wood, valued at £40 per tonne, total £418, delivered to the Earl of Cumberland by warrant of the Lord Admiral.
    Custom of these prizes paid by the Earl of Cumberland.

2. One small Leaguer prize:
    788 roons [casks] of oil

    Tenths   79 roons at 6s. 8d. per roon, £26 6s. 8d., delivered to to the Earl as above.
    Custom paid by the Earl of Cumberland.

By the *Pilgrim* of that port, Francis Slingsby captain, John Dix master.

1. One small West Indiaman, a Spanish frigate:
    821 raw hides
    115 tanned hides
      3 tons of blockwood [logwood, used in dyeing]

    Tenths   82 raw hides, 12 tanned hides at 9s. 6d. per hide, 6 cwt of blockwood, £57 6s. 4d., delivered to the Earl as above.

2. More, out of the *Pilgrim*:
    4 chests of Domingo sugar
    7 lbs weight of pearle
    1 ingot of gold
    9 buttons of gold set with Emrods [emeralds]

    Tenths   of the pearls delivered unto you by the Earl of Cumberland.
    Custom paid by the Earl of Cumberland.

TABLE 3 continued

JUNE

By the *Anthony* of that port, James Langton captain, John Paul master.

One West Indiaman, which had in it:
- 4,333   India hides, raw and tanned
- 57   chests of Indico [indigo]
- 64   bags of the same
- 6½   tons of blockwood
- 6   chests of Domingo sugar
- 23   lbs 8 oz of pearl

Tenths   433 hides good & bad, 11 kintals 33½ lbs Indico, 13 cwt blockwood, one chest of Domingo sugar (for 6 chests out of the *Anthony* and 4 out of the *Pilgrim*).

Value				
	hides, at 9s. 6d. per hide	£205	13s.	6d.
	Indico, at 5s. per lb.	£316	7s.	6d.
	one chest of Domingo sugar	£12	0s.	0d.

The tenths of the blockwood being allowed in the *Pilgrim*'s prize.

For my patent, at £5 per cent, by your Lordships appointment at the hands of Thomas Cordell, merchant £51 15s., being the twentieth part of these 5 prizes, the whole sum of your Lordships tenths amounting to £1,035 14s.

(*Source*: BL, Harl. MS 598, fols 28v–29)

Most grievous was the death of the *Mayflower*'s captain, William Anthony, while the admiral, George Cave, was sorely hurt by a musket shot, languished with a festering wound and died on 5 December, being interred in St Gregory's church, London. The third commander, Nicholas Downton, was wounded by a shot in the belly which put him out of action, but he recovered on the journey home. Captain Thomas Greenwell took over from Anthony while Lieutenant Thomas Baker substituted for Cave.

Having re-united with the carvel and pinnace the fleet sighted another large ship. They were chary of tackling her at first, because they thought she was one of Philip II's warships, but on the second day, Sunday 30 June, the *Mayflower* ascertained she was a 1,500 ton carrack, the *San Felipe*, and fought with her all day. On the Monday, first the *Royal Exchange* and then the *Sampson* joined in the battle until all three and the carrack also were forced to break off to repair damage. In calm, the admiral's boat went to parley, displaying their two important captives from the *Cinco Chargas* to persuade the *San Felipe*'s captain to surrender. But he, Don Lewys de Costinio, was a resolute naval commander, proud at having been present at the destruction of the *Revenge*. He not only refused to surrender but renewed the fight with a broadside at the *Mayflower*.

Tuesday 2 July blew a gale. The Earl's ships were more handicapped than the carrack by the damage they had suffered in two battles. The *Sampson* in particular had received a shot in the foremast and was lost sight of. The *Mayflower* and *Royal Exchange* shadowed the carrack until the next day, then gave up to search for the *Sampson* and happily found her. Meanwhile, the *San Felipe* 'with large spred sayles winde convenient and sea room at will' got so far away she was beyond pursuit. The London ships arrived in the Thames on 6 August, the *Sampson*, carvel and pinnace a month later at Portsmouth.[12]

For the Earl and his co-investors this had been a financially disastrous voyage. Their ships had been heavily damaged and they had captured only a few small prizes to compensate for their stern and costly actions and the loss of two front-rank captains. It does not look as if the Earl was able to repay on 22 October, the appointed date, the £1,000 and £50 interest due to Cordell, Bird and Paradine. It was just as well that illness prevented his journeying to Scotland to act for the Queen, the godmother, at the christening of Prince Henry in the Chapel Royal, Stirling, on 30 August. Her choice of him was apposite because he was her Champion, there was the touch of cousinage through Lady Margaret and James VI had a high regard for him. Although he missed meeting the future King of England, George avoided the big outlay which so worried his replacement, Robert Radcliffe, Earl of Sussex. With Lord Wharton also present, Cumberland's family was in a sense represented.[13]

By 1594 the unfolding saga of Earl George's maritime career had attracted the attention of a chronicler, Richard Robinson, a freeman of the Leathersellers Company in the city of London and an industrious author who collaborated on occasion with the poet Thomas Churchyard. Though Robinson may have intended his compilation eventually to be published with the Earl's aid, it remained in manuscript in versions differing mainly by the addition of the later voyages. For his description of the first seven voyages he relied on the knowledge of Captain William Middleton gent., who had been secretary to the late William, 1st Earl of Pembroke, afterwards ensign bearer to Sir Philip Sidney at Zutphen and then captain under Earl George. For the eighth voyage, Robinson also drew on the personal experiences of Thomas Greenwell, the gentleman who had taken over as captain of the *Mayflower* and was to accompany the Earl on his subsequent expeditions.

If published in 1594 Robinson's manuscript would have been another in the stream of promotional and patriotic writings urging the English to greater endeavours in the struggle against Spain. In his florid dedication to the virtuous-minded noblemen and gentlemen of England, he proferred the Earl as an example to follow, 'a loadstarr of Lightsome vertue, and a pereless precyous Ruby of Renowme.' He rendered to the Earl his ample due, as he deserved, for adventuring his noble person, sparing no charge, neglecting no labour, pains nor toil 'to pursue, assayle, encounter, surpryse, daunte, Repress and suppress the Idolatrus, malignant, prowde, ambitious, Crewell & tyranous Spanyardes'. He continued in similar vein, yielding nothing in hyperbole to the most inventive of his contemporary writers and possibly not to Earl George's literary taste. Yet Robinson's descriptions of the voyages are commendably terse and factual, an

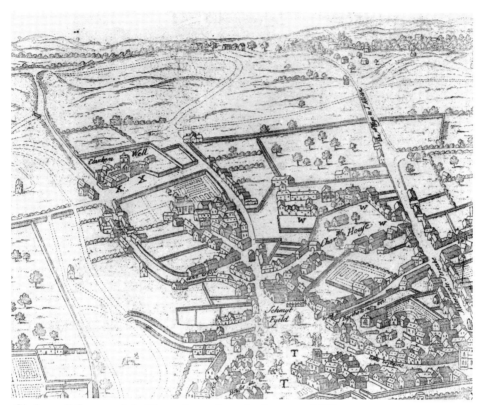

Clerkenwell Green and the Charterhouse, from the Agas map, 1633

invaluable source for reconstructing the Earl's maritime career. Moreover, the manuscript is a tract for the time, an insight into the state of mind and the current anxieties of a man who in many ways would be representative of the committed Protestant and patriotic adherents of the war against the threatening Iberian powers.[14]

The Earl was almost continuously at Court from the autumn of 1594, needing to be there in part in the interests of his relatives, the Derbys and Dacres, using his good offices on their behalf as nobility were obliged to do. From September, he was constantly aiding his nephews Ferdinando, 5th Earl of Derby until his death later in the year and then his brother William, 6th Earl, proferring advice and practical help. Ferdinando precipitated a long and tortuous family dispute by seeking to exclude his brother from inheriting his properties in favour of his widow Countess Alice and his daughter Anne, Lady Chandos. It was a case of the rights of an heir male over the heirs general, made more confusing by the current uncertain state of the law on such matters. For Earl George, this was a salutary exercise, because his intentions were the opposite, excluding his heir general, Lady Anne, for the benefit of his brother, his heir male. All his later dispositions had this intention and the Derby case he constantly bore in mind. With the

Dacres, the issue was political and straightforward: to persuade the Queen to grant pensions to Francis Dacre's daughters, because he was in voluntary exile abroad. The girls had been farmed out to other relatives; for example, Anne entered Francis Clifford's household. Eventually, in April 1595, the Queen gave in to George's and Lord Montagu's pleading and gave the girls £40 a year 'for their relief'.[15]

George led the jousting in Whitehall on Accession Day and St Elizabeth's Day, 19 November, Essex as usual being the challenger. The Earl was also present on 3 January in the great assemblage of nobility and others for the entertainment the Gray's Inn law students bravely presented before the Queen. This was rounded off with fighting at the barriers, Essex and other challengers against the Earl and his company. At Shrovetide, 5 March 1595, the sports and revels included more fighting at the Whitehall barriers. Yet, what was germinating and requiring his attention throughout these months was a new approach to his privateering which came to fruition when the Court was at Greenwich in the spring of 1595.[16]

CHAPTER 8

The Disastrous Years: 1595–7

It is appropriate to review here the course of the sea war against Spain because that is the setting in which Earl George and his fellow privateers operated and it will place in context the analysis and re-assessment which followed the return of his 1594 fleet and the changed attitude as to how he should conduct his own campaign. After the 1588 débâcle Philip II had quickly built up another formidable navy with better-designed galleons. He had responded imaginatively to the threat to his plate-fleet convoys by sending the American bullion in fast *gallizabras*, 'treasure-frigates', to beat the English blockade. Speedy *avisos* improved military, naval and commercial communications between his Atlantic possessions. He strengthened the fortifications of the port-cities in the Caribbean and on the Spanish Main, of which more will be said later. By contrast, for financial reasons and worries about losing her warships, Queen Elizabeth had virtually withdrawn the royal navy from confrontation after the fright to Lord Admiral Howard in the Azores in 1591. Indeed, as commented upon earlier, the government concentrated most of its limited resources on the land war in Brittany. The immense strain of this military conflict became worse from 1594 when bad weather brought four successive years of ruined harvests and associated inflation, hardship, poverty and disease; a wretched time for many of the populace.

From 1592 to 1596, therefore, it was the English privateers who largely shouldered the burden of the war at sea which stretched from European waters through the Azores to the Americas. Earl George's fleets were but a few of the many which did great harm to Iberia's coastal and inter-island trading but their main targets, the huge carracks, proved fast and formidable and, even when overcome, unwilling to surrender their riches. Since 1590, the Queen had employed neither Drake nor Hawkins, considering their notions of sea-warfare, using the precious royal navy, too risky and costly. However, by 1595, with Spain's power again menacing, Elizabeth reluctantly accepted the need for a large expedition under their joint leadership which would attack shipping off Spain's coast, intercept if possible the *flotas* and then raid the Caribbean. This was to set off in August, the first of successive annual royal expeditions seeking to damage

Philip II's maritime power which marked the later stages of the war as they had done the early years from 1585 to 1589.[1]

Earl George's analysis of his own contribution similarly underlined the need to change his approach if he was to hope to succeed. In particular, he was conscious of the shortcomings which had handicapped his fleets in waylaying and grappling with the carracks, notably their lack of sheer size, strength, fire-power and enough soldiers for boarding. There was also the unreliable victualling. Lack of adequate store of good salt beef, biscuit, beer and, especially, water was the chief cause of ill-health and discontent shipboard and the squandering of time searching for supplies instead of the enemy. These problems plagued the royal navy and the Council constantly issued directives to halt the abuses of hoymen and others, though ineffectively.[2] Only the plundering of wine and corn ships had, at times, kept some of the Earl's fleets at sea. Oceanic voyaging was to be bedevilled by these difficulties long after the Elizabethan era, when it was in its infancy.

For the Earl, however, there was the additional pitfall of royal and rival political interference. The novel and ambitious scheme he devised to overcome past deficiencies also had the advantage in theory of making him less dependent on the Queen through having to hire big ships from her. In practice the scheme did not work. He decided sometime in the late autumn of 1594 to build a large admiral's ship of his own. How long its construction took is not recorded, but it would have been months rather than weeks and at a cost of £6,000. Fine timbers for it were obtained from the royal Deptford and Woolwich yards. It was launched by the Queen at Deptford in the spring and appositely named the *Malice Scourge*, the scourge of malice, for 'by that noune it seemed he tasted the envy of some that repined at his honourable achievement'.

Samuel Purchas says that the 600 ton *Malice Scourge* was the best ship hitherto built by any subject, better therefore than Raleigh's *Ark Royal*. It certainly proved its worth as the flagship first of the Earl's fleet and afterwards of the East India Company. Its dimensions are not precisely known, perhaps 100 ft in length at the keel, 35 ft in beam and 17 ft deep in the hold, the ratios then best favoured by naval architects. Though still with the tubby look of contemporary naval design, it would have had the longer, sleeker lines of the late Elizabethan galleon, low at the head and high at the stern, and the Earl had it painted black to give it a deceptively lower and smaller silhouette. Its powerful armament, as inventoried in 1600 (see Appendix III), comprised 34 pieces in its two-tiered gun decks and four more at the stern. With two demi-cannons, 16 culverins, 12 demi-culverins and 8 sakers it was equal to the stronger warships in the royal navy. It had a long-boat, which would be towed behind, and two small row-boats stored on deck between forecastle and poop. The inventory shows that the galley had two furnaces. The Earl's great cabin in the poop, furnished with table, chairs and stools, would be decorated with his hangings depicting in red, gold and silver the Clifford and Cumberland coats of arms and the dragon crest. Among the pennants and streamers at the mast head would fly his own 'bloody' flag, retained from his Armada service, since the red dragon symbol was a royal preserve at sea.[3]

The commission the Queen granted the Earl on 28 March, 'knowing your

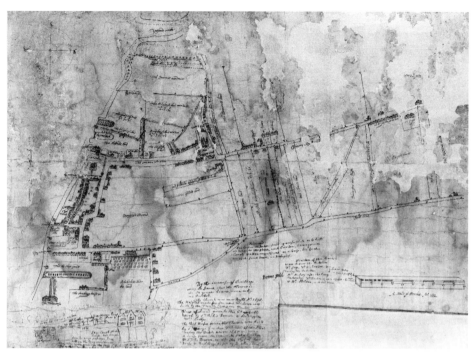

Deptford Strand in 1623

approved fidelity and valour', and enlarged in April, permitted him as usual to raise volunteers to man six vessels and, with the conflicts of 1592 in mind, gave the adventurers the value of any prizes taken saving £10,000 on every carrack bound from Portugal to the East Indies and £20,000 on any from the Indies to Portugal, with similar authority to any deputy should the Earl not sail in person.[4] One volunteer was a countryman of the Earl's, a scion of the Stricklands of Sizergh in Westmorland, probably the twenty-one-year-old Robert, whom he was glad to have 'for their be many good parts in him, and verie honest'. But young Mr Strickland held a royal office and the Earl had to write on 15 June from Bedford House to Sir Robert Cecil and the Lord Admiral to obtain a licence for him to join his crew. The Earl was much in demand in another sense. He had quality pearls to spare which he sold to his relatives and friends. Lady Mary Stanley, Northumberland's daughter who was also related to the Derbys, sent £20 to Sir Henry Slingsby to buy good, fair pearls for 12d. or 18d. apiece from the Earl, because she knew he had sold such to Sir Henry Constable much under the normal value.[5]

The *Malice Scourge* was an expensive ship to maintain at sea, requiring 400 crew at a cost of £600 a month with commensurate costs to replace equipment and repair damage. During May, when the Earl was going about his ordinary purchasing to equip his fleet, he had the tiresome additional worry of the first of several judgements against him in this and subsequent years over the plunder of

Dutchmen's goods taken out of flyboats and a Hamburg ship, for which he eventually had to give restitution in the form of bonds totalling £7,519 18s. 10d. Nevertheless, these were paper debts and he never honoured them. Twenty-five years later Earl Francis did pay most after compositions which reduced them to a quarter of their original values.[6]

There was a flurry of financial activity at the end of May and early June, much of it concerning his fleet but one separate project also. This was an agreement with Sir Robert Cecil to build ironworks. Profit was the objective though they had an eye on the strategic need for iron with the war at its height. As a preliminary, the Earl, on 28 May, purchased, for £1,250, a lease of the Earl of Northumberland's woods in Spofforth Park in the West Riding which his servants William and Sampson Ingleby had obtained for him. But, because of his current expenses, he deferred the project and then, in May 1596, had to give the Inglebys bonds to pay them the sum they had laid out for him. This was another big debt he passed on to his officers and, in view of his current financial position, quite understandable. For the project to go ahead the Queen's approval was required because the iron ore was on the lands of the Duchy of Lancaster in the Forest of Knaresborough. Though the Earl was steward there, she failed to respond to his requests for access to the ore, perhaps another sign of her attitude now towards him. Only when Cecil became Chancellor of the Duchy in October 1597 was she persuaded to assent and then laid down tough terms in her grant of mining rights to the Earl.[7]

How heavy the cost was of building and equipping the *Scourge* and

'Will' Ingleby (1546–1618), artist unknown

Sampson Ingleby (1569–1604), artist unknown

provisioning his fleet is evident from his new borrowing which totalled £10,100. On 29 May he revoked his 28 February 1592 deed concerning the manors of Eshton, Gargrave and Flasby to allow him to mortgage them on 2 June for £4,600 to Thomas Cordell for eight months. Four days later, he raised another £3,500 from Cordell on a statute and £1,000 on the mortgage of Nesfield and Westhall to Thomas Bird, Thomas Paradine and another leading London merchant, Thomas Symonds, skinner. Finally, with his cousin Henry Cholmley, he borrowed £1,000 more on two obligations from Richard Humble, citizen and vintner.[8] These London merchants, in effect, were financing the Earl's reconstituted fleet with the Craven manors and recorded obligations as security. On this voyage they do not appear to have invested to any great extent, if at all. They had committed all they could in ships and cash to Drake's and Hawkins's Caribbean enterprise which set out on 29 August from Plymouth.

Recruiting, even in competition with others, proved no problem. In the Earl's view, he had in the *Scourge* the best manned ship that ever went out of England. Drake told him he knew there were four score men in her crew able to take charge. 'For good sailing and excellent working', the Earl commented, 'it is not possible to amend her' and he was as healthy and fit now as at any time in his life. In the event, his excitement at commanding his great ship's maiden voyage was quickly dulled. News came as he was about to leave that a carrack had been seen by the Rock and he feared he had missed those leaving for the Indies. Moreover, with reports of Drake's imminent arrival, all Portuguese shipping was stayed for three months and the fortifications strengthened in the Canaries and the Azores.

Once again the Earl had been stymied by royal policy. With prospects unfavourable, he could not justify sailing in person but he was apprehensive that Elizabeth, unless she heard some reason for it, would misconstrue his return. To Cecil, his friend, confidant and now business partner, he wrote from Tavistock on 30 June, knowing his words would reach her ears, that another journey might recover what he lost, if he lost, 'but my own going, idly, I will not, upon slight grounds adventure.' His mood was one of despondency. He was particularly upset that the Queen was offended by reports that he had carried his flag in the same harbour as a royal warship, the *Swiftsure*, an act which could be interpreted as lese-majestie. Sir John Burroughs had done so, he argued, and Captain Crosse in the *Swiftsure* had agreed to it. But well, he confided,

it is my fortune, who will ever strive to deserve as well, whatsoever disgrace is laid upon me, as any that liveth. Excuse me for going into the North, necessity forced, being without money, having much to pay, presently, there only to get it, and from this place London 9 or 10 score mile about.

Quitting the *Scourge*, with the excuse to his crews that the Queen had commanded his return to Court, caused him further trouble. His appointment of James Langton as his deputy was so resented by Captain Monson that he left in the *Alcedo*, bore a lifelong grudge against the Earl and thereafter served the Earl of Essex. Langton sailed to the Azores with the *Scourge*, *Anthony* and *Discovery*, captured a carvel of 100 tons and then attacked but after a fierce fight lost in the fog a Spanish vice-admiral's ship, the *Saint Thomas*. Her escorts, it was reported, 'were loath to come within daunger of this his Honoures Fleete'. Having spent their victuals, Langton had to return home, but captured three Dutch ships laden with wheat, copper, munitions and provisions for Spain and so contraband.[9]

The nature of Langton's plunder is partly known from lists taken when he reached harbour in October. A Flemish ship he brought into Portsmouth carried 885 bags of woad. The *Scourge* itself had on board large quantities of cloths. The most timely capture was a Flemish flyboat laden with wheat which was taken into Plymouth where 200 quarters were off-loaded with Lord Burghley's permission quickly given to succour the inhabitants suffering from food shortages. Corn had already risen to 9s. or 10s. a bushel and was set to become dearer still. The flyboat with its remaining 323 quarters of wheat was then taken to Portsmouth where the Lord Admiral's tenths were assessed before its cargo could be sold to bring relief there also. The *Scourge*'s first exploits could not have covered costs, yet they were not entirely fruitless and the ports' inhabitants had particular cause for gratitude.[10]

Earl George spent the late summer months in a Yorkshire, he told Cecil on 15 August, 'barren of all news' which afforded nothing worth his knowing. He wanted to visit Cecil in secret, not yet willing to go near the Court for reasons he would not state. Later in the month he intended to hunt towards Bath and spend some time in the spa town to confirm his already good health. He was at Court for the Accession Day tournament where he entered with a device representing his castle, its treasure guarded by a dragon. When Elizabeth arrived, he rode out from the castle in his gilded armour to do her service. But he was upstaged by Essex who presented an elaborate show with a political message both before and after the tilting and banquet, though in the end, Alan Young concludes, it was 'an expensive flop.'[11]

He had recovered his enthusiasm by now and, early in December, was provisioning the *Scourge* and the refurbished but relatively lighter-armed royal ship the *Dreadnought* of 450 tons which required a crew of 200 and cost £300 a month at sea. This was not a front-rank warship, which was probably why it was available, six being with Drake and Hawkins. For the outlay, the Earl on 2 December borrowed £2,000 on two recognizances, one for five months, the other eleven months, from Edward Greville Esq., of Milcote, Warwickshire, who had sat as member for Warwick in the 1593 parliament.[12] His intention was to attack Spanish shipping or suppliers carrying contraband to the great armada Philip II was again preparing. A fleet of Hamburg ships, laden with cordage and other 'warlike provisions' for Spain, had taken the westerly route round Scotland and Ireland so as to avoid interference from the English privateers in the Channel. The Earl with the Queen's direction or approval wished to pursue them. But on 21 December, ready to sail at Portsmouth, he still had not received her commission. It grieved him, he told the Lord Admiral and Cecil, that he could not do her the service he wanted, yet he worried less because no one was paying for the delay but himself. All he needed to proceed was two lines under the Queen's hand to extend his last summer's commission. But he dare not sail without her warrant for though he was as careful of her subjects as he was of

TABLE 4 *Prizes brought into Portsmouth by the Earl of Cumberland's ships, October 1595*

1. One prize of oade, being a Fleming, John Birch captain and master.
    885 bags of woad, net weight 1,216 quintals [cwt] 3 qrs 14 lbs, disposed of as in the corn prize below.

2. By the *Malice Scourge*, James Langton captain, John Greenaway master.
    259 pices of barras cloth [coarse linen fabric], of 4,328 ells [45 in.]
    13 bolts of Holland [cloth] and one piece of Holland of 30 ells
    59 pieces of Hanscotte Sayes [fine serge cloth]
    122 pieces of striped canvas
    54 pieces of buckram
    42 pieces of buffens [coarse cloth]

    Tenths as below.

3. By the *Malice Scourge*, one corn prize being a Fleming:
    323 quarters of wheat

    Tenths   of the woad, of the goods in the man of war and this corn prize were wholly left in the Earl of Cumberland's hand to be accompted for between your honour and him.
    Note: 200 quarters of wheat were unladen in the west country before she came to Portsmouth, as reported.

(*Source*: BL, Harl. MS 598, fol. 36)

himself the danger to him if he lost but one man would be more than he would willingly risk.[13]

At last, on 4 January 1596, he was granted his commission, with the proviso that he return before the end of March in time for the projected attack on Cadiz where Philip II was gathering his armada.[14] The Earl's idea now was to catch up with three of the Hamburg stragglers, but adverse winds prevented his sailing for two more weeks. He was annoyed by criticism that he was tardy to set out, replying that his big ships had already wastefully lain at anchor for six weeks and now dare not attempt to leave harbour. He pointed out to Cecil on 16 January that all the expense of preparing his ships to do Her Majesty service was borne by him but, revealing a conscience not always matched by honouring his bonds, that 'upon my credit there are many poor men whose living is only trading in small barks along the shore'.

He managed to depart early in February for the French coast and hoped this would silence the innuendo against him 'of unjust informers who seek credit by depraving others.' He captured three Flemings which had traded with Spain, took out sugar and other Spanish commodities, though leaving the oranges, and was so pleased to have discommoded foreigners overtly hostile to the Queen that the small value of his plunder he discounted since, he reminded Cecil, he strove more 'to serve Her Majesty than profit myself.' His notion now was to await a fair wind and then head for Lisbon, where the carracks were due to leave on their outward journey, and take any of the returning Hamburg ships laden with rich Iberian merchandise he met on the way.[15]

His private actions against the enemy were suddenly subsumed by a national crisis. News came of the Spanish investment of Calais which, if successful, would give Philip II the cross-Channel base for an invasion of England he had lacked in 1588. the Queen instructed the Earl to bring his fleet with all the ships and soldiers he could find to Dover where an English force was hastily being assembled to bolster Calais' defence. He collected two good ships at Portsmouth and three at Cowes carrying nine companies of soldiers under their Colonel, Sir Henry Power, newly returned from France. Burghley for once overcame Dutch objections to the Earl as commander. However, Elizabeth and Henry IV could not agree over the sovereignty of Calais, she held back the English reinforcements and consequently the city and its fortress fell in April. After all his recent frustrations, Cumberland had been eager for battle. The Lord Admiral told Cecil on 17 March that he had come to see him aboard the *Repulse* 'and seemed to me to be much grieved at that he is stayed, but I dealt so with him as he knoweth how it must be.'[16]

For Earl George as well as Elizabeth's government the spring of 1596 was an unhappy and fraught time. News of Drake's death, following that of Hawkins and other fine commanders on their West Indian voyage, brought sadness. With Philip II now established at Calais and his burgeoning strength in Spain, a pre-emptive Cadiz assault was more imperative than ever. Two commissions appointing the Lord Admiral and the Earl as leaders were secretly prepared and signed by the Queen. However, once their contents became known the usual rivalries broke out and the Queen rescinded the order, to the Earl's chagrin. Worse followed. He was ruled out when preparations began because of Dutch participation. The Lord Admiral, Essex and Raleigh had the honour of leading the great expedition of 17 royal ships, 47 others, 18 Dutch vessels and 8,000 men which sailed on 1st June.[17]

A seemingly trivial incident arising from the preparations for this fleet had led on 29 April to a Star Chamber action in which Earl George was named. In the trial, one Smithe confessed to spreading slanderous news. He had been a pressed soldier at Dover and swallowed the soldiers' tittle-tattle that the Lord Admiral's ship had been searched by the Earl of Essex who found ashes, dust and powder instead of gunpowder and called Howard traitor. This was not so far-fetched or as colourful as the rest of his tale. Both Howard and Essex had returned to Court where the latter and Earl George had dragged the Lord Admiral by the beard before the Queen and exclaimed 'ah thou Traytor!'. Smithe, travelling home, had stopped at the house of a justice of the peace at Windsor for a drink and foolishly repeated the slanderous story to him and was immediately apprehended. The Councillors, solicitous as ever of their dignity, gave Smithe an exemplary sentence, to lose one of his ears upon the pillory at Westminster, the other at Windsor, to be whipped, wear a paper on his head showing his crime, imprisoned and fined £20. This punishment, they considered, would have been greater had it not been for Smithe's 'baseness', because he was only a peasant and a boy at that.[18]

By spring 1596 Earl George was in a sense on a treadmill, and one of his own making. Had he wanted, he could not retire to Skipton Castle in dudgeon at his exclusion from the Cadiz expedition, nor could he abandon his own sea-warfare. It says much for his resilience that he was keen to continue his activities. The 'great charge' of the *Malice Scourge* and her consorts for four months, mostly lying at anchor, the limited plunder and no help from the royal coffers had plunged him even further into debt. On 2 April he obtained a licence of alienation for Bolton Priory and exactly a month later mortaged it for £5,000 for six months to the London merchants Alderman Peter Haughton and Nicholas Stevens. The Priory's value was then stated to be £300 a year above charges and its woods worth at least £2,000. He extended his debt to the Inglebys by giving them bonds for the £1,250 he owed them for the lease of Spofforth Woods to repay them between 1599 and 1600, a longer-term and so realistic commitment.[19]

Part of the mortage money he used to equip one of his ships – not named – for an unrecorded voyage to the Azores in the early summer. A report to Essex on 30 June about Portuguese vessels reaching Lisbon from the Azores mentioned one which had fought the Earl's ship, lost sixty of her men and received a shot under water. By September, when the Cadiz raiders had returned, leaving the Queen disillusioned at their lost opportunities, the Earl was eager to take advantage of the confusion they had caused and seek out the treasure ships they missed. For this he wanted to hire merchant-privateers' big Levanters and would have to act quickly to bespeak them before they were freighted for the Straits of Gibraltar and the Eastern Mediterranean. He sought the Queen's licence on 25 September, again with Cecil as intermediary, which in her current tetchy humour would not be easy.[20]

He had been at Court himself earlier in the month and present in the royal chapel at Greenwich on the 8th when Elizabeth consented to a common guarantee with Henry IV.[21] Then Lady Derby's illness took him to her side. Her death on 29 September put an end to his plans for a major voyage. Apart from seeing to her speedy burial, he was her sole executor, obtained probate on 22 November and in December took a lease of her Clerkenwell mansion, making it his London home. Her most noteworthy bequests were to Francis Clifford of a gilt bowl with cover which the Queen had given her and to Countess Margaret 'a Tablett of gold with her Lords picture in yt', possibly a Hilliard: miniatures were very personal gifts intended to be kept secret. Attending to his late sister's affairs brought him closer to Countess Margaret and, in an emotional letter of 28 November, he pleaded with her not to let 'this good course begun die in its first beginning, but go forward in doing to me as thou oughtest to a husband whom solely and wholly will be thine as he is bound, both by God and right courses to the world'.[22]

The set-back to his reputation Earl George had experienced during the past year and his fruitless heavy investment in the *Malice Scourge*'s voyages continued during the early months of 1597 when his career reached rock-bottom. He was again denied the chance of royal service. The Privy Council had agreed a further expedition to destroy what survived of Philip II's third armada which storms had scattered in October 1596 and now was anchored at Ferrol. In January, the Earl and Essex submitted rival projects for this official enterprise. The Earl's offer to take two royal warships, some of his own fleet and twenty Hollanders had the merit of being the cheaper. Both his and Essex's plans were initially rejected but another attack on the lines of the 1587, 1589 and 1596 raids could not long be delayed if Philip's dogged preparation of yet another armada was to be disrupted.

In the competition for who should lead, Earl George was quickly disposed of. The States General refused to co-operate if command was given to a privateer whom they held responsible for depredations against Dutch merchantmen. The Earl was deeply humiliated. He now sought Burghley's furtherance for his 'reputation and estate' of his quest for the governorship of the Isle of Wight, a prestigious appointment in view of its strategic position, the garrison of 3,000 troops at Carisbrooke Castle and a programme to strengthen the castle's defences over the next few years. As it turned out, the replacement of the current governor, Lord Hunsdon, was only a rumour and, in any case, Earl George was too useful as a privateering admiral to appoint him to a shore command. Yet his letter to Burghley on 26 April, at first sight a typical depressed courtier's plea and probably dismissed as such, reveals him in an unfamiliar frame of mind. He promised to tie himself to the island and 'not with such eumerrs to sea-journeys as heretofore', the first written expression of doubts about his privateering obsession. He affirmed the primacy of his aim to do the Queen service but felt so disgraced by his rejection that 'if hir majestie dooe not showe me sum other token of hir favor, I shall as often wyshe myself dead as I have houres to lyve.'

Thrown back on his own initiative once again, he prepared another enterprise, writing to Cecil on 25 March for help in buying corn stored at Portsmouth for biscuit which he urgently needed for his voyage, the borough officers obviously not happy about releasing their reserves. This, his tenth, consisted as in 1596 of the *Malice Scourge* and the *Dreadnought*. Their voyage was short and unsuccessful. No more than forty leagues out at sea they met a storm and the *Scourge* lost her main mast, which compelled the Earl to transfer to her consort and return to port. With his ship undergoing repairs, he now hired from the merchant-privateer William Garraway his *Ascension*. This 400-ton, 34-gun merchantman, manned by 120 men, was taken out by Captain Francis Slingsby to search mainly for ships sailing from Lisbon. Slingsby was a Yorkshireman, of the notable gentry family of Scriven. Gales ended his first essay and he had to replenish at Plymouth. On the second, he had the misfortune to run into a Spanish squadron under Admiral Pedro de Zubiaur, but beat off the six galleons which attacked him. Two weeks later the *Ascension* returned to port 'having made noe profitt to his Lordshipp towardes all his charge expended in that Shippe . . . and many maymed and many hurte and all without meanes to mayntayne then at their Cominge on Shoare.'[23]

The Earl had other ships at sea in 1597 about which a little is known. One, sailing in consort with Sir Thomas Gerrard's ship (probably his *Scorn*) captured a Hamburg flyboat belonging to Middleburg merchants with a cargo of sweet wines and raisins from Malaga in Spain. Unfortunately for the privateers' owners, the merchants, who included Arnold, Peter and Hans Lulls, won a judgement in the Admiralty Court for restitution of their goods. The mayor of Plymouth was ordered to take the cargo into custody and get back what had been sold to William Lewis or take a bond to the same value. The Earl had pinnaces – and presumably other vessels – operating off Fayal in October, as Essex reported from the royal expedition. Yet only one prize, brought into London in May, is recorded as taken by the Earl's ships this year, a trifling return from six months' efforts severely hampered by misfortune.[24] One reason is that, with the great English fleet at sea, ordinary shipping, on which privateers like the Earl preyed, tended to be chary about leaving harbour. But it looks as if the random privateering he had to indulge in during 1597 was fast losing its old profitability. Spain was strong at sea and more protective and neutrals were well-honed to litigation in the English courts to recover their merchandise.

Earl George devoted much time to Court. He had been in the garter procession on 23 April at Whitehall Palace. On 23 October, he carried the new earl's sword when the Queen raised Lord Admiral Howard to the earldom of Nottingham and carried the sword the day after when parliament commenced.[25] But he also gave much attention throughout the year to pecuniary matters. For him and his advisers 1597 was a year of unprecedented financial juggling to cope with exceptional demands caused by his continuing privateering failures. His known debts had risen from £20,200 in December 1595 to £28,450 a year later. In addition, he had mounting obligations to the Dutchmen, the Earl of Northumberland and the Queen, though he was making a token effort with small sums to clear the account with the Court of Wards. What he owed the often poor tradesmen in London and the southern ports cannot even be guessed. His servants had lent him money, such as Richard Musgrave perhaps £500 on the mortgage of the Hawhouse and Henry Denton, his brother's steward, much more on Eshton demesnes and mill, the Inglebys £1,250 on Spofforth.[26] To gain relief from the accumulation of London loans and their crippling annual interest the Earl for the first time since 1588, but now on a far bigger scale, turned to his Craven tenants for cash relief from them.

He had instructed his estate commissioners in 1596 to look into the question of tenant-right and, by the end of the year, they had begun to raise money by negotiating mortgages with 335 tenants on 21 manors in Craven. The basis was the grant of a lease of 5,000 years in return for a payment of usually 40 years' rent due for the tenement. The Earl reserved the right to redeem these long leases by repayment of the full amount in two instalments five years later, on 30 February and 25 June 1602. On redemption, the tenancies would revert to their existing terms. By this means he raised £8,775 13s. 6d. interest-free and by May was in a position to come to terms with his major creditors.[27] In the meantime, his finances had again deteriorated. The early receipts from the Craven mortgages allowed him to repay £500 owed to Richard Humble on 3 January 1597. Yet to send out the *Malice Scourge* and her consort he had borrowed more on 15 April, this time from his steward of the Courts in Westmorland, Thomas Braithwaite gent., who lent him £1,000 for five years on the mortgage of Winderwath, the only manor there not part of Countess Margaret's jointure estate.[28]

The preliminary stage in the series of new financial arrangements the Earl entered into in the spring and early summer was a new rental of all his properties compiled on 26 March which showed his net yearly receipts from Craven and Westmorland as £2,329 16s. 1½d. This sum did not include revenues such as entry fines or woodsales, two of the larger though variable sources of income, the former of which would be now truncated with the mortgages. On the debit side, however, would be the high cost of the upkeep of his houses and other properties, Countess Margaret's and his own household expenses, lawsuits and other incidentals. It is not hard to see how threadbare his means were in relation to his London and privateering outlays, let alone servicing the interest payments on his major borrowings. Even the apparent annual totals shown in the rental are misleading because so much of the manorial and tithes revenues had been assigned to Francis and others to pay the debts and the many mortgaged manors were vulnerable should his London creditors choose to foreclose.[29]

The next step was to alter the existing terms by which Francis and his officers dealt with his finances. On 2 April he obtained a licence of alienation and on 3 May revoked by deed poll the previous indenture concerning his Yorkshire lands. On 7 May, he entered into a new indenture tripartite between himself and Clifford; William Ingleby and Ferrand; and all his creditors, the four most important being named, that is Lindley, Cordell, Paradine and Bird. However, as in the past, this was not just a private arrangement between the Earl, his officers and creditors for management of his finances. It had required the consent of Lord Keeper Egerton, Lord Burghley, Anne, Countess of Warwick and 'other good friends' of the Earl who represented the interests of the Queen and Privy Council, Countess Margaret and Lady Anne, and any one else of note affected by the Earl's financial predicament.

Since the previous indenture made in 1588, Clifford, Ingleby and Ferrand had sold only one property, Idle, a testimony to their astute handling of the family's affairs during the Earl's long absences. However, the estate assigned to them by that first indenture now needed enlarging to bring it into line with his far greater current indebtedness. By this time the Earl had full possession of Buckden and Starbotten because he had bought the leases made in 1535 and 1536 and they had also terminated. These two lordships, the Littondale manors of Hawkswick and Arncliffe and, for the first time, the mineral rights and other royalties on all the named properties were added when the new assignment was made on 7 May to William and Sampson Ingleby.

The manors assigned were stated to be worth £1,000 a year clear and £30,000 if sold – about the same amount as the Earl's total known debts. Of the Earl's other Craven possessions, Bolton Priory, Eshton, Gargrave, Flasby and Westhall were, as has been seen, separately mortgaged. Only the original 1311 estates of Skipton, Barden and Silsden with their honorial jurisdiction were exempted and in the last two many tenants had taken individual mortgages. Every other part of the Earl's great Craven estates might now be sold or foreclosed on to clear his debts.

TABLE 5 *Rental and valuation of Earl George's Estates, 26 March 1597*

CRAVEN

		Rents	
	£	s.	d.
Skipton	416	8	8
Gargrave	72	18	9
Silsden with Holden	112	13	0½
Barden Forest	82	11	0½
Stirton & Thorlby	11	4	2
Elso & Crookrise	35	3	4
Embsay	17	11	2
Eastby	12	12	9
Cononley	9	19	7
Carleton	65	5	4½
Lothersdale	19	7	7½
Bradley	28	18	2½
Nesfield & Langbar	13	12	11
West Hall	49	0	0
Steeton	15	8	10
Bolton	356	13	7
Halton	18	1	10
Storithes & Hazlewood	13	17	8
Woodhouse cum Appletreewick	6	6	4
Cracoe & Threapland	37	14	6
Grassington	37	13	4
Eshton	114	12	5
Flasby	7	6	8
Scosthrop	3	9	7
Malham and Malham Moor	1	16	3½
Arncliffe	1	13	4
Hawkswick and Oldcoates	5	4	7½
Littondale	59	6	8
Newhall and Cowlinghead	6	1	2
Glusburn	0	15	2
Draughton	0	15	0
Settle, with Cleatop and Langcliffe	50	17	6½
Giggleswick, with Rathmell, Neweth and Stainforth	47	4	9
Long Preston	31	7	2½
Birks (worth)	40	0	0
Middlesmore (worth)	30	0	0
Greenfield (worth)	23	13	4
Langstrothdale	74	17	4⅓
Buckden and Starbotton	42	16	10
Hens in Clifford Fee	10	10	4

TABLE 5 continued

		£	s.	d.
Profits of courts and wapentake fines		30	0	0
Clifford's Inn, Middlesex		4	0	0
Tithes		321	11	7
	Sum total	2,340	11	0½
Payments, deductions and allowances		787	13	0½
	Net total	1,552	18	0

WESTMORLAND

	£	s.	d.
Mallerstang	43	16	2
Kirkby Stephen	28	7	0½
Winton	32	13	7½
Sowerby	24	0	3¼
Brough Over and Nether	44	8	0
East Stainmore	107	16	1
Stainmore mill	2	0	0
South Stainmore	34	13	7½
Scattergate and Burrells	22	13	8
Bongate	19	15	6
Appleby demesne lands	6	6	8
Brampton	5	14	1½
Knock	23	18	8
Kings Meaburn	30	6	2½
Moorehouse with Hornby	17	11	2
Whinfell and Cliburn moss (besides £1 6s. 8d. decayed)	2	0	0
Kendal Town	1	2	0
Burton and Helton	0	7	4
Herbage in Whinfell, by estimation	51	0	0
Herbage of Brougham demesne, by estimation	53	6	8
Profits of Brougham corn mill, by estimation	12	0	0
Profits of agistments at Langton and Flakebridge, by est.	48	0	0
Profits of Bongate mills, by estimation	16	13	4
Profits of Winderwath, by estimation	100	0	0
Profits of sales of corn and tithe wool	46	13	4
Newhall	11	11	7
Brougham coney warren	10	0	0
Southfield at Appleby	20	0	0
Profits of courts and sheriffwick	13	6	8
Neatgeld, serjeant food and rent hens, Milburn Fell and Sandfordwood	56	0	3
Sum total	885	2	0¾

TABLE 5 continued

			3
Payments in Westmorland	113	8	8
Net total	771	13	4¾

CUMBERLAND

	£	s.	d.
Carleton and Penrith	2	8	7
Skelton and Lamonby	2	16	2
Sum total	5	4	9
Total rents in Yorkshire, Westmorland, Cumberland and Middlesex	3,230	17	9½
Total payments and allowances in Yorkshire and Westmorland	901	1	8
Net receipts	£2,329	16	1½

(*Source*: YAS, DD121/76)

Implicit in the 7 May agreement was that the Queen could envisage this. She had no obligation to bail out her Champion. Once again, however, and no doubt with the London merchants' collusion, the Earl's hard-pressed officers avoided all but minor disposals of his lands over the next five years.[30]

However, the Earl had personal debts which were even more a matter of honour and he set aside other future income to settle these. In a separate indenture also concluded on 7 May, he demised his lease of Christ Church tithes to Ingleby and Ferrand specifically to satisfy the former, his friend as well as servant. They were to raise the greatest sums they could by letting the tithes and use them to pay first the £664 10s. the Earl owed Ingleby on the Spofforth deal and then £325 he owed Ingleby and John Hodgson jointly. Afterwards, the tithe revenues were to be added to the main assignment for repayment of the debts. One consequence of this arrangement was the rackrenting of tithe leases, bringing them into line with inflation which was then at a high point in the Tudor century.[31]

With the later instalments of the tenants' mortgage payments and other rents due, the Earl and his senior officers managed to reduce his commitments over the next few months. Brancepeth was redeemed on 14 May, £3,000 capital and £1,200 interest being paid in cash and statutes given for the rest – for £900 in two instalments on 31 January and 31 July to Sanders, Young and Wright, and £1,100 to Standen. In fact, Arden Waferer took over the £900 debt with the usual proviso that he would start an action against Ingleby and Ferrand in case of non-payment. At the end of June, the second loan of £500 from Richard Humble was repaid. Temporarily flush with money, Earl George threw caution to the winds, betting at bowls in June with a dubious character, one Rechin, and lost £600. He did not pay up and when Rechin was later convicted and executed for coining and clipping the debt was forfeited and added to the list of what George owed the Queen.[32] In September, more of his own creditors were satisfied; £4,000 was repaid with £600 interest to Thomas Cordell on the redemption of Eshton; two days later, £1,000 was paid to Bird, Paradine and Symonds to redeem Nesfield. In October, the Earl's estate commissioners renewed their work of concluding mortgages with the Craven tenants and continued on a smaller scale until 12 August 1598, which brought in the last £700 of the total given above.[33]

Although the transactions of late 1596 and 1597 merely transferred a part of Earl George's borrowings from his creditors in London to his tenants in Craven, they reduced the pressure of his indebtedness and the demands for payment of interest. In the four months following the May indenture, he lowered his recorded debts nominally at least by £8,500 capital and made provision to pay off others. Besides Eshton demesnes, only Bolton, albeit a vital property, remained in mortgage. His other debts were still enormous in comparison with his revenues but, judging by the credit allowed him in the past, he had given himself the scope to invest in another, major enterprise to attempt to recover what he had lost through privateering over the past twelve years. The outcome was his great Puerto Rican expedition of 1598 which, as the most crucial of his career and one of the outstanding enterprises of the Elizabethan sea-war, merits detailed consideration.

CHAPTER 9

The Great Puerto Rican Expedition: Preparations, 1597–8

While storms battered the Anglo-Dutch fleet under Essex, Raleigh and Lord Thomas Howard and delayed their departure, Earl George was planning an expedition which, in its final shape, was to be the most important of his whole privateering career. He was, Cecil confided to Essex on 19 July, a suitor to go a 'royal journey' in October. He thought Raleigh would adventure his *Roebuck* and he might do the same with his *True Love*. Foremost in his mind, Cumberland explained, was the obligation of discharging his duties to Queen and country and in the eyes of God, denied him by his exclusion from both the 1596 Cadiz and now this 1597 Ferrol attack. It was the disgrace which rankled with him, a matter of pride most of all. Cecil, appreciating this, commented to Essex 'it is to be wished that his spirit which loves action should be cherished.' Queen Elizabeth, adept at deflecting courtier enthusiasms to her own ends, encouraged the Earl to proceed. What they agreed in their private conversations was never revealed and may only be inferred, and as the Earl interpreted it, from his later actions and assertions. In Cecil's words, the plot was 'very secret between Her Majesty and him.' Certainly she offered no help, either in cash or ships, the Ferrol fleet monopolising both. Cumberland's would have to be an entirely private joint-stock venture, his own ships and capital supplemented by what Raleigh, Cecil and especially his London merchant-privateer associates would venture.[1]

The influence of the latter is evident from the chosen target, Pernambuco with its port-town of Recife in Brazil, a repeat therefore of Captain James Lancaster's 1595 raid which brought back over £50,000 worth of plunder, when his four backers were the Earl's close city associates John Watts, Paul Bayning, William Shute and John Moore.[2] In July 1597 this new project might have been regarded as no more than the usual follow-up to a royal expedition, exploiting the confusion so as to damage Spain and her possessions further at no cost to the Queen and with the chance of riches for the Earl and his fellow investors. Yet he was later to assume that Elizabeth was ready to support him in the establishment of an English base in the Americas, the ultimate goal of the Atlantic strategy long advocated by the aggressively expansionist courtiers and sea-dogs over which the Queen blew hot and cold. He was to be mistaken. When he sent for royal help in July 1598 Queen and Council had new pre-occupations and were indifferent to what befell his enterprise. In the event it did not matter. But for so experienced a courtier to be under that illusion as late as March 1598 when he eventually set sail suggests that his discussions with the Queen had given him grounds to expect she would back up his success.

The great Ferrol fleet did not set sail again until August and then quickly abandoned its purpose and instead attempted to capture the Spanish treasure ships in the Azores. Earl George was busy that month helping to settle the problems of the Derbys, showing himself, wrote Edward Mylar to Cecil, 'a kind friend to my Lady and a good uncle to the Earl.' Cumberland was by now fully committed to his voyage. His commission from the Queen on 7 October authorised him to fit out a small fleet – the *Malice Scourge* and six other ships – appoint captains and other officers, levy men for his service by sea and land, and gave him the necessary powers of life and death to maintain discipline on the voyage.[3]

His preparations were slower than he had perhaps expected. First cause of the delay was the threat at the end of October of Philip II's last armada sent, it was feared, to capture and garrison Falmouth as a base for the conquest of England soon after Essex's fleet had returned to harbour. All available English forces were hurriedly assembled to repel the Spanish. Fortunately they were not needed, the enemy fleet being scattered by a storm.[4] The Earl, too, may have had difficulty in obtaining provisions for his ships in this fourth successive year of bad harvests and food shortages with hard-hit local communities unwilling to let go what they badly needed to eke out the winter. The Council lent their weight to his efforts on 3 November because the Earl was 'forthwith to goe to the sea for her Majesty's speciall service'. They published an open warrant requiring royal officers in Suffolk and Essex, who were probably siding with the local people in their obstruction, to suffer his employees Covell and Skelton to transport 200 quarters of pease, 200 bushels of oatmeal, 60 firkins of butter and 40 way of cheese to his ships.[5]

The chief cause of the delay, however, was a change in the scale of the whole project. More of the merchant-privateers were attracted to join his venture either by his or their fellows' persuasion. This called for a far higher order of planning and organisation, a much bigger investment by the Earl and concomitant changes in his financial and testamentary arrangements, as will be seen. One advantage was that with no rival fleets at sea there would be plenty of officers and seamen eager to join his big enterprise. Conversely, the Earl knew he had lost his chance to cross the southern Atlantic to Brazil. He discussed this with Essex and adopted instead the latter's suggestion of an attack on one of the West Indian cities, a plan similar to that of Drake and Hawkins on their last voyage in 1595 which Essex had likewise greatly influenced. Essex was currently the foremost advocate of the notion of an English base overseas to counter Philip II's power, either Lisbon or

Cadiz on the mainland or one of the Atlantic islands. The Council were at odds
among themselves over policy, as Burghley told the French ambassador de Maisse
in January 1598. He and the Lord Admiral desired peace, whereas others, the
young Essex among them, wanted war. The Queen, judging by her
encouragement of Earl George's project, was then inclined to pursue the conflict
with Spain. Indeed, among de Maisse's coterie she was held to be sending out the
fifteen ships under the Earl.[6]

This new objective in effect substituted the aggressive courtier strategy for the
mercantile, though in practical terms it made sense. Cumberland kept this switch
secret, except perhaps from Essex, Raleigh, Cecil and the Queen herself, until he
had passed the Canary Islands in April 1598. He had learnt the virtues of
reticence yet his reason may have been less to deceive his city backers – who had
lost heavily on Drake's ill-fated last voyage – than to keep his real purpose from
the ears of Spanish spies who were quick to pass on rumours of his fleet. Indeed,
their reports led Philip II to send reinforcements to Pernambuco.[7] In the winter
months of 1597–8 it was the prospect of plunder at sea and in Brazil and
confidence in Earl George as admiral and general which brought solid support
from Thomas Cordell and his fellow city investors.

It was a much enlarged fleet and forces which the Earl began to gather early in
the New Year 1598. Thomas Cordell and William Garraway's big Levanter the
Merchant Royal was ready by 10 January. The royal patent, granted on 14 January,
permitted the Earl to take the *Malice Scourge*, twelve other ships and two
pinnaces at the most, though his fleet was to exceed that number. He was now

Robert Devereux, 2nd Earl of Essex
(1566–1601)

authorised to recruit as many crews and troops as he required, appoint officers and captains as he chose, and 'to invade and destroy the powers forces preparations or provisions' of the King of Spain or people not in league or friendship with the English Crown, which gave him a free hand for whatever actions he decided. There was no lack of volunteers to serve under him, including typical mariners like Abraham Birch 'whose life is only to be at sea and upon shore in a short time will spend more than his reward will come to.'[8]

The composition of the fleet and the adventurers emphasise the close interrelation of the financial and privateering aspects of Earl George's connections with the City of London. For the first and last time all the ships of his private fleet sailed together – the *Malice Scourge* 600 tons as his admiral's ship, the *Sampson* 300 tons captained by his relative Henry Clifford gent., the *Anthony* 120 tons, his frigate the *Discovery*, his black pinnace the *Scout*, with the *Guiana* 200 tons borrowed from Raleigh, and two barges for landing men. The largest city contributor, almost rivalling the Earl, was John Watts, the greatest of all privateering promoters, with six ships, the *Alcedo* 400 tons, *Consent* 350 tons, *Margaret and John* 200 tons, *Galleon Constance* 250 tons, *Affection* 120 tons, and *Pegasus* 80 tons. Moreover, Watts's son John, who had sailed with Lancaster in 1595, captained the *Scourge*. Garraway and Cordell's *Merchant Royal* 350 tons was the vice-admiral's ship. Garraway's *Ascension* 400 tons, which the Earl had twice sent out in 1597, was the rear-admiral's vessel. Garraway also contributed with William Cockayne the *Royal Defence* 190 tons, and Cordell his own *Centurion* 300 tons, the 'slug' of all the fleet. William Shute's *Prosperous* 400 tons was the other large merchantman. John Ley, captain of the *Alcedo*, had with him his own pinnace, the *Bark Ley*.

Cumberland's fleet, comprising fifteen ships, two frigates, a pinnace, and two barks, had a total burden of about 4,600 tons. Its real strength was the powerful *Malice Scourge* supported by the eight large consorts between 300 and 400 tons. The total complement of 1,790 comprised about 1,000 seamen and 700 soldiers, with many gentlemen volunteers in addition, the essential surgeons, carpenters and coopers, and two Portuguese pilots, one of whom, an elderly man, had been to Brazil twenty-eight times. The Earl sailed with the full dignity of one of the leading peers of the realm, with eighteen of his household on the *Scourge* and as his chaplain Dr John Layfield DD, Fellow of Trinity College, Cambridge, whose detailed description of the whole voyage is the most reliable as well as the most complete of the extant accounts. The captains and masters were men of long experience in sea warfare and oceanic privateering, such as John Watts jnr, James Langton, Robert Careless, William Wynter and Richard Knottesford; the boatswains, master gunners and most of the crews likewise.

On the other hand, the two regiments of 'soldiers' were described as largely raw and untrained, men who had been attracted to the Earl's colours by the prospects of adventure, plunder and alternative employment, as on most Elizabethan privateering ventures. Even if many had handled pikes, bills and muskets either at musters or on the recent royal expeditions, drilling would be essential to weld them into disciplined fighting companies. Their commanders were professional military men, veterans of the Spanish war, yet they too, as was

TABLE 6 *Cumberland's 1598 Fleet*

Ship	Size (tons)	Owners	Captains (O=Outward; H=Homeward)	Masters
Malice Scourge	600	Cumberland	O John Watts H James Langton	John Ellyot
Sampson	300	Cumberland	O Henry Clifford* H Christopher Colles	Andrew Shilling
Anthony	120	Cumberland	O Robert Careles* H Andrew Andrewes	O William Wynter H Anthony Danyell
Discovery (frigate)[1]	(50)	Cumberland	William Harper	Edward Smith
Scout (pinnace)	(20)	Cumberland	Henry Jolliffe	Henry Lake
Guiana[2]	200	Cumberland	O Christopher Colles H Gerard Middleton	Edward Godderd
Alcedo	400	John Watts	John Ley/Thomas Coche[3]	John Pokam
Consent	350	John Watts	Francis Slingsby	Samuel Spencer
Margaret & John	200	John Watts	Edward Dixson	John Newman
Galleon Constance	(350)	John Watts	Hercules Fulgeam	O Richard Knottsford* H Walter Pryse
Affection	120	John Watts	William Fleming	O Thomas Harding* H ?
Pegasus[1]	80	John Watts	Edward Goodwyn	R. Carr
Ascension	400	William Garraway	Robert Flick	O John Graunt* H William Wynter
Royal Defence	190	William Garraway & William Cockayne	Henry Bromley	Phillip Hilles
Merchant Royal	350	William Garraway & Thomas Cordell	Sir John Berkeley	Wyllyam Parfect
Centurion	300	Thomas Cordell	O Henry Palmer* H William Palmer (son)	O John Peryman H Bartholomew Keble
Prosperous	400	William Shute	O James Langton H John Watts	Robert Thornton
Bark Ley (pinnace)[3] Two barges[4]		John Ley		

Total 16 ships, two pinnaces, two barges – 20

Additions   Flemings and carvels captured off Portugal and Lanzarote. One Fleming was sunk at San Juan, two more, the *Kesar* and *Dove*, were among the nine prizes brought back.

Notes: * Died at San Juan.
1. *Discovery* lost off Ushant and the *Pegasus* on the Goodwin Sands, with forty men drowned.
2. Borrowed from Sir Walter Raleigh.
3. Ley left the fleet in his pinnace after Lanzarote.
4. One was deliberately sunk in the harbour entrance at San Juan, the other lost off Bermuda.

(*Source*: Richard Robinson's account (Williamson, pp. 178–9), with additional details on tonnage and owners.)

to be seen at Lanzarote, required firm control if they were to perform their tasks efficiently. Sir John Berkeley was second in command to the Earl, vice-admiral and colonel-general of all the forces, with sixteen land captains holding designated posts under him and others without specific duties. The senior officers were Captain William Meysey, lieutenant-colonel of the forces, Captain Hercules Foljambe, sergeant-major general, Captain Arthur Powell, lieutenant-colonel of the Earl's regiment, and Captain Arthur Milles, master of the artillery and provant master. Foljambe also captained the *Galleon Constance*.[9]

With two exceptions it was the city merchants who provided the capital for the Earl to equip and provision his own ships. In November he raised his first new loan by redeeming Eshton demesnes from Henry Denton and re-mortgaging them with the manor of Flasby for seven years to Robert Bindlose Esq., a northern gentleman, for £2,000, which gave him £1,500 in cash to pay for the early victualling mentioned above. Brancepeth again provided the largest sums for this enterprise. On 20 December the Earl sold the farm of Binchester to its occupant, Charles Wren, for £800, and mortgaged the rest of the property for £4,400 for one year to Bayning, Watts and Thomas Allebaster.[10] There was a difficulty over the Bolton Priory mortgage and again the city men came to his aid. Peter Houghton, the mortgagee, had died. There may have been a demand for the repayment of the loan; in any case, the previous arrangement could not stand. On the following day, Thomas Cordell and Robert Chamberlain, ironmonger of London, took over the Bolton mortgage and the property was conveyed to them and John Bird, William Shute, Haunceus van Huste, Giles Fleming, John Newton and Thomas Paradine. Huste was, rather surprisingly, a Spaniard, though long resident in London, the others all notable merchant privateers.[11]

Some of the £6,700 the Earl raised in November and December would meet his living expenses in London. Most, however, was used to furnish his ships. But this was not the sum of his new borrowings. William Shute supplied goods for his vessels worth £1,000 and also £200 in ready money on the Earl's own bond which he himself had taken up on credit.[12] Other merchants may have done likewise. It would be natural for them and in their interest to equip and victual his ships as well as their own. The Bolton mortage may have been largely credit for goods from Watts, Bayning and their fellows. This is another aspect of the merchants' collaboration with Earl George in his 1598 enterprise, besides contributing ships, financing him and, at the end, disposing of the plunder through their established market outlets. On the outward journey at least this fleet appears to have been quite well-victualled, with none of the common complaints about inadequate food and drink, as well it might with so many traders involved. Yet its relatively trouble-free voyage in this respect may have owed much to its success in capturing corn and wine ships off the Iberian coast.

The joint financial responsibilities for this business venture shared by the Earl and his fellow mercantile investors were delineated in a formal document. The agreement settled such essential questions as the conduct of the voyage, the valuing of prizes and the distribution of profits. The latter, after the payment of the Queen's dues, were to be divided into ten shares. What the Earl was entitled to and what proportion his was of the total investment are not recorded, judging

TABLE 7 *Cumberland's land captains, 1598*

Sir John Berkeley, Knt.	Colonel General (and captain of the *Merchant Royal*)
Captain William Meysey	Lieutenant Colonel and Marshal
Captain Hercules Fulgeam [Foljambe]	Sergeant Major General (and captain of the *Galleon Constance*)
Captain Arthur Powell	Lieutenant Colonel of the Earl's Regiment
Captain Lewys Orrell	
Captain Thomas Robartes	
Captain Henry Gill	
Captain Thomas Coche [Coache]	(captain of the *Alcedo* from Lanzarote)
Captain Hugh Starckey	
Captain Rookesby	
Captain Roger Tyrwhitt	
Captain Andrew Andrewes	Leader of the Earl's Company (and captain of the *Anthony* homeward)
Captain James Tottell [Tothill]	Leader of Sir John Berkeley's Company
Captain James Evans	Corporal of the Field
Captain George Carrell	Corporal of the Field
Captain John Man	Provost Marshall
Captain Arthur Milles	Master of the Artillery and Probant Master

Lieutenants included Cholmley and Belings

(*Source*: Robert Robinson's account (Williamson, pp. 178–9))

by the tonnage at least a quarter and possibly two-fifths. He was said to have 'the chiefest charge', with Bayning and Sir John Hart, a Yorkshireman and London grocer, as co-investors in the *Scourge*. The commissioners appointed to act for the merchants included four who contributed ships – Watts, Cordell, Garraway and Shute – together with Bayning, Lancaster, Moore, Allebaster, Leonard Holliday and Robert Walden. Allebaster was placed in charge of the records and accounts.[13]

Over a six-week period starting the same day as the Brancepeth mortgage – a busy time for his officers – Cumberland brought his private family financial and estate arrangements into line with his new commitments outlined above, making alterations as his circumstances changed. His prime concerns were to safeguard his Skipton estate and provide for his daughter. In an indenture tripartite concluded on 20 December between himself and the seven-year-old Lady Anne of the first part, his brother of the second, and William Ingleby, William Ferrand and Laurence Lister of the third, the Earl revoked the 1591 indenture and settled on his officers the castle, Honour and borough of Skipton in Craven with the manors of Silsden, Barden, Stirton, Thorlby, Crookrise, Embsay, Eastby,

Skibeden, Malham and Malham Moor, Halton, and other lands in Carleton and Broughton for 140 years. As before, male inheritance had precedence. The profits of these lands were to go first to the Earl during his life, then to his heirs male, then to the heirs male of Francis, then to his own right heirs. Lady Anne was to be provided for, though only as the Earl's daughter, not his sole heir. On his death, the assignees were to pay her £100 a year for her education until the age of seventeen or her marriage, and £3,000 within three years of her marriage if he got a son as heir, £6,000 if he did not. Francis had to enter into an obligation with Lady Anne for the payment of these sums with the revenues of Bolton Priory demesnes and various manors including Gargrave as her safeguard. These terms were subject to modification when he made his will and this he did within a month.[14]

Christmas and the New Year festivities perhaps came as a welcome break for Earl George and his advisers immersed in intricate and sensitive financial and family matters. The earliest of their tasks in the New Year was to assure the Yorkshire gentleman Henry Lindley, Essex's officer, that he for certain would get back all his money whatever the Earl's fate. Lindley was still owed £700 for the loan first negotiated in 1591 and he required a specific promise of repayment. This the Earl, Clifford, Wright and Ferrand gave him in an indenture dated 4 January 1598, whereby the money was to be handed over on the following 1 December at Lindley's dwelling house in the Poultry, London, commonly called the Sign of the Blue Bull. The statute he held from Earl George would then be cancelled.[15]

On 16 January, two days after the grant of the royal patent, the Earl made a new will, revoking all previous wills, including that made before his 1595 voyage and added to during his last sickness. Its only uncontroversial statement was his wish to be buried in Skipton parish church with as little cost as possible, saving some charitable contribution to the poor. For the rest, as in his earlier arrangements, there was a current of conflict between his duties to his wife and daughter and what he regarded as prior responsibilities to the Clifford inheritance, his brother, his officers and his many creditors. Although coolness in his letters to his wife already presaged their later separation, his dispositions in this will were generous to her. He requested his executors not only to ensure she enjoyed her Westmorland portion fully but also to recompense her for any loss she might suffer from encumbrances on her jointure lands. This she had a legal right to, by the jointure act. Earl George now also bequeathed to her for life his tithes in Westmorland. Furthermore, he allowed her all the household stuff at Skipton she would need to furnish her dower house, Brougham Castle, provided she did not alter that dwelling. He left to her the valuable lease of his house at Clerkenwell and – not a wife's entitlement in Tudor England – all her jewels and household stuff which were in the South at his death, except those things he gave to his brother.

Earl George was, likewise, more generous to his daughter than in the recent December indenture. Yet the new terms must have been even more unpalatable to Countess Margaret and Lady Anne. The Earl's more expansive attitude had a purpose, part bribe, part deterrent, to enforce their acceptance of his conviction that the inheritance must stay in the male line. Its effect was to emphasise the growing chasm between them. The Earl added to the £6,000 allowed Lady Anne in the indenture £4,000 more, when she married or reached the age of sixteen, to be paid in two instalments, the earlier obligation to ensure this still applying. The proviso was that she should not make claim as heir general to any of his castles and lands after his death while Francis or any of his male heirs were alive, or in any way disturb his possession. If she did, then payment of any sum was to be void. It had, he asserted, 'of late happened in lyke cases being a thing I have long feared, and which I seke by all meanes I can to prevent.'

The Earl's bequests to Francis give a special insight into his concept of obligation to his noble lineage and forbears and of his brother as the proper recipient of Clifford chattels accumulated over the generations instead of allowing them to go to his Bedford wife and a daughter who, if she married, would take them out of the family. Francis was by this will to inherit with the earldom the sheriffwick of Westmorland, the Christ Church tithes, all the furnishings in the Cliffords' castles and houses (other than what Countess Margaret needed), and the cannons, guns and armours stored there. Furthermore, Francis was to have the Earl's ships and whatever they brought back from this voyage, his apparel, jewels, parliament robes, coats, suits of armour, guns, swords, saddles and other military equipment, the appurtenances of a high Elizabethan nobleman.

He spelt out his maritime obligations, requesting his executors to ensure his followers in the forthcoming voyage received their due 'according to the Sea Custome' as by their agreement with him. He made the usual provision for his estate and household officers and servants, with special consideration for his 'trew kynde and old servants' Anthony Wright and Thomas Wilkes. John and Stephen Taylor were to enter Francis's service. His old servant Robert Oglethorpe was to have a gelding, Watty and Fergus Gleadstone given a house, and others, such as Richard Herbert, a tenement. His brother, Ingleby and Ferrand were to be the sole executors and 'with all diligent and honest care looke to the preservacon of the estate of my howse left behind me'. The two officers were to 'gyve honest and wyse Counsell' to Francis, a reminder of the burden his brother would bear should he inherit. Richard Hutton, left £100, was requested to continue giving his best advice, as the man with the deepest knowledge of the state of the House of Clifford.

Earl George's dispositions in 1598, however hurtful to his Countess and Lady Anne, were given weight, even royal sanction, by his choice of two of his four supervisers, his good friends and in some respects mentors, the two most influential of Queen Elizabeth's courtiers, Lord Treasurer Burghley and her favourite the Earl of Essex. The other supervisers were his 'loving and trew frendes' Judge Walmesley, to look after his concerns, and Sir Dru Drury to represent Countess Margaret's interests in the execution of the will. To show his love for them, Earl George left Burghley his best garter George, Essex a jewel worth £100, Walmesley his 'Germayne Clocke with two Bells' and one of his young horses at Skipton, and Drury £40. His other chief bequests were to his brothers-in-law Lord Wharton and Sir William Russell, who were to have his best and second best stoned horses, and to Sir William Bowes a gelding called Bay

Mettam. The Countess of Warwick, his most private confidante, was to have his board of mother of pearl.

It was on Burghley, Essex and the Countess of Warwick that Earl George thrust the most taxing responsibilities, that of advising and strengthening his brother in upholding the House of Clifford, serving the Queen and preventing disharmony in the family. 'I doe earnestly desyre and begg of them', he wrote, 'that if any unkyndnes happen (which I hope well shall not) betwixt my deare wyfe and loving brother, that they will use there best meanes both by persuations and aucthorytie to end yt'. He concluded by praying his wife and brother to shun occasions which might breed dissension between them. The elderly Burghley, who had kept an avuncular eye on George since his early wardship days, was to die in August 1598, while Cumberland was still at sea.[16]

The dispositions in the will were to be superseded in a minor way before the Earl sailed from the Thames for Portsmouth in the middle of February. The protection to Ingleby and Ferrand given in 1596 was now insufficient and had to be extended because of the Earl's much greater indebtedness and the reduced value of the Craven lordships due to mortgaging so many tenements. In a deed signed on 1 February 1598, he made the lands previously conveyed to Ingleby and Ferrand subject also to these new debts and, to give them added protection as well as enable them to pay the debts, he granted to them – instead of to Francis, as in the will – all his ships, their equipment and the proceeds of the enterprise, also his leases of Christ Church tithes and Spofforth woods and his ironworks just built there. The Earl's senior officers in London witnessed this deed, John and Stephen Taylor, Stephen Tempest, the lawyers Richard Hutton and Thomas Pickering, and two of his close personal servants, Richard Herbert and Richard Johns. The diversion of so much of his estate revenues to service his debts was to leave his officers in Craven short of ready money to pay day-to-day expenses there. William Ferrand the younger had to dig deep into his pocket for these, providing £1,000 on 29 April on a three-years' mortgage to him of the manors of Nesfield and Westhall, another hidden cost of the 1598 enterprise.[17]

Many of the Earl's companions also took the precaution of making their wills before they sailed. Sir John Berkeley's grounds were that he was 'uncertaine howe it will please god to dispose of me' on his intended voyage. His main bequests, to his brother, included 'my adventures', indicating he had a stake in the enterprise. The sergeant-major general, Hercules Foljambe Esq. of Moorhall, Derbyshire, from a substantial family in that county, took the extreme course of selling his estates, that is his capital messuage of Moorhall, his Yorkshire manor of Adwick-upon-Dearne, Sandal and Long Sandal and his other Derbyshire lands for £1,000 to Godfrey Platts of Whittingham, Derby. The cash would help cover his expenses and perhaps an investment too. The unstated terms of the bargain, 'for divers other good considerations', probably allowed his re-purchase should he return safely and with the means to do so.[18]

The 'extreme toil of infinite business and deep engagement in a sea preparation' was completed when Earl George wrote on 14 February to his old friend Archbishop Hutton of York, his last chance perhaps to wish 'your Grace best health, all happiness and long life to God's pleasure'. For the Earl himself, there was a parting shot from the quarrelsome Captain Monson, still resentful, who sent a challenge 'for having used some disgraceful words of him and his doings' when they failed to capture the treasure in Terceira in 1589. Cumberland ignored this and went on his way.[19] He could set sail with his mind at rest that, should he die, the original Clifford Westmorland and Skipton estates were protected from litigation by his creditors; his wife and daughter were provided for; his officers, who were friends as well as servants, would not lose their own estates and fortunes as guarantors of his great debts, and Francis would not lack support in inheriting the problems as well as the titles. Yet, apart from Westmorland and the Skipton Fee, all else was now at risk. What was at stake in 1598 was, unlike at any earlier period in his career, the survival of the landed estate which had sustained the eighth-ranking English earldom for over half a century.

As it happened, his fleet all but made a false start which might have jeopardised the whole venture. Thirty-eight Spanish flyboats were heading for Calais and, because his was the only available strong force equipped and ready, he was ordered by the Queen on 17 February to put to sea to do what service he could against them. Lord Admiral Howard's sensible opinion was that he should be told to keep to his purpose by which he would light on them in any case. This, indeed, is what happened after the merchantmen which had been at anchor in the Thames joined his fleet at Portsmouth and he set sail on 8 March 1598.[21]

There can be no doubt that, once at sea, Earl George was in complete command of the direction and conduct of the voyage. He had a clear idea from the outset of what he wanted to achieve and at every stage the decisions were entirely his. The advantages of undivided leadership by a resolute and, as it proved, resourceful and courageous commander are plain to see. There were five phases of action during the seven months voyage: off the Iberian Peninsula; at Lanzarote; at Dominican and the Virgin Isles; the main activity on Puerto Rico; and on the return journey at Flores in the Azores.

The Earl met but did not interfere with twelve Dutch vessels bound for England, other than to purchase two butts of wine on a bill of exchange. The *Sampson* also checked on two other Flemings and two Scottish ships from Leith, under Captain James Robinson, homeward bound with wine from Bayonne. The fleet called briefly at Plymouth to pick up more mariners before proceeding with a favourable wind to the Spanish coast. The first incident notable to Dr Layfield was at prayer on Monday 13 March, when the Earl noticed a gallant reading Ariosto's *Orlando Furioso*, popular courtier fiction which contained a risqué tale, of Giacomo.[22] After the service, with all the company present, he told the young gentleman 'that we might looke that God would serve us accordingly, if we served not him better', and warned that if he saw him do the same again he would throw the book overboard and turn him out of the ship.

The Earl's immediate objective was to try to capture the Portuguese carracks laden with European commodities and large quantities of coin as they set out from Lisbon bound for the East Indies. Were he to succeed, he would return to England with his great prizes after a short and triumphant privateering voyage. Trouble with the *Scourge*'s masts, especially the mainmast – a weakness of contemporary English naval design – forced the Earl to anchor off the Burling Islands near the Portuguese coast with only the *Guiana* and *Scout* as consorts and concealing his presence as best he could while his carpenters worked to make the mast safe by lashing ropes round it. 'I protest', he wrote, 'I would have given five thousand pounds for a new one; the greatest part of my strength both by Sea and Land having beene lost, if that ship had returned in this extremitie'. However, it was a relief, as Dr Layfield confessed, for the raw mariners like him who were seasick. They were taken ashore to recover, the Earl courteously visiting them briefly each day to check on their condition.

The rest of the fleet, beating up and down at sea well out of sight of the coast, captured some of the Calais ships, three Flemings carrying wheat and a French wine vessel, while the *Affection* took another Fleming which, unknown to the Earl, it sent back to England. On one of the shallops also captured was Garcia de Valdes, an old soldier whom Cumberland decided to keep with him on the *Scourge* because of his knowledge of the Spanish colonies. The Spaniard's description of the voyage both corroborates and adds to Layfield and the other English sources.[23] Another useful man taken later in a ship bound for Angola and added to the ship's company was Antonio Robles, a licentiate in physick.

The *Scourge* was sighted and joined at the Burlings by an English ship returning home, the *Hope Bonaventure* 180 tons owned by Richard Cornelius, a Southampton merchant, and captained by his factor Richard Duncombe. The Earl knew both men well. His servant James Whitley bought £30 worth of beer for the *Scourge* from Cornelius, who owned a brewery supplied by the brewer Thomas Heath, giving a bond for repayment. The *Hope* may have been the ship of similar name hired by the Earl in 1595. Duncombe gave the Earl the news he most wanted to hear, that the carracks had not yet left Lisbon. When 'a tall and stowte' ship came sailing towards them, the Earl sent the *Hope* to investigate. Duncombe requested the ship to strike for the Queen of England. Instead, he got 'foul words' and a shot from the ship's great ordnance.

Fearing it was too strong for the *Hope*, the Earl sent the *Scout* to help. But it fought so well that he suspected it was a king's man o'war and hastily slipped anchor to join in the struggle. It turned out to be a 240 ton Hamburg Levanter, the *St Marie*, which got in the first shots against the *Scourge* before the latter raked it. In the fight lasting two and a half hours the *St Marie* was shot through eight times before some of the *Scourge*'s crew lept from the forecastle onto her. Even so she got free and continued desultory firing until suddenly she yielded. The Earl's men had suffered casualties, three killed and five or six wounded, including Captain Greenwell, a veteran of Cumberland's 1594 voyage, who had a leg shot off. The *Scourge* had been hit in six or seven places, some of them very dangerous.

The *St Marie* was laden with corn, gunpowder, copper, sails and other merchandise for the West Indies which she meant to discharge at Lisbon on her way to the Levant. Since all were prohibited commodities, the Earl discounted the master's licence to trade issued under the great seal of the city of Hamburg. The next day was a Sunday and, after divine service, the rest of the day was spent removing those goods the *Scourge* required and setting aboard a prize crew to sail the *St Marie* to England. Juan Bocquel, a Brabant seaman taken from it was, like Valdes, to write a report on Cumberland's voyage for the authorities in Seville.[24] The *Hope* meanwhile recovered the *Scourge's* anchor from the Burlings shore.

Since both the *Scourge* and the *Scout* had used up much equipment and ammunition in the fight and put men aboard their prize, the Earl turned to the *Hope* for what else he needed. He told Duncombe he was 'in dannger to be cast awaie for want of victuall municon and other Tackle' to manage so large a warship as the *Scourge*. He persuaded the factor to let him have 80 men and all his other needs valued at £800 which made the *Scourge* again fully fitted out for a long voyage. He gave Duncombe a bond, and his word of honour, for repayment. Cornelius was later to claim in his lawsuit to recover this money that his ship, now short of seamen, was driven ashore and wrecked before it reached England. The *Hope* was therefore another casualty of the itch for adventure and plunder which took Duncombe and his crew, like so many Elizabethan merchantmen, away from their workaday trading into risky ventures and in this case disaster.[25]

With the *Scourge* now fully seaworthy, the Earl captured a French vessel carrying salt which, with his men on board, in turn surprised a Portuguese carvel fishing. Her crew confirmed that the five carracks and twenty-five other ships bound for Brazil were still at Lisbon. He rejoined Berkeley and the rest of his fleet wishing 'for nothing but an happy houre to see those long-looked-after Monsters, whose wealth exceedes their greatnesse, yet bee they the greatest ships in the world'. Unhappily, he learnt soon after, from another captured carvel, that his presence, suspected by the Portuguese, was now known owing to the garrulity of an English ship's master, Woosley, who had brought Spanish prisoners from England and had seen the Earl's fleet passing Plymouth.

On the off-chance the carracks were moored where they could be boarded, the Earl took the *Scourge* alone into Lisbon Bay to within sight of the ships – four carracks and a Molucca galleon laden with silver – which Captain Andrews scouted in a boat. He considered an attack on the castle of St Julian with its valuable 100 pieces of ordnance but the conditions were against him and he rejoined the main fleet to continue the voyage past the Rock to the Canary Islands. He chased two other shallops round the Cape until they came near the Sagres fortress, which fired a shot through the *Scourge's* sail and drove him away. Here ended the first phase of his enterprise, unlucky to fail in its surprise attempt on the carracks, yet with several prizes to its credit, two of which were added to the fleet as well as replenishing it with corn, wine and munitions.

The fleet, sailing down the eastern coast of the Canaries, reached Lanzarote Road on 13 April. Earl George had hopes here of capturing its governor, Marquis Agustin de Herrera, whose reputed great wealth would have brought a fine ransom. He landed his soldiers for training on a beach ten miles from Guarapay Castle, knowing 'many of them to bee very raw and unpractised'. Then he became unwell and was confined to his cabin with a cold for two days, leaving the vain search for the governor and the easy capture of the town and Guarapay Castle with its dozen brass pieces to Sir John Berkeley. The island, being poor, yielded little other than wine which the troops indulged, becoming disorderly, and some of their commanders too. Skirmishes with the inhabitants cost a few lives with others wounded. Informed by Berkeley of the trouble with the men the Earl went on shore on Easter Day to see the soldiers drill. He gave his first warning over discipline to the paraded forces, rebuking the captains for allowing the misbehaviour. Reading out the royal commission empowering him to act, he assured them that he would not be slow to punish offences. But for a good reason, which he was to explain to them later, he took no action this time.

Next day the fleet resumed its journey and was coasting off Tenerife when the *Royal Defence*, which had left Plymouth late, caught up with them, bringing word from a party of Frenchmen employed in Weymouth who had recently escaped from captivity in Lisbon that the carracks would, indeed, set sail. The Earl met his ships' commanders and they agreed it was worth spending a few days longer there in case the East Indiamen passed. However, they did not leave the safety of Lisbon Bay. Cumberland explains in his own account that missing such a 'fair fortune' did not much trouble him. The Caribbean was now his target. But, first, he had to convert his commanders to the new direction of the voyage. He called another meeting with all his captains and masters and encouraged full discussion on the question of continuing the voyage to Pernambuco. He then gave them his own reasons for not proceeding – that it was now too late for the best passage, the sickness aboard their ships might jeopardise the whole enterprise on so long a crossing, with their destination known the Spanish had sent 600 troops to strengthen Recife and would be ready to hide or destroy the sugar and brazilwood when they arrived.

Taking their silence as agreement, he surprised them by announcing that the West Indies, not Brazil, had been his real destination. Always a persuasive speaker, he won them over, soldiers, seamen and merchants' representatives, with a strongly-argued appeal to their eagerness for booty, reminding them of the plunder the Spanish settlements offered – the richness of Margarita, the pearl island, Puerto Rico with its silver mines, Santo Domingo, and the homeward-bound *flotas* to intercept in late July or August. Commanders and crews responded enthusiastically and the ships set off individually 'with greedie desire, and hopeful expectation' to rendezvous at Dominica. The courtier, mercantile and the Earl's private ambitions fused in a common purpose. Captain John Ley, disagreeing perhaps, left the fleet, sailing alone to the Orinoco in his pinnace, the *Bark Ley*.

The Earl himself was not quite done with the Canaries. He despatched the reliable Captain Slingsby in the *Consent* with Captain Jolliffe in the *Discovery* and the *Scout* as its eyes on a special mission to Las Palmas. What his instructions were and whether they accomplished the mission are not recorded. On the way to Puerto Rico the two small vessels parted company with the *Consent* to chase a prize, which they caught. Then the pinnace, leaking badly, had to be abandoned, her crew taking over and re-naming the prize which outsailed the *Discovery* to reach Puerto Rico first, but not until the fighting there was over.

With excellent navigation, the *Scourge* accompanied by the *Alcedo, Centurion* and the two Flemish corn ships reached Dominica on 23 May, the others mostly arriving the following day, anchoring in a bay large enough to take the whole fleet.

The men, especially the sick, refreshed themselves in a spring, as hot as that at Bath in Layfield's judgement, and huts were put up for the ill and wounded. The Indians, who according to the Earl hated the Spaniards and loved the English very much, traded potatoes, other foods and tobacco for swords, hatchets, knives, clothes and trifles. A couple of the captains enterprisingly rowed up river to a town where they were entertained by the local King with a meal and afterwards danced with his naked daughters.

Dominica, with its thick forests, was not suited for preparing the soldiers for the attack on Puerto Rico, so, after six days there, and with only Slingsby's ships and one of the Flemings missing, Cumberland led the fleet to the Virgin Islands which were uninhabited and had the space to muster the men ashore. All his attention now was on organising and planning the landing on Puerto Rico. He appointed field officers and the troops were divided into a dozen companies of eighty, the gentlemen volunteers making up numbers where needed. With Berkeley's own company exceeding eighty, there were almost 1,000 soldiers in the force. They were mustered – on Whitsunday – and trained in all sorts and phases of fighting. When this was completed they were all called together by drums.

Earl George now delivered to the assembled forces a second, much sterner warning on discipline, standing on a rock so that all might hear him. He explained that hitherto he had been lenient and patient because he had hoped for a short journey ending in the capture of the carracks and he 'thought it better to returne with everymans good word, then by just punishing of any to have their ill word at any returne.' Now, he stressed, they were on a different course which, though it might not prove so rich, would keep them abroad longer and bring more glory to God, more service to the Queen and country and more honour to themselves. Yet to achieve success he had to govern and direct while they had to obey. He had circulated the articles of discipline twenty days previously. From now on, he assured them, he would neither overlook ill-doing nor let any go unpunished. He was to be as good as his word.

All was set now for the attack on San Juan de Puerto Rico, though there was a difference of opinion between the Earl and his experienced officers on how to reach the island. Captain Langton and William Wynter, master of the *Anthony*, Edward Goodwin, captain of the *Pegasus*, who had sailed with Drake and Hawkins in 1595, and Richard Knottesford, master of the *Galleon*, Hawkins' pilot then, were all familiar with navigating the narrow channels through the Virgin Islands. The Earl, aspiring to be the first man to capture Puerto Rico and not the second through the Virgins, rejected their advice to follow the quicker if more dangerous passage, opting for the safer, circuitous route round the islands. This brought his fleet to Puerto Rico on its north-east coast on the direct approach to its fortified capital city of San Juan.

The Earl sent his knowledgeable officers, Langton and Knottesford, in a pinnace to seek a landing place, but they failed to discover one with night approaching. At dawn on Tuesday 6 June, the Earl himself spied a flat beach, ignored contrary opinions and with Sir John Berkeley rowed ashore where they found the long, smooth, sandy Bay of Cangrejos on which they could march towards the city. He again overruled objections, this time about the distance, saying that, having been sick and not being strong, he would himself lead at a moderate pace. 'Let me have no more speaking', he told his officers, 'but get your men all into your Boates, and follow in order as I have directed you.' With good heart and courage, he promised, they would have the maidenhead of Puerto Rico and with it the keys of all the Indies.

CHAPTER 10

The Great Puerto Rican Expedition: Defeat in Victory, 1598

The target of Earl George's forces was the military base of Puerto Rico, the small island of San Juan off its northern coast.[1] Less than three miles long by half a mile wide, it forms in its lea the natural, sheltered, deep-water harbour of El Tejar, entered through the broad harbour mouth to the west. The eastern arm of the sea is much narrower and shallower and was crossed by a bridge onto a causeway, the only link from the island to the mainland. El Tejar was, with Cartagena, one of the two great fortified harbours of the Spanish Caribbean. Its strategic value was constantly stressed and its importance as a port of call for the *flotas* from New Spain and Peru.

San Juan city, the second city of the Indies, stood on the side of a hollow hill in the western part of the island and was invisible from the sea except for the Dominican Friary on the hill, whose white outline was a guide to mariners approaching the harbour. Its population in 1590 was perhaps 765, dwelling in 170 houses.[2] Dr Layfield judged the city, with its handsome cathedral, three or four chapels, broad straight streets and houses in the Spanish style, as bigger and fairer than Portsmouth within its walls, though less so than Oxford. It had grown in size by a quarter in the past three or four years. The brick-built friary was 'a pretty Colledge'. With his scholar's vision, he thought it would stand well in the orchard of Queen's College, Oxford though doubting the gain if the orchard were to be lost. San Juan was 'exceedingly delightful' in its situation. Coconut trees, their fruit excellent, graced the city's avenues, and in the orchards and woods to its east grew limes and the 'goodliest Orenges' Layfield had ever seen.

Unlike Portsmouth or Oxford, however, San Juan's role was essentially military and administrative. Its men, involved in those duties, were of Spanish gentle and noble status brought up and trained in the skills of war and they also formed the island's militia. There were four small settlements and various scattered groups on the Puerto Rican mainland. This was sparsely populated, its gold mines worked out or stopped by royal command, what riches it had being raw commodities such as sugar, ginger and hides from its haciendas. These were owned by the leading families, who mostly lived in their San Juan town houses, and worked by negro slaves. Puerto Rico's importance was not economic but strategic, as 'the entrance and key to all the Indies', a base and harbour which as Captain Diego Menendez de Valdes, a former governor, affirmed Spain could not allow to fall into enemy hands.

San Juan's defences had developed slowly during the sixteenth century as the perceived threats to the island changed. Casa Blanca, a square crenellated building constructed about 1523 for the family of the first governor, Juan Ponce de Leon, was a fortified house rather than a fortress, a refuge from the attacks of the Carib Indians. The first permanent fort, La Fortaleza, begun in 1537 and essentially for the same purpose, had two-storey, medieval-style round towers facing the harbour and could shelter two hundred people within its courtyard behind its thick square walls. A ravelin and semi-circular parapet protected its doors. By 1570 it had become the King's House, a palace and residence of the governor (as it still is) and of other officials with charge of the documents and the royal strong box – the Chest of Three Keys – holding the island's subsidy from Spain's Council of the Indies. Its vaulted lower chambers were used as a munitions store and a prison.

La Fortaleza was badly sited and out of date as soon as it was built. Marauding corsairs, French first, then English, were the danger then. In 1539 work started on a new fort on the best site, El Morro, the headland overlooking the harbour entrance. There, where the land fell sharply a hundred feet down to the sea, a platform for a battery was made at the foot and a masonry tower built against the cliff connecting with a second gun emplacement at the top. El Morro fort, commanding the narrowest part of the entrance, was improved gradually during the next four decades.

It was the threat from the English privateers which forced Philip II to fortify San Juan island during the 1580s. Governor Menendez de Valdes identified the vulnerable places on the island and started work on them in 1582. Four years later Fieldmaster Juan de Tejeda and his Italian military engineer Juan Baptista Antoneli came to the Caribbean to draw up plans to establish defences at ten key sites to protect the Spanish settlements and shipping, the *flotas* most of all. These included San Domingo, Cartagena, Havana, Panama and San Juan. They returned in March 1589 to lay out the main defences at El Morro. The island's fortifications were largely completed when Sir Francis Drake made his vigorous but unsuccessful attack in November 1595, but other improvisations made then became permanent. Cumberland's forces were thus committed to breaking through well-planned defensive sites which had already been put to the test by the greatest of the Elizabethan naval commanders.

The premise on which Philip II's military experts based their plans for San Juan was that the city and port could be assaulted in only two ways, through the harbour entrance or over the causeway and bridge from the mainland. To protect the harbour mouth, they completed the citadel of El Morro by enclosing the promontary with a landward wall, creating a fortress triangular in shape. El

Morro was impregnable seawards because of the steep cliffs, shoals, rocks and pounding surf. Most of its thirty cannon were housed in three tiers of outward-facing gun emplacements, one at sea level, a second higher up the cliff and on the headland itself two more, the smaller directed towards the sea, the larger towards the harbour. These emplacements thus controlled the approaches and harbour entrance. Furthermore, to anchor at sea out of range of these guns was dangerous, as Drake found in 1595. Layfield regarded El Morro to the seaward as the strongest fortification he had ever seen – more impressive, therefore, than Dover Castle, Lisbon or Sagres – and fitted with 'the goodlyest ordyneence' placed to the best possible advantage. He considered no ship could pass without being sunk.

Landwards, El Morro was less formidable, as Layfield noted, but the form of its construction gave an appearance of solidity. There, Tejeda had laid out a single wall in the form of a hornwork across the headland to protect the seaward batteries and enclose an area large enough to hold 3,000 people. The wall, set on properly-laid foundations, was constructed of mamposteria, a concrete of lime mortar mixed with stone or brick spalls, faced with coursed, dressed stone and had a slight batter. It was essentially a parapet, without shelter for troops. The two half-bastions, faced with kiln-baked Roman-Spanish bricks, had platforms and embrasures for landward-facing cannon, the stronger on the harbour side named 'Austria' in honour of Philip II's dynasty, the other, 'Tejeda', on the Atlantic. In front was a narrow moat to add height and give protection to the walls. The central gate was guarded by a small ravelin with cannon embrasures to cover the approaches.

Within the citadel were the guardhouse, two magazines for ammunition and food for either bulwark, and a large cistern for the water supplies. From its heights, El Morro landwards overlooked the city and could only be approached over a long expanse of open ground. Properly garrisoned and victualled, Layfield reckoned, it was capable of withstanding a long siege. Sir Thomas Baskerville recorded the impression the citadel made on Drake's men. They found it 'otherwise fortefied then we expectid, for upon the entrance of the harborow stod a castell of quarid stone having 2 greatt Bolwarkes with Cavalliers towardes the Land and 3 plattformes on above the other towardes the sea upon which stod mor then 30 pecis of cannon and collvering.'[3]

Any fleet which succeeded in running the gauntlet of El Morro faced three more gun emplacements. One was next to the citadel, the others on small headlands at Santa Elena, a four-gun battery which inflicted most of the damage and casualties during Drake's night attack in 1595, and Santa Catalina. There was no redoubt on the low-lying land at El Tejar. The practice was to dig trenches there for artillery and musketeers to stop an enemy force getting a foothold and reaching the city by way of the harbour. La Fortaleza had walls seven feet thick and, properly garrisoned, could hold out against all but siege artillery.

San Juan's northern coast was regarded as too hazardous for ships to essay a landing because of its shallow waters, reefs and rocky shoreline. San Domingo friary, on its hill almost level with El Morro, could be fortified, and a gun platform below it looked out to the Atlantic. On a foreland at the eastern end of the coast stood another gun emplacement, El Morrillo, whose three cannon were intended to drive enemy ships away towards the harbour. The sea at the eastern approaches was only a few fathoms deep and rocky. It was held that even ships' boats would have difficulty in reaching land there. Even so, because that was feasible, an emplacement for two pieces at El Cabron, and a fort at El Boqueron, where the arm of the sea narrowed to the distance of a caliver shot, covered the shoals there and in the small bay leading to the causeway. El Boqueron fort, housing five cannon, was called 'Mata Diablo' – 'devil killer' – by the Spanish because it was thought (mistakenly) that Sir John Hawkins had been killed by fire from its guns. To Cumberland's men this two-storey enclosed building was the Red Fort, probably because it was constructed or faced with red brick, like the bastions; if so, this was a recent strengthening of the eastern defences.

It was a shot from a demi-culverin taken to El Boqueron which killed Sir Nicholas Clifford and Mr Brute Brown, wounded other officers and knocked Drake off his stool at supper in the *Defiance* on 12 November 1595, the day Hawkins died. Sir Francis was considering landing on the coast until the cannon fire from these eastern defences forced him to stand off. Not until his fleet anchored off El Cabron was it realised in San Juan that the sea there was just deep enough for big ships, which soundings later confirmed. This was one lesson the defenders learnt from Drake's attempt on the island. Even so, the eastern gun emplacements had proved their worth and persuaded Drake to attack past El Morro instead.

The island's most vulnerable point was at the causeway and bridge, El Puente, on its south-eastern corner. To force a passage there, however, would be difficult. The causeway on the mainland side was narrow and rough, with room for only three men abreast. Where the bridge joined the causeway midway, progress was obstructed by a barricado – a strong, lockable timber gate. On the island stood a fort, known to the English as San Antonio, constructed of timber palisades and housing six pieces of cannon, with wooden sheds to protect them from the weather. Its guns and the muskets of the garrison covered the bridge, causeway and the mainland approaches.

Compared with the time of Drake's attack, San Juan's defences were more secure, because of recent work on them, and were well equipped with cannon, altogether eighty good brass pieces. The garrison comprised 14 artillerymen and 334 infantrymen. In other ways, the island was less prepared to face a concerted attack. The population had been weakened by one of the periodic outbreaks of dysentery as well as a severe shortage of corn in the city and the whole countryside, the garrison as much as the civilians, though Layfield was informed that only two people, both elderly, had died in the city. Lack of pay besides the rationing of bread, it has been claimed, put the troops in a truculent mood; certainly, the ship carrying the money from Havana had not yet arrived. However, these and other shortcomings were not articulated until Earl George's tactics had effectively delivered the island to the English troops.

He was obviously aware of El Morro's reputation, because he chose his own course, different from both of Drake's lines of attack. He and his officers, however, had no inkling of what his mainland advance entailed, except that San

Juan island was linked to the mainland by a bridge. The English commanders were to be unpleasantly surprised when they came to El Boqueron and then El Puente. It may seem odd that the Earl had neither procured nor appears to have been aware of Sir Thomas Baskerville's *Discourse*, his description of San Juan's defences based on Antoneli's which he had purloined at Panama on Drake's voyage. Both Burghley and Francis Throckmorton had copies.[4] Possibly the secrecy of the Earl's real objective, keeping it from the Lord Treasurer's ears, also deprived him of this exceptional source of military intelligence, although the Baskervilles were servants of Essex. Likewise, the Earl was ignorant both of conditions and the strength of the Spanish military in the city; hence the combination of dash and caution which characterised his assault on the island's defences.

The governor of San Juan de Puerto Rico was Captain Antonio de Mosquera, a forty-four-year-old professional soldier with thirty-two years service in Philip II's armies and as governor in Flanders and other regions of the Spanish Empire, who had arrived on the island on 9 April 1597. Present in the city also were his immediate predecessor, Captain Pedro Suarez Coronel, who had been in charge when Drake was beaten off, and the other former governor, Diego Menendez, on whose original ideas the island's defences were based. In terms of experience, the citizens could hardly have been better served. But Diego Menendez, a strong personality and a veteran of the Florida campaigns before he became the first captain-general of Puerto Rico, had quarrelled with at least one of his successors, a matter of professional jealousies. Governor Mosquera, likewise, was at odds with Diego Menendez, the latter's son-in-law Captain Francisco de Lanzos, and Judge Alcazar de Villasenor, who seem to have looked down on him as a 'gallego' even if the main issue between them was rivalry over authority and jurisdictions. At one stage he had, in fact, arrested Menendez and Lanzos for disrespect and they were regarded as his enemies. This disharmony among the island's leaders played some part in their failure to withstand the Earl's attack. Their later recriminations have to be viewed with caution. Mosquera's opponents, seeking their own exculpation, blamed him for their collective defeat, Villasenor itemising his supposed errors. The former governor's shortcomings became more apparent after the loss of San Juan than before the conflict began, a common fate for the vanqished in any age.

As with Drake, the island had early warning of Earl George's fleet. News reached San Juan from the Canaries at the end of May – the source being two Scottish ships – and later sightings confirmed the Earl's presence in the vicinity. Mosquera's response was energetic and confident. He informed the city militia captains and municipal authorities at once and discussed with them the defensive measures to take. In both these and his troop dispositions, Mosquera followed precisely the lines of the successful commanders in 1595, with some changes based on the experience gained then. He called a general muster, assembling 150 of his own soldiers and perhaps another 600 men from outside as well as within the city. Because of the food shortage he lodged his men outside the city. Compared with the raw English troops, the San Juan militia were veterans, having helped fight off Drake's much bigger force only a good two years earlier.

Anticipating an attack by Cumberland similar to Drake's at the harbour entrance, and fearing a landing on the mainland there beyond the range of El Morro's guns, Mosquera blocked the Channel at El Canuelo with stones and brush and prepared to hang a chain across (brought with him from Spain for that purpose) so as to make it impassable to boats. He built a blockhouse on El Canuelo islet to defend it and a gun emplacement on the mainland to cover the chain's anchorage. He erected another blockhouse at the mouth of the Bayamon river and a series of elaborately contrived trenches with eleven-feet terreplanes where harquebusiers could bar any advance along the shore. By the waterside at El Tejar, he had a strong ditch dug to impede any landing, as in 1595.

A second danger would be the seaward entrance at El Boqueron. Mosquera claimed he built the fort there. If this was the brick edifice replacing a gun platform, he may have been correct. He mounted three brass pieces at El Boqueron (the English said five) and sank stakes in the shallows to obstruct boats. When a lookout and then his cavalry brought news of Cumberland's landing in Cangrejos Bay, the Governor mustered 60 or 70 sailors from the six or seven ships in the harbour and employed some of them to hang the chain at El Canuelo. Others would be specialist gunners. Because San Antonio fort's cannon faced mostly south and could not fully cover the bay, he ordered the lightest draught frigate to move in near El Puente to give support, but it took two days to work it through the shallow waters into position, by which time the attack had begun. He inspected the defences before the Earl's fleet arrived.

As the English troops disembarked, Mosquera distributed arms, powder and ammunition and assigned his captains and men to their posts. Captain Bernabe de Sierralta, a municipal councillor of the city and commissioned to be Alcalde (mayor) of La Espanola, garrisoned San Antonio fort with 50 soldiers and militia to hold the bridge. Captain Don Gaspar Troche with Captain Lanzos's sergeant Hernan Sanchez and a number of musketeers manned El Boqueron fort. Captain Alonso de Vargas took charge at El Cambron, as in November 1595. Captain Lanzos himself held El Morrillo. Mosquera made similar dispositions at Bayamon and, where necessary, at the other redoubts. The remaining forces he held together in the city, to guard the harbour and reinforce where necessary, just as Coronel had done against Drake. He went round to inspect the defences in person.

It took Cumberland's officers two hours to land his 700 soldiers in pinnaces and boats onto Cangrejos beach, nine miles from San Juan city, unopposed; not one got his arms or powder wet. The troops formed up in seven companies of musketeers, harquebusiers and pikes, and the volunteers joined on behind, making almost 1,000 in all. With St George and personal banners aloft, they marched up the sandy shore following the Earl's blood-red colours carried at the head by Captain Andrews, with El Morro in sight all the way and the sea to cool themselves in. When they reached El Boqueron inlet, the Red Fort with its ordnance and musketeers prevented their crossing the mere sixty yards of the Channel. The gunners fired a piece or two at them. At first nonplussed, Cumberland and Berkeley began to look for the place where the horsemen who had watched them disembark must have crossed. At the flat bay a little beyond, they were fired at with one or two shots from the great ordnance at San Antonio fort.

A captured negro told them about the bridge and guided them further round the narrow headland through the 'wickedest' wood the Earl had ever seen, and then several miles more round the lagoon. Many of the troops, burdened by their heavy pikes, muskets and other arms, came near to fainting in the great heat and only the large number of horses they captured enabled the weariest, Layfield among them, to keep going. About sunset they reached the causeway where they found Aguilar bridge drawn up, the barricado shut, and Sierralta's garrison with their six cannon in the fort barring their passage, five Spaniards observing their approach. With their troops exhausted and the defenders alerted, Cumberland and Berkeley could do nothing more. But from another negro they learnt that the sea channel could be waded beside the causeway at low tide, the next being early morning, at two o'clock. They set a watch for it and led their columns back to a large grassy space beside the lagoon, to rest and eat after their gruelling day's trek.

The prospects for the Earl's force had now proved daunting. There was no chance of a successful storming of San Antonio or El Boqueron in daylight against cannon and muskets firing at point-blank range. The odds were heavily against taking the bridge even under cover of darkness, with the water in the inlet still deep even at low tide, but this they had to attempt. Two hours before dawn, the soldiers were awakened and fallen in. Berkeley, fearing exclusion from the honour and glory of battle, questioned whether Cumberland's company should have the van for the second day and the Earl expose himself to danger. They compromised. Earl George conceded the van but insisted on being at the front. He donned his fine starred armour and others followed suit.

For two hours or more in the dark Berkeley's company attacked the causeway 'with great spirit', as the militia captain Francisco Delgado, who commanded at

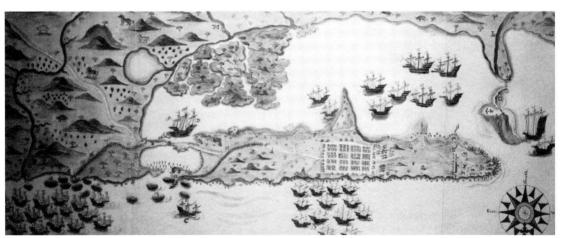

Cumberland's attack on San Juan, 1598. The illustration includes: the landing; the causeway at El Puente; the Flemish ship grounded; the Spanish frigate; El Boqueron, 'The Red Fort', 'Mata Diablo'; El Morro; Cumberlands's siege batteries; La Fortaleza; the friary; Rivers Toa, Bayamon, Piedras, Luiza; the 'Governor's island' and El Canuelo

Santa Elena, recorded. But there was no way they could enter the gate. Many of the men waded through the water to get at it because of the ruggedness of the causeway. Twice Berkeley himself went so far that had he not been able to swim he would have drowned. There was close-quarter fighting at the gate with English bills against Spanish pikes. The company suffered losses from the cannon shot as well as musketfire from the fort. A piece called a murtherer, sited at a port by the gate, caused most casualties.

The Earl himself was at the forefront of the assault, encouraging his men, and drove his dagger into the bridge. But he came close to losing his life when he overbalanced into the water, struck by a musketball or pike which his good armour withstood, so Garcia de Valdes and the Spanish defenders thought, or accidentally tripped by the man who bore his target according to Layfield. Borne down by the weight of his armour he would have drowned but for Serjeant-Major Hercules Foljambe (aptly named) who struggled to hold him up until others helped carry him onto the causeway, where he was still exposed to bullets, very sick from the sea-water he had swallowed.

Berkeley's men called for dry shot and pikemen to help them and the Earl's own company came up under his colours to reinforce them. But as day began to break and the tide turned they were in greater danger from the rising waters and the gunners, who could now better sight their targets. Fifty musketeers were left in ambuscades near the causeway to keep up fire on the fort while the rest of the companies were withdrawn to the grassy area where the surgeons attended the wounded. From there they were marched back to the sea where the Earl had arranged for victuals to await them, brought from the fleet which was now anchored off El Boqueron beyond cannon range. In this first attack, Berkeley's troops alone had spent over 3,000 bullets, the Spanish, defending well, hardly fewer. Cumberland's forces had suffered in casualties under fifty dead and wounded, among them Lieutenants Cholmley and Belings. San Antonio's garrison lost five dead and nineteen wounded, including Captain Sierralta with a musket ball through both legs. Mosquera sent the former governor Diego Menendez to replace him with 150 reinforcements. Cumberland's first attack thus ended in failure against the sturdy resistance of Sierralta's soldiers and militia; the weak point of the San Juan's defences had held and appeared likely to do so again if the Earl mounted any more direct assaults whether by night or day. The Spaniards rejoiced, mocking his musketeers in English.

A 'murtherer' of the kind used at the barricade on the causeway

Earl George was still very ill and had to be taken aboard the *Scourge* to recover. However, his mind was too restless to sleep. Balked at Aguilar bridge, he conceived a plan to turn the defences by landing men above El Boqueron fort, then capture it, which would enable him either to land all his forces there or continue his attack on San Antonio fort. He really needed the bridge, intact, to march his companies across more speedily and safely than ships' boats allowed. After a few hours rest he came ashore to put his scheme into effect, at whatever cost. To keep the Red Fort's garrison occupied, he placed fifty musketeers on the shore opposite, and from an entrenchment built with large stones, they opened up fire. The musketeers near the causeway likewise pinned down the troops at San Antonio and prevented them going to the aid of those at El Boqueron. He ordered one of the big Flemings to run close in to the shore (where such a ship had never before ventured) and after it wrecked the distance of a musket-shot from the beach it played its cannon onto both the Red Fort and also the bridge itself. One shot dislodged a gun in the fort and killed two of the troops manning it.

At five o'clock in the afternoon, under cover of the Fleming's artillery fire and the musketeers' bullets, five pinnaces carrying 200 men, under Captains Coach and Orrell, came up behind the ship and landed on the little beach at Escambron only a musket-shot from the Red Fort. Don Gaspar Troche led out twenty men to resist and 'skirmished gallantly' for a while, supported by Sergeant-Major Juan de Cavillas, but they were heavily outnumbered and retreated. The defenders now abandoned the fort and disappeared into the woods, the English soldiers taking possession 'with shouts of victory.' One Spaniard who was in hiding in an upper room they killed. Their orders were to make the place good and occupy it, since it was vital for the next phase of the Earl's attack and he had no means of knowing Spanish strength and the likelihood of a counter-attack.

With control of the bridge his objective, the next stage of his plan was to ferry more soldiers across the bay from a neck of land nearer San Antonio so as to take that fort and the bridge from the rear, while his garrison at El Boqueron protected his flank and also covered the sea approaches and the Channel. He ordered Captain Langton, in charge of the boats, to bring them into the bay. As he did so, the frigate fired five or six shots from its great ordnance without doing any damage to the boats, and Langton's men in turn killed some of the garrison passing from the fort to the frigate. With the water again at a low ebb, the stakes hampering the boats and the moon bright enough for the frigate's cannon to be dangerous, Cumberland deferred crossing until nearer dawn the next day. But from the neck of land with its clear view of San Antonio, his troops perceived that the fort was now empty. The Earl sent Captain Rookesby with three or four men to investigate and the captain got no answering fire when he threw stones over the wall. The garrison had, in fact, been evacuated by the frigate and the bridge was now undefended. Not knowing what kind of resistance he would meet on the island and in the city, Cumberland returned his weary troops back to the grassy place so that they would be fed and fully rested for the morrow's advance.

In fact, the shock of the invasion of San Juan island and the loss of El Boqueron had disheartened Mosquera and the other leaders. San Antonio fort was abandoned on his orders and the garrisons at El Cabron and El Morrillo withdrawn – some soldiers and militia deposed that their commanders had fled on seeing the enemy had landed. Mosquera himself fell back to the city and then retreated further with all his available soldiers and militia, women and children too, into El Morro. There was some panic in San Juan. Many soldiers and citizens took boats to the mainland or into the mangroves, among them Captain Vargas, who went to Bayamon, Judge Villasenor to St German, and the treasurer, Gutierre Munoz de Moya who, under the pretext of conveying the Chest of Three Keys to safety, fled with his family and household belongings. The Bishop went into the country. All the friars, except for one old man, left San Domingo convent for safer havens.

While it was still dark the English forces re-formed, and on Thursday at daybreak, Cumberland and Berkeley led their two columns, one across the bridge and the other from El Boqueron, converged and then marched the mile and a half to the city with flags flying and drums beating. It was on this stretch, Layfield concurring with Mosquera's critics, that the Spanish missed their best opportunity to counter-attack by ambushing while the English could advance only three abreast over a narrow road and were wearying themselves dragging with them the captured cannon. A determined stand here might have inflicted heavy casualties. Instead, the English companies entered the city unopposed. All the able-bodied men had left. The women, elderly and disabled men who remained were put in the charge of the Provost.

The Earl quartered his officers in the principal houses of San Juan, where he set up seventeen corps de garde, with their flags flying. For himself, he chose the Bishop's residence which he made his own headquarters. His soldiers took over La Fortaleza, where they found 200 barrels of powder, ball and cartridges, spades and other implements. To secure their position, the Earl and Berkeley fortified the city, setting up barricades in the principal streets beyond the houses. From there, following standard practice in laying siege, they extended trenches to within a musket shot of El Morro. One trench was based on the Dominican Friary and another lay between the Casa Blanca and the enclosing wall which ran towards El Morro. Here again Mosquerra missed an opportunity, failing, except now and then, to fire his cannon at the English as they dug their earthworks (with spades from the castle) and took up position in them. His critics were to claim that the gun carriages had rotted and they could not properly be used. A more cogent reason will become plain later.

Earl George's object, now that he was firmly in control of the island, was to establish an English garrison. He therefore wanted to seize the citadel with as little loss of life and damage to its fortifications as possible. But there was some urgency because his fleet, his life-line to England, would be endangered at its anchorage out to sea should a storm blow up. His plan was to invest El Morro, using numerous boats rowed in via the El Boqueron channel to keep watch day and night to prevent food supplies reaching the besieged. To hasten the surrender, he brought ashore four of the *Scourge*'s large iron guns – two culverins and two demi-culverins – which, with four of the captured brass pieces, formed two batteries of siege artillery on gabions constructed for them in trenches, one in front of the monastery, the other Casa Blanca. The strenuous job of unlading and hauling the 14-ft, 2-ton cannon with plenty of shot and implements via Aguilar bridge and readying them took a full week. His emplacements were completed on Saturday 17 June, but the Earl delayed opening the bombardment until after the Sabbath.

On Monday 19 June his culverins battered all day at El Morro's Austria half-bastion until all their shot was used up and then the other pieces continued. Spanish troops who appeared on the parapet were driven off by the cannon-fire, the bulwark's guns dislodged and the wall itself breached. On the Tuesday the culverins' target was the Tejeda bulwark, whose guns covered both the gateway with its ravelin and the breach already made. By mid-day they too had been dislodged. When it next rained, Layfield believed, the cavaleros on which the Spanish guns had stood, being sandy earth, would crumble.

Unbeknown to the English, El Morro was ill-prepared to withstand a long investment. It lacked food and especially water for the garrison, let alone the citizens who had crowded in. The city itself had suffered a severe shortage of flour and maize and supplies had only just arrived. Mosquera had neglected or just had no time to move the ships' cargoes into the magazine. Instead, the meal fed the English. Water was even scarcer. The citadel's cistern was defective. There was only one day's supply inside El Morro and another five days' in a deposit outside, got only by skirmishing. Although it was the rainier season, none had fallen for a month. The 400 people inside soon suffered privation. The English had no such problems; there were wells and a large stone conduit on the mainland and every house had its own cistern, the underlying water being brackish.

Mosquera was to be criticised for not occupying La Fortaleza which had plentiful supplies of food and water, besides arms and ammunition. However, it would have been equally at the mercy of Cumberland's culverins. Captain Lanzos, the defiant spirit among the defenders, begged the governor to give him 150 soldiers, of his selection, for a night sortie against the English in the city when, he argued, they would as usual be drunk. Mosquera refused this, but let him have 50 harquebusiers, which he led out of El Morro in search of water. In a skirmish, it was claimed, he captured one of the English captains and put his men to flight.

Bad as were the shortages in the citadel, worse was the morale. Coronel was heard to say openly to soldiers after the fall of El Boqueron 'We'll go to El Morro and we'll eat four grains of maize and make an honourable showing against the enemy and then we'll abandon the place because we cannot do anything else.' The soldiers and householders were unwilling to risk their lives in a lost cause. Mosquera might just have hoped Cumberland would plunder and then move on. The turning point in the siege was the desertion of two foreigners in the garrison, a Flemish artilleryman named Lorenzo and a French soldier, who described conditions inside El Morro and stated that the beleaguered occupants were dying of hunger.

Mosquera and Coronel, resigned to the fact that Cumberland would now be aware of the privations, sought and obtained a truce from him, offering to capitulate on honourable terms. The parley took place in a large, fair room in the Bishop's house, crowded by the English captains and masters. The Earl rejected their demands, refused to use any language in the negotiations but English and imposed his own surrender terms. These allowed the defenders to retain their flags, wear their rapiers and daggers, and thirty harquebusiers carry their guns and short match. The Earl, furthermore, promised them passage from Puerto Rico to another Spanish possession. Mosquera and Coronel accepted, dined with the Earl on the morning of Wednesday 21 June and then yielded the citadel, marching out with 260 soldiers besides citizens and womenfolk, perhaps 400 in all and many of them sick and sore. Cumberland and Berkeley took over El Morro and raised the flag of St George to signal occupation in Queen Elizabeth I's name. Next day, the Earl's fleet sailed into El Tejar harbour. He housed Mosquera, Coronel and Captain Lanzos under guard in Juan Lopez Correa's house and dined with them daily. The rest of the prisoners, disarmed now, were confined in La Fortaleza. The English casualties in the siege could hardly have been lighter, only two men lost, killed by a cannon shot from El Morro.

Earl George had attained in a two weeks campaign what he had confidently promised, the capture of the Virgin City of the Indies which had thwarted Sir Francis Drake two and a half years before. No matter the island's weaknesses or the errors of its leaders, it was the unexpected direction of the Earl's attack and, especially, his tactics which the soldiers and householders later testified opened up San Juan's defences. Mosquera's severest critics, Judge Villasenor included, had anticipated a direct assault on the lines of Drake. They had no qualms about El Morrillo, El Cabron, El Boqueron and the bridge defences holding off the English. The Earl, rejecting the advice of Drake's associates and his professional colleagues, pressed ahead with his own considered eastern thrust and, when balked by El Boqueron and San Antonio forts, switched to an amphibious attack with the Fleming's guns and his musketeers neutralising the Spanish garrisons. Thereby he gained a strong point on the island and control of the sea arm towards the bridge. With this surprise move he wrested the initiative from the defenders, whose nerve failed them. At the last, Mosquera might have denied Cumberland the thirty pieces of artillery on El Morro's platforms, as Villasenor claimed. But the latter was safe at St German and anxiety for an honourable surrender dictated otherwise to Mosquera and Coronel.

Cumberland's was a spectacular success, one of the considerable achievements of the English oceanic effort in the Spanish war. As he himself was to point out, San Juan had been thought impregnable. He had captured the stronghold with largely untrained men who had never seen land-service and when the garrison had twenty days notice of his coming. Never anyone, he thought, had lost fewer men. His care for his troops and his personal behaviour had been exemplary. The authorities in San Juan had learnt the lessons of Drake's attack, but Cumberland even more so, because it was the originality of his tactics which negated Mosquera's careful dispositions and, the mark of an able tactician, wrong-footed the defenders. The Earl brought tenacity and subtlety both to the invasion of San Juan island and then the investment of El Morro; the qualities of a careful and determined commander with a mind of his own. As Michael Oppenheim concluded, the Earl had shown 'capacity for command of a very high order both in governing his force and in handling it.' Captain Monson was large-minded

Thomas Cockson's equestrian engraving of Cumberland, with the San Juan campaign as background

enough to call his expedition the greatest undertaking by any subject without the help or assistance of the Queen and achieved by so great a person who, by his earlier voyages, had attained a 'perfect knowledge' of maritime affairs.[5]

In control of San Juan island, the Earl directed himself to strengthening its fortifications, helped by the large quantities of captured munitions, and to easing the occupation. His intention, to garrison the island with 500 or 600 men until the Queen ordered otherwise, was common knowledge to his soldiers and to Spaniards like Garcia de Valdes who were kept informed by the Catholics in his forces. The English soldiers said that if they remained they would send for their wives. It was understood, too, that the Earl had ordered a ship home to ask for reinforcements and that, if they came, his intention was to attack Cartagena or perhaps San Domingo. The Earl certainly considered this, looking for greater profit than Puerto Rico offered and with the 'desire hee had his Adventurers should become gayners.' But he had the full support of his officers and soldiers in staying at San Juan. They, too, were infected by enthusiasm to hold the island as an English base after their resounding victory. All were eager to remain there in the garrison in surroundings which were most pleasing to the eye and the senses.

As he had threatened on the Virgin Isles, the Earl kept firm discipline. He publicly disarmed a very good soldier 'for over-violent spoyling a Gentlewoman of her jewels.' At a court-martial he enforced the articles against defacing churches and molesting women. He hanged a soldier in the market square for the latter offence, who had shown notable courage in the fighting, and reprieved a sailor for the former only because of his dependence on the crews for the return to England. As Layfield recorded with relief, these 'few but notable examples of justice have since held us in much better terms of ruly obedience.' But he noted the damage done by soldiers to the shrines in the cathedral, a sign of hatred and Protestant animosity towards Spanish imperialism and Catholicism.

Good order was also a prerequisite for the cooperation of the San Juan citizens which the Earl sought. By proclamations he offered them passage to leave the island or kind treatment if they decided to reside under his government. The negroes and negresses, all slaves, he freed, telling them they were not subject to service or captivity and giving them clothing and other gifts. With this they went over to his side, as Francisco Delgado bitterly reported, serving as guides and showing his men the sugar estates, farms and roads on mainland Puerto Rico. Some of the English soldiers lost their lives, killed by villagers as they searched for food, sugar, ginger, the non-existent gold mines and other plunder on the mainland. There was some pillage and the sparse population of Puerto Rico suffered from the occupation. Some of the accounts were no doubt exaggerated, special pleading when requesting aid from the Spanish Crown. The church authorities, for instance, claimed that their two sugar plantations had been burnt by the heretics and the haciendas and other buildings destroyed, which meant loss of most of their revenues in 1599.

How far Cumberland was aware of this is uncertain, for he never left San Juan island. The churches were stripped, perhaps by Berkeley's men after the Earl himself had quitted Puerto Rico. The holy altar pieces, other ornaments, the fine organs, choir stalls, small bells, wrought iron work in the windows and the door locks were taken, with everything else of value, from both the cathedral and convent church it would seem. Images were defaced. But the city itself was unscathed; not a single house was burnt, even if the contents such as copper kettles were purloined and coins, mainly copper, collected in chests as legitimate booty. This ransacking happened probably because the soldiers were frustrated by the lack of the expected treasure in the island. But Cumberland himself brought back at least one valuable object, a gilt coffer which he passed onto his daughter who still possessed it sixty years later.[6]

The Earl took as prizes the half-dozen Spanish ships in the harbour, all empty so of little worth, and two more which sailed in – a frigate with negroes aboard and a great ship of 200 tons with meal, oil and other necessaries laden for Brazil. The Havana ship with the soldiers' pay did not appear. The Earl used the Brazil ship and two of the other vessels to convey the 300 captives – soldiers, citizens and women – who desired it to Cartagena. The *Prosperous* and *Affection* escorted them and provided the better accommodation for the governor, Captains Lanzos and Ayela and the other officers (with their flags) and set them ashore on 26 July. The Earl intended taking the former governor, Coronel, to England to relate the events to the Queen before sending him thence to Spain. But, old and sick though he was, he contrived to escape, with the connivance of his keeper. At Cartagena, Captain Mosquera was imprisoned and then sent to Spain to await trial. After two years in gaol, he was exonerated and proved to have been a good governor, though an appeal was lodged against that verdict. His successor, Captain Alonso de Mercado, another Flanders veteran, was at pains to explain how easy it was for San Juan island to be invaded; again, a matter of being wise after the event and, in his case, with an eye to his own position.

San Juan's location, fine, strongly-defended harbour and the mainland's thin population made it far more suitable than San Domingo or Havana as an English base, self-financing by playing havoc with enemy shipping in the Caribbean. But Spanish troops knew all too well they had drawn the short straw when drafted there. After only a few weeks of the English occupation, neither military, strategic nor economic considerations counted for much. Disease first undermined then made Cumberland's position untenable. By early July 200 of the English soldiers and seamen were dead of dysentery and another 400 seriously ill, among them Sir John Berkeley. Nor were the Spanish spared by the pestilence which this time was to save them from the enemy but was an affliction they had regularly to endure. The English dead included old campaigners such as Henry Clifford, captain of the *Sampson*, Henry Palmer, captain of the *Centurion*, and John Peryman its master, Richard Knottesford, master of the *Galleon Constance*, Thomas Harding master of the *Affection*, Robert Careless, captain of the *Anthony*, and John Graunt, master of the *Ascension*. The gallant Captain Sierralta also succumbed, having survived his wounds. A later report said that all but two of the eighteen of the Earl's household on the *Malice Scourge* with him also perished. Any succour or reinforcements from the Queen or the Earl of Essex would have been wasted. Royal reaction to an established English base in the Americas was not, as it turned out, to be put to the test, rather the Queen's scepticism was once more justified.

The advantage now began to swing back to the islanders. Yet, without arms and outside help they were incapable of ousting the English. Eager to be rid of them and knowing of their heavy losses through illness, the Teniente, Pedro Garcia, and other men of standing accepted the Earl's offer to negotiate ransom for the city and island, but tried his patience by prevaricating to avoid any payments, still uncertain of his real intentions. As late as 11 August, Judge Villasenor, appealing to Philip II from St German for galleys and military aid to enable the mainland people to resist, warned that if Cumberland remained 'nothing is safe in all your majesty's colonies and fleets.'

By late July, the Earl had gained little from the bargaining with the Teniente. He could not long delay his departure for fear of shortage of crews to sail his large ships home. With the main object lost, his mind turned again to a privateering coup. The *Prosperous* and *Affection* were expected to proceed to Cuba on their way back from Cartagena, to capture a man who could say whether the West Indiamen were at Havana or New Spain. From a carvel which unsuspectingly entered El Tejar with medicinal pearls, Cumberland learnt that Philip II's pearl store at La Margarita had been stayed because of his presence and was filled with several years collections. He therefore attempted with three ships to reach the island, well to the South off the coast of the Spanish Main, until the seasonal contrary winds forced him back.

With 400 of his men dead and as many ill, Earl George left San Juan in some haste on 14 August in the hope of reaching the Azores in time to meet a carrack, taking along with the *Scourge* only the *Sampson* of the great ships, and of the lesser the *Royal Defence*, the *Discovery*, the new *Scout*, the *Elizabeth*, the *Guiana* and two smaller vessels, one a Frenchman, the other a Spanish frigate taken in the harbour. His manner of going convinced the Puerto Rican officials that he intended to return. Beaten by tropical diseases and not the Spanish foe, the Earl ensured that Imperial Spain would not easily re-establish itself in San Juan. He instructed Berkeley to follow him with the rest of the fleet and men when he had sufficiently recovered from his illness but to erase El Morro's landward side before he left, which he did with great effect. The Earl also sank one of the two barges in the haven as an obstruction to shipping. Reports from the island stated that enough negroes accompanied him to England to denude the plantations of workers during the next year. But the happier side of the occupation was also remembered. He potted up sensitive plants, *mimosa pudica*, which grow wild on the promontary and intrigued his men, and brought them back to England.

The Earl's small fleet, returning past Bermuda, was becalmed for thirteen days. Approaching the Azores, they were scattered by a great storm with vast seas rising above the *Scourge*'s mast tops which again proved to Layfield's comfort how good a ship she was, 'the remembrance whereof yet maketh me quake' he confided in his account. At Flores the *Sampson* and several of Berkeley's ships caught up, recognising each other by the pennants Cumberland had ordered them to fly on their fore-top masts. They obtained water and victuals peaceably and learnt there was no chance of meeting either the carracks or the Mexican fleet. The Earl left Flores on 16 September, reached Portsmouth on the 23rd with fifteen of his ships, a bark, pinnace and 1,000 men, and landed in person at Blackwall on the Thames on Monday 1 October, a fortnight after the death of Philip II. Of the 700 men lost, only 60 had been killed in the fighting, 40 more on the return when the *Pegasus* sank on the Goodwin Sands and his old frigate the *Discovery* upon Ushant. The other 600 had succumbed to the dysentery and fever contracted in Puerto Rico.

Cumberland's great enterprise was the dominating event of the sea war in 1598 and its tactical success can hardly be overstated. His fleet terrorised the Iberian coast, prevented the Portuguese carracks for the first time ever from leaving Lisbon for the East Indies and stopped the West Indian trade, the treasure ships being ordered by Philip II to remain in Havana. By this, the Spanish Crown lost half a year's bullion in 1598, later a full year's return on its far eastern commerce just when the Dutch were beginning to break in. The Spanish merchants were denied incalculable profits from the re-sale of pepper, other spices and exotic tropical produce in the European markets. All this caused great hurt to the Iberian countries' trade and war effort and precarious mercantile position in the Orient. The Venetian ambassador in Madrid reported, on 27 September 1598, that the wealthier Spaniards were thinking of selling large quantities of jewels because the gold and silver from the West Indies had not arrived. Thus, wrote a correspondent in Lisbon on 1 May, 'the small forces of an English Earl can shut in both the East and West India Fleet.'

The capture of San Juan, one of the major cities and strongly fortified havens in the West Indies, was a severe blow to Spain's prestige. The restoration of its fortifications, replacement of the lost artillery and increased garrison, 400 soldiers, were hurriedly undertaken, an additional strain on Spain's resources. The strategic potential of Earl George's feat was fully appreciated by the Iberian authorities as well as by islanders like Judge Villasenor. In the words of the Venetian ambassador, 'if Cumberland can stay at Porto Rico the danger will be immense.' It was fully believed in Madrid as late as October that Puerto Rico would be held, that England and the Dutch were making an extraordinary effort to maintain the garrison and lead an assault on Spain. Philip II died in the belief that the English had at last gained a foothold in the Indies. The new king raised great forces at his own cost in readiness; unnecessarily, his spies' alarmist reports exaggerating as usual.[7]

The Earl himself argued the case for following up his success in his apologia to the Countess of Warwick, devised in part with the intention that through her it would reach the Queen's ear. With only nine strong ships, he pointed out, he had stopped Spain's trade and opened up gaps to the enemy's ruin. What, he rhetorically asked, would the Queen's warships be able to do if they were rightly set to the task. He echoed the expansionist English writers from Robert Thorne to Richard Hakluyt in his belief that England could disrupt and supplant the Spanish and Portuguese in oceanic trade. He offered to undertake two courses of action which would halt Spanish trade and force the King to sue for peace: a blockade of Portugal using only six royal and six merchant ships – the greatest of all West Indian fleets was due to cross now in 1599 – and the capture of Havana, where all Spain's Oriental and American riches were gathered.

The strategic notions which Earl George overtly espoused at San Juan and re-iterated to his sister-in-law had the fault common to the English expansionists of elevating aspirations over realities. They had, moreover, been overtaken by the drift towards peace in Europe following the Treaty of Vervins between France and Spain on 2 May 1598, as his fleet sailed towards the Caribbean. Neither the

English Crown or nation, let alone private groups, could muster adequate forces, naval power or finances during the 1590s to maintain a permanent base in the Americas. A decade later, Jamestown in Virginia, almost outside Spanish intervention, barely scraped survival.[8] Nor could the English mount a Hawkins-style blockade of the Iberian coast or the Azores; that had been tried and discarded by 1591. Had it been possible, then the fears expressed in Madrid over Earl George's interruption of commerce would have been justified. It had suited the Queen's purposes – embarrassing Philip II and pleasing her Champion – to let the Earl's private expedition go ahead. She never had any thoughts, whatever impression she gave to the Earl, of committing Crown resources to follow up his unexpected success. Moreover, there was now internal danger from Tyrone's rebellion in Ireland which would absorb all that might be spared and much more besides and permit Spain one last effort to interfere in the Queen's realm, in 1601.[9]

The populace, in any event, was suffering in 1598 from the fourth successive bad harvest, food shortages, severe inflation and plague. Peace from exhaustion was on the horizon, in Castile more than anywhere. Cumberland's was almost the last blow in a sea-war which was on the verge of transmutation into far eastern commerce and American colonisation.[10] The Earl was glumly aware of having 'been onlie a Fyre maker for others to warme themselves at, when I was thruste out of doores to blowe my fingers in the coulde, and I thinke was borne like Watt of Greenwiche to dye carryinge the Colebaskett.' The feeling of having been let down by Elizabeth long persisted. His great Puerto Rican enterprise was yet another instance, and still not the last, supporting the premise that the closer to Court and higher in status an entrepreneur was, the more he became the unwitting instrument of the immediate policy favoured by the Queen and her narrow circle of Privy Council advisers.

The greatest ambiguity in the 1598 enterprise is its financial aspect and in the city's collaboration with the Earl. Their monetary rewards fell far short of the merit of the whole endeavour. Earl George stripped San Juan's fortifications of their eighty brass cannon and ammunition, collected (according to Judge Villasenor) 8,000 cwt of ginger, many hides and much sugar. He was to sell thirty-one of the pieces to the royal ordnance. Yet the value of the plunder and nine prizes brought back, estimated at £16,000, was not half the cost of setting out, besides the loss of his frigate. One report said that the merchants who adventured with him would be content to take eight per cent of their principal. A gentleman soldier's share came to only ten shillings.

Without doubt Earl George was unlucky. He just missed both the outward and the inward bound carracks and thirty corn vessels off the coast of Spain which one correspondent in Lisbon said would have 'furnished his country but famished this.'[11] Yet it is apparent that the Earl, all but unanimously supported by his officers and by the merchants' representatives on the ships such as Captain Flick and John Watts, allowed the possibility of long-term plunder to prejudice the immediate financial return. He was to claim that, had he decided to quit San Juan quickly, he could have had all the ginger and sugar on the island, worth £500,000, brought to him, besides good store of jewels and plate; as well he might, though that figure is grossly inflated. The very success of the attack went to the heads of the whole force and subverted the attainable objective of striking hard, pillaging and returning with a profitable haul into the uncertain prospects of widespread plundering from an English privatering base in the Indies. Granted the state of the Earl's own finances, if this was a gambler's last throw, he strangely took his eye off the main chance.

In the end, Cumberland had little other than the honour and glory of his personal achievement, the second reason for his great enterprise. He had proved his worth to the Queen and his courtier rivals as much as to himself and his mariners. His triumph was commemorated in an engraving by Thomas Cockson depicting the Earl in his starred armour mounted on his rearing steed with his forces in the background in the act of invading San Juan island. His hat, surcoat and saddle are lined with silk emblazoned with armillery spheres, olive branches and caduci, the royal emblems. The engraving was printed and sold, appropriately, at the Golden Anchor in Paternoster Row. It was also, uniquely, skilfully sculpted on to a small plaque, which still survives in Bolton Hall.

The Earl's capture of San Juan added to his reputation on the Continent. To England's opponents he was 'the archpirate Earl of Cumberland'. In Antwerp he was popularly regarded as 'the English Lord that doth great harm to the Spanish at sea.' How the Earl was received by Elizabeth in October 1598 is not recorded, but, to judge by her pleasantness to those who had fought with him, the Queen received him warmly.[12] His subsequent employment both by her and, after 1603, by James I indicates that both monarchs were duly impressed by his military skills and powers of persuasion. The Earl was slow to come to terms with the financial reckoning. When he did, it was to have a devastating effect on the Clifford inheritance.

A stone plaque of Cockson's engraving (reproduced on p. 169), artist unknown

CHAPTER 11

Mercantile Promoter and Privy Councillor: 1598–1605

The Puerto Rican expedition was the great watershed in Earl George's life. With it ended his maritime career and optimism about regaining his lost fortune. A shift now occurred in the direction and emphasis of his main concerns. Freed from his time-absorbing obsession, he could devote his energies to public affairs as well as his own pressing problems. What is worth stressing here is that his final years, far from being an inglorious anti-climax to a decade of renowned command at sea, were distinguished by involvement in government and commerce which contributed to long-lasting achievements. By contrast, in his private affairs, except for one redeeming gain, the story is one of immense harm to both his estates and family relations as he finally faced up to the financial consequences of his privateering failures.

This was not to happen for more than three years, for reasons which will be explained, and in the meantime Earl George could not resist gambling on a privateering success, starting almost as soon as he returned from San Juan. On 9 December 1598, having perhaps sold some of his older vessels, he purchased, for £500 from Thomas Dykes gent. of Frant in Sussex and William Burrell, shipwright of Ratcliffe, Middlesex, the 'good ship' *Elizabeth Guiana* of 140 tons burden, then at anchor in the Thames. With its captain, John Martyn, its master, Spenser, and others as fellow adventurers, he sent out the *Guiana* with a crew of seventy and at a cost for the victualling of £300. Its capture and spoil of a French ship, the *Maria*, laden with goods valued at £3,000, embarrassed the Privy Council whose concern was for amicable relations with Henry IV. The French ambassador sought redress on behalf of the *Maria*'s owners, John Crosmer and Peter Grout of St Malo, and the Council were keen to make it clear to him that French subjects would find ready justice in England. For the Earl, making restitution, this was another wasted investment.[1]

Bearing in mind Cumberland's pleading at the Accession Day celebrations in

1600, there is a sense of unreality in the alacrity with which he once again responded to the Queen's request in private conversation on 3 May to send his ships to sea and to list for her the victualling costs. All the outlay was to fall on him. He reckoned the *Malice Scourge*, with a crew of 400, and two merchantmen with 150 men apiece would cost about £3,000 for a four months' voyage and so, he informed Sir Robert Cecil, he dare undertake it. But he wanted to sell the *Scourge* and in its place take a royal warship. He had word of a Flemish merchant who had long wanted to buy her and he had made his mind up to agree whatever price the man asked even if he lost on the deal for he now had to turn 'from interceptyng of Carrackes to sowinge of corne from Rigging Shippe to Breedyng sheep and from Honour to Clownysh cogitations'.[2]

Not yet awhile, though, and never completely; privateering was too much in his blood to abandon it, no matter what his circumstances. In March 1601 he put forward, by request, a plan for the Queen to equip a large fleet to intercept either the outward-going *flotas* for New Spain or the carracks off Florida or at St Helena, the cost as much as £15,000 or as little as £8,000. It was not implemented and looks like one of Elizabeth's whims or a contingency plan in case peace negotiations with Spain foundered. Moreover he continued to invest, this time with Cecil, in successive voyages of the *Watt* of Plymouth. On the second, it was in Sir John Gilbert's fleet of seven ships which captured three Portuguese prizes, the *St Mark*, *St Anne* and *Suttea*, off Lisbon in March 1602 and brought them back to Plymouth. There was intense personal, political and legal wrangling over the *St Mark* but in the end the Earl received £141 17s. 1d. as his third share in the *Watt*'s adventure. The Lord Admiral commenced suit in the Admiralty Court for his tenths which he asserted Cecil, Gilbert, Cumberland and the other captains and masters had evaded. The Earl disbursed £60 of his profit from the *Watt* to send out a pinnace from Padstow, his last effort because James I's accession put a swift end to English privateering on both sides of the Atlantic, formalised in the peace treaty with Spain in 1604.[3] The future lay in oceanic trade and western colonisation. Earl George's final gesture as a private entrepreneur was to help pioneer the English cross-Atlantic trade which grew out of the sea-war. He dispatched a small merchantman, the *Pilgrim*, under the *Sampson*'s former captain Nicholas Downton, on an illicit trading voyage to Cumana and other Spanish ports in the Caribbean. It came home with a cargo of tobacco probably obtained in Trinidad.[4]

However, it was in the thrust for eastern trade that Earl George, more than any other nobleman and even non-city man, epitomises the transformation of English maritime enterprise at the close of the Tudor era. He was an active participant in the founding of the East India Company in December 1600. The London merchants, galvanized by the return from Asia of the richly laden Dutch fleet in July 1599, had hastened to follow suit. At the forefront were the Levant traders who stood to lose their advantage in importing exotic eastern goods via the Mediterranean. The original subscribers to the proposed East India Company were dominated by the Earl's Puerto Rican co-adventurers, Sir John Hart, Aldermen Paul Bayning and Leonard Holliday, Thomas Symonds, Thomas Cordell, William and Thomas Garraway, Augustine Skinner, Bartholomew

Barnes, William Offley and two other old acquaintances, Alderman Nicholas
Mosley and the Leeds-born Sir Richard Saltonstall.

For a year the project was held back because of the Queen's fears that it might
obstruct her peace negotiations with Spain. When these collapsed, the subscribers
met, with Privy Council approval, to elect committees on 23 September 1600.
Four days later they decided to purchase the *Malice Scourge*. The Earl took a
tough stand on the price, demanding £4,000, refusing £3,000 after an inventory
had been taken, and then on 7 October agreeing to arbitration. Bayning and
Holliday acting for the merchants, Garraway and Allebaster for the Earl
suggested £3,700, which he accepted; a fair price considering that her necessary
repairs cost the company £1,000. He used £2,200 of the sale money to repay
some of the debts or interest he owed, £1,000 to Bayning, £700 to Holliday and
£500 to Cordell, which they took in stock in the company's first voyage. With the
remaining £1,500 he bought stock for himself.

As a major subscriber, Earl George now joined the court of the company and
attended its meetings. His investment, however, was whittled down under the
pressure of his debts. On 1 April 1601 £200 of his stock was assigned at his request to
William Bublock, a goldsmith; on 6 July £570 to Alderman Bayning, and on
5 January 1602 £230 to Holliday. But in March that year he adventured £500 in the
Company's second voyage and Countess Margaret, independently, £50. These two
voyages together realised a 95 per cent profit from their cargoes of pepper, though the
Earl was dead long before final returns were made. Earl Francis was to be fortunate in
his investment in the fifth voyage in 1608 since it made 234 per cent profit.

The charter of incorporation of the East India Company on 31 December 1600
was granted to the Earl, the only noble member, and 215 knights, aldermen and
merchants. The cask mark adopted for shipping the company's goods shared his
initials, GCE or GEC, though it is believed to stand for the Governor and
Company of East Indies merchants. His stock apart, the Earl's link with the
Orient was his great ship the *Malice Scourge*. Re-named the *Red Dragon*, a fusing
here of the Earl's and the Queen's Tudor symbols in their last joint maritime
concern, she proved her worth as the company's flagship over the next two
decades. With James Lancaster as captain, John Davis as pilot-major, and the
Earl's boatswain William Burrage, she left Woolwich with her three consorts on
13 February 1601 on the first and, as it turned out, successful English trading
voyage to the Far East, completed on 11 September 1603. She led the second
voyage in 1604 and the third in 1607.[5]

It was on her fourth voyage in 1612 under Captain Thomas Best that the
Dragon's fire-power proved decisive in helping establish the company in the East.
With the *Hosiander* as companion, she fought a month-long battle with the
Portuguese at Swally Roads which opened up English trade with India at Surat.
In the words of an eye-witness, the *Dragon*'s culverins and demi-culverins 'gave
them such banges as maid ther verie sides crack'. She led the fleet of four ships
which escorted Sir Thomas Roe, the first English ambassador to the Court of the
Great Mogul in 1615. But eventually the *Red Dragon* came to a sorry end. She
was one of the four company vessels surprised and taken with their valuable
ladings at Tiku in western Sumatra in October 1619 by the Dutch who had now

resorted to war to protect their own East Indian commerce. Already an old ship, she was worn out by the Dutch over the next few months ferrying materials to build their fort at Batavia in Java. At the conclusion of peace, the English opted to be recompensed with her value, not the creaking vessel itself, so there she remained, in Dutch hands.[6] The names of the archetypes of Elizabethan maritime enterprise, Drake's *Golden Hind*, Grenville's *Revenge* and the *Ark Royal*, today have greater resonance. But the *Red Dragon* deserves to stand beside them, because no other ship straddles those twin peaks of Elizabethan success, the sea-war against Imperial Spain and the company's nascent Far Eastern trade. From El Morro to Swally Roads she demonstrated the maturing skills of the English shipwrights, navigators and mariners and of the city merchants in their trans-oceanic trading organisations.

Much of Earl George's attention after his return from Puerto Rico was taken up with royal duties. He performed regularly at the Accession Day tilts and on other special occasions. He was appointed to the High Commission for the province of York in November 1599, whose members also included Richard Hutton and Christopher Shute. He was a guest with Countess Margaret and attendant on the Queen at the great wedding on 16 June 1600 of Lady Anne Russell with Lord Herbert, the Earl of Worcester's son. Among the routine courtier tasks the Queen assigned to him was chaperoning visiting dignitories such as the Duke of Biron in September 1601 whom he conducted, with his twenty French noblemen and 400 other followers, from London into Hampshire where the Queen was on progress. The Earl was one of the noblemen in attendance on the Queen when she dined and banquetted on Twelfth Day 1601 and then, after a grand ball and dancing that evening, watched the first perfomance of Shakespeare's *Twelfth Night*. The visiting celebrity Don Virginio Orsino supped with Cumberland and later reported 'with him I had some speech which will be to the taste of his Highness [his uncle Ferdinand, the Grand Duke of Tuscany] since that man is the greatest corsair in the world.' On May Day 1602, when the Queen went a-maying at Sir Richard Buckley's house at Lewisham, it was George who organised the elaborate show on horseback at which the *Ode to Cynthia* in praise of her was performed.

The Earl's age, experience, reliability and proven military skills brought him close to the fringe of the Privy Council in Elizabeth's last years and then into it immediately after James I's accession. The Queen favoured a small, tightly-knit Council. The Earl had been one of the courtiers she occasionally called on to bolster the Councillors in their deliberations, as at the trial of Mary, Queen of Scots, and he now played a prominent part in the crises which beset the last years of her reign. In August 1599, when an attack by the Spanish fleet then off the coast of France was feared imminent, the Earl and the Lord Mayor were directed to take steps to defend London. He tackled the problem with his usual verve. He planned to block the Thames with a bridge of boats and cables at Gravesend, as had been successfully deployed to defend Antwerp. With 1,500 musketeers he pronounced he would hold the barricade or lose his life. But his plan was deemed too costly and a simpler alternative was to sink boats. As it happened, the threat passed before any serious preparations had been made.[7]

Queen Elizabeth going in Procession to Blackfriars in 1600, *attributed to Robert Peake the Elder. Knights of the Garter are leading, with Cumberland third from left*

What must have been Cumberland's most distressing duty was attendance and judgement at the trials of his friend and jousting partner the Earl of Essex, whose brashness and pride brought him to a tragic end. The royal favourite had unwisely importuned the Queen into making him governor-general of Ireland, where only strong military action would put down the revolt. Having failed to subdue the rebels, he returned to Court with his close friends without first obtaining royal permission. For this dereliction of duty he faced censure on 5 June 1600 by a commission of eighteen councillors, judges and others, including Earl George, at Lord Keeper Egerton's residence, York House. It was a fatiguing session. As Archbishop Hutton recorded, 'wee sate from viii of the clock in the morning till it was almost ix at night, without either eating, drinking, or rysing.' Predictably, the commissioners found Essex at fault, the sentence being to lose his offices and be kept prisoner in his own Essex House on Thamesside. Earl George's was the only dissenting voice. Essex's servant Sir Gelly Meyrick reported to Henry, 3rd Earl of Southampton, another adherent, 'My Lord of Cumberland dealt very nobly'. In fact, demurring at the severity of the sentence, he bravely commented that he knew how easily a general commander might incur censure; but, confident in the Queen's mercy, he agreed with the rest of the commissioners.

True to form, the Queen kept Essex under restraint only until August. At liberty though humiliated and facing financial ruin, he was an easy prey to the malcontents who sycophantly gathered round him at Essex House. Putting undue faith in them and his popularity in London, Essex chanced all in a rebellion on Sunday, 8 February 1601. Cumberland, the Lord Mayor and the Bishop of London hastily collected forces to bar Essex's 200-strong company at the city's gates and compel their retreat by boat to Essex House. He was one of the group of leading nobility who laid siege to the house and negotiated the surrender. The verdicts at the state trial of Essex, Southampton and others on Thursday, 19 February, an occasion of pageant and dignity, were inescapable and Earl George concurred with his peers. To the Queen at least it was appropriate that he should be the senior of the handful of noblemen she ordered to attend Essex's execution on Wednesday, 25 February at the Tower of London. Sir Gelly Meyrick was one of Essex's four henchmen who shared the same fate a month later. Southampton and the others were imprisoned.[8]

The death of Essex and disgrace of Southampton cleared the way for Earl George to obtain the royal manor of Grafton Regis in Northamptonshire which he had been seeking since June 1599, when he offered £500 to Sir Edward Carey for it. The competition for Grafton is typical of the jostling for royal offices and properties which was endemic in the Elizabethan Court but the outcome is an insight into the hierarchy of power and patronage in the last years of the reign. Southampton also desired Grafton but Sir Charles Danvers reminded him that no man would dare buy it without the consent of Essex, who was warden of the adjoining Forest of Salcey. Earl George, too, had to hang fire while the favourite lived. After Essex's execution, Sir Robert Cecil held the Queen's ear over patronage and his intimates like George had the best chance of obtaining the offices and properties they desired.

Cumberland was granted not only the keeperships of Grafton House and its park on 30 May 1602 but also the wardenship of Salcey Forest. An obstacle was Sir Arthur Savage who had a lease of the park. He tried to eject Savage who complained to Cecil and sought his help. Sir Robert made quite plain to Savage that he would in no way cross the Earl and pointed to the great difference between them when their affairs were in the balance. Savage then appealed to the Queen who first promised to write to the Earl and request him to let Sir Arthur keep the park or repay him what the lease had cost him. Then, being importuned on the Earl's behalf, she changed her mind, comforting Savage that the Earl would deal well with him. This was the situation in March 1603 when the Queen died and the Earl was able to eject Savage.[9]

Grafton House, that 'ruinated place' he called it, had a fine setting and a big park well-suited to the boisterous and bucolic style of James I's Court, which was much swollen in numbers and excess compared with the old Queen's. Twice on royal progresses the Earl entertained the Court at the house. On the first visit, 27 and 28 June 1603, Lady Anne writes, he banquetted the King and Queen with great royalty, speeches and delicate presents. The outdoor sports in which the courtiers delighted included jousting during which the Earl hurt Henry Alexander very dangerously.

The second, longer visit in 1605 would have required far more elaborate

Sir Robert Cecil, 1st Earl of Salisbury
(1563–1612), by John de Critz the Elder

preparations at high cost and certainly caused the Earl a great deal of trouble to organise. The king and his entourage were at Grafton for four full days from Friday 16 August until Tuesday, Queen Anne joining him with her party for most of the time. The royal household's expenditure was £651, normal for four days, but the host's outlay on feasting, banquetting, music and other entertainments always far exceeded that. The Earl ruefully commented that his frequent royal occasions were the main cause of his continued borrowing, even when the huge amounts of cash collected from his tenants were now flowing down to London. Among his new loans in 1605 were £1,000 from Peter Van Lore on 2 February and another £1,000 from Bess of Hardwick on 23 October, just a week before his death.[10] The Earl had wanted Grafton, or so he claimed, less for himself than as a residence for Francis and Lady Grisell so that he could stay with them now that he lacked a London home. During his last illness he pleaded with the King for Francis to be allowed to retain Grafton. There was no hope of that because James had already promised it to his cousin, Ludovic Stuart, 2nd Duke of Lennox, but Earl Francis was allowed to use it as an occasional residence until at least 1609.[11]

Earl George's royal duties in Elizabeth's last years may appear to have taken precedence over his private affairs yet it was the latter which principally tied him to the capital for nearly three and a half years. He well appreciated that to raise the huge amount of cash he needed from his estates would permanently cripple the Clifford inheritance. Large-scale help from the Queen was imperative in the form of an office or licence which would yield a big yearly income over a long term. Many courtiers had benefited from such royal munificence, for instance Leicester and Essex with successive leases of the customs on sweet wines which brought them £2,500 annually. Earl George had been denied that kind of aid so far. His initial difficulty now would be to locate a suitable and available licence, the best already being in the courtiers' clutches. Then he would have to lobby the Queen for a grant and fend off rival claimants, a test for his endurance and skills in argument.

His old friend Thomas Caesar and Robert Webbe, clothier of Somerset, unwittingly perhaps pointed the way. They anticipated one of the most lucrative recurring opportunities to acquire cash in quantity – at the expense of the Merchant Adventurers, the wealthiest of all the English trading companies. The merchants had a virtual monopoly of the export of undressed, that is undyed and unfinished, woollen cloths which, by the Tudor era, constituted the bulk in quantity and value of England's export trade. The cloths were finished and dyed on the Continent, mainly in the Low Countries. The merchants' weakness was that their licence from the Crown, granted in 1564, allowed them to transport annually only 30,000 cloths whereas in a normal year their trade was more than double that number. The deficiency was remedied by the Queen's frequent grants of similar licences to noblemen, foreign rulers and others who sold them to the merchants; an established Elizabethan practice of rewarding the deserving without incurring cost to the royal treasury. The most recent nobleman to benefit was Lord Admiral Howard who had made a quick profit by selling his licence for 100,000 cloths to Sir Edward Stafford.

Caesar and Webbe raised deep issues because the patent they requested was a radical departure from previous grants. They wanted a term of twenty-one years in which exports on their licence would be unlimited, whereas earlier grants had been for specific, though often large, numbers of cloths. For the first time the Queen was offered a rent, £2,000 a year. The merchants, who, always on the occasion of new grants, fought to get them into their own hands, countered by offering £1,000 rent. Caesar's petition was referred on 17 January 1600 to the Master of Requests, his brother Sir Julius, Lord Treasurer Buckhurst and Lord Chief Justice Popham for decision. There the petition must have foundered because no more is heard of it. Yet with it began a new phase in the recurrent struggle over the next grant and, even more important, the form the licence would take.

Earl George now took over from Caesar whose consolation, if it were such, was to sit in the 1603 Parliament as his nominee for the borough of Appleby. His first petition was a strange combination of provisions taken from earlier grants as well as Caesar's with little to commend them except that altogether the income would be high. He requested a patent to buy and sell 1,000 sarpcloths (coarse wrapping canvas) each year, as in a licence to Walsingham in 1572; to prohibit aliens from buying wool without his licence; to have the moiety of the penalties arising from the statute against woolbroggers (brokers) and, finally, a licence to export unfinished white cloths. The term would be for twenty-one years and he offered £500 annual rent. Soon after, he considered it wiser to confine his proposals to the main provision and in a second petition offered a rent of £1,000 for a licence to export undressed white cloths for twenty-one years.

He proferred this suit to the Queen in person on 1 May 1600 and was greatly discouraged by her manner of rejecting it two days later when, as mentioned above, she tried to sweeten him by asking him to equip a fleet. It would never have troubled him, he told Cecil, if the rent he had offered had been thought too small or any other detail objected to, but it hurt him to be at once judged a cosener and so absolutely denied. Wherefore, he wrote,

> since after my long attendance, with neglect of my poor estate, adventure of my life, hate of all thoughts that were not for her Majesty's service or profit, I have gained no better opinion than to be a deceiver, it is time for me to creep into a corner, where, hiding myself from company my frugal course out of my own shall pay what down my last breathing I will heartily wish for.

When, 'urged by grievous necessities', he approached the Queen again after dinner on 13 July, stressing he wanted the licence to satisfy his creditors, she raised the old objection of her gracious dealing over the *Madre de Dios*. He walked with her in the garden that evening but dare not mention the matter again. He would, he confided to Cecil, 'rather become a country clown with husbandly care to work out of my own in long time what shall pay my debts' rather than risk displeasing the Queen by badgering her. He regarded Cecil as his best, indeed at this juncture his only, hope of persuading her to relent and he urged the Secretary to plead with her on his behalf.

At this moment, 30,000 cloths, a full year's trading, had still to pass on Stafford's licence so the Queen would feel no compunction about shelving the matter. More worrying for the Earl would be the objections the merchants had raised to his patent. A hard-fought polemic now developed between them with the Earl eventually winning the argument without any certainty it would tip the scales with the Queen. The Accession Day celebrations of 1600 gave him the ideal opportunity to regale her publicly about his desperate plight. With Essex disgraced, Cumberland had all the limelight. Gone now are his Arthurian conceits and all but a few of the obligatory flattering allusions to Cynthia's brightness and 'your highnes beautie and vertue'.

His speech dwelt almost unrelievedly on his melancholy, misfortune and discontent in a succession of vivid aphorisms, Elizabethan prose at its most muscular and evocative. He had 'made ladders for others to clymbe' and likened himself to 'him that built the ancker to save others' only to be drowned himself. He reminded the Queen 'Is it not, as I have often tould ye, that, after he had throwne his land into the sea, the sea would cast him on the lande for a wanderer?'. His resentment, even bitterness, at his fate came out sharply in quoting the Spanish proverb 'Let them hold their purses with the mouth downeward that hath filled them with mouth upwards.' His fall, losing his estates, would be all the harder for a nobleman imbued like him with 'Northeren thoughtes, that measures honnor by the acre'. But, with the disgrace of Essex in mind or not, he carefully set bounds to his expression of discontent, reassuring the Queen that his eyes, thoughts and actions were tied to her in an undissoluable knot.

The speech (or Cecil's quiet words) persuaded Elizabeth to relent, although Cumberland had to wait almost nine months before Stafford's licence ended. In the patent granted on 7 August 1601, he got all the main provisions he wanted, except for the twenty-one years' term, his licence being for an unlimited number of cloths for ten years paying £1,000 rent per annum. He was given extensive administrative powers, with an office in the Custom House, the right to appoint up to eight officers in London and two in any other ports, with full rights to search for and seize the cloths of traders evading payment and to prosecute them. The Earl had achieved half his goal. As tough a proposition was getting the merchants to pay him a good price for the right to export cloths under his licence. This was a matter of serious contention and bitter negotiations. The Earl eventually forced a decision by making his licence available to all shippers, which would free trade and undermine the merchants' monopoly, the action they feared most of all. However, this threatened a disruption in England's greatest overseas trade which in the national interest the Privy Council could not allow to happen. The controversy had become a cause of state which only the Council could settle.

The end came in March 1602. The Council decided the merchants should pay the Earl 2s. 2d. per cloth and confirmed their monopoly. Cumberland could be well satisfied with the outcome, for which he had fought hard. As John Taylor declared, the merchants 'are a great adversary and an overmatche almost for any particular person. Yf ever my Lord had gone away before this Matter had been decyded his Patent would sure have been overthrown'. His problems did not end then. After James I's accession he had to defend his patent afresh against other courtiers. In December 1603 the King granted Sir James Hay and Sir Philip Herbert an old-style licence to export 15,000 cloths, and another to the merchant and moneylender Peter Van Lore. After the Earl's protests, helped now by his place in the Privy Council, these grants were altered so that they fell within his patent without any of the parties losing the intended monetary gain. On 18 May 1605 the Earl had a greater triumph. He managed to get his licence renewed and for a twenty-one years' term, starting then. How he did this is not certain, though it coincided with a confirmation of the Merchant Adventurers' licence and they now appreciated the advantages of dealing with a single, supportive licensee.

Earl George's perseverence was amply rewarded by the £2,000 a year profit he and his brother received on average throughout the quarter of a century they held the licence. This more than any other single source of income saved their family from complete financial disaster. What it cost George in private hardship to hang on in Westminster till he was certain the licence and the price were secure is revealed in John Taylor's report to Francis from the Court on 7 January 1602. We have, he wrote, 'with muche adoe Rubbed owte, to Lyve, the Parliament and Christemaes and god knowes miserably enough.' Over Christmas there had been gambling as great as any he had ever seen. The Earl had declined to join in at first, despite being urged by the Lord Admiral and Secretary Cecil, until he saw how many lords were doing so. Then he made great shift to find £100, had good fortune and bettered his stock; 'he plaies much warelyer, methinkes then heretofore', continued Taylor, 'he can Leave a wynner, and so was he not wonte, and yet hathe furnished him self with Clothes and other Necessaries.' Adversity had tempered his recklessness. He could at last control his gambling; much too late, though, for the good of the Clifford patrimony.[12]

Queen Elizabeth's death in March 1603 may in a sense have released the Earl from a life-long bondage to her; it certainly brought a new focus to his royal service. He was a signatory to the proclamation of James I's accession and travelled north to meet the King. Francis Clifford crossed the border to be in attendance on James from Scotland, Francis Dacre too. Countess Margaret paid her respects to, and joined the entourage of, Queen Anne when she arrived in the South. At York, the King settled the usual altercation over the Earl's claim to carry the city's sword before the monarch, this time with the Lord Mayor and Thomas, Lord Burghley, Lord President of the Council in the North. He delivered it publicly 'to one that knew wel how to use a sword, having beene tryed both at sea and on shoare, the thrice honoured Earle of Cumberland, who bore it before his Majestie, ryding in great state from the Gate to the Minster.' For the whole of the visit, the Earl preceeded with the sword wherever the King went within the city. Among the gentlemen James I knighted in Yorkshire were the Earl's cousin Henry Cholmley of Whitby and his officers and friends Richard Musgrave of Norton Conyers, where the King had halted en route, and William Ingleby of Ripley Castle, where he had stayed the night.[13]

The King had developed in Scotland a much broader concept of Privy Council composition and work than Elizabeth I and this he implemented as soon

Ripley Castle, c. 1780, unaltered since James VI spent the night of 15/16 April 1603 there

as he reached Whitehall. He directed on 10 April that the Earl be made a Privy Councillor and he was sworn at the 26 April meeting. In addition to Earl George, James brought into the Council Henry, 9th Earl of Northumberland, Lord Thomas Howard and Charles Blount, Lord Mountjoy. All four had fought against the Armada, Howard was second only to Earl George as a noble privateering entrepreneur and Mountjoy had proved his ability as a military commander by subduing the Irish rebels. These men of action with military and naval expertise strengthened the Council where it had been weak under Elizabeth, but there was also an added social and geographical dimension. Cumberland and Northumberland were the heads of great noble families who owned widespread estates with big gentry followings in the north of England. In the context of James I's two realms the north was near his heart not, as the Tudor monarchs usually viewed it, too remote from Westminster to bother visiting.[14]

James I's rather old-fashioned reliance on traditional families like the Percys and Cliffords had an instrumental bearing on the policies which had to be implemented, as will be seen in considering Earl George's work. Its corollary was his profuse, some would argue over-indulgent, granting of titles. This created bonds of obligation and gratitude and released some of the pent-up urges for social advancement ignored by the old Queen. When James knighted over 300 gentlemen and others in the garden at Whitehall Palace on 23 July, Earl George sponsored twenty-three from Yorkshire, including the current head of the Cliffords' long-serving gentry family in Craven, Stephen Tempest of Broughton, notwithstanding his Catholic recusancy. The Earl's relatives George Wharton (Lord Philip's son), Gervase Clifton and Richard Cholmley, and his legal advisers Judge Walmesley and Thomas Crompton were others who bent the knee that day.[15]

The specific duty the King had earmarked for the Earl was the wardenship of the Borders. Although, since the 1586 Treaty of Edinburgh, the old threat of war between England and Scotland had receded, the Marches were still a lawless region, a barrier to trade and communication and a blight on nearby communities. James's accession had been marred by widespread plundering and even murder by the unruly English and Scottish border surnames who went on the rampage as soon as the news broke of Elizabeth I's death. Military action temporarily quelled the clansmen after this notorious 'busy week' raiding. James had envisaged in his *Basilicon Doron* the methods to suppress the surnames and incorporate their homelands into his kingdom. On 8 June 1603 he appointed Earl George Lord Warden of the English Marches and Captain of Carlisle with the job of implementing the first stage of the pacification of the whole border region. Granted the size of his entourage and their household and stable costs, his 1,200 marks allowances may not have left him any profit. Lord Robert had been the first to hold those posts, under Edward I; Earl George was the last. Sir William Bowes had suggested Cumberland as the best nobleman for the wardenship in June 1592 but the Council were loth to lose his maritime aggression and instead had appointed Thomas, 10th Lord Scrope in succession to his father. Earl George brought to the office the ideal qualities needed for this work – high rank, military renown, powers of persuasion and solid local gentry backing – and, equally vital, his link with and presence in the Privy Council. He appointed as his deputy his old companion Sir Richard Musgrave, who was well-versed in Border matters from his service at Berwick and proved equally firm and energetic in dealing with the errant clansmen.

Earl George's wardenship lasted until February 1605 when a new administrative structure was created for the Borders, James I's 'Middle Shires', in which Earl Francis and Henry, Lord Clifford were to be actively involved. How well Earl George in particular acquitted himself and the eventual success of the King's policies have been examined in detail elsewhere. The two Earls benefited by territorial gains on the Cumberland Borders, in part rewards for their labours but also necessary to aid their difficult administrative work. George was granted the royal property of Nichol Forest in 1604; Francis in 1606 the Debatable Lands, for which George had petitioned the King before his death. In 1610 James granted a sixty years' lease to Francis and his heir Lord Clifford of the Captaincy of Carlisle Castle and its socage manor and, finally, in 1614 a forty years' lease of the border lordship of Bewcastle. All these properties needed careful surveying and letting for a decade or more by the Earls' estate officers and relentless litigation by Francis before their depressed state could recover and begin to yield profitable revenues. A metropolitan viewpoint might well underestimate the urgency and the achievement of the pacification of the Borders. James I did not do so, nor the local noble and gentry landowners, farmers, townspeople and traders who had suffered three centuries of invasion and rapine, the unhappy legacies of Edward I's Scottish ambitions which had given Lord Robert his

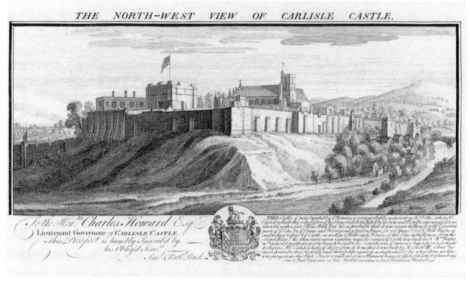

Carlisle Castle, Cumberland, Earl George's headquarters as warden, drawn by Nathaniel Buck, 1739

family's first opportunities of service at Carlisle.[16]

One incident in the city during the Earl's wardenship throws light on current social attitudes. The castle garrison had been left without pay; not the Earl's fault though he understandably got the blame. Three former soldiers, all local men, Richard Hardewyke, Francis Collingwood and Thomas Wilkinson, and John Cooke, butcher, met at the home of Rowland Gryffin, citizen and tailor, for a drink and a chat on Sunday 26 August 1604. Wilkinson, letting his tongue run away with him, accused the Earl of deceit over the lack of pay and called him dishonourable, a disrespectful comment in itself. Worse followed, which led Gryffin and the others to inform on him to the city authorities. Wilkinson was brought before the mayor, Henry Baines, three days later. His companions averred that he had claimed the Earl had received enough money to pay all the troops but had not done so, the implication being he had stolen the cash. Wilkinson had called the Earl 'the basest of all the privie Counsell' – no high opinion of them either – and asserted that he 'haith both Cozened the kings Majestie, and the souldiours'. When Gryffin riposted that he dare not say that to the Earl in person, Wilkinson answered 'what I have spoken I will speke before my Lord Lieutenntes face and before a better man than him, and before the king and a better man than the king'. To these near-treasonable words Collingwood had retorted 'then thou must speeke them before Themperour'. What is revealing is not just their perception of hierarchy, but that Wilkinson's assertions had so offended his companions they disowned him and went so far as to denounce him to the authorities. How Baines, a Clifford estate officer, dealt with the matter is not recorded. A fine, imprisonment, even flogging would have been justified for the comments about the Earl and Privy Council, worse if his outburst was adjudged treasonable.[17]

Because of his long absences dealing with Border affairs, Earl George's attendance at both Council and Star Chamber tended to be intermittent. One of his first duties, on 19 June 1603, was to help suppress disorders in the Queen's Court.[18] He was one of the Councillors at the Court at Wilton on 30 November 1603 who signed Lord Treasurer Buckhurst's letter to the East India Company, following the return of its first fleet, on the disposal of its main cargo, pepper, of which he had first-hand experience. To help the company recoup its investment, the Council restricted sales until the grocers had cleared what the company and the King jointly owned.[19] It was on the Council's initiative but in his capacity as Lord Lieutenant of Westmorland that he wrote, on 14 April 1604, to the mayor and council of Appleby to take more care than in the past about enforcing the statutes concerning petty chapmen and warning them of likely punishment if they ignored the request. The chapmen's private trading was held to be undermining the markets in towns and boroughs, which thereby lost revenue.[20] He was one of seventeen councillors and judges present in the Star Chamber early in May 1605 to hear the cause between Lord Sidney and Sir Robert Dudley, the Earl of Leicester's illegitimate son by Lady Douglas Sheffield. He intervened at the end of the sitting on 8 May because one of the witnesses, Mrs Chancellor, had, by casual reference, impugned the honour of his late sister, Lady Derby.

Mrs Chancellor had repeated what one Dennie had told her and had affirmed its truth, that Leicester also begat a bastard on Lady Derby. George reminded the court that his sister had been 'a ladye of as greate blood as any subiecte in Englaunde', had lived many years in virtue and great honour and had died 'never spotted or blemished'. He was very upset at the allegation and demanded punishment. The Earls of Salisbury and Northampton supported him and the latter pointed out that another witness had said Lady Douglas had conceived a second base child by Leicester, which 'was most false to that honourable Lady'. The ethical code by which the nobility judged themselves excluded comment by their social inferiors. The Earl sat in the Court the following week when Lewis Pickering, a Northampton gentleman, was found to have libelled Archbishop Whitgift. All this was routine Privy Council work. His greatest influence at the Council table may have been as one of the few survivors with Popham and Cecil of the westward expansionists who persuaded King James to renew the quest for an American colony. It was the London project, supported by George's associates the city merchants, which was incorporated in the Virginia Company's charter granted in April 1606 and led to the first successful English settlement on the North American continent.[21]

The Earl's high profile as a courtier, councillor and marcher warden tends to mask his private affairs which were dominated by the state of his finances. The turning point was winning the cloth licence. Until then, Francis and John Taylor – on whom most of the responsibility fell – had only the ordinary receipts from the Craven estates to clear the bonds and statutes. Then from 20 March 1602, as soon as the price was agreed by the Merchant Adventurers, the Earl granted Francis the cloth licence with its £2,000 a year income specifically to pay the debts 'for the discharge of my constience and respect of my Honor'.[22] Whether his brother guessed it or not, that was to become a life-time's obligation. However, the bulk of the cash had to come from Craven. The Earl took the first steps in spring 1602 and, a year later in March 1603, a plan was drawn up to raise £30,000. How the estates had fared during his twenty-five years' tenure, what policies George and his officers devised, their implementation and the far-reaching consequences will be considered in detail in the next chapter.

CHAPTER 12

The Craven and Westmorland Estates: 1579–1605

Freed from all commitments at Court in May 1602 Earl George rode to Skipton, content that the receipts from the cloth licence would more than double his clear yearly income and be devoted to satisfying his creditors. He now approached in a throughly business-like way the question of making his estates yield what the sea had denied him. Yet he persistently underestimated his needs. He first told Cecil that the encumbrance of his debts had long distracted his mind but did not doubt that 'a small time will clear these mischiefs'. Late in August, he reported that his work at Skipton was proving much more tedious than he had expected and he would leave the 'weightiest' unfinished if he returned south then.[1] This first intense dealing with his tenants proved no more than preliminary. When his Court and Border duties permitted he regularly returned to Skipton to continue his activities and had barely completed them at his death in October 1605.

Because he had sold off all his outlying properties by now, Craven and to a lesser degree Westmorland were his only remaining landed resources. With the latter largely, though, as will be seen, not entirely barred by the jointure act, Craven was the prime source. Since the careful valuation in 1597 his assets there were yielding much more than previously.[2] The Leeds and Craven tithes and also some demesne leases granted for twenty-one years in 1578 had fallen in and annual lettings by Francis, Ingleby and Ferrand had brought their rents into line with inflation. On the debit side, Eshton demesnes, Flasby and Bolton Priory were mortgaged, though the Earl still occupied the latter with its revenues, and looming large was the issue of the many tenancies mortgaged. For at least two years the Earl's officers had refrained from re-granting messuages and other holdings which had fallen in on the death of the tenant, awaiting his decisions about the policies to follow. He was obviously aware that much had to be done but it seems certain he did not fully appreciate the enormity of the task facing him when, after organising the fete at Sir Richard Buckley's at Lewisham on May Day,[3] he at last returned north.

The Earl's intentions were common knowledge in Craven and his choice of outside commissioners, Mr Richard Russell, Mr Webb and others, who preceeded him to Skipton caused alarm. Thomas Ferrand reported to Clifford on 12 April: 'It is a wonder to heare the murmering of the people & especially of the porer sort, what ffeare allredy possesseth them'. They longed to see Francis and wanted the estate officers they knew – Ingleby, Eltoftes and Lister – to be on the commissions. John Taylor, who best understood the state of the Earl's finances, was thought responsible for suggesting the use of outsiders.[4] He had good cause to do so. Francis and the local gentry had served the Earl well in managing his lordships for the past twenty years. But they were both too familiar and too close to the tenants for the hard bargaining which lay ahead. The new commissioners took charge, stiffened the local gentry's attitudes and oversaw much of the rigorous surveying and valuing which were the prelude to all the leasing and selling over the next three years. Russell posed unusually searching questions about the tenures and holdings for the juries of enquiry on each manor to respond to, as the detailed entries in the books of survey of 1602 and subsequent years show. It was Russell's servant Henry Plukenett who compiled the Estate Ledger which recorded many of the leases granted. A Kentish man, Samuel Peirce, was employed to do some of the thorough manorial surveys, notably that of Grassington in 1603.

It is worth considering in broad terms the kind of estate and tenures Russell and his fellows had to deal with in April 1602. A characteristic of the Craven property, which has been noted earlier, was the big expanse of demesnes from Barden through Bolton to Skipton, much of it arable, with good meadow and pasture land, and plentiful rougher grazing in the enclosed woody parks. The Earl kept a large part of these demesnes in his own hands to provide corn for his household's needs and grazing and hay for winter fodder for his horses, deer, cattle and sheep. His officers decided every autumn which demesne holdings he would not require during the next year and these were let to whoever would bid the most. With this 'economic' renting the income from the demesne holdings kept pace with the rising prices. The same applied to the Craven tithes. In theory these had been assigned specifically to pay his London debts; in practice, some of the tithe crops were reserved for the household's use, though this was minimal between 1598 and 1602 when the Earl only once visited Skipton. Russell and his colleagues took over the yearly lettings from the commissioners and continued to rackrent whichever demesnes and tithes were not retained. The income from these lettings certainly increased after 1602 as prices continued to rise but also because of the more searching valuations made by Russell, more in line with national than local levels.

The many messuages or farmholds, cottages and other lands in the townships (as distinct from the demesnes) were held by a variety of tenures. As the 1597 valuation shows, in every manor there was a handful of freeholders, who paid small, set rents totalling about £11. The combined rents of about seventy-five tenants who held by fee farm or long lease, mostly granted in the Airedale manors between 1588 and 1592, came to £30. However, the predominant form of tenure was by warrant for the term of the life of the Earl or the tenant, whichever ended first. These warrant-

TABLE 8 *Craven rents and tenures, 1597*

	£	s.	d.
Free rents	11	0	8¼
Fee farms	30	2	8½
Rents of tenants for the life of Lord or tenant	541	5	4¾
Rents by lease or term of life	334	15	5
Rents of tenants at will or from year to year	377	13	1
Rents of corn mills (besides Embsay mill, charged above amongst tenants for life)	69	0	0
Rents of the walkmills		18	0
Rents of tolls of fairs and markets	11	0	0
Rents of improvements, besides the new rents in Silsden	47	5	10
Profits of boon hens, geese, capons and eggs	13	19	0
Yearly value of grounds in my Lord's hands	546	19	4
Rents and profits of tithes assigned to Mr Clifford and Mr Ingleby	121	11	7
Rents and profits of tithes assigned to the Earl of Kent and Lord Wharton	201	0	0
Rent of Clifford's Inn in London	4	0	0
In wapentake fines and profits of courts	30	0	0
Sum total	2,340	11	0½
From which, in payments and deductions for rents, fees and allowances	787	13	0½
Net total	1,552	18	0

(*Source*: YAS, DD121/76, fols 6, 13)

holders contributed £541 to the rental. A considerable number of the remaining tenants held indentures for two lives, usually their own and a son, or for twenty-one years, most of them being for the latter term. Together, their rents exceeded £334. The yearly rents did not reflect the true value of the estates or the revenues the Earl could expect from them. The rents reserved in the tenancy agreements were mostly the low 'ancient' rents dating from medieval times. They could be and, over a period, were added to by 'improvements', which were enclosures taken in by the tenants from the rough pasture land and moors and eventually incorporated in the main holdings. Otherwise, they tended to remain static. What brought the Earl extra income were the entry fines (gressums) which the warrant and indenture holders paid him on entering their tenements.

   Many of his current tenants had paid them in 1579–80, the others at some subsequent date when taking over the holding, either by assignment or, usually, following their father's death. Entry fines allowed the landlord to anticipate future income from the tenements, in effect taking part of the rents in advance. It was a traditional method, accepted by the tenants, with the current value of the holding as the basis for agreeing the size of the fine. As land values rose, fines also increased, but, because they had to await the death of the lord or tenant, always tended to lag behind. In a period of high inflation, as in Elizabeth I's later years, these 'beneficial' leases as they are known, by which the tenants enjoyed longish tenures and paid low rents and fines on death or assignment, worked to the benefit of the tenants and to the disadvantage of landowners. Earl George had enjoyed a windfall in 1579–80 when the new leasing had brought him big sums from fines. Thereafter, the beneficial leases in Craven and Westmorland were a contributory factor to his perennial cash shortage. Economic rents, with their annual or frequent increases in response to changing land values and market demand, were not charged on the township holdings except when they were vacant and awaiting re-letting.

The big share of the rents, £377, contributed in 1597 by tenants at will and on yearly leases is rather misleading. Many of those who held at the will of the lord were the poorer, sometimes older people, cottagers and small-holders who could not afford the fines to buy warrants or leases. Hitherto they had been fairly secure because it was in the Cliffords' interest as much as theirs for them to continue undisturbed. They were most at risk in 1602; hence the 'fear' among them which Ferrand reported. However, what artificially bulked up the income from these tenancies in 1597 was the manors of Buckden and Starbotton in Langstrothdale, which the Earl had only recently obtained. The holdings there had reverted to him but no warrants or leases had been granted because, as is explained later, he was at loggerheads with the tenants.

The immediate problem for Earl George in May 1602 was the re-leasing of the many holdings which had reverted to his hands, mostly small tenements, closes and improvements but some tithes and mills. The thrust of his policy, to raise cash by granting new tenures with longer terms than in the past, was apparent from the start. The new terms, taken from July, varied between twenty-one years, one, two or three lives, and 99 years limited by two or three lives. The last was a novelty, introduced for the first time on the Craven manors. The entry fines paid could be as low as twenty and as high as sixty years' rents, reflecting Russell's valuations and no doubt the Earl's social conscience. The average rate was forty, with the much more profitable mills and tithes bringing in the most from the better-off bidders. Getting some of his tenants to accept the new leases for three lives and his demands for higher entry fines may explain the delay before he was able to seal the first leases, which was not until 16 July. But there was also the tricky question of good lordship. As Ferrand had pointed out 'the poore hopeth my Lord wilbe both Honorable & pitiful to them & in some respect respect their habilities.' This he appears to have done.

The main hurdle facing him and his advisers was the mortgages he had negotiated in 1597 with 335 tenants on twenty-one manors. He could not afford to repay the £8,775 he owed on them and he needed to raise money by persuading these tenants also to take longer leases instead of the warrants which they would revert to on redemption. The tenants, well-aware of his objectives, were in a strong bargaining position. Much depended on his powers of argument. His continuous presence at Skipton was essential because the tenants dug their heels in, resisting, if not the new leases, then the price the Earl wanted them to pay. He succeeded, though with what mutual concessions is not recorded. As he informed Cecil on 26 August, he was spending his days doing nothing but making bargains with his tenants 'who now (though it were long ere I could draw them to it) are yielding to so good a course as I hope will effect the purpose I came down for and clear my debts.'[5] That last optimistic note may have been to impress his friends but if he meant it he was still blinkered about the real state of his finances.

The principal redemptions he made between August and October were in Silsden, with others in Gargrave, Cononley, Giggleswick and Haltongill hamlet in Littondale. The first redemptions were ad hoc, with the Earl and his commissioners obviously feeling their way, and then they established a standard formula. By this, the tenants surrendered their mortgages and warrants and paid twenty years' ancient rent for new leases of 99 years and three lives. Added to the forty years' rent advanced in 1597, they had now paid sixty years' ancient rent for much more favourable leases. Because the three lives specified usually included

The first entry, William Wilson of Silsden, in the 'Estate Ledger', in which 429 leases granted from 1602 to 1606 were recorded

their children, continuity of tenure of their farmholds was assured for at least another generation, a big improvement on even the beneficial leases they had been accustomed to. For his part, the Earl would be relieved at his prospective cash receipts and also at the precedent for granting new leases to his many Percy Fee tenants.

The other feature of his policies in 1602 was his resort to sales. He disposed of Nesfield capital messuage, the small manor of West Hall, his moiety of the manor of Steeton, the rent of Cracoe capital messuage and various woods, as shown in Table 9. His long summer's and autumn's work negotiating face to face with groups of tenants and flanked by his gentry commissioners in the Great Hall of the Castle had saved him the mortgage money and in addition brought the promise of £7,309 17s. 8d. in cash. A third of the money would be paid him at once, the rest in two instalments over an eighteen months' period. Even that considerable sum would make little more than a dent in his debts, but he had now established the lines of the policies to follow up the next year, so prospects for him were far better than in May. The Earl tried to wriggle out of his royal duties to continue his work and free himself from the financial 'miseries' he had endured, but he was ordered back to Court, leaving on 7 November for, as it turned out, his last Accession Day appearance and jousting as Queen's Champion.[6]

It would be at John Taylor's prompting that a target was set for the total sum the estates would have to yield if the Earl were to succeed in paying off his major creditors. In March 1603 Russell or one of the other commissioners drew up a plan to raise £30,000 from Craven and Westmorland which included what had already been agreed in 1602. A few week's later this estimate was amended to £35,809 17s. 8d. Two major developments in leasing were to produce the bulk of this cash. The first, during 1603, was the opportunity given to all the remaining Clifford Fee tenants, that is those who had not held mortgages, to take leases for 99 years and three lives. Consequently, a further 145 now converted to this form of lease, compared with the 122 who had held mortgages. This lease now became the standard form of tenancy throughout the Clifford Fee, only the very poor remaining as tenants-at-will.

The second development concerned the Percy Fee manors of Settle, Giggleswick, Long Preston and Litton. By the time the Earl was free to deal with them, in September, October and November 1604, his perceived cash needs had grown much more urgent, one factor being his expenses at the coronation and in entertaining the Court at Grafton. He persuaded the Percy Fee tenants who held mortgages to pay forty years' rent for fee farm grants or long leases of several thousand years. Some of the other tenants who in 1602 had taken different kinds of lease on redemption or had not held mortgages also bought fee farms and long leases and the mills were granted out in the same way. Fee farms and leases of 6,000 or 7,000 years now became the near-uniform tenancies in the Percy Fee so that the traditional distinction between that and the Clifford Fee was maintained; here as always a matter of practicality as well as sentiment. On all these manors the ancient rents were retained, many now as quit-rents, and clauses in the leases reserved the Earl's manorial rights.

The other proposals in the £35,000 estimate involved the conversion into cash

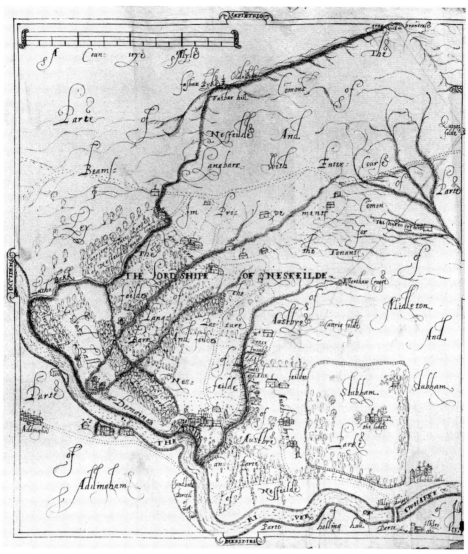

The lordship of Nesfield, c. 1580, showing Nesfield manor house, West Hall and the Sandbeds, all sold by Earl George in 1602

of some of the most valuable assets of the Craven estates; individual manors, capital messuages, demesnes and woods, by a variety of methods – outright sales, fee farm grants and long leases with nominal rents reserved. Here again what dictated the choice of manors was their origin because those most affected were the more recent acquisitions, mainly from Sir Ingram Clifford, that is Grassington, Eshton and Gargrave besides Nesfield, West Hall and Steeton where the process had begun in 1602. As in the past, the Skipton, Barden and other demesnes and parks and woods were protected as much as possible. The one big inroad into Skipton's demesnes was the Earl's lease for three lives of the former granges of Elso and Holme to Michael Lister Esq. Woods were among the patrimony's most precious assets but necessity forced the Earl to continue his 1602 policy of selling entire woods. The biggest and most vital of his enclosed demesne parks he obviously had to keep, but he did sell much felled timber from them. From all this leasing and selling in Craven he received £33,539 15s. 9 ½d, the last instalments falling due in 1606, after his death. The details are summarised in Table 9.

One of the intriguing aspects of the contracts is how so many tenants found so much ready money for their purchases in so short a time. Some of the richer, the yeomen as well as gentry, paid out very big sums. Cecilie Wright, Anthony's widow, paid £320 in cash (with the release of £80 mortage money extra) for her fee simple grant of Nesfield capital messuage. William Ferrand gent. paid £1,300 for the manor of West Hall, Thomas Ferrand gent. £850 for the fee farm of Carleton capital messuage and its two mills, Edward Malham Esq. £800 for Bradley and Gargrave, Michael Lister Esq. £700 and Stephen Tempest gent. (soon to be Sir Stephen) £366. Big buyers below the rank of gentry included Miles Fawcett who paid at least £1,500 for 6,000 years' leases of Upper Hesledon and Sleights in Littondale. There is a suspicion that the Earl's biggest customer, Robert Bindlose Esq., borrowed in London to cover the £1,444 he had paid out by March 1606, which would not be surprising because he was a financier and property-speculator as well as landowner. The only local man known to have borrowed was barely of gentry status, Richard Burton, the vicar of Linton, and he still owed the money at his death in 1615.[7] Some of these men had in the past lent the Earl considerable sums, even at times when agriculture was hard hit. But all the gentry and yeomen purchasers give every indication of enjoying revenues from land and cash in their coffers which were hardly tapped by parliamentary taxation and county and parish dues. Protests vouched by them or on their behalf sound like special pleading when one considers what funds they could dispose of for their private advancement.

Where the husbandmen, craftsmen, tradesmen and even cottagers found so much spare cash between 1597 and 1606 is a mystery. It points to a hidden economy which no other contemporary sources such as inventories reveal and of which historians remain in ignorance. Most leases were paid for in three instalments, the first immediately, the others over the next two years. True, some of the existing tenants-at-will (the poorest cottagers, small-holders and widows) remained as such, but a considerable number of them did find the wherewithall to buy leases. There are only seven recorded cases from 1602 to 1605 of tenants having difficulty in paying and they were treated by the Earl and his officers with their usual sensitive consideration. Three whose rates initially had been set higher than average were reduced, *ex grac comit*; Thomas Paradine intervening for Robert Craven of Woodhouse & Appletrewick on behalf of his uncle, Sir William Craven, mercer, money-lender, Lord Mayor of London in 1611, and benefactor of his home village, Burnsall. One has to conclude that many Craven inhabitants had cash reserves, assets of their own and annual incomes greater than is supposed. Raising money by marketing cattle and sheep or by credit, borrowing from

TABLE 9 *Earl George's receipts from sales and leases, 1602–5*

CRAVEN

Property	Receipts (to nearest £)	Individual purchasers

1602
Sales

Steeton (moiety)	296	William Garforth Esq., moiety of the capital messuage with 330 acres £200
Nesfield capital messuage	384	Cecilie Wright, widow of Anthony
West Hall manor	1,300	William Ferrand gent.
Cracoe Capital messuage rent	150	George Burton gent.
Total	2,130	

Leases

On redemption of mortgages	326	
Other leases	2,223	
Tithes	966	
Total	3,515	

Woods sold

Long Preston	135	Thomas Heber gent.
Others	120	
Total	255	

Small tenement and tithe leases and woods sold	1,410	
1602 total	*7,310*	

1603–6
Sales

Steeton (moiety)	944	William Slater of Keighley and John Midgley, moiety of 34 tenements, £700
Gargrave capital messuage	830	Edward Malham Esq. the capital messuage £300 and £100 release of mortgage. Caleb Waterhouse Rayburge Close £300 William Bentley Hawes Close £170
Eshton capital messuage	100	Robert Bindlose Esq., with £2,000 pre-paid on mortgage
Nether Hesledon	960	Robert Bindlose Esq.
lambert Hall, Skipton	210	
Total	3,044	

TABLE 9 continued

Property	Receipts (to nearest £)	Individual purchasers
Long leases with nominal rents reserved		
Grassington	4,391	George Lister gent., capital messuage and corn mill £800
Over Hesledon and Sleights	1,500	Miles Fawcett
Eshton	457	
Total	6,348	
Long leases and fee farm grants with full rents reserved		
Nesfield	530	
Carleton capital messuage and two corn mills	850	Thomas Ferrand gent.
Bradley capital messuage and mill	500	Edward Malham Esq.
Green Field	200	Exchanged with Thomas Heber gent. for Marton Woods sold for £200
Appletreewick	155	
Cononley	37	
Settle, on redemptions	1,086	
Giggleswick, on redemptions	1,368	
Long Preston, on redemptions	145	
Litton, on redemptions	172	
Corn mills	709	
Total	5,752	
Other leases (21 years, 99 years and three lives and variations)		
On redemptions	1,602	
Silsden	1,313	
Other tenants	3,785	
Home and Elso	700	Michael Lister Esq.
Corn mills	486	
Total	8,586	
Woods sold	2,500	
1603–6 total	*26,230*	

WESTMORLAND

1602 Receipts	3,000	
1603–5 Projected receipts	9,000	
Total	12,000	
GRAND TOTAL	*45,540*	

(*Sources*: YAS, DD121/31/8; 32/3; 34/1, and the Estate Ledger)

relatives and neighbours, was normal and the complexity of such transactions in rural communities is becoming better known. But to do this on the scale to produce £8,000 in 1597 and then £19,000 only a few years later would not have been feasible because whole townships throughout Craven were involved. What makes it all the more remarkable was that the region, indeed the country at large, had barely recovered from the four worst years of the Tudor century for harvest failures and disease.

With changes on such a massive scale, some tenants were almost certain to be hard done by. The evidence indicates it was not the Cliffords' officers but the new owners who were unsympathetic. But in the case of the half-manor of Steeton Earl George may be regarded as equally to blame. Between 1596 and 1600 the tenants there had purchased one quarter of the manor from its owner, William Oglethorpe Esq., the owner of the other quarter being Sir Gervase Clifton. In the autumn of 1602, the Earl persuaded seven tenants to purchase the fee of his moiety of their holdings, which would give them ownership of three-quarters of their farmholds. Others, like Widow Hustler, were too poor to buy theirs. The next stage in the sale of the property was delayed until 1604. Then William Garforth, already owning one quarter of the manor house, its demesnes and 330 acres of ground, purchased the Earl's moiety for £200. The Earl repudiated his previous agreements with the other 34 tenants and sold his moiety of their farmholds for £570 to William Slater of Keighley. He paid Slater what the tenants had already handed to him in fines, and Slater allowed those sums in the new leases he now granted. Slater and William Midgley also bought the moiety of the water corn mill.

As was usual in a change of ownership, there were competing claims for tenancies and Slater, essentially a land speculator, took the options which best suited him. Widows were protected on the Cliffords' manors by clauses in the leases which guaranteed them the moiety of the holding to enjoy during their widowhood. Slater, having purchased the moiety of the fee, was not bound by this custom. One widow, Ann Smith, owning one quarter of her late husband's farm and Clifton the other, was put under pressure by Slater who made a quick profit by selling his moiety to John Hargreaves. After two years, she was ready to move. She importuned Earl Francis, who paid her £2 on 28 March 1607 to quit the tenement quietly. But she was still in financial trouble and, on the following 24 September, she was 'so Clamoras about the gates' of Skipton Castle that he gave her a further £2 to clear her debt to Henry Currer. This time he made it conditional that she relinquish, that day, all her rights to the tenement. What happened to her thereafter, or to Widow Hustler, is not recorded. As for the manor, Garforth bought Slater's and Midgley's part in 1607 and his son obtained Clifton's in 1613, so that his family became the new manorial lords there.[8]

The damage Earl George did to the Clifford inheritance in Craven was enormous. The annual rental was reduced by a quarter – more if the rise in land values from 1597 to 1602 is taken into account. Three quarters of the entry fines were lost, another severe limitation on future revenues for his successors. Capital messuages, with their mansions and the best manorial land in their large demeses, had been surrendered to local gentry. The manors of Grassington, Eshton, Settle,

Giggleswick and Long Preston were but empty shells, with little more than manorial and mineral rights retained, entry fines a thing of the past and yielding only their traditional low ancient rents or even less, not up-to-date economic rents. In Grassington quit-rents of 1d. or 2d. were reserved. Earl George had liquidated much of the capital assets in Craven, crippling the revenues permanently for short-term ends. In addition, he had placed some of the best surviving assets beyond Earl Francis's immediate reach by granting twenty-one years' leases of some of the demesnes and tithes. Another consequence, a transformation which made itself felt very soon, was the sense of independence the new tenancies gave to the populace throughout Craven and especially in the Percy Fee. The tenants had never been docile. Now, though they were still subject to manorial and honorial courts and minor impositions, the strongest restraints imposed on them by tenure had been permanently weakened, as Earl Francis was to find to his cost.

Yet, at the very end of Earl George's life, there was a glimmer of recovery in Craven in several respects. The Buckden and Starbotten men who had refused new tenures, claiming tenant-right, lost the lawsuits he and his brother initiated against them and, in 1607, purchased long leases like the rest of the Percy Fee tenants, though from Francis not George. In 1605, James I sold George the manors of Rylstone, Hetton, Linton and Threshfield with lands in Flasby, all forfeited by the Nortons after the 1569 Rebellion, for £5,143, reserving to the Crown their £128 11s. 7d. rents. The purchase price was largely, though perhaps not entirely, recouped by granting the sitting tenants leases for 99 years and three lives. The Cliffords had waited long to obtain their old enemies' manors. In the intervening thirty-five years they had been badly supervised by the Exchequer[9] but at least they had been protected from Earl George and in 1605 they were new assets giving Earl Francis scope for exploitation. The third development was the building of a lead-smelting mill at Grassington between 1605 and 1606 which enabled Earl Francis to open up lead-mining on the pastures and moors.[10] To judge by the conditions of his sales of the tenements, George had intended this but died before his plans could start. Furthermore, although the inheritance had suffered, the best had survived. The Barden, Bolton and Skipton demesnes and the Leeds and Craven tithes remained as jewels in Earl Francis's tarnished coronet and could be burnished further by him and his Burlington, Devonshire and Thanet successors.

In Westmorland the situation in 1602 was different, estate policies having diverged from Craven's almost from the start.[11] Countess Anne and Earl George had all but withdrawn from direct farming and become absentee, rentier landlords. Their large demesnes around Brougham, Appleby and Brough castles, with some good arable, meadow and abundant pasture land, had mostly been let out, the rents from them contributing over half the total income in 1597. Under Earl George some corn was grown at Appleby, and Ramgill Close in the great 321-acre Southfield there was retained for grazing and hay for his stewards' and commissioners' and the judges' horses at the regular manorial courts and yearly assizes. He had pasture for 800 sheep on Little Fell in Burton and kept sheepwalks and rakes on Middle Tongue on Milburn Fell, Sandford and East Stainmore, though in practice his flocks were modest in size. More important were his two remaining enclosures for fallow deer, in Whinfell Forest in the North and Newhall in East Stainmore. Haunches of venison and pies and pasties graced his table at Brougham on the rare occasions he visited and satisfied the judges and local gentry with traditional aristocratic munificence. Philip, Lord Wharton was master of the game with a £2 fee and Robert Leigh gent., tenant of the capital messuage at Newhall, looked after the herd there. Camden was impressed by the goats, red deer and enormous stags he spied running wild on Mallerstang Edge. How they fared under Earl George is not recorded. In Westmorland, as in Craven, he had regularly to prosecute deer-stealers in the Star Chamber, many of them local gentry or their servants, their derring-do also a profitable pastime with much of the venison ending up on their tables. Unlike the old days, George was rarely in residence to feast them, so even more than in the past they helped themselves.

Earl George's tenure is a graphic illustration of the perils of absentee landlordism. Absorbed in privateering, he paid little attention to his Westmorland lordships until in 1602 necessity forced him to act. The revenues he had lost were then mostly beyond his reach. In a period of high inflation, the gross rental had increased from £623 in 1572 to only £800 in 1597, far less than it should have done with such a high proportion of demesnes let, and £200 below what Countess Margaret was soon to collect. The story revealed by the 1604 survey, the only important document extant, is that George showed interest in Westmorland only when he entered into a major financial arrangement in London, which in turn gave a temporary jolt to his estate officers in the county. The thorough work of leasing in 1582, when novelty and necessity engrossed the Earl, was followed by a two-year gap before the first Book of Dimissions was compiled in 1584 just at the time he was running up his first biggish debts in London. There was then a three-year gap before new books were started in 1587 and 1588, his officers in Westmorland also feeling the pressure which the Queen, Burghley and his creditors put on the Earl to enter into the first of the important indentures to pay his debts. New books were begun in the three consecutive years 1590–92, coinciding with the flurry of activity over the Earl's indenture tripartite and his grant of the Westmorland properties as Countess Margaret's dower estate. Her legal and gentry advisers, if they were diligent, would have examined the accounts if not the properties themselves. The next new start was not until 1596 and 1597 when the Earl was mortgaging the farmholds in Craven and negotiating his financial arrangements prior to the Puerto Rican expedition.

Another hiatus followed, five years certainly and, in terms of arrears, seven, because of George's pressing affairs in London, Craven and the Borders, during which the effects of the mortality and debilitation of the famine and plague years of 1597–98 on his tenants and their tenancies were ignored.[12] The long-overdue thorough investigation of all his Westmorland interests did not come until 1604, two years later than in Craven, while he was spending most of his time at Carlisle dealing with Border affairs. A new rental was made in April and the survey taken between 19 and 25 September by commissioners chosen from his most trusted servants – his feodary and steward of courts Thomas Braithwaite, Christopher Pickering Esq. of Ormside, Andrew Oglethorpe gent., George Heles and John Cocke.

As in Craven, the commissioners superseded the local men. They enquired meticulously, with the aid of large juries drawn from four areas, Brougham, Appleby, Brough and Kirkby Stephen, into the management of the estates since 1582 and the collection of rents and gressums. Their survey is a record of laxity and venality for over two decades, with a hint of an over-sympathetic attitude by the receiver-general, Thomas Hilton gent. of Hilton, and his fellow officers towards the tenants. They displayed a certain closeness in outlook to the tenants which was to the detriment of the Earl's proprietary interests. Among the many tenants in arrears for rents or gressums was John Addison, bailiff of King's Meaburn, who still owed 6s. 8d. of his fine due in 1582. Henry Dethick, bachelor at law, a justice of the peace for Cumberland and Westmorland, agreed he owed £5 6s. 8d. of his gressum for his tenement at Palyeat Green in East Stainmore and his predecessor there, Richard Johnson, 15s. 4d. The smallest sums were not overlooked. Even Thomas Birkbeck gent., found to owe 2d. a year rent for the past twenty years for a house in Knock, had to pay the debt and the rent in future.

Certain demesne assets had suffered badly. Formerly profitable eel arks at the foot of Sowerby Tarn, an eel and fish tarn and pond in Whinfell where once there was 'great store of fish', and a tarn at Langton were all now decayed. This was in part due to the low household demand, yet they could have been rented out. Unwisely, Earl George had ignored one of the best sources of income, woodsales, his receipts as recorded in the 1597 rental being nil. Yet the woods, as Countess Margaret pointed out, were worth between £1,000 and £1,200 and he could have made £300 a year from the underwoods and left the woods in good condition.[13] Instead, because of ill-supervision, the local people had helped themselves. The commissioners noted 'great spoil' for instance at Flakebridge, in Luckman Flat, where no spring had been made and the ash trees wasted, and at Knock, where a hundred oaks and ashes had unlawfully been cut down.

As usually happened when estate officers were easy-going, there had been many unlawful encroachments on the Earl's moors and wastes, especially intakes, and building houses without licence. A typical case was John Jackson of Over Brough who had set up the third part of a 'faire hous' of two couples using stones taken without authority from the ruins of the castle. Most audacious was Richard Leysenbie who, trying to avoid his dues, had shifted his entire dwelling house from the Earl's land in Bongate onto the property of the Dean and Chapter of Carlisle, even more slumbering landlords no doubt. In Mallerstang alone, four firehouses and five other houses had been constructed on the Earl's waste without consent or rent since 1582 and thirty-five illegal improvements made. All these and many more elsewhere were incorporated into the rental in 1604; recovery and increase of the Earl's revenues being the prime objectives of the commissioners' work.

The chief culprits, they discovered, were the men best able to indulge themselves at the Earl's expense: his own estate officers. Not content with their fees and legitimate perquisites they had in a variety of ways deprived the Earl of his due revenues. Robert Leigh enjoyed the large and profitable leaseholds and fine dwellings at Winderwath and Newhall and wages as storer and for long had been a welcome guest at Skipton Castle where a chamber was reserved for him. Yet he had failed to pass on to the Earl £20 of a fine given him about 1594 by a former tenant of the messuage in King's Meaburn which Leigh himself held in 1604. Much the worst was Thomas Hilton. Since the death of Jane Hartley on 1 July 1599 Thomas had let part of Southfield in Appleby to several tenants for £16 a year, though it was worth £20, and the rest of the pasture he had kept for himself without paying rent. The jury averred that the winter and spring fogg, worth £25, had been 'lost by evill husbandrie & eating the same in Somertime'. The commissioners calculated that Hilton owed £189 in rents unpaid over nine years and required him to re-imburse the Earl. Hilton had also helped himself on other properties. In Burrell demesnes in Appleby he had intruded on the Earl's land by stopping a way for the past twenty years, forcing travellers to make another route. He promised to open up the way after he had gathered the crop growing on it.

There were accusations also that Hilton, like Leigh, had held onto gressums, the commissioners being sufficiently convinced not to press the tenants to pay, although they could not prove the receiver-general had failed to account for them. Richard Dent of King's Meaburn was one of these men. He claimed he was admitted to the second moiety of his tenement in 1594 in Hilton's chamber in Appleby Castle at night with the candles lit, in the presence also of George Salkeld Esq. of Corby, one of the stewards, Thomas Braithwaite and Henry Denton, and had paid the receiver-general £4 in two instalments. This Hilton denied. Andrew Hilton had taken advantage of his brother's protection to help himself to land. He had pulled down the houses of one messuage he held from the Earl in Burton and laid down the fences of its grounds so that they could not be distinguished from his own demesnes. He had paid no rent for the messuage for fourteen years and claimed it as his own. On Langton Moor, Hilton had interfered with the tenants' commoning of cattle and turbary, they being denied redress for these wrongs because of the Hiltons' standing.

The commissioners recovered over £825, owed to Earl George since 1582, taking the money in cash or bonds, although many debts must by then have been written off for lack of proof. They also increased some rents to catch up with inflation; that of Robert Leigh for Newhall from £2 to £13 11s. 7d. This necessary action was one aspect of the Earl's great efforts to find cash to reduce his debts between 1602 and 1605. Yet it may have been the lesser part of the commissioners' work which started, as in Craven, during 1602 and then was delayed by the Earl's royal duties. The evidence is not easy to interpret. In the 1602 plan to raise £30,000 from the whole of the Earl's estates, his officer entered the sum of £4,000 'ffor estates to be made in Westmorland for which all the tennants there have sealed Covenants until my Lord have time to seall their Assurances.' In the later revision, he crossed out this entry and substituted £3,000 which by then – 1604 or 1605 – had been collected and he expected to receive more. The jointure act preserved the Westmorland lordships from the massive selling and leasing the Earl achieved in Craven, but he may have got round it to some degree by other means.

The tenants were later to complain that 'before the saide late Earles death they were assessed to paye theire ffines' and paid them accordingly. Some, indeed, were still paying instalments of gressums in January 1607 which, Stephen Taylor noted, were 'due of the Contracts with the Tennants for Warrants in the last yeare of my late Lord'.[14] This seems to have been more than the granting of new tenancies on warrants to catch up with the seven years' backlog of vacancies, even allowing for the heavy mortality of 1597–8. It is conceivable that the Earl hoodwinked his tenants into taking new warrants, they perhaps not expecting him to die so soon afterwards. For his part, George had learnt too late for his own financial good that his reputation as a successful commander, Queen's Champion, even titular sheriff, counted for nothing with the farmers of the Eden Valley and Pennine fells, or for that matter with his own officers there. What did carry weight was firmness and persistence by dedicated subordinates and with proof of customs, precedents and right title presented by sworn juries, their whole proceedings regularly backed by his own presence and understanding.

CHAPTER 13

Retrospective

If there was a star in the firmament guiding Earl George's fate and fortunes it was the Virgin Queen herself. His life and her reign virtually coincided. He was but three months old when she ascended the throne and survived her by only two and a half years. His beliefs and outlook were moulded during his youth and early manhood in the direction she wanted. He was imbued with the ferment of ideas and cultural flowering of the high Elizabethan renaissance, personifying through his voyages the expanding horizons of the real world of Hakluyt and in the symbolism of his jousting armours, pageants and portraits the romantic idealism of Sidney's *Arcadia* and Spenser's *Faerie Queene*. His career was given shape and substance by the unfolding crises and call to arms of the later 1580s. His most vigorous and mature years were devoted to the dangerous and, in the end, triumphant defence of the realm against Imperial Spain. His achievements and his failings are synonymous with the most lauded and the more sombre features of the closing years of her reign.

Tudor monarchs regarded the nobility as their family, cousins who had to be favoured but also controlled and put down when they posed a challenge to their own power. Queen Elizabeth, safer and more relaxed after the fraught first decade of her reign, treated the rising generation of nobility as her surrogate children.[1] Nowhere perhaps are the wiles of her management of them more exposed than in Earl George's life. The circumstances of his wardship and his half-sister's blood-royal link predisposed Elizabeth to have a special regard for him and his affairs. She often acted as if she were his godmother with a divine dispensation to intercede and direct or cajole him as she thought fit, either in person or through the agency of Burghley and the Lord Admiral and the weighty authority of the Privy Council. George's career, embracing the roles of courtier, Champion, privateer and spendthrift, lent itself more than most to royal manipulation. the Queen's influence could be beneficent or baleful because she necessarily placed the good of her realm above the well-being of a valued warrior. The mutual interplay which permeated all facets of their relationship allowed the Earl to express his views and feelings privately in the seclusion of a palace garden, lobby her through her ministers and his friends and publicly exploit royal celebrations with speeches and presentations entreating her favours. Yet she was always the mistress and he the servant and, unlike Essex, he knew better than to step over the bounds set by the implicit rules defining a subject's subordination to his monarch.

Under Queen Elizabeth Earl George remained no more than a trusted courtier who was frequently consulted but never had any overt influence on the direction of royal policy. Even had the Queen wished it, and there is an element of reserve in her regard for him, his restlessness for action and his rash plundering of Dutch merchants early disqualified him from being drawn into the Privy Council because the alliance with the United Provinces was vital to the war against Spain. His cavalier attitude towards continental traders was an expression of his pronounced xenophobia. Where its roots were is not clear; perhaps in Bedford's circle of Puritan expansionists.[2] It was strong enough for him to refuse to let his daughter learn a foreign language and, in San Juan, to demand that all negotiations should be conducted in English. There was even less likelihood of his taking a central role from 1592, the unfortunate episode of the *Madre de Dios* casting a shadow over his relations with the Queen until at least 1601. Moreover, although courtier dalliances were commonplace, his treatment of Countess Margaret, one of the Russell coterie among the ladies-in-waiting, could not have endeared him to the Queen. The slate was cleared when James I succeeded. He was more attuned to George's attitudes and qualities and his style of kingship at last gave the Earl the opportunity to show his worth in government.

What drove George, from the time of his return to Court in 1582, was more than the motives Fulke Greville listed, that is curiosity, necessity, ambition, covetousness, a desire for false greatness and disdain for the lesser things in life. Above these, for George, stood the higher callings of family honour and pride and a sense of tradition, and 'Honour' in the chivalric sense espoused by Greville's mentor, Sidney, in *Arcadia*.[3] Intertwined through all George's actions was a deep sense of loyalty and service to the Queen's person. Had he ever been allowed royal command, which was his due, then his incessant striving to uphold his honour and prove his value to himself, to the Queen and Court and his fellow mariners would probably have deflected him from his costly private endeavours. It might, too, have earned him the fruits of office such as Leicester, Essex, Raleigh and Howard enjoyed, which would have sustained his courtier life and saved his estates. There is some justification, allowing for the anachronism of the concept, for Williamson's conclusion that with Cumberland 'patriotism was the aim, if privateering was the means.'[4] But it misses the personal dimension, a kind of Arthurian questing to achieve self-fulfilment through honourable deeds.

Much that the Earl achieved in the broad span of a varied career enriched the Elizabethan scene. Three spheres of action had lasting influences. Firstly, his maritime exploits contributed to the undermining of Philip II's thrust for the hegemony of Western Europe and the Atlantic ocean, an immense and exhausting struggle which England could not afford to lose, whatever the cost. Secondly, the Earl was prominent in the exploitation of the victory; in the birth, through the East India Company, of England's oriental trade and in the pressure group advocating western expansion. Finally, there was his essential work in the pacification of the Borders which resulted in the opening up of safe travel and trading between James I's two kingdoms, uniting them in a real, practical sense. His interests thus spanned England's forced emergence, under foreign threat, from its insular chrysalis, and his own contribution to the process was distinctive.

Assessments of Earl George's career have inevitably focused on his maritime exploits. Contemporary and later Jacobean writers fairly appraised his worth. To the poet John Davies of Hereford he was 'Neptunes vice-gerent' whose merit was honour, glory and fame.[5] Camden linked him with Essex and Nottingham as one of the three earls who 'for the honour of their Queene and Country' adventured their lives and spent their blood in battles on land and at sea and in the mouth of cannon. He pithily described George as 'renowned for sea-service, armed with an able bodie to endure travaile, and a valerous minde to undertake dangers'.[6] Dr Layfield regarded George's achievements as undervalued. He recorded in his private history of the Puerto Rican expedition, 'I professe I would have his Lordships service done to his Countrye thought of according to the great desart thereof.'[7] Later historians of the Spanish war have perhaps granted him less than his due. Corbett acknowledged his high skill in capturing San Juan de Puerto Rico yet surmised that if the government had been disposed to a vigorous renewal of the war he 'might well have supplied the place of Essex', a view Oppenheim endorsed. As a charismatic leader perhaps, but Cumberland proved himself much the superior commander and tactician and incomparably the more responsible. Those writers who, like Williamson and even more Tenison, looked in detail at his career formed better appreciations of his abilities, while Andrews emphasises the exceptional nature of his privateering.[8]

On the Earl's whole career, the comments of two eighteenth-century researchers have never been bettered. To an unnamed chronicler of the Clifford family, the kernal of the Earl's attainment in national and personal terms was that of a man eminent in our ancient annals, 'by deeds of arms of use to his country, of honour to himself'; an epitaph which, placing him alongside his most notable martial ancestors, would not have displeased him. The learned Dr Whitaker, who made full use of the Clifford archives (more than now survive) in compiling his massive *History of Craven*, wrote of him: 'If we trace him in the public history of his times, we see nothing but the accomplished courtier, the skilful navigator, the intrepid commander, the disinterested patriot. If we follow him into his family, we are instantly struck with the indifferent and unfaithful husband, the negligent and thoughtless parent. If we enter his muniment-room, we are surrounded by memorials of prodigality, mortgages and sales, inquietude, and approaching want. He set out with a larger estate than any of his ancestors, and in little more than twenty years he made it one of the least.' Whitaker was given to moralising and full-blooded comments. It would be impertinent to quibble, in the light of this study, at his choice of phrases; better to remark that the individual strands in the Earl's life on which he focused were in reality interwoven, the causes and effects a seamless web, and if they are picked out for too close scrutiny the rounded picture can all too easily be lost.[9]

Earl George's pursuit of his ends was at enormous cost to himself and his family. His privateering caused the chief damage. The financial failure of his voyages has been delineated above. Ill-luck is a partial explanation, especially as regards the carracks. One contemporary stressed this. He wrote that the Earl was so excellent a person it could hardly be said what was wanting in him, 'but still there was a very considerable thing wanting him – namely a steady gale of good

Earl George 'Like Mars in valour . . .', engraved by William Rogers

fortune.'[10] It is a judgement which carries weight. Andrews has pointed to the near-impossibility of large fleets like the Earl's ever being profitable, yet from 1589 to 1593 arguably they were, or would have been but for the Queen.[11] The changing nature of the sea-war thereafter counted against him. Fundamental, however, was the conflicting duality of his objectives, profit being too often subordinated to royal service. Even more constricting was the Queen's calculating direction. Noblemen and other courtiers placed their persons and wealth at the disposal of the Crown; that was one of their functions. The Earl had even more to offer than that, the rarity of powerful private warships, at the Privy Council's beck and call from the time of the Armada. Dr Layfield would have extended the principle further. He could see no reason 'why the goodes of great rich men in a state may not rightlye be called the goods of the state, seeing where there are wealthye subiectes the state ys truelye called wealthy'.[12] The Earl would not have taken issue with that. What he begrudged was the many who filled their purses while he emptied his for the good of the realm.

George himself claimed he had spent £100,000 on his voyages and there is no reason to dispute that. Besides his losses privateering, there were the usual courtier indulgences, his gambling infusing all in the manner John Taylor described. His daughter recalled that his extreme love of horseracing, tiltings, bowling matches, shooting, hunting and 'all such expensive sports did contribute the more to the wasting of his estate.'[13] As many great landowners before and since have done, the Earl regarded his inherited wealth as the means to live his life to the full. His fellow courtiers regularly ruined themselves by building prodigy houses, entertaining the Court, and spending out of their own coffers what the Crown should have provided for them when on embassies and military campaigns. A feckless few merely followed a wastrel's life.[14] George left no great mansion and precious few artifacts as tangible evidence of his extravagance, but it is hard to deny him equal merit for throwing his private resources against a foreign foe instead. Not until the close of his career did he master the damaging flaw in his nature, his lack of self-restraint; earlier he had to be reined in by the Queen and Burghley, the Countess's friends, even Francis and his officers. Yet, as soon as he reached the limelight he craved for, as Champion, his financial fate was sealed. He might bewail his losses thereafter, but he could not reform his ways because he was forever tied to the Court.

How great the debts he had accumulated by 1602 is conjectural. The best guess is the cash available to reduce them before 1613, when they still totalled £18,000. By then, his leasing and sales of lands in Craven and the yearly income from the cloth licence had brought in £60,000. The £6,000 owed on the Bolton mortgage and its accumulated interest had been separately paid off. Much of his £4,400 Crown debt for subsidies, victualling and port bonds was written off by James I. The £1,000 due on the Winderwath mortgage was cleared when he failed to redeem it, the manor another forfeited property. His later debts to his brother, never paid, were large enough for Francis to set up a commission to enquire into them. Making allowance for George's extra outlay on twice entertaining James I at Grafton, his debts and accumulated interest may have exceeded £80,000.[15]

A balance sheet of which of the Earl's many associates gained and who succumbed because of his actions puts the broad consequences of his prodigality in perspective. Francis must be included in the count. He sacrificed a gentleman's estate in sharing his brother's early courtier flamboyance. Prominent among the unfortunate was their cousin Henry Cholmley who lost heavily because of his expensive outings with the Earl. Henry's chief creditor, Richard Humble, pursued him in the Courts for his debts.[16] Hercules Foljambe petitioned James I for reward to recompense him for the £10,000 he claimed he had spent privateering, drawing the King's attention to his saving the Earl's life at the assault on the bridge at San Juan. The merchant William Shute was incarcerated in the Fleet prison because of the Earl's default on the £1,200 he owed from the 1598 expedition. He won redress against Earl Francis yet had to settle for half that sum in composition.[17] Other people of note whose debts were never paid included

Lady Hawkins, owed £66 13s. 4d.; Sir Robert Dormer of Wing, £200 lent to Countess Margaret when she was in want; Bird and Newton the privateers, £417, and Sir Michael Stanhope, the £125 arrears of George's rent for Gresham House. Lady Montagu assigned the note for the £80 he owed her to one of her ladies, but it was never honoured.

Much the hardest hit were the many tradesmen in London and elsewhere whose debts were never or only partially satisfied following similar litigation – tailors, drapers, apothecaries, sadlers, innkeepers and even painters such as Isaacson. Those who suffered most from the Earl's broken pledges were his creditors, mainly ships' suppliers, at Plymouth where £370 was still owed in 1620, at Portsmouth £670, Southampton £140 and Rochester £150. These men were all economically vulnerable, as the Earl well knew. By his dishonourable defaulting, they did much to subsidise his maritime adventures and, with their families, paid an unfair price. Not George himself but Earls Francis and Henry and Richard, 1st Earl of Burlington had the problem of giving them some recompense, the last of the debts not finally cleared until the 1660s.[18] In all this, George was no different from many Elizabethan and Jacobean courtiers, who went through life like comets, leaving trails of debris in their wakes.

Outweighing the unfortunate, both in numbers and in the extent of their gains, were the multitude who made the most of the Earl's wastefulness. His major creditors, whether nobility, gentry, lawyers, government officials or city merchants, all profited and in many instances got far more than they deserved, witness the undervaluing of the manor of Hart. Wright, Walmesley and Bindlose stand out among George's officers and other northern gentry who made the most of their chances to buy Clifford properties. However, it was the middling and lower social orders in Craven who in the long run were the greatest gainers, no matter their immediate qualms and reluctance to hand over their hard-won cash reserves for better tenancies. Earl George's sales and leases gave many of them and their successors a degree of independence never previously enjoyed, with management of their own farming and far higher retained profits from it. This was the beginning of a social revolution on the Clifford estates which was largely completed by the time of the Civil War.

Earl George's disposal of his Yorkshire lands, starting with Cowthorpe in 1586, and his Craven sales and leases put a different complexion on the role of the gentry, lawyers and merchant-privateers from whom he borrowed so much. They merely provided short-term credit, whereas it was the purchasers of his Yorkshire properties who ultimately financed his voyages. Theirs was a considerable, if unknowing, contribution to the maritime war against Spain. The Earl might grieve that he had thrown his lands into the sea, yet what he had in fact done was sponsor a property redistribution from his own great noble family into the hands of lesser men. This was an almost irreversible switch in land-holding. Although Lady Anne Clifford did her utmost to put the clock back,[19] in reality her father had thrown away the proprietorial dominance in Craven he had inherited. The baronial and manorial super-structure largely remained, but over most of the Percy Fee and in parts of the Clifford Fee there was a tenurial hollowness beneath. War, it is often remarked, is an accelerator of change. Earl George was the principal conduit by which Philip II's war reached into Craven and permanently altered its society and economy. Only Countess Margaret's jointure prevented a similar process in Westmorland.

It remains to consider what effect George's career had on his immediate family. His marriage was to be a casualty. The fluctuating relationship between him and Countess Margaret has been recounted above. During the 1590s they kept up appearances and the Earl's letters exude a warmth which was belied by the increasing distance between them in attitudes and lifestyles. That the Earl had a mistress was common knowledge. Lady Anne later wrote of her with delicate reticence: 'But as good natures through human frailty are oftentimes misled: so he fell to love a Lady of Quality; which did by degrees draw and alienate his love and affection from his so virtuous and well deserving wife, it being the cause of many discontents between 'em for many years together.' Williamson depicts her as a young, comely and ambitious woman who died about the same time as the Queen, yet cites no source for that assertion.[20] She may have been the mother of George's elder natural child, Frances, who would have been born about 1601, but not of the younger, George. His mother – and more likely Frances's also because no Court scandal is recorded – was still alive in 1634 and receiving a pension from Earl Francis, though she was then in straightened circumstances. Francis brought up both the children and they entered his household.[21]

Countess Margaret's marital plight inspired one notable writer, Samuel Daniel, and, it has been postulated, Fulke Greville also, to pen works of quality in moral support. The long-standing nature of the relationship with the lady of quality gives some credence to Joan Rees's tentative attribution of Countess Margaret as the would-be recipient of Greville's incomplete 'A Letter to an Honorable Lady'. On the other hand, Ronald Rebholz considers it more likely a fictional creation of a personal nature which also reveals the Christian stoical phase in Greville's development as a writer. His dating of its compilation as between 23 December 1588 and 2 August 1589 does not fit Countess Margaret's life if the reference to the noble lady's children is taken literally. That reference would place it either before 8 December 1588 or to the fifteen months from Lady Anne's birth on 30 January 1590 to Lord Robert's death on 24 May 1591, which is still feasible. Greville's denunciation of the lady's husband as 'evill', corrupt and crafty, would be intemperate language to apply to Earl George, whom he knew well, yet this was a private letter, not published until 1633. Greville's listing of the errant husband's motives and use of the phrase borrowing 'wodden feet to walke over . . . movinge waters' may be thought more apposite to the Earl than most noblemen then at Elizabeth's Court. What is striking is Greville's depiction of the manner of the lady's separation and his advice on how to come to terms with the fact of the mistress. These are so close to Countess Margaret's known position that if she were not the intended recipient she shared the identical dilemma and, even more, the temperament of the lady in question. Greville stresses that the lady's husband 'hath neither life, love, nor sense to you' and his devotion and affection had long since been transferred from her to his mistress. After rehearsing the actions the lady might take to win him back, such as competing with the mistress in beauty (the Countess in 1591 was still only thirty-one) and even combining with her, his advice was to attack her husband over his estates and, instead of trying to master him, master herself. 'My councell is therfore *Madame*! that you enrich your selfe upon your owne stocke, not looking owtwardlie, but inwardlie for the fruit of true peace, whose rootes are there.' This is precisely the Puritan sentiment and course of action which would appeal to the Countess. According to Lady Anne, it is what she did. As to why Greville left the 'Letter' unfinished: the death of Lord Robert and the jointure agreement which gave the Countess financial security might be thought reason enough. It may be, in the end, that the Countess's life paralleled Greville's fictional perception of how a noble lady of Puritan persuasion would behave when betrayed by her husband. If so, then Lady Anne would have recognized the analogy. A copy of Greville's published works is prominent among her books depicted in the Appleby triptych.[22]

Because Samuel Daniel was under Greville's patronage from 1594 to 1595 and shared his literary and political associations, including antipathy towards Sir Robert Cecil, there are grounds for seeing continuity between the 'Letters' they composed. Daniel, furthermore, had been connected with Countess Margaret before 1592. She appointed him Lady Anne's tutor in 1598 and he subsequently dedicated two works to her which obliquely drew attention to her unhappy condition. 'A Letter from Octavia to Marcus Antonius', published in 1599, is a metaphor for Earl George's neglect of his Countess. Octavia is the faithful, deserted and wronged wife who, though she detests what Antony has done, bears him no ill-will and 'still is thine though thou will not be hers.' Daniel's fine verse epistle to the Countess, published in 1603, concludes in praise of her,

> You that have built you by your great deserts,
> Out of small meanes, a farre more exquisit
> And glorious dwelling for your honoured name
> Then all the gold that leaden minds can frame.

Earl George's reaction to Daniel's literary comment on his marriage is not recorded. To his credit, he did not dismiss him as Anne's tutor. There is, in Daniel's espousing of the Countess's cause, not just servility to a patron but the whiff of Puritan and political oppositionism, aping Greville's, to the dominant Cecil faction at Court which included the Earl.[23] Neither then nor since has George won literary plaudits for his treatment of his Countess. She and Lady Anne have always been accorded the ethical high ground, gained for them by the power of the printed word, both Daniel's and even more Lady Anne's, with her gift for self-justification.[24]

The Earl's family suffered as his debts mounted during his final years. Countess Margaret had great difficulty in getting him to maintain her and Lady Anne. Although they were still together at the start of 1600, when they exchanged New Year's gifts with the Queen, and in the following June when they supped together as guests at the great wedding of Lady Anne Russell to Henry, Lord Herbert, the Earl of Worcester's son,[25] they had separated by the end of the year. George was generous in allowing the Countess the use of Clerkenwell House, well-furnished except for bedding, linen, brass and pewterware, which he formally agreed to supply on 8 April 1601 but which were still deficient in 1603. He promised to assign her £1,000 a year for her upkeep and to enable her to pay her debts, a level of income she would have received had she been widowed. Yet, getting him to pay much, if any, of this money was all but impossible; not surprising, because his own purse was empty. Her entreaties and the pressure of Sir Dru Drury and her other friends forced George to draw up an agreement and give bonds to keep to it. But he still could not perform.

Counsels of patience from him exasperated her when what she desperately needed was the wherewithall to maintain her in dignity, especially at the Coronation, and to rent a residence in the country when the plague drove her and Lady Anne out of the capital. George's excuses were not entirely specious. On 16 April 1604 he explained his failure to send any part of the £500 due for her allowance from Craven (when she knew he had agreed terms with his tenants) on the grounds that they would not pay any part of their fines until their assurances had been formally completed and that could not be done until the law term began, which was indeed the case. He promised to satisfy her with the first money to reach London. On 20 July he was again apologising for the late payment.[26]

These were years of deep sadness and humiliation for Countess Margaret, separated, kept short of money, incessantly pleading, ousted by her husband's mistress and denied her role as wife and hostess on the King's 1603 visit to Grafton, although she was there in attendance on the Queen. Yet no solicitous intervention by James I himself and concern by Lord Treasurer Buckhurst and other interested parties could wring from Earl George anything more than good intentions until well into 1604. Lady Anne noted that when her mother and father did chance to meet, 'their countenance did shew the dislike they had one of the other', but he would speak to Anne and give her his blessing. When the Countess died in 1616 she blamed her debts, which had grown without any fault of hers, partly on the 'want of those meanes which my late lord should have paid me'.[27]

Earl George was in good health during the summer of 1605. He visited Bess of Hardwick with Francis late in July, discussed with her Lady Anne's marriage to Lord Cavendish's son, and hunted in the park where he killed the great stag, which had been long preserved, with twelve couples of hounds. From there he made his way to Grafton to prepare for the royal visit in August. Lady Anne stayed with him at Grafton until 1 September, and departed from him at Greenwich Heath to join her mother at Sutton-in-Kent.[28] Then, early in October, he was suddenly taken ill at Oxford with a 'Bloody flux', dysentery perhaps, his life was despaired of, and he hastily made his final dispositions. In a flurry of indentures he assigned his cloth licence, tithes, ironworks and other lands in Yorkshire and Westmorland (jointure apart), a hundred years lease of Holden and Carleton in Craven, his Cumberland properties, and all his goods, jewels, household stuff and other chattels to Sir Robert Cecil, now Earl of Salisbury, Edward, Lord Wotton (who married Lord Wharton's daughter Margaret), Francis Clifford and John Taylor for the purpose of paying his debts and Lady Anne's portion. He settled the Skipton and other Craven lands on Sir William Ingleby for the same dual purpose.

Lady Anne Clifford (1590–1676), aged fifteen, by Sir Peter Lely

On 18 October he reaffirmed the succession in a new deed to the male line, his own male heirs first, then Francis and his male heirs, remainder to Lady Anne and her right heirs, then to Francis and his right heirs. This was enrolled in Chancery. In his last will, drawn up on 19 October, the Earl lamented that his debts had 'growen farre greater than heretofore, they were, by reason of my many occasons of charges and greate expence of late, and within a fewe yeares paste'. These had forced him to make changes he had not intended. At its heart, as in 1598, was the request to his daughter to accept cash in recompense for any part of his inheritance, lands, jewels, plate or chattels. He now bequeathed her £15,000, to be paid in instalments which he and Francis must have at that moment considered practicable: £3,000 within two years of his death; £3,000 a year later; £4,000 a year after that, and the final £5,000 in two sums the year after she attained the age of twenty-one. She was to be given £200 annual allowance for each of the first two years after his death. The rub was that Lady Anne should agree not to molest or cause trouble for Francis in his tenure of the estates. The Earl made the payment of the last £5,000 of her portion conditional on that. He also required her to deliver up to Francis the bond by which assurance had been made to her in 1598 for payment of her portion from the Bolton demesnes.

Whatever was left after the debts and Anne's portion had been paid, and he did not envisage a great deal, he bequeathed to his brother, 'to whome I have left all to thende he may paie all'; honour at stake, with its moral imperative. Should Francis die without male heirs and Lady Anne inherit after him, then his daughters Margaret and Frances should each receive £4,000 from the estates. Salisbury, Wotton, Francis and John Taylor were to be the executors and the first two he asked to remind the King to grant to Francis the Crown's Debateable Lands on the Cumberland Borders, as he had promised. Salisbury, to the King's relief and gratitude, acted as a buffer between him and George, but confirmed the

Cup and cover, made in Norwich in 1583, given by
Earl George to Lady Anne

grant would be made. The Earl rewarded his faithful servant John Taylor with a twenty-one years' lease of the New Park (Park George) at Skipton. He gave £20 to the poor of Skipton parish and the parish where he died, and worried he could not afford legacies to his other friends. As in 1598, he called on Richard Hutton to advise Francis on the burdens he would have to shoulder.

In a touchingly penitent letter to his wife, he begged her to 'take as I have me[an]t in kyndnes the course I have sett downe for disposinge of my estate and thynges lefte behinde', assuring her he had dealt most kindly with her. Out of love, he requested her not to have a hard opinion of his brother or start suit against him. 'Thou hast conceved wronge of him', he continued, 'for his nature is Swite and though wronge concet might well have urged him yet hath he never to my knowledge sayde or donne anythynge to harme thee or thyne.' His expressions of love and his homily to wife and daughter were to prove in vain. The will and its dispositions could hardly have upset them more, even though they must have long been aware of what he had in mind. Francis's assumption of his brother's part and sharing his problems since the early 1580s had caused Countess Margaret to distrust him and now the weight of her umbrage fell on him as she challenged on her daughter's behalf his right to the Clifford inheritance.[29]

George's letter, however, brought a death-bed reconciliation, the Countess and

Earl George's tomb, erected by Lady Anne Clifford between 1654 and 1655, in Holy Trinity Church, Skipton

Anne being present at his bedside in the Duchy House near the Savoy when he died on 29 October 1605, aged forty-seven. A little before his death, Anne records, he expressed 'much affection to my Mother and me'. He made to Dr Andrews, as Salisbury told the King, 'a religious and penitent confession in a faith constantly and clearly condemning all popish and corrupt opinions.' Although he requested the Countess to join him in his last communion, she would not do so. His bowels were buried in the Savoy chapel and his body was escorted to Skipton by William Graham and other servants for burial on 29 December in Holy Trinity. His funeral was solemnized in noble style on 13 March 1606 though his widow and daughter did not attend.[30]

No one had a better appreciation of the parlous state of the inheritance than Francis, or had been more supportive of his brother over the past quarter of a century. His reward for graft and loyalty was a *damnosa hereditas*, not just the burden of indebtedness and shrunken estates but a long, complex and acrimonious dispute over possession of the patrimony and its revenues, which were essential to him to clear the debts. The task was to prove to daunting for him and his son Henry over the next forty years. Lady Anne never wavered in her conviction that she was the true inheritor, through her father, of the centuries-old Clifford traditions, estates and titles. The breach in the family and its associated litigation, which lasted well into the eighteenth century, was Earl George's bitterest legacy.

Appendix I

ROYAL JEWELS, PLATE AND OTHER STUFF BORROWED BY SIR ANDREW DUDLEY FOR HIS MARRIAGE TO LADY MARGARET CLIFFORD, JUNE 1553

One fair tablet of gold to open in the back, made like a castle, garnished with 27 diamonds, 8 rubies and 4 sapphires cut lozenge-wise, with a picture of a woman and an agate holding a small diamond in her hand like a glass.

One fair brooch of gold set with 7 emeralds and 18 pearls.

A fair brooch of goldsmiths work set with 12 table diamonds and a diamond in the middle lozenge-wise.

One ring with a table diamond, another with a rock ruby, and another with a garnet.

Four rings with two pointed diamonds, one with a table diamond, and one with a diamond cut lozenge-wise.

One salt of crystal garnished with gold, set with small pearls and counterfeit stones like rubies, the foot enamelled green.

Forty-seven links of a small chain of gold containing 87 links, and 139 links of another chain containing 184 links to lengthen a chain to hang his garter George at when he was made Knight of the Garter.

One girdle containing 25 pieces of agates and 28 pieces of goldsmiths work enamelled black and 8 pieces of gold enamelled blue and black, with a great knob like a bell pendant garnished with small chains and pearls.

A girdle of gold having 23 pieces of gold set with 9 pearls in every piece and 24 pieces of gold enamelled black, with a pendant of gold like a lily pot garnished with small chains and pearls.

A girdle of goldsmiths work enamelled black, containing 16 pieces of gold, set in every piece a diamond, and 15 pieces of the same work this French pose *Ung sans chaingier*.

An upper habiliment containing 25 pieces of goldsmiths work enamelled black and white with a French pose written therein *Ung sans chaingier*, of which 25 thirteen pieces have set in them table diamonds.

A coronet of 15 pieces of goldsmiths work set with 15 table rubies, and 11 pearls between every piece, with 13 pearls at both ends set in collets of gold, with a flower pendant set with a rock spinel, a fair lozenged diamond, and 3 small table diamonds and a pearl pendant.

A flower of gold with a rose of diamonds in the middle and 8 small table diamonds on the borders, and three pearls pendant.

A clasp of goldsmiths work enamelled black, set with a table diamond.

Twenty pieces of aglets of gold, enamelled black with billets.

Twenty-eight pieces of fair aglets of gold enamelled white like biskets.

Sixty-three triangle buttons of gold enamelled black.

Two crepon partlets of cypress wrought with gold.

One pair of sleeves of linen wrought with gold.

One emerald set in gold.

Two fair table diamonds set in rings enamelled black.

A fair ring of gold with a blue sapphire, enamelled black and white.

One pair of plain perfume gloves.

One pair of gloves of white silk knit, garnished with gold, lacking the tops of the fingers.

A brush of hair with a handle of purple velvet, garnished with passement lace of silver and gold.

Sleeves of cambric and calico cloth for plucking out of French sleeves as following, viz. two pair wrought with black silk, three pair wrought with blue silk, and two pair wrought with red silk.

Two pairs of sleeves wrought with silver.

A smock of cambric wrought with red silk, and four other smocks of cambric wrought with black silk,.

A fine smock of holland edged with passement lace of gold, the collar ripped off.

Three linings for partlets of nettlecloth, wrought with red silk.

One lining for a partlet of cambric wrought with flowers of damask gold, being in three parts.

A pair of shears of iron for a woman, parcel gilt.

A table of Diana and nymphs bathing themselves, and how Acteon was turned into a hart.

Two partlets of fine holland, the collars wrought with silver.

Two coverpanes, the one wrought with gold and silk, and the other with black silk.

One cupboard cloth of fine holland plain, of one breadth.

Two targets of steel lined with velvet.

One pair of knives garnished with damascene work, the sheath velvet.

One cassock of black velvet all over embroidered with Venice gold.

An ewer of antique work of silver and gilt, garnished with pearls, jacinths, amethysts and other stones of small value – 22½ oz.

Three bowls with a cover of silver and gilt, weighing 97½ oz.

Three spoons of gold taken out of the green coffer in the silk house.

One Almayne cup with a cover thin beaten of silver and gilt, in a case.

Six lancegays with brazilwood staves, trimmed with green velvet and fringe of green silk, save one is with blue silk and velvet.

One remnant of bridge satin purple – 17½ yards.

One remnant of white bridge satin – 15¾ yards.

One remnant of black velvet containing 6 yards

Two remnants of black velvet, being velvet on both sides, together 5 yards 1 nail [one sixteenth of a yard].

One remnant of black velvet containing 2¼ yards scant.

One remnant of black satin containing 3½ yards.

One remnant of crimson satin containing 3 yards.

One hat of black velvet crossed over with passement lace of gold and black silk.

A hat of black velvet all over embroidered with twists of gold.

One case of knives of black leather printed with gold, furnished with knives tipped with metal gilt.

Two pair of fine bain sheets of three breadths.

Two pair of black silk hose knit.

A case of leather furnished with fine tools.

Three combs, a glass, an ear pick and a bodkin, all of white bone garnished with damascene work.

Two old garters.

Fifty-one ostrich feathers.

Two pair of black silk hose knit.

A comb case covered with crimson satin embroidered.

A Flanders chest.

Three collars of green and white velvet.

Six leames [collars for hounds] and collars of red velvet.

A wagon of ironwork.

(*Source*: Hatfield House MSS. CP 198/107–9)

Appendix II

MUNITIONS AND PROVISIONS DELIVERED TO MR JOHN WINGFIELD, CAPTAIN OF THE RED DRAGON OF THE EARL OF CUMBERLAND, AT PORTSMOUTH 25–9 JULY 1588 FOR THE QUEEN'S SERVICE AGAINST THE SPANISH ARMADA

	£	s.	d.
Thursday, 25 July			
Of Joshua Savoure,			
8 crossbar shot for demi-culverins			
70 crossbars for sakers			
70 crossbars for minions			
10 crossbars for falcons			
47 shackled shot for sakers			
50 round shot for sakers			
Of Thomas Beare of Fareham two hundred and a quarter and twelve pounds of beef at 13s. 4d. the hundred	1	11	1½
Of Gefferie Gaskin of Fareham two hundred and a half and three pounds of beef at 13s. 4d. the hundred	1	13	8
Of John Edmondes of Havant half a hundred and seven pounds of beef at 13s. 4d. a hundred	0	7	5½
Friday, 26 July			
Of John Lardner of Portsmouth thirteen hundred and a half and four pounds of beef at 13s. 4d. the hundred	9	0	5½
Of William Torye of Portsmouth six hundred three quarters and twenty-two pounds of beef at 13s. 4d. the hundred	4	12	7
Of Thomas Thornye two tuns and a hogshead of double beer without cask at 36s. the tun	4	1	0
Of Owen Totty a barrel of pitch to trim the ship	0	9	0
More of him, a coil of ropes weighing 25 lbs at 23s. the hundred	0	5	0
Of Rice Woodes of Gosport four hundred of bricks to make up the *Dragon's* hearth and back at 15d. the hundred	0	5	0

Of Edmond Monmouthe a hundred of laths for the said back	0	1	0
Of John Alawe four iron rakes to make clean the ship weighing 8 lbs at 3d. the pound	0	2	0
Of Lyonell Slade a tap bore, a spike gimlet and a small gimlet	0	1	0
Of John May half a dozen trussing hoops for the *Dragon's* tops	1	6	0
More due to him for hooping the beer and water casks and setting in the heads of the beef tubs for four ships and barks	0	3	0
Of Henry Mericke of Gosport one coil of ropes	0	5	0

Saturday, 27 July

Of Andrew Studley of Hampton a hundred and a half of dry fish at 12s. the hundred	0	18	0
More of him in Large bank fish one hundred and a half at 36s. the hundred	2	14	0

Sunday, 28 July

Of John Jenners' widow a tun of beer and cask at 28s. the tun and 8s. the cask	1	16	0
Of William Jones of Gosport 25 couple of bank fish called newland fish priced at	1	0	0
Of William Ryman five butts of wine at £6 the butt	30	0	0

Delivered to Mr John Wingfield, Captain of the *Dragon*
  20 demi-barrels of corn powder
  20 demi-barrels of fine corn powder
   2 budge-barrels
   2 quire of royal paper
   1 pound of glue
   1 dozen bowstrings
  100 twopenny nails
  218 crossbar and chain shot for sakers and minions
Received of Mr William Wallop out of the shire's provision 18 barrels of fine corn powder double casked at the charge of the shire.

Monday, 29 July

Of Henry Feelder a tun of beer and cask at 32s. the beer and 8s. the cask	2	0	0
Of Lawrence Inglebert 4,500 of bisket at 6s. 8d. the hundred	15	0	0
Of Peter Cooke for the Captain of the ship two dozen of bread	0	2	0
Of Mathewe Watkins 15 hundred of wood at 9s. a thousand	0	13	6
Of John Elliott			
100 sixpenny nails	0	0	6
100 fivepenny nails	0	0	5
4 candlesticks at 2d. the piece	0	0	8
taps and brimstone	0	0	4

	£	s	d
2 padlocks	0	0	8
sail needles and glue	0	0	3½
500 spike nails	0	0	8
20 ells of canvas for cartridges at 11d. the ell	0	18	4
a pound and a half of thread at 2s. 4d. the pound and 24 needles at 2d.	0	3	8

Of John Jenners these parcels, viz.

	£	s	d
4 coils of ropes weighing six hundred and a quarter and one pound at 23s. the hundred	7	13	11½
8 bushels of salt water measure at 20d. the bushel	0	13	4
3 hoggs and a punch to powder beef	0	6	8
3 tun of casks for beer	1	8	0
a butt of oakum weighing three hundred at 9s. the hundred	1	7	0
26 lbs of candles at 4d. the pound	0	8	4
a pottle of salad oil at 14d. a quart	0	2	4
4 lambskins at 5d. a piece	0	1	8
delivered to six of the company to buy them victuals	0	1	0
half a bushel of hair	0	0	3
2 rands of twine weighing a pound and a half	0	2	4
1000 scomp nails at 6d. the hundred	0	5	0
1000 twopenny nails	0	3	4
4 baskets for the gunners at 4d. a piece	0	1	4
Of Henry Filder 5 tun of casks for beer and water at 8s. the tun	2	0	0
More, one truss of hoops	0	3	4
Of Robert Woodes of Langstone 6 cords of 21½ ft a piece at 1½d. a foot	0	16	1½

Delivered to Mr John Wingfield, Captain of the *Dragon*, of powder and shot from Her Majesty's Tower of London
- 70 demi-barrels of corn powder double casked
- 50 round shot for demi-cannon
- 50 culverin shot
- 50 demi-culverin shot

Received of Richard Rogers, boatswain of the *Prudence*, of Captain Ryddesdale for the *Dragon*

	£	s	d
2 lists and a maintop sail halyard	0	13	4
2 maintop sail bowlines	0	6	8
a pair of main martinets and four martinets	0	15	0
2 maintop sail braces	0	4	0
2 clew lines and a mizzen lift	0	13	4
a coil of small ropes weighing a hundred and a quarter	1	0	0
a rope to make stoppers	0	2	6
a great copper kettle	4	0	0
2 dozen platters	0	3	0
a dozen small cans	0	2	0
9 bread baskets	0	1	6
3 lanterns	0	1	6

a great bowl	0	0	10
a frying pan	0	2	0

Note: all the ropes were half-worn

Total cost of setting forth the *Dragon*, besides her own store   £106   17   6

Delivered to the Master Gunner of the *Dragon* William Maddocke
    the store of the ship belonging to the gunners' room
        7 muskets and 7 bandoliers
        36 calivers, 21 flasks, 13 touch boxes and 8 bandoliers to them
        3 cases of pistols
        6 demi-barrels of gunpowder of a hundredweight apiece or thereabouts
        3 humber barrels of gunpowder
        a small barrel of match

Delivered to Morris Jones, boatswain of the *Dragon*, all the said ship's sails and ropes and a piece of new canvas belonging to the ship and a topsail of the *Bark Clifford*.

Munitions delivered from the Bark Clifford *to the* Flyboat
        2 castiron minions mounted
        40 round shot for minions
        12 crossbars for minions
        6 crossbars for falcons
        1 crow of iron
        4 minion and ladle sponges
        1 falcon ladle
        1 wadhook with a staff
        and 2 bonnets priced at £2

(*Sources:* PRO, SP12/214/28 fol. 1;/215/87 fol. 1;/215/88)

Appendix III

A fore course, bonnett and drabler little used
A maine course bonnett and drabler little used
A maine Topsaile little used
a missen and a missen bonnett little used
a newe spritt saile little used
an olde maine course bonnett and drabler
more another maine course
more an olde forecourse
more a Top gallont saile
a spritt saile Topsaill
x Iron scantions
2 Iron cheines 4 nettinges
3 Cables by which the shipp rides broken
2 ankers of 30 cwt or thereaboutes a peece
1 anker of 16 cwt
1 anker of 12 cwt
3 olde muckes
   a whole sute of rigging as the ship came from Chatham saving that the most
      part of the small runing ropes is spent and hath bene otherwise used
   A sewt of winding tackle blockes with 4 shevers of brasse
   Brasse shevers more 50
x Iron pompe staves
3 Iron pompe brakes
3 Crowes of Iron
2 paire of Cannon hookes
1 paire of billowes
5 esses of maine cheines of iron
3 dead mens eies with cheines of iron
6 tackell hookes
5 port hinges
4 boat hookes
2 fidd hammers
2 fiddes

   4 capsquares for carriages
      a Loose hooke
   2 dipsy leades
   1 harping iron
   1 fisgig
   1 hawser of 7 inches
   2 hawsers one of 7½ inches thother of 7 inches
  40 gunners tackles
120 roles of matche decaied
   4 dossen of plate Cartringes which are in 2 chests
  14 exceltries
  17 plates of leade to lay over the peeces
   5 great brasse bolles
   3 old brasse ladles
  36 sprigges and runners
   4 ladles
   2 wadhookes
   3 cwt of square shott
  16 breechinges
   1 table in the great Cabin with 4 stooles and one chaire
   2 earthen great pottes for water
   1 pompehooke
      A Bell of brasse
      A Longe boate lying at Plimoth verie little used
   2 fornaces in the Cookerome with iron worke to binde the Cookerome
      The top mastes and yerd serviceable
      Demi Cannon shott 49
      Culvering shott 162
      Demi Culvering Crosse barre 49
      Demi Culvering rounde 34
      Sacre Crosse barre 14
      Sacre round 12

Demi cannons	2, of 60 cwt apiece, total weight 6 tons.
Culverins	16, of which 8 of 42 cwt apiece, 8 of 36 cwt 2 qrs apiece, total weight 31 tons 8 cwt.
Demi culverins	12, of which 2 of 29 cwt 2 qrs, 10 of 29 cwt, total weight 17 tons 8 cwt.
Sacres	8, of 20 cwt 2 qrs apiece, total weight 8 tons 4 cwt.

Sum total of the tons of ordnaunce, 62 tons 27 cwt.

(*Source:* Stevens, *Court Records*, pp. 42–4)

Notes

1. George, Lord Clifford, and his Heritage: 1558–70

1. Clay, p. 386.
2. Helen Miller, *Henry VIII and the English Nobility* (Oxford, 1986), pp. 2–3; L. Stone, *The Crisis of the Aristocracy 1558–1641* (Oxford, 1965), Appendices VI, XIV.
3. GEC, iv, 26; S. J. Gunn, *Charles Brandon, Duke of Suffolk c. 1484–1545* (Oxford, 1988), *passim*.
4. Clifford, chaps 1–23; Clay, pp. 355–81; R. T. Spence, *The Shepherd Lord* (Skipton, 1994), *passim*.
5. Spence, 'Earls', pp. 6–13; Clay, pp. 375–86; Whitaker, pp. 11–13. For Suffolk's role, see Gunn, *Suffolk*, pp. 209, 220.
6. R.T. Spence, 'Tithes and Tithe-holders in the Parish of Leeds from the Dissolution to the Restoration', *Publications of the Thoresby Society*, 134 (1990), 1–6; Currey, 26/5.
7. Lond. K. For the other third, see *VCH*, East Riding, iv, 46.
8. Clay, p. 382.
9. BL, Lansdowne MS 75, no. 29. Winchester was the marquess and the senior earls Oxford, Northumberland, Shrewsbury, Kent, Derby, Worcester and Rutland.
10. Whitaker, pp. 391–3.
11. Bodleian, MS Dodsworth 118, fol. 160v; Clifford, p. 84.
12. BL, Harleian MS 6177, fol. 33; YAS, MS 338, fol. 423; Whitaker, pp. 398–402, 430–3, 486–8.
13. Stone, *Crisis*, chap. II.
14. Lambeth Palace Library, Shrewsbury Papers, 695, fol. 92.
15. G.R. Elton, *England under the Tudors* (1960), pp. 202–14.
16. Bodleian, MS Dodsworth 88, fol. 105.
17. C.C. Stopes, *Shakespeare's Environment* (1918), pp. 248–57; G. C. Williamson, *Lady Anne Clifford, Countess of Dorset, Pembroke & Montgomery 1590–1676. Her Life, Letters and Work* (Kendal, 1922), pp. 23–4; *CPR*, 1554, p. 117.
18. PRO, State Papers Supplementary, SP46/8/5.
19. *The chronicle of Queen Jane. . .* , ed. J. G. Gough, Camden Soc. old ser. XLVIII (1850), 169.
20. CSPD, Venetian, 1556–7, p. 1,077.
21. *The diary of Henry Machyn . . . 1550–63*, ed. J. G. Nichols, Camden Soc. old ser. XLII (1848), 82. The marriage terms are noted in Bodleian, MS Dodsworth 88, fol. 104.
22. Lond. G/2 (1572 Inventory). On the Earl's hostility to a foreign marriage, see M. A. R. Graves, *The House of Lords in the Parliaments of Edward VI and Mary I* (Cambridge, 1981), pp. 85–96, 289, n. 72.
23. Neville Williams, *All the Queen's Men* (1974), pp. 59–62; Barry Coward, *The Stanleys Lords Stanley and Earls of Derby 1385–1672*, Chetham Soc. 3rd series, XXX (1983), 31–2, 144–5.
24. Lambeth Palace Library, Shrewsbury Papers, 696, fol. 39; *CPR*, 1554–5, p. 247; Clay, p. 386.
25. Clifford, p. 91; Clay, pp. 379–83.
26. *Clifford Letters of the Sixteenth Century*, ed. A. G. Dickens, Surtees Society, CLXXXII (1962 for 1957), 149. Some of the alchemical works he owned survive in KRO, WD/Hoth/A988/1,2,3.
27. Williams, *All the Queen's Men*, pp. 91–106; P. Collinson, *The Elizabethan Puritan Movement* (1967), pp. 26–27.
28. Whitaker, p. 338; Williams, *All the Queen's Men*, pp. 105–110; *DNB*, VII, 40, XLIX, 431–3; Susan E. Taylor, 'The Crown and the North of England 1559–70: a study of

the rebellion of the Northern Earls, 1569–70, and its Causes' (unpub. PhD thesis, Manchester University, 1981), p. 52; P. W. Hasler, *The House of Commons, 1558–1603*, History of Parliament, 3 vols (1981), I. 264–5; J. M. Robinson, *The Dukes of Norfolk* (Oxford, 1982), p. 59.

29. YAS, DD203/11.
30. Miller, *Nobility*, pp. 83–4; Williamson, p. 3; *An Elizabethan Recusant House*, Richard Smith's 'The Life of the Lady Magdalen Viscountess Montague (1538–1605), ed. A. C. Southern (1954), pp. x–xi, 43.
31. Clay, pp. 381–5; Leeds City Archives, Ingilby Records, 3098 (Tankard).
32. PRO, State Papers Domestic, Addenda, Edw. VI to Jas. I SP15/15/111, 121, 127; /21/63, 20; *Memorials of the Rebellion of 1569*, ed. Sir Cuthbert Sharp (1840), *passim*; Taylor, thesis, pp. 294–5; J. T. Cliffe, *The Yorkshire Gentry from the Reformation to the Civil War* (1964), pp. 168–76.
33. Clay, p. 381; Whitaker, p. 338; Williamson, pp. 5–6. Wardship is explained below, chapter II.
34. PRO, SP15/17/35.
35. *DNB*, VII, 40; GEC, iv, 23–7; Clay, p. 385; PRO, Wards 9/150B, fol. 298 (Wharton); R.T. Spence, 'The Pacification of the Cumberland Borders, 1593–1628', *Northern History*, XIII (1977), 66, 74–5. Henry, 8th Earl of Northumberland was allowed to succeed after his brother was beheaded at York in 1572.

2. Guardianship and Tutelage: 1570–9

1. Bolton MSS, Book 13**, May–July 1576.
2. Bedfordshire County Record Office, Box R262, I, m. 2. The most valuable horse listed was 'Grey Cumberland' (m. 8).
3. J.H. Wiffen, *Historical Memoirs of the House of Russell*, 2 vols (1833), I, 473–4; *DNB*, XLIX, 431–3.
4. John Nichols, *The Progresses and Public Processions of Queen Elizabeth*, 3 vols (1823), I, 299–300.
5. Stone, *Crisis*, pp. 734–9; *DNB*, XXVII, 56; Collinson, *Elizabethan Puritanism*, p. 22.
6. Wiffen, *Russell Memoirs*, p. 474.
7. *Les Reportes del Cases in Camera Stellata 1593 to 1609*, ed. W. P. Baildon (1894),

p. 228; Peter Lake, *Moderate Puritans and the Elizabethan Church* (Cambridge, 1982), pp. 57–9.
8. Dickens, *Letters*, p. 149; Lambeth Palace MS 807, also printed in S.R. Maitland, 'Archbishop Whitgift's College Pupils', *The British Magazine*, XXXII (1847), 360–5; XXXIII (1848), 17–29; Williamson, pp. 7–11; *DNB*, XIV, 614–21 (Lord North). Courses at Trinity are discussed in Joan Simon, *Education and Society in Tudor England* (Cambridge, 1967), pp. 108–12, 251–3, 316.
9. Victor Morgan, 'Cambridge University and "The Country" 1540–1640', *The University in Society*, I, ed. L. Stone (1974), 190.
10. PRO, Signet Office Docquet Books, SO3/1. Musgrave was the son of Sir William of Edenhall who obtained the Nortons' property of Norton Conyers in the North Riding (*The Visitations of Yorkshire 1584–5 and 1612*, ed. Joseph Foster (1875), p. 143) and a descendant of both Thomas, 8th Lord Clifford and Lady Vescy. Venn identifies him with the Richard who matriculated from Jesus College aged 8 in 1566 (*Alumni Cantabrigienses*, ed. J. and J.A. Venn, Pt I, vol. III (Cambridge, 1924), 229). For Shute, see *DNB*, LII, 169, and for Brogden and others named, see W.J. Sheils, *Archbishop Grindal's Visitation, 1575*, Borthwick Texts, 4 (York, 1977), p. 16, and *Admissions to Trinity College, Cambridge*, ed. W. W. Rouse Ball and J.A. Venn, II, 1546–1700 (1913), 70, 76, 86, 96, 105.
11. Williamson, pp. 10–11; John Parker, *Books to Build an Empire: A Bibliographical History of English Overseas Interests to 1620* (Amsterdam, 1965), p. 144; John Sugden, *Sir Francis Drake* (1990), p. 3.
12. Bedford CRO, Box R262, I, m. 7; II, m. 1.
13. G.B. Parks, *Richard Hakluyt and the English Voyages* (1961), pp. 65–7; R. Hakluyt, *The Principal Navigations Voyages Traffiques & Discoveries of the English Nation*, 12 vols (MacLehose edn, Glasgow, 1903), I, xviii.
14. *The Three Voyages of Martin Frobisher. . . 1576–8*, ed. R. Collinson, Hakluyt Society 38 (1867), 163, 167–9.
15. Parker, *Books to Build an Empire*, pp. 70–1; BL, G.6479; PRO, C54/1214.
16. Woburn Abbey MSS, Earl of Bedford Papers, 2.

17. PRO, Wards 9/380, fols 103v to 386, fol. 283v; 7/13/53, 54. The social aspects of wardship are explored by Joel Hurstfield, *The Queen's Wards: Wardship and Marriage under Elizabeth I* (1958).
18. Woburn Abbey MSS, Earl of Bedford's Papers, 2.
19. Gervase Holles, *Memorials of the Holles Family 1493–1656*, ed. A.C. Wood, Camden Soc. 3rd ser. LV (1937), 41; *Staffordshire Pedigrees*, ed. Sir George Armytage and W. H. Rylands, Harl. Soc. LXIII (1912), 215.
20. Diana Poulton, *John Dowland* (1972), p. 315; Williamson, pp. 19–20.
21. Wiffen, *Russell Memoirs*, pp. 507–8; *DNB*, XLIX, 433.
22. Williamson, pp. 11–12. Wharton's recognizance for £4,000 to Countess Anne and Viscount Montagu on 18 June would be to ensure his provision of a jointure. He also borrowed £400 from Sussex on 6 July, secured by a £1,000 recognizance (PRO, C54/1019).
23. Spence, *NH*, XIII, *passim*.
24. Woburn Abbey MSS, Earl of Bedford's Papers, 2; PRO, C54/1021; Chatsworth, BAS, Box B3/2 (grant 6 July, 1577), witnessed among others by Richard Musgrave. The Russell mansion later became known as Corney House (T. Faulkner, *The History and Antiquities of Brentford, Ealing and Chiswick* (1845), p. 368.
25. PCC, 45, Windsor.
26. Williamson, pp. 12, n. 1, 286; *DNB*, LII, 169; Nichols, *Progresses*, II, 68, 83.
27. KRO, Hothfield MSS, WD/Hoth, Box 44.
28. *HMC, Ninth Report*, Corporation of Plymouth, p. 277.
29. Williamson, p. 286.
30. Claire Cross, *The Puritan Earl* (1966), p. 264.
31. Williamson, p. viii.
32. Chatsworth, G.R. Potter's lists, p. 115.
33. Whitaker, p. 399; Clay, pp. 383, 387; KRO, WD/Hoth, Books of Record, III, fol. 32. Marton was one of the founder trustees of Ermysted's School, Skipton (Whitaker, p. 437).
34. *The Register of Admissions to Gray's Inn, 1521–1889*, ed. J. Foster (1889), p. 54; KRO, WD/Hoth, Books of Record, III, fol. 186.
35. Bolton MSS, Books 13B, 13*, 13**.
36. Elton, *Tudor England*, pp. 303–5; J. J. Cartwright, *Chapters of Yorkshire History* (Wakefield, 1872), pp. 149–50; BL, Lansd. 30, no. 54; *The Memoirs of Sir Hugh Cholmley Knt. and Bart* (1777), p. 9; Cliffe, *Yorkshire Gentry*, pp. 168–76, and for the Moncktons, p. 376.
37. Stone, Crisis, chap. II.
38. For some of the men who served the Earls, see Clay, p. 384.

3. Landowner and Courtier: 1579–86

1. *Longleat Papers*, ed. J.E. Jackson, Wiltshire Archaeological Magazine, XVIII (1879), 269.
2. Whitaker, p. 354.
3. *HMC, Salisbury*, XVII, 461.
4. E.M. Tenison, *Elizabethan England*, 13 vols (Royal Leamington Spa, 1933–60), VIII, pt VI, 189.
5. Whitaker, p. 430.
6. Williamson, p. 276.
7. PRO, Wards 9/140, fols 291–4; YAS, DD121/29/3.
8. Clay, pp. 383–4, 386–7; PRO, C54/777.
9. Currey, 28/138, fol. 125; Bolton MSS, Sundry, IV (Petitions); Book 13*, 22 Feb. 1575–6.
10. Currey, 28/138, fols 79–80; Bolton MSS, Sundry.
11. Christ Church, Oxford, MS 109, fol. 7; Chatsworth, BAS, Box B3/2.
12. D. Welch, 'Three Elizabethan Documents Concerning Milburn Fell', *Transactions of the Cumberland and Westmorland Antiquarian and Archaeological Society*, new series, LXXXV (1985), 136–49.
13. Bolton MSS, Book 250.
14. Currey, 28/6; Bolton MSS, Sundry, 237, 238, 240; Currey, 46/13; Lond. PB/29965/41.
15. Bolton MSS, Sundry IV, 67, 161.
16. *HMC, Belvoir*, IV, 206; Sheffield Central Library, Bagshawe, I, 1026; Currey, 28/138, fols 73–4.
17. Clay, p. 383; Currey, 28/138, fol. 92; KRO, WD/Hoth, Books of Record, III, fol. 145.
18. Currey, 28/138, fols 92, 125; Bolton MSS, Book 212. As earl, George was entitled to £20 per annum fee from the Crown to sustain his title, which was paid from 1584 (PRO, C66/1245).

19. Currey, 28/138, fol. 73; YAS, DD121/31/9.
20. Bolton MSS, Sundry.
21. Bodleian, MS Dodsworth 88, fols 102, 105; Bolton MSS, Sundry, IV (Petitions); Chatsworth, BAS, Box B3/2.
22. KRO, WD/Hoth/34.
23. *Yorks. Fines, Tudor*, II, 149; PRO, C54/1111; Whitaker, pp. 90, 242; Lond. E/8.
24. *Yorks. Fines, Tudor*, II, 187; PRO, C54/1185, 1252; J.P. Steele, *Feet of Fines, Cumberland, during the Reigns of Edward VI, Mary, Philip and Mary, and Elizabeth*, (n.d.) p. 23; D. Lyson and S. Lyson, *Magna Britannia*, 6 vols (1813–22), IV, 145.
25. Lond. PB/221165/107.
26. PRO, Lists & Indexes, IX, Lists of Sheriffs for England and Wales (1898), p. 151; Sir Robert Somerville, *History of the Duchy of Lancaster*, I, 1265–1603 (1953), 523, 525; *Calendar of Letters and Papers Relating to the Affairs of the Borders of England and Scotland*, ed. Joseph Bain, 2 vols (Edinburgh, 1894–6), I, 35.
27. Williamson, pp. 13–14; Hasler, *House of Commons*, pp. 264–6; Spence, *NH*, 1977, pp. 64–7.
28. Williamson, pp. 14–15; *CSP, Spanish, (Elizabeth)*, 4 vols (1892–9), 1580–6, p. 552.
29. *HMC, Salisbury*, X, 138.
30. Clay, p. 396.
31. *HMC, Various Coll.*, IV (1907), 229; Jackson, *Longleat Papers*, XVIII, 269.
32. *The Roxburghe Ballards*, ed. W. Chappell, 9 vols (1888–97), I, 1–9.
33. Bolton MSS, Book 99, fol. 119r.
34. PRO, C54/1170, 1198, 1214; C. Whone, 'Christopher Danby of Masham and Farnley', *Pub. Thor. Soc.*, XXXVII (1945), 3.
35. Williamson, p. 13.
36. Alan Young, *Tudor and Jacobean Tournaments* (1987), p. 52.
37. YAS, DD121/29/4.
38. Spence, 'Earls', pp. xxiv–xLviii, explains them in relation to Earls George and Francis.
39. PRO, C54/1117, 1156, 1196; *HMC, Salisbury*, IV, 554–5.
40. PRO, Exchequer, Plea Rolls, E13/351, m. 2.
41. BL, Add. MS, 6707, fol. 18v; 6668, fol. 449; Sheffield Central Library, Bagshawe Coll. 696, 1027, 1028a; PRO, St.Ch.5/C32/6; C54/1799.
42. *Yorks. Fines, Tudor*, III, 29.
43. Williamson, p. 298.
44. Beverley Record Office, Constable Papers, DDCC/132, 9; PRO, C54/1238, 1236, 1247, 1248, 1250; Bolton MSS, Sundry, 256; YAS, DD121/29/4; *Yorks. Fines, Tudor*, III, 43.
45. PRO, C54/214; Williamson, pp. 287–9. the Queen gave 140 oz of gilt plate at Robert's christening (Nichols, *Progresses*, II, 424).
46. Williamson, p. 287.
47. PRO, C54/1237, 1240, 1238, 1263, 1250, 1257.
48. YAS, DD121/29/4; G. R. Batho, 'The Household Accounts of Henry Percy, Ninth Earl of Northumberland, 1564–1632' (unpub. MA thesis, London University, 1953), p. 395.
49. PRO, Wards 9/386, fol. 51v; Alnwick Castle, Syon MSS, X.II.6, Box (14), fol. 1r.

4. Promoter and Commander: 1586–8

1. Andrews, pp. 6, 24–31, 89.
2. *CSP, Spanish*, 1580–6, p. 578; PRO, SP12/215/88; Williamson, p. 44.
3. *HMC, Salisbury*, X, 138–9.
4. Lond. M/4.
5. CSP, *Spanish*, 1580–6, pp. 586, 578; Hakluyt, *Principal Navigations*, XI, 202–7.
6. Williamson, pp. 27–8, 32.
7. PRO, C54/1244, 1248, 1249, 1250.
8. Andrews, pp. 46–50.
9. PRO, C66/1287; Williamson, p. 34.
10. PRO, C54/1250; YAS, DD121/3/29; *Yorks. Fines, Tudor*, III, 88.
11. *CSP, Scotland*, IX, 102, 262, 308, 346, 353; *HMC, Salisbury*, III, 224.
12. Williamson, pp. 18, 31.
13. Currey, 28/138, fol. 60; PRO, C54/1248, 1296.
14. Williamson, p. 287; YAS, DD121/67/15.
15. PRO, C66/1294; *Yorks. Fines, Tudor*, III, 77.
16. *The Memoirs of Robert Carey*, ed. F. H. Mares (Oxford, 1972), pp. 5–6.
17. Hakluyt, *Principal Navigations*, VII, 420; BL, C.21 c.41.
18. Hakluyt, *Principal Navigations*, XI, 224–5.
19. Williamson, p. 18; *Calendar of Border Papers*, I, 289; Tenison, *Elizabethan England*, VIII, pt VI, 189.
20. YAS, DD121/67/18; Lambeth Palace Library, Shrewsbury Papers, 698, fol. 47.

21. YAS, DD121/29/4; Currey, 28/138, fol. 25.
22. Clay, p. 397.
23. Currey, 24/64.
24. PRO, C54/1296, 1288.
25. PRO, SP12/213/4; A. Ryther, 'A Discourse Concerninge the Spanish Fleet . . .', *Tracts on the Spanish Armada* (1588–90), pp. 25–7.
26. Williamson, p. 17; *APC*, 1588, pp. 175, 178; Mares, *Carey Memoirs*, pp. 9–10; *State Papers relating to the Defeat of the Spanish Armada Anno 1588*, ed. J. K. Laughton, Navy Records Society, II (1895), 249, 324–31, 338.
27. Mares, *Carey Memoirs*, pp. 9–10; Michael Lewis, *The Spanish Armada* (1966), pp. 154–90; Ryther, *Armada Tracts*, p. 22; BL, Add. MS, 33740, fol. 6; Petruccio Ubaldini, *A Narrative of the Glorious Victory . . . 1588* (1740), p. 37.
28. Mares, *Carey Memoirs*, p. 10; Miller Christy, 'Queen Elizabeth's Visit to Tilbury in 1588', *English Historical Review*, 34 (1919), 55–6; Laughton, *Defeat*, II, 59, 69, 84.
29. PRO, SP12/215/55 I.
30. PRO, SP12/214/28; 215/76, 87, 88. Cf Michael Lewis, *Armada Guns* (1961), pp. 120–2.
31. Laughton, *Defeat*, II, 96–7, 330. See Appendix II.
32. *CSP, Spanish*, 1587–1603, p. 419.
33. Nichols, *Progresses*, II, 580.
34. Ryther, *Armada Tracts*, p. 54. The Earl's portrait is shown in Ryther's engravings of Robert Adam's maps of the Armada, which were later woven into the tapestries lost in the House of Lords' fire in 1834 (D. Shrire, *Adam's & Pine's Maps of the Spanish Armada*, Map Collectors' Circle, 4 (1963)).
35. *CSPD*, 1581–90, pp. 530, 550; PRO, SP12/217/7, 32; 237/34.
36. Currey, 28/1; 46/9; Leeds City Archives, Ingilby Records, 2790; Chatsworth, BAS, Box 3/2 (indenture 7 Oct. 30 Eliz.).
37. *CSP, Spanish*, 1587–1603, pp. 478, 485, 504–5; Williamson, pp. 38–9; Laughton, *Defeat*, II, 296–7.
38. Williamson, p. 37; *APC*, 1588, p. 356; H. E. Rollins, *An Analytical Index to the Ballad-Entries (1557–1709) in the Registers of the Company of Stationers of London* (Hatboro, Pennsylvania, 1967), no. 816.
39. YAS, DD121/67/18; PRO, C54/1288.

5. Privateer and Queen's Champion: 1589–91

1. Elizabeth Davies, *A Memoir of Robert Davies: The Pretensions of the Cliffords, Barons Clifford* (1876), p. 27; Williamson, pp. 287–8.
2. Andrews, p. 72; *The Expedition of Sir John Norris and Sir Francis Drake to Spain and Portugal, 1589*, ed. R.B. Wernham, Navy Record Soc. 127 (1988).
3. Except where otherwise noted, this discussion of the 1589 voyage is based on Williamson, chap. 5; Wright's account and Linschoten's discourse in Hakluyt, *Principal Navigations*, VII, 1–31, 62–87; *The Naval Tracts of Sir William Monson*, ed. M. Oppenheim, 6 vols, Navy Records Soc. (1902–14), I, 226–37; and *Arqivo Dos Acores*, II (Ponta Delgada, 1980), 304–6. For the *Victory*, see Williamson, pp. 41–3 and PRO, SP12/238/43.
4. Tenison, *Elizabethan England*, VIII, pt VI, 190–1. Wright's famous world map was published in Hakluyt, *Principal Navigations*, I (1598) and the second edn. of his *Certaine Errors . . .* (1610); PRO, High Court of Admiralty, HCA 13/27, fol. 324 (I owe this reference to Geoffrey Harris).
5. Williamson, *Lady Anne Clifford*, p. 56.
6. Andrews, pp. 41–2, 134–5; BL, Lansd. MS 145, fol. 101.
7. Williamson, p. 65.
8. *The Third Book of Remembrance of Southampton, 1514–1602*, III (1573–89), ed. A.L. Merson, Southampton Records Series, VIII (Southampton, 1979), 59–60; Southampton Record Office, Burgess Admission Register 1496–1704, fol. 56r.
9. PRO, Chancery, Signet Office Docquet Books, Index 6800, April 1591.
10. *List and Analysis of State Papers Foreign Series Elizabeth I*, ed. R. B. Wernham, I (1964), nos 275, 768; *CSP, Foreign*, 1589, p. 162.
11. BL, Add. MS 5664, fols 165–7.
12. E.P. Cheyney, *A History of England from the Defeat of the Armada to the Death of Elizabeth*, 2 vols (1914–26), I, 527.
13. PRO, C54/1399.
14. PRO, HCA 24/68, no. 179.
15. *CSP, Scotland*, XI, 36.
16. Williamson, p. 66; Andrews, pp. 19–20.
17. Andrews, pp. 72, 248, 250; *CSP, Foreign*,

1590–1, p. 177; Rollins, *Index to Ballad-Entries*, no. 1623.

18. Lond. M/19; Andrews, pp. 116, 247.
19. Young, *Tournaments*, pp. 165–9; Nichols, *Progresses*, pp. 45–50, 69–70; Williamson, pp. 66–7, and for the speech (wrongly dated) 108–9.
20. Sir Roy Strong, *The Cult of Elizabeth. Elizabethan Portraits and Pageantry* (1977), p. 156; Erna Auerbach, *Nicholas Hilliard* (1961), pp. 112–15.
21. PRO, SP12/238/17, 63, 102, 239; Cheyney, *History*, I, 533; Williamson, pp. 66 n. 1, 70–2.
22. PRO, LC4/192/40.
23. Currey, 28/138, fols 60, 61; 24/24.
24. Currey, 28/138, fols 125–6; PRO, Common Pleas, Feet of Fines, CP25/254/83 Eliz. Trinity. For Hutton, see *The Diary of Sir Richard Hutton 1614–1639*, ed. W. R. Prest, Seldon Society, Supplementary ser. 9 (1991), xiii–xvii, where the Cliffords' patronage is noted.
25. Williamson, p. 77; PRO, C54/1399; *CSPD*, 1591–4, pp. 6, 15, 21, 37; *Extracts from the Portsmouth Records*, ed. Robert East (Portsmouth, 1891), p. 137; Clay, p. 396.
26. Williamson, pp. 72–81; G. Robinson, 'The Loss of H.M.S. *Revenge*, 1591', *The Mariner's Mirror*, 38 (1952), 149.
27. Andrews, p. 262; *CSPD*, 1591–4, pp. 67, 77; Williamson, p. 80.
28. *CSP, Foreign*, 1591–2, nos 178, 846; 1592–3, no. 672 (iv).
29. Williamson, pp. 78, 122.

6. The Elusion of Riches: the Capture of the Madre de Dios, 1592

1. Currey, 28/138, fol. 126.
2. J.P. Gilson, *Lives of Lady Anne Clifford Countess of Dorset, Pembroke and Montgomery (1590–1676) and of Her Parents* (Roxburghe Club, 1916), p. 25; Alnwick, Syon MSS, X. II. 4, Box 1b; *Statutes of the Realm*, iv, pt 2, 841 (35 Eliz. c.14).
3. Williamson, p. 110.
4. Williamson, pp. 83–6, 90, 103; Clay, p. 386; *Further English Voyages to Spanish America 1583–1594*, ed. I.A. Wright, Hakluyt Soc. XCIX (1951), 290, 293.

5. Williamson, pp. 109–110; Nichols, *Progresses*, pp. 144–60.
6. Tenison, *Elizabethan England*, pp. 198–9.
7. The following discussion is based on C. Lethbridge Kingsford, 'The Taking of the Madre de Dios, Anno 1592' in *The Naval Miscellany*, II, Navy Records Soc. XL (1912), 87–121; E. W. Bovill, 'The Madre de Dios', *The Mariner's Mirror*, 54 (1968), 129–52; and Hakluyt, *Principal Navigations*, VII, 105–18.
8. The 'Black Book' of Plymouth recorded 'In September 1592 the Earle of Cumberlande took a greate Carricke of 16 or 17c tonnes richelye laden and broughte her into Dartmouthe.' (Devon Record Office, W46). Details of the plunder given here are from *HMC, Salisbury*, IV, 226–55.
9. Williamson, pp. 96, 111.
10. Hatfield MS, CP21/110, calendared in *HMC, Salisbury*, IV, 233. All but one signed their names.
11. Kingsford, *Naval Miscellany*, II, 111.
12. Williamson, p. 112.
13. M. Oppenheim, *A History of the Administration of the Royal Navy 1509–1660* (1896), p. 166; Williamson, p. 94.
14. PRO, Chancery Masters Reports, C38/1, Carew 25 Jan. 1593; *HMC, Salisbury*, IV, 233; Kingsford, *Naval Miscellany*, II, 118.
15. Andrews, p. 75.
16. *HMC, Salisbury*, IV, 287, 289.
17. *Yorks. Fines, Tudor*, III, 191; Longleat, Devereux Papers, III, fol. 72.
18. *Middlesex County Records*, I, ed. J.C. Jeaffreson, Middlesex County Record Society (1886), 211–12.
19. Hakluyt, *Principal Navigations*, VII, 116.
20. *CSP, Foreign*, 1591–2, nos 177, 178; 1592–3, nos 146, 170, 617, 672 (iv).
21. BL, C.60, fol. 8.
22. Wright, *Further English Voyages*, pp. lxxix, xci, 293.

7. The Undaunted Earl: 1593–4

1. Elton, *Tudor England*, pp. 380–1.
2. Williamson, pp. 104–5, 117; *Statutes of the Realm*, iv, pt 2, 847–9 (35 Eliz. c.4).
3. Kingsford, *Naval Miscellany*, II, 111; Lambeth Palace Library, Shrewsbury Papers, 700, fol. 17.
4. Williamson, pp. 113–16; PRO,

LC4/192/248; C54/1458; *Foedera* . . . , ed. Thomas Rymer and Robert Sanderson, 20 vols (1727–35), VII, pt 1, 120–1.

5. Williamson, pp. 115–18.
6. Young, *Tournaments*, p. 169; Williamson, pp. 121–3; Jackson, *Longleat Papers*, XVIII, 269.
7. *HMC, Salisbury*, XVII, 585–6; PRO, Wards 9/387, fols 268–9; 388, fols 63–4.
8. Alnwick, Syon MSS, X. II. 6, Box (14), fol. 1r; Williamson, pp. 124–5.
9. Andrews, chap. 6.
10. Andrews, p. 76; Williamson, p. 128; PRO, C54/1486, 1485, 1458.
11. Andrews, pp. 39, 74; Williamson, pp. 118–20, 137. The prizes and cargoes are listed in BL, Harl. MS 598, fols 28–9.
12. Richard Robinson's narrative, printed in Williamson, pp. 128–36; Hakluyt, *Principal Navigations*, VII, 118–22.
13. *CSP, Scotland*, XI, 367–8, 407; GEC, XII, pt II, 600.
14. BL, Add. MS 64870, fols 86–91v; Williamson, pp. 21–6
15. *HMC, Salisbury*, IV, 620; V, 83; Coward, *Earls of Derby*, chap. 4; GEC, IV, 23–7; PRO, SO3/1, April 1595.
16. Young, *Tournaments*, p. 204; Nichols, *Progresses*, III, 281.

8. The Disastrous Years: 1595–7

1. R.B. Wernham, *After the Armada* (Oxford, 1984), pp. 555–9; Andrews, pp. 9–10, 19–21.
2. BL, Add. MS 64870, fol. 114.
3. Williamson, pp. 142, 148; *The Dawn of British Trade to the East Indies. Court Minutes of the East India Company, 1599–1603*, ed. Henry Stevens (1886), pp. 42–5.
4. Williamson, pp. 143–4; *CSPD*, 1595, no. 74.
5. Chatsworth, BAS, B3/1; E. Bellasis, 'Strickland of Sizergh', *Trans. Cumb. and West. Ant. and Arch. Soc.*, old ser. X, 75; *The Diary of Sir Henry Slingsby, of Scriven, Bart*, ed. Daniel Parsons (1836), p. 248.
6. PRO, SP12/261/80; Bolton MSS, Sundry, 257–69.
7. R.T. Spence, 'Mining and Smelting by the Cliffords, earls of Cumberland, in the Tudor and early Stuart Period', *YAJ*, 64 (1992), 163–5.

8. Currey, 28/138, fol. 126; PRO, C54/1495, 1579; LC4/192/417.
9. Williamson, pp. 145–7.
10. BL, Harl. MS 598, fol. 36; *HMC, Salisbury*, V, 433.
11. Williamson, p. 154; Young, *Tournaments*, pp. 169, 176.
12. PRO, C54/1545.
13. Williamson, pp. 169, 144, 156–7.
14. PRO, Signet Office Docquet Books, Index 6800, 4 Jan. 1595.
15. Williamson, pp. 144, 157–8.
16. Williamson, p. 160; *HMC, Salisbury*, VI, 102; G. B. Harrison, *The Life and Death of Robert Devereux, Earl of Essex* (Bath, 1950), pp. 95–100.
17. Williamson, pp. 158, 162; *HMC, Salisbury*, VI, 145; Harrison, *Essex*, chap. VIII.
18. Baildon, *Camera Stellata*, p. 39–40.
19. PRO, C54/1524; Leeds City Archives, Ingilby Records, 3475, 3476.
20. *HMC, Salisbury*, VI, 231, 399.
21. P.P.L. de Kermaingaut, *L'ambassade de France en Angleterre sous Henry IV. Mission de Jean de Thumery, Sieur de Boissise (1598–1602)* (Paris, 1886), p. 56.
22. Williamson, p. 167; PCC, PROB 11/88/79; Clay, p. 386.
23. *CSPD*, 1595–7, p. 350; *HMC, Salisbury*, VII, 130; Williamson, pp. 241–2, 169–72.
24. *APC*, 1597–8, pp. 17, 19–20, 171–2; *CSPD*, 1595–7, p. 432; *HMC, Salisbury*, VII, 439.
25. Baildon, *Camera Stellata*, pp. 75, 85; Cheyney, *History*, II, 445.
26. YAS, DD121/76, fols 3r, 5v.
27. Bolton MSS, Sundry, 52; Book 249; YAS, DD121/67/3. The manors were Long Preston, Settle, Giggleswick, Grassington, Storiths, Hazlewood, Halton, Cracoe, Woodhouse, Appletreewick, Eastby, Embsay, Littondale, Nesfield & Langbar, Cononley, Glusburn, Bradley, Gargrave, Silsden, Carleton, Lothersdale, and two messuages in Barden.
28. PRO, LC4/192/417; Leeds City Archives, Ingilby Records, 3477.
29. YAS, DD121/76.
30. PRO, C66/1464; Currey, 28/1, 21; 46/9.
31. YAS, DD121/76; Spence, *Thoresby Society*, LXIII, 8–9.
32. *HMC, Salisbury*, XIX, 419.
33. PRO, C54/1548; Currey, 26/4; 28/138, fol. 96.

9. The Great Puerto Rican Expedition: Preparations, 1597–8

1. Harrison, *Essex*, p. 145; Williamson, pp. 174, 224.
2. Andrews, pp. 211–12.
3. Harrison, *Essex*, pp. 153–67; *HMC, Salisbury*, VII, 344; *The Egerton Papers*, ed. J. Payne Collier, Camden Soc. old ser. 12 (1840), 263–6.
4. Harrison, *Essex*, pp. 168–71.
5. *APC*, 1597, pp. 90–1.
6. *Hakluytus Posthumus or Purchas his pilgrimes*, ed. Samuel Purchas, 20 vols, (MacLehose edn, Glasgow, 1905–7), XVI, 35–7, 77; L. W. Henry, 'The Earl of Essex as Strategist and Military Organizer (1596–7)', *English Historical Review*, LXVIII (1953), 363–3; Andre Hurault, *De Maisse's Journal*, ed. G. B. Harrison and R. A. Jones (1931), pp. 10, 67, 107.
7. Purchas, XVI, 36.
8. Williamson, pp. 172–3, 199–200.
9. Williamson, pp. 178–9, 223.
10. Currey, 28/138, fol. 62; PRO, C54/1578, 1579; Leeds City Archives, Ingilby Records, 3481.
11. PRO, LC4/193/330; C66/1480; *Yorks. Fines, Tudor*, IV, 89. On Huste, see *Returns of Aliens in London 1571–1579*, ed. R. E. G. and E. F. Kirk, Huguenot Soc. Publications X, pt II (1902), 92.
12. Bolton MSS, Sundry 273.
13. Williamson, pp. 200–2.
14. Leeds City Archives, Ingilby Records, 3479.
15. Currey, 26/1.
16. Currey, 26/5, 6.
17. Leeds City Archives, Ingilby Records, 3482; Currey, 28/138, fol. 75.
18. PCC, PROB 11/100/59; C54/1578.
19. Williamson, pp. 179, n. 1, 54.
20. *CSPD*, 1598–1601, pp. 24–6.
21. Except where otherwise noted, the following discussion is based on Cumberland's account in Purchas, XVI, 29–42, and his apologia in Williamson, pp. 220–5; Layfield's account in BL, Sloane MS 3289 (an abridged version is in Purchas, XVI, 43–106); and Richard Robinson's account in Williamson, pp. 177–85.
22. The first translation of *Orlando Furioso*, by

Sir John Harington in 1591, had a title page by Thomas Cockson and engravings by William Rogers, illustrated in Neville Williams, *All the Queen's Men* (1974), pp. 193–5.
23. See below, chapter X, n. 1.
24. See below, chapter X, n. 1.
25. PRO, Chancery, Series II, C3/265/76; *The Book of Examinations 1601–2*, ed. R. C. Anderson, Southampton Record Soc. 26 (1926), vi–ix.

10. The Great Puerto Rican Expedition: Defeat in Victory, 1598

1. Except where otherwise noted, this chapter is based on the English sources given in chapter IX, n. 21, and the following Spanish sources which Professor Andrews kindly made available to me: Biblioteca Naccional de Madrid, MS 775, fols 407–9 (Bocquel's account); Archivo General de Indias, Seville, Santo Domingo, Legajos 70 (Alcazar de Villasenor); Santa Fe, Legajos 38 (Francisco Delgado and Garcia de Valdes); 134, Pieza 2 (Governor Mosquera's deposition and soldiers' depositions). San Juan's defences are described in Edward A. Hoyt, *A History of the Harbor Defenses of San Juan de Puerto Rico under Spain 1509–1898* (San Juan, 1944), pp. 30–55; A. Manucy and R. Torres-Reyes, *Puerto Rico and the Forts of Old San Juan* (Old Greenwich, Connecticut, 1982), pp. 27–51; Andrews, *Last Voyage, passim*.
2. Adolfo de Hostas, *Historia de San Juan Cuidad Murada* (San Juan, 1983), p. 21.
3. Andrews, *Last Voyage*, docts 20, 28, and for a critical assessment, pp. 8–9.
4. Andrews examines the history of the *Discourse* in *Last Voyage*, pp. 159–60.
5. Oppenheim, *Monson's Tracts*, II, 223.
6. KRO, WD/Hoth/Account Book, 10 April, 1665.
7. *CSP, Venetian*, IX, no. 744; Williamson, pp. 202–3. A letter sent from San Juan on 1 Sept. 1598 is in BL, Add. MS 64871, fol. 7.
8. J. A. Williamson, *A Short History of British Expansion I. The Old Colonial Empire* (1965), pp. 169–80.
9. Elton, *Tudor England*, pp. 384, 391–2.
10. Andrews, pp. 222–8.

11. Williamson, pp. 205–6. Richard Cornelius claimed that Cumberland's return was at least £8,000 (PRO, C3/265/76).

12. Williamson, p. 203; *HMC, Salisbury*, VIII, 98.

13. Williamson, p. 173.

11. Mercantile Promoter and Privy Councillor: 1598–1605

1. Bolton MSS, Sundry 266; *APC*, 1599–1600, pp. 388–9; PRO, HCA, 13/34 (I owe this reference to Professor Andrews).

2. Williamson, pp. 234–6.

3. *HMC, Salisbury*, XII, 114, 425; PRO, HCA 24/69, no. 123.

4. *The Voyage of Nicholas Downton to the East Indies 1614–15*, ed. Sir William Foster, Hakluyt Soc. ser. II, LXXXII (1939), xiv.

5. Stevens, *Dawn of British Trade, passim*. For the cask mark, see p. 107.

6. Purchas, IV, 128–32; Sir William Foster, *England's Quest of Eastern Trade* (1966), pp. 154–5, 236–7, 274, 282.

7. Williamson, pp. 225–30, 234, 244–5; Leslie Hotson, *The First Night of Twelfth Night* (1954), p. 201; Strong, *The Cult of Elizabeth*, pp. 29–30, 46.

8. Harrison, *Essex*, chaps XIII, XIV; *The Correspondence of Dr Matthew Hutton, archbishop of York . . .*, ed. James Raine, Surtees Soc. XVII (1843), 157; *HMC, Salisbury*, X, 178; Cheyney, *History*, II, 515.

9. *HMC, Salisbury*, IX, 198; XII, 539, 648, 674–5; XVII, 459–61; XXI, 39; PRO, C66/1571; P. A. J. Pettit, *The Royal Forests of Northamptonshire A Study in their Economy 1558–1714*, Northamptonshire Record Soc. XXIII (1968 for 1963), 14, 21 n. 8.

10. Joseph Hunter and Alfred Gatty, *Hallamshire* (1969), pp. 120–1; *The Diaries of Lady Anne Clifford*, ed. D.J.H. Clifford (Stroud, 1990), p. 24; Clay, p. 387; PRO, Exchequer, Accounts Various E101/433/3; LC4/195/374, 460.

11. *HMC, Salisbury*, XVII, 460; Bolton MSS, Book 228, fol. 212v.

12. Spence, 'Earls', chap. IX; Williamson, pp. 68, 242–3; BL, Althorp, B2.

13. *HMC, Salisbury*, XV, 20; *CSP, Venetian*, IX, 563; Clifford, *Diaries*, pp. 23–4; John Nichols, *The Progresses of King James The First*, 4 vols (1828), I, 77–82.

14. Penry Williams, *The Tudor Regime* (1979), pp. 427–8; *APC*, 1601–4, p. 496. The despatch of packets of letters to him when absent on the Borders is recorded in H. V. Jones, 'The Journal of Levinius Munck', *English Historical Review*, 68 (1953), 249, 253.

15. Nichols, *Progresses of James I*, I, 205.

16. Spence, *NH*, XIII (1977), 59–160; PRO, Chancery, Index 6801.

17. CRO, Carlisle City Records, CA/3/2, 37, 38.

18. *CSPD*, 1603–10, p. 15.

19. *The Register of Letters &c of the Governour and Company of Merchants of London trading into the East Indies, 1600–1619*, ed. Sir George Birdwood (1893), pp. 42–44.

20. YAS, MS 784, fol 14.

21. Baildon, *Camera Stellata*, pp. Lxvii, 204–22; D. B. Quinn, *England and the Discovery of America, 1481–1620* (1974), pp. 482–8; Williams, *All the Queen's Men*, p. 158.

22. This was done by a codicil to his 1598 will. With Burghley and Essex dead, he appointed three new supervisers – William, 2nd Lord Burghley, and Sir Robert Cecil, and Lord Chief Justice Popham. William was to receive his best George and Robert a jewel worth £100 (Currey, 26/6).

12. The Craven and Westmorland Estates: 1579–1605

1. *HMC, Salisbury*, XII, 227, 574.

2. Except where otherwise stated, the following discussion is based on analyses of DD121/24/6 (1605 Rental); /28/6 (1603 Craven Rental); /29/23 (1603 Craven Rental); /32/11 (Grassington Survey); /32/41 (1608 Survey); /34/26 (Book of Grants, 1602–5); /76 (1597 Rental); /Estate Ledger; Bolton MSS, Books 249 (1596 mortgages), 253 fol. 1 (tenants dead); Ingilby Records, 2813 (tithes leasing). For details, see Spence. 'Earls', chaps IV, V.

3. Strong, *Cult of Elizabeth*, p. 46.

4. BL, Althorp, Cumberland Papers, letters of 12, 13 April, 1602,

5. *HMC, Salisbury*, XII, 321.

6. *HMC, Salisbury*, XII, 438, 459.
7. Burton's will, 11 Feb. 1614/15 (Borthwick Institute, York, York Wills Chancery, 1610–14).
8. *Yorks. Fines, Tudor*, IV, 53, 151–3; DD121/34/26; /36A, fol. 234; Bolton MSS, Book 226, fol. 258; W. H. Dawson, *Loose Leaves of Craven History*, 2nd ser. (Skipton, 1906), p. 254.
9. PRO, C66/1714; YAS DD121/32/49; /34/26.
10. Spence, *YAJ*, 64, pp. 168–9.
11. The following discussion is based on the 1604 Westmorland Survey and Rental (KRO, WD/Hoth/34) and the 1597 Craven and Westmorland Rental (DD121/76).
12. Andrew B. Appleby, 'Disease or Famine? Mortality in Cumberland and Westmorland, 1580–1640', *Economic History Review*, 2nd ser. XXVI (1973), pp. 414–20.
13. PRO, Chancery, Entry Books of Decrees and Orders, C33/117, fols 947, 991.
14. PRO, Chancery, Decrees and Orders, C78/153/4; Bolton MSS, Book 226, fol. 104.

13. Retrospective

1. Christopher Haigh, *Elizabeth I* (1988), *passim*.
2. Cf. Parker, *Books to Build an Empire*, p. 144.
3. *The Prose Works of Fulke Greville, Lord Brooke*, ed. John Gouws (Oxford, 1986), pp. 151–2; Mervyn James, *English Politics and the Concept of Honour 1485–1642*, Past & Present Supplement 3 (1978), pp. 68–72.
4. Williamson, p. 278.
5. John Davies, *Microcosmos* (1602).
6. W. Camden, *The Historie of the Most Renowned and Victorious Princess Elizabeth, late Queene of England* (1630), dedication; *Britannia* (1610), p. 788.
7. BL, Sloane MS 3289, fols 75v–76r.
8. J.S. Corbett, *The Successors of Drake*

(1900), p. 239; Oppenheim, *Monson's Tracts*, II, 223–4; Tenison, *Elizabethan England*, VIII, pt VI, 187; Andrews, p. 70.
9. Beverley Record Office, DDCC/144, 4; Whitaker, p. 354.
10. Unnamed writer, quoted in W. H. Dawson, *History of Skipton* (1882), p. 237.
11. Andrews, p. 74.
12. BL, Sloane MS 3289, fol. 79r.
13. Williamson, pp. 17, 240.
14. Stone, *Crisis*, chap. X.
15. Spence, 'Earls', pp. 169–70.
16. Whitaker, p. 354.
17. *Cholmley Memoirs*, pp. 10–11; *English Reports*, vols 72, p. 778; 123, p. 509; Williamson, p. 191, n. 1; Bolton MSS, Sundry, 273.
18. Lond. M/19; BL, Althorp, Box 3.
19. Spence, 'Earls', pp. 349–51.
20. Williamson, p. 264.
21. Bolton MSS, Books 230, fol. 271r; 172, fol. 72v.
22. Ronald A. Rebholz, *The Life of Fulke Greville First Lord Brooke* (Oxford, 1971), pp. 82–5, 328; Gouws, *Greville's Works*, pp. xiv–xxx, 138, 142, 145, 147, 154, 160–1; Williamson, *Lady Anne Clifford*, p. 344.
23. Joan Rees, *Samuel Daniel* (Liverpool, 1964), pp. 76–7; *The Complete Works in Verse and Prose of Samuel Daniel*, ed. A. B. Grosart, 4 vols (1885), I, 207; James, *Concept of Honour*, pp. 72–7.
24. Clifford, *Diaries, passim*.
25. Williamson, pp. 233–4; *HMC, Salisbury*, X, 176.
26. *HMC, Salisbury*, XII, 617–18; Williamson, pp. 265–9, 299–301.
27. Clifford, *Diaries*, p. 26; Clay, p. 393.
28. Williamson, p. 261; Lambeth Palace Library, Talbot MS 3203, fol. 308.
29. Clay, pp. 387–92; YAS, DD121/67/6; Currey, 28/138, fol. 127; 26/13, 14.
30. Williamson, p. 271; *HMC, Salisbury*, XVII, 459–61; *The Letters of John Chamberlain*, ed. N. E. McClure, 2 vols (Philadelphia, 1939), I, 214; Bolton MSS, Book 226, fol. 226v; Clay, p. 387, n. 2.

Bibliography

Except where otherwise stated, the place of publication is London.

PRIMARY SOURCES

Manuscript

1. English

British Library
Althorp Papers
Additional MSS, 5664, 6707, 33740, 64870,
64871
Harleian MSS, 598, 6177
Lansdowne MSS, 30, 75, 145
Sloane MS 3289

Public Record Office
C3	Chancery, Proceedings, Series II
C33	Chancery, Entry Books of Decrees and Orders
C38	Chancery, Masters Reports
C54	Chancery, Close Rolls
C66	Chancery, Patent Rolls
C78	Chancery, Decrees and Orders
CP25	Common Pleas, Feet of Fines
E13	Exchequer, Plea Rolls
E101	Exchequer, Accounts Various
HCA 13	High Court of Admiralty, Examinations
HCA 24	High Court of Admiralty, Libels
LC4	Lord Chamberlain's Office, Recognizances
PCC	Prerogative Court of Canterbury, Wills
SO3	Signet Office Docquet Books

SP12	State papers, Domestic, Elizabeth
SP15	State Papers, Domestic, Addenda, Edward VI to James I
SP46	State Papers Supplementary
St. Ch. 5	Star Chamber Proceedings, Elizabeth I
Wards 9	Court of Wards, Miscellaneous Books

Alnwick Castle
Syon MSS

Bedfordshire County Record Office
Box R262	Chenies Inventory

Beverley County Record Office
DDCC	Constable Papers

Bodleian Library, Oxford
MS Dodsworth 88, 118

Borthwick Institute of Historical Research, University of York
Wills in the York Registry

Chatsworth
Bolton MSS
Bolton Additional Series, BAS
Currey Papers
Londesborough Papers
Londesborough papers, G.R. Potter's
  transcripts

Christ Church, Oxford
MS Estates 109

Cumbria County Archives
Carlisle   Carlisle City Records
Kendal   Hothfield MSS

Devon Record Office
W46   The 'Black Book' of
                 Plymouth

Hatfield House
Hatfield MSS

Lambeth Palace Library
Shrewsbury Papers 696, 698, 700
Talbot MSS
MS 807   Archbishop Whitgift's
                 Accounts

Leeds City Archives
Ingilby Records

Longleat
Devereaux Papers

Sheffield Central Library
Bagshawe Collection

Southampton Record Office
Burgess Admissions Register, 1496–1704

Woburn Abbey
Woburn Abbey MSS, Earl of Bedford's Papers

Yorkshire Archaeological Society
DD121   Skipton MSS
DD203   Calton Deeds
MS338   Dodsworth's Book of Arms
                 and Monuments
MS784   Notes for a history of
                 Appleby by C.B. Norcliffe,
                 1875

2. Spanish Sources

Archivo General de Indias, Seville
Santo Domingo, *Legajos* 70
Santa Fe, *Legajos* 38, 134
Biblioteca Naccional de Madrid
MS 775   Juan Bocquel's account

Printed

Acts of the Privy Council, 1547–1604, HMSO, 1890–1907
Anderson, R.C. (ed.), *The Book of Examinations 1601–2*, Southampton Records Society, 26 (1926)

Andrews, K.R. (ed.), *The Last Voyage of Drake and Hawkins*, Hakluyt Society, 2nd Series, 142 (1972)
Argivo Dos Acores, vol. II, Ponta Delgado, St Michael, 1980
Armytage, Sir George and Rylands, W.H. (eds), *Staffordshire Pedigrees*, Harleian Society, LXIII (1912)
Baildon, W.P. (ed.), *Les Reportes del Cases in Camera Stellata 1593 to 1609*, privately printed, 1894
Bain, J. (ed.), *The Border papers. Calendar of letters and Papers Relating to the Affairs of the Borders of England and Scotland*, 2 vols, Edinburgh, 1894–96
Ball, W.W.R. and Venn, J.A. (eds), *Admissions to Trinity College, Cambridge*, II, Macmillan, 1913
Birdwood, Sir George (ed.), *The Register of Letters &c of the Governour and Company of Merchants of London trading into the East Indies, 1600–1619*, Bernard Quaritch, 1893
Bourne, W., *A Regiment for the Sea . . .*, 1592
Brigg, W. (ed.), *Feet of Fines of the Tudor Period, 1486–1603*, 4 vols, Yorkshire Archaeological Society, Record Series, II, V, VII, VIII (1887–90)
Calendar of the Patent Rolls Preserved in the Public Record Office, Philip and Mary, Elizabeth I, HMSO, 1936–82
Calendar of State Papers, Domestic Series, 1547–1602, Longman, 1856–7
Calendar of State Papers, Foreign, 1547–95, Longman and HMSO, 1863–1993
Calendar of State Papers relating to Scotland and Mary, Queen of Scots, 1568–1603, Longman, 1858
Calendar of State Papers, Spanish, 1580–1603, HMSO, 1896–99
Calendar of State Papers, Venetian, 1581–1603, HMSO, 1894–97
Chappell, W. (ed.), *The Roxburghe Ballads*, I, Ballad Society Publications, 1888
Cholmley, Sir Hugh. *The Memories of Sir Hugh Cholmley Knt. and Bart*, 1777
Clifford, D.J.H. (ed.), *The Diaries of Lady Anne Clifford*, Gloucester, Alan Sutton Publishing, 1990
Cokayne, G.E. (ed.), *The Complete Peerage*, 13 vols, 1910–59
Collier, J.P. (ed.), *The Egerton Papers*, Camden Society, old series, 12 (1840)
Collinson, R. (ed.), *The Three voyages of Martin Frobisher . . . 1576–8*, Hakluyt Society, 38 (1867)

Dickens, A.G. (ed.), *Clifford Letters of the Sixteenth Century*, Surtees Society, CLXXXII (1962)

Dictionary of National Biography

East, R. (ed.), *Extracts from the Portsmouth Records*, Portsmouth Corporation, 1891

English Reports, XIII

Foster, J. (ed.), *The Visitations of Yorkshire 1584–5 and 1612*, privately printed, 1875

—— *The Register of Admissions to Gray's Inn. 1521–1889*, privately printed, 1889

Foster, Sir William (ed.), *The Voyage of Nicholas Downton to the East Indies 1614–15*, Hakluyt Society, 2nd Series, 82 (1939)

Gough, J.G. (ed.), *The Chronicle of Queen Jane . . .*, Camden Society, old series, 48 (1850)

Gouws, J. (ed.), *The Prose Works of Fulke Greville, Lord Brooke*, Oxford University Press, 1986

Greepe, T., *The true and perfecte newes . . .*, 1587

Grosart, A.B. (ed.), *The Complete Works in Verse and Prose of Samuel Daniel*, 4 vols, privately printed, 1885

R. Hakluyt, *The Principal Navigations Voyages Traffiques & Discoveries of the English Nation*, 12 vols, MacLehose, Glasgow, 1903

Harrison, G.B. and Jones, R.A. (eds), Andre Haurault, *De Maisse's Journal*, 1931

Hasler, P.W. (ed.), *The History of Parliament: The House of Commons, 1558–1603*, 3 vols, HMSO, 1981

Historical Manuscripts Commission:
Ninth Report, Part I: Manuscripts of the Corporation of Plymouth, HMSO, 1883
Salisbury MSS: Manuscripts of the Marquess of Salisbury at Hatfield House, 24 vols, HMSO, 1883–1976
Twelfth Report: Manuscripts of the Duke of Rutland at Belvoir Castle, HMSO, 1888–89
Various Collections, IV: Manuscripts of the Corporation of Salisbury, HMSO, 1907

Jackson, J.E. (ed.), *Longleat Papers*, Wiltshire Archaeological Magazine, XVIII (1879)

Jeaffreson, J.C. (ed.), *Middlesex County Records*, 1, Middlesex County Record Society, 1886

Kirk, R.E.G. and Kirk, E.F. (eds), *Returns of Aliens in London 1571–1579*, Huguenot Society Publications, X, pt II (1902)

Laughton, J.K. (ed.), *State Papers relating to the Defeat of the Spanish Armada Anno 1588*, Navy Records Society, I, II (1894–5)

McClure, NE. (ed.), *The Letters of John Chamberlain*, 2 vols, Philadelphia, 1939

Mares, F.H. (ed.), *The Memoirs of Robert Carey*, Oxford University Press, 1972

Merson, A.L. (ed.), *The Third Book of Remembrance of Southampton*, III (1573–89), Southampton Records Series, VIII (1979)

Nichols, J.G. (ed.), *The Diary of Henry Machyn . . . 1550–63*, Camden Society, old series, 42 (1848)

Oppenheim, M.M. (ed.), *The Naval Tracts of Sir William Monson*, 6 vols, Navy Records Society, XXII, XXIII, XLIII, XLV, XLVII (1902–14)

Parsons, D. (ed.), *The Diary of Sir Henry Slingsby, of Scriven, Bart*, Longman, 1836

Prest, W.R. (ed.), *The Diary of Sir Richard Hutton 1614–1639*, Seldon Society, Supplementary series 9 (1991)

Purchas, S. (ed.), *Hakluytus Posthumus or Purchas his pilgrimes*, 20 vols, MacLehose, Glasgow, 1905–7

Raine, J. (ed.), *The Correspondence of Dr Matthew Hutton Archbishop of York . . .*, Surtees Society, XVII (1843)

Rymer, T. and Sanderson, R. (eds), *Foedera . . .*, 20 vols, 1727–35

Settle, D. *A true report of the late voyage into the west and northwest regions* (1577)

Sharp, Sir Cuthbert. (ed.), *Memorials of the Rebellion of 1569*, Nichols, 1840

Southern, A.C. (ed.), *An Elizabethan Recusant House*, Richard Smith's 'The Life of the Lady Magdalen Viscountess Montague (1538–1605)', Sands & co. 1954

Statutes of the Realm

Stevens, H. (ed.), *The Dawn of British Trade to the East Indies. Court Minutes of the East India Company, 1599–1603*, Stevens, 1886

Wernham, R.B. (ed.), *List and Analysis of State Papers Foreign Series, Elizabeth I*, I, 1589–90, HMSO, 1964

—— (ed.), *The Expedition of Sir John Norris and Sir Francis Drake to Spain and Portugal, 1589*, Navy Records Society, CXXVII (1988)

Wood, J.C. (ed.), Gervase Holles, *Memorials of the Holles Family 1493–1656*, Camden Society, 3rd series, 55 (1937)

Wright, I.A. (ed.), *Further English Voyages to Spanish America 1583–1594*, Hakluyt Society, 2nd Series, 99 (1951)

SECONDARY SOURCES

Andrews, K.R. *Elizabethan Privateering*, Cambridge University Press, 1964

Appleby, A.B. 'Disease or Famine? Mortality in Cumberland and Westmorland, 1580–1640',

Economic History Review, 2nd series, XXVI (1973), 403–32

Auerbach, E. *Nicholas Hilliard*, Routledge & Kegan Paul, 1961

Bellasis, E. 'Strickland of Sizergh', *Transactions of the Cumberland and Westmorland Antiquarian and Archaeological Society*, old series, X (1889), 75–94

Bovill, E.W. 'The Madre de Dios', *The Mariner's Mirror*, 54 (1968), 129–52

Camden, W. *Britannia*, 1610

—— *The Historie of the Most Renowned and Victorious Princess Elizabeth, Late Queene of England*, 1630

Cartwright, J.J. *Chapters in the History of Yorkshire*, Wakefield, B.W. Allen, 1872

Cheyney, E.P. *A History of England from the Defeat of the Armada to the Death of Elizabeth*, 2 vols, Longman, 1914–26

Christy, M. 'Queen Elizabeth's Visit to Tilbury in 1588', *English Historical Review*, 34 (1919), 43–61

Clay, J.W. 'The Clifford Family', *Yorkshire Archaeological Journal*, xviii (1905), 355–411

Cliffe, J.T. *The Yorkshire Gentry from the Reformation to the Civil War*, The Athlone Press, 1969

Clifford, H. *The House of Clifford*, Chichester, Phillimore, 1987

Collinson, P. *The Elizabethan Puritan Movement*, Cape, 1967

Corbett, J.S. *The Successors of Drake*, Longman, 1900

Coward, B. *The Stanleys Lords Stanley and Earls of Derby 1385–1672*, Chetham Society, 3rd series, XXX (1983)

Cross, C. *The Puritan Earl; the Life of Henry Hastings, third earl of Huntingdon, 1536–1595*, Macmillan, 1966

Davies, E. *A Memoir of Robert Davies; The Pretensions of the Cliffords, Barons Clifford*, York, privately printed, 1876

Davies, J. *Microcosmos*, 1602

Dawson, W.H. *History of Skipton*, Skipton, Edmonson, 1882

—— *Loose Leaves of Craven History*, 2nd series, Skipton, 1906

Elton, G.R. *England Under the Tudors*, Methuen, 1960

Faulkner, T. *The History and Antiquities of Brentford, Ealing and Chiswick*, Simpkin, Marshall, 1845

Foster, Sir William. *England's Quest of Eastern Trade*, A. & C. Black, 1966

Gilson, J.P. *Lives of Lady Anne Clifford Countess of Dorset, Pembroke and Montgomery (1590–1676) and of Her Parents*, Roxburghe Club, 1916

Graves, M.A.R. *The House of Lords in the Parliaments of Edward VI and Mary I*, Cambridge University Press, 1981

Gunn, S.J. *Charles Brandon, Duke of Suffolk c.1484–1545*, Oxford, Blackwell, 1988

Haigh, C. *Elizabeth I*, Longman, 1988

Harrison, G.B. *The Life and Death of Robert Devereux Earl of Essex*, Bath, Cedric Chivers, 1970

Henry, L.W. 'The Earl of Essex as Strategist and Military Organizer (1596–7)', *English Historical Review*, 68 (1953), 363–93

Hostas, A. de. *Historia de San Juan Cuidad Murada*, San Juan de Puerto Rico, I, 1983

Hotson, J.L. *The First Night of Twelfth Night*, Hart-Davis, 1954

Hoyt, E.A. *A History of the Harbor Defenses of San Juan de Puerto Rico under Spain 1509–1898*, San Juan, Puerto Rico Coast Artillery Command, 1944

Hunter J. and Gatty, A. *Hallamshire*, Pawson and Brailsford, 1869

Hurstfield, J. *The Queen's Wards: Wardship and Marriage under Elizabeth I*, Cape, 1958

James, M.E. *English Politics and the Concept of Honour 1485–1642*, Past & Present Supplement 3 (1978)

Jones, H.V. 'The Journal of Levinius Munck', *English Historical Review*, 68 (1953), 234–58

Kermaingaut, P.P.L. de. *L'ambassade de France en Angleterre sous Henry IV. Mission de Jean de Thumery, Sieur de Boissise (1598–1602)*, Paris, Firmin-Didot, 1886

Kingsford, C.L. 'The Taking of the Madre de Dios, Anno 1592', *The Naval Miscellany*, II, ed. Laughton, J.K., Navy Records Society, XL (1912), 87–121

Lake, P. *Moderate Puritans and the Elizabethan Church*, Cambridge University Press, 1982

Lewis, M.A. *Armada Guns*, Allen & Unwin, 1961

—— *The Spanish Armada*, Pan, 1966

Lyson, D. and Lyson, S. *Magna Britannia*, 6 vols, Thomas Cadell, 1813–22

Maitland, S.R. 'Archbishop Whitgift's College Pupils', *The British Magazine*, XXXII (1847), 361–5; XXXIII (1848), 17–29

Manucy, A. and Torres-Reyes, R. *Puerto Rico and the Forts of Old San Juan*, Old Greenwich, Connecticut, The Chatham Press, 1982

Miller, H. *Henry VIII and the English Nobility*, Oxford, Basil Blackwell, 1986

Morgan, V. 'Cambridge University and "The Country" 1540–1640', in Stone, L. (ed.), *The University in Society*, I, Oxford University Press, 1974, pp. 183–245

Nichols, J. *The Progresses and Public Processions of Queen Elizabeth*, 3 vols, Nichols, 1823

—— *The Progresses of King James The First*, 4 vols, Nichols, 1828

Oppenheim, M.M. *A History of the Administration of the Royal Navy 1509–1660*, Bodley Head, 1896

Parker, J. *Books to Build an Empire: A Bibliographical History of English Overseas Interests to 1620*, Amsterdam, N. Israel, 1965

Parks, G.B. *Richard Hakluyt and the English Voyages*, New York, Frederick Ungar Publishing, 1961

Pettit, P.A.J. *The Royal Forests of Northamptonshire A Study in their Economy*, Northamptonshire Record Society, XXIII (1968)

Poulton, D. *John Dowland*, Faber, 1972

Quinn, D.B. *England and the Discovery of America, 1481–1620*, Allen & Unwin, 1974

Rebholz, R.A. *The Life of Fulke Greville First Lord Brooke*, Oxford University Press, 1971

Rees, J. *Samuel Daniel*, Liverpool University Press, 1964

Robinson, G. 'The Loss of H.M.S. Revenge, 1591', *The Mariner's Mirror*, 38 (1952), 148–50

Robinson, J.M. *The Dukes of Norfolk*, Oxford University Press, 1982

Rollins, H.E. *An Analytical Index to the Ballad-Entries (1557–1709) in the Registers of the Company of Stationers of London*, Hatboro, Pennsylvania, Tradition Press, 1967

Ryther, A. 'A Discourse Concerninge the Spanish Fleet . . .', *Tracts on the Spanish Armada*, 1588–90

Sheils, W.J. *Archbishop Grindal's Visitation, 1575*, Borthwick Texts, 4, York, 1977

Shrire, D. *Adam's & Pine's Maps of the Spanish Armada*, Map Collectors' Circle, 4 (1963)

Simon, J. *Education and Society in Tudor England*, Cambridge University Press, 1967

Somerville, Sir Robert. *History of the Duchy of Lancaster*, I, 1265–1603, 1953

Spence, R.T. 'The Cliffords, Earls of Cumberland, 1579–1646: a study of their fortunes based on their household and estate accounts' (unpublished PhD thesis, London University, 1959)

—— 'Mining and Smelting by the Cliffords, earls of Cumberland, in the Tudor and early

Stuart Period', *Yorkshire Archaeological Journal*, 64 (1992), 157–83

—— 'The Pacification of the Cumberland Borders, 1593–1628', *Northern History*, XIII (1977), 59–160

—— *The Shepherd Lord*, Skipton Castle, 1994

—— 'Tithes and Tithe-holders in the Parish of Leeds from the Dissolution to the Restoration', *Publications of the Thoresby Society*, LXIII (1990), 1–26

Steele, J.P. *Feet of Fines, Cumberland, during the Reigns of Edward VI, Mary, Philip and Mary, and Elizabeth*, n.d.

Stone, L. *The Crisis of the Aristocracy 1558–1641*, Oxford University Press, 1965

Stopes, C.C. *Shakespeare's Environment*, Bell, 1918

Strong, Sir Roy. *The Cult of Elizabeth. Elizabethan Portraits and Pageantry*, Thames and Hudson, 1977

Sugden, J. *Sir Francis Drake*, Barrie & Jenkins, 1990

Taylor, S.E. 'The Crown and the North of England 1559–70: a study of the rebellion of the Northern Earls, 1569–70, and its Causes' (unpublished PhD thesis, Manchester University, 1981)

Tenison, E.M. *Elizabethan England*, 13 vols, Royal Leamington Spa, privately published, 1933–60

Ubaldini, P. *A Narrative of the Glorious Victory . . . 1588*, 1740

Welch, D. 'Three Elizabethan Documents Concerning Milburn Fell', *Transactions of the Cumberland and Westmorland Antiquarian and Archaeological Society*, new series, LXXXV (1985), 136–49

Wernham, R.B. *After the Armada: Elizabethan England and the Struggle for Western Europe, 1588–1595*, Oxford University Press, 1984

Whitaker, T.D. *The History and Antiquities of the Deanery of Craven in the County of York*, 3rd edn, ed. Morant, A.W., Joseph Dodgson, Leeds, 1878

Whone, C. 'Christopher Danby of Masham and Farnley', *Publications of the Thoresby Society*, XXXVII (1945), 1–29

Wiffen, J.H. *Historical Memoirs of the House of Russell*, 2 vols, 1833

Williams, N. *All the Queen's Men*, Cardinal edn, Sphere Books, 1974

Williams, P. *The Tudor Regime*, Oxford University Press, 1979

Williamson, G.C. *George, Third Earl of*

Cumberland (1558–1605) His Life and Voyages, Cambridge University Press, 1920

—— *Lady Anne Clifford, Countess of Dorset, Pembroke & Montgomery, 1590–1676. Her Life, Letters and Work,* Kendal, Titus Wilson and Son, 1922

Williamson, J.A. *A Short History of British Expansion I. The Old Colonial Empire,* 3rd edn. Macmillan, 1965

Wright, E. *Certaine Errors in Navigation,* 1610

Young, A. *Tudor and Jacobean Tournaments,* George Philip, 1987

Index

Page numbers in italics denote illustrations. Bold numbers refer to colour plates. Names in Appendix II, local to Portsmouth, are omitted.